Acknowledgments

My heartfelt thanks to the many people who, knowingly or unknowingly, gave me their support and assistance during the last decade. It is impossible for me to mention all of them by name.

I am especially grateful to Annemarie Bjerg, who never wavered in her unconditional support and love for me throughout this journey, and to whom I attribute my survival; to my mother who kept the wolves from howling at the door many a time; to Leslie for his support; to my dogs Jessie Alabama and Musie, who prevented agoraphobia, and whose love and antics soothed my spirit and made me chuckle on occasion; to the wonderful Kincaid Awareness Center, where light, love, healing, compassion and tolerance abounds; to my physicians Samuel Segal and William Courtney for doing their utmost to protect me from my opponents; to Antonia di Palma for sharing her research materials on air quality with me; to my friends Monica Escudero and Michael Manley-Casimir for their encouraging feedback on the first, voluminous manuscript; to my opponents, who made it possible for me to write Broken Wings; to my editor Carol Sheehan of CS Communication Strategies, Inc., and my agent Johanna Bates of Johanna M. Bates Literary Consultants, Inc., for their patience, support, tolerance, compassion and nurturing while guiding me through the traumatic editing process, and for putting all aspects of the publication process into place.

May balance, peace, and harmony fill your lives to abundance.

BROKEN WINGS
A Flight Attendant's Journey
by Nattanya Andersen

Publisher:
Avia Publishing Inc.
205–329 North Road
Coquitlam, British Columbia, Canada
V3K 3V8

Editor: Carol Sheehan, CS Communication Strategies, Inc., Calgary, Alberta, Canada
Cover Design: ThinkDesign Ltd., Calgary, Alberta, Canada
Printing: AGMV Marquis Imprimeur Inc., Cap-Saint-Ignace, Québec, Canada

ORDERING INFORMATION:
Fax: 604.931.3695
Internet: www.brokenwings.com
Email: amore@bc.sympatico.ca

CANADIAN CATALOGUING IN PUBLICATION DATA
Andersen, Nattanya H., 1943–
      Broken wings: a flight attendant's journey

          1. Post Traumatic Stress Disorder. 2. Flight Crew—Health
          3. Andersen, Nattanya, 1943- I. Title.

      RC552.P67A53 1999   363.12'4'092   C99-900277-5

ISBN: 0-9684976-0-8

Printed in Canada

TABLE OF CONTENTS

To
the world's flight attendants–past, present, and future.

Broken Wings

A Flight Attendant's Journey

by
Nattanya Andersen

Introduction

Awake from the dream
in which you sleep
and you will triumph over all
that is done against you.

–Inscription from a Bronze Age Egyptian ornament[1]

Unlike many other youngsters, I never had to ponder what I wanted to be when I grew up. I knew almost from the cradle that I would be a stewardess. Too young to pursue my destiny, but with wanderlust already deeply ingrained in my being, I left school and, with my mother's reluctant consent, was hired by Dansk Fransk Dampskibsselskabet, a shipping line out of Copenhagen, Denmark. At the tender age of seventeen, I set sail out of Hamburg, Germany for West Africa via various ports of call accompanied by one other stewardess, thirty sailors and no passengers. My life as a world traveler began.

During twelve months onboard ship, I was treated like everybody's little sister and the crew took it upon themselves to educate me as quickly as possible about journeying through the world's perils. Encounters with harbor police in European ports became common as we hung out at the less fashionable establishments close to the docks. Invariably, my obvious youth compelled authorities to check if I really was on the crew list. As a traveler, I was maturing quickly, though in hindsight, my innocence, fearlessness, and ignorance saved me in some rather tricky situations. I crossed the Bay of Biscayne in hurricane winds as if I were born to it, learned to swab decks, and even to paint the 15,000 ton vessel from bow

3

to stern (with the captain's permission). The journey was filled with memories. Mesmerized by my slender, blond, green-eyed presence, Canary Islanders offered me gifts of perfume and flowers; I graciously declined their gifts of live canary birds. I climbed Cape Verde's extinct volcanoes, swam in the wonderful but shark-infested waters off Pointe Noire, and crossed through jungle roads to the mouth of the Congo River. Often when I roamed the countryside around Boma and Matadi, Nigerian Ibo UN soldiers would stop their jeeps, curious about what I was doing in places far away from the vessel. And on every trip, I visited orphanages run by nuns to deliver some presents, inquire about the state of affairs, and practice my French. While in the company of "my" sailors, I learned Danish at a fascinating speed, my paternal grandmother having originated from that country. Throughout my journeys, wherever I went, I felt I belonged; to whomever I spoke, I could relate somehow. Nothing ever fazed me.

Then the inevitable happened. I fell in love; we were engaged and went to Copenhagen. There, with stewardess aspirations still firmly anchored in my mind, I became an *au-pair* to the children of an American three-star general and began to hone my English skills. When Pan American Airways conducted interviews that autumn, I promptly went but was gently rejected with a "We'd take you, but you're too young. Come back next year." By then I was married and working for Danish Rigstelefonen, the government-owned telephone company. I did everything I could to stay in touch with the beckoning world beyond.

When my husband and I discovered that children were not in our cards, my wanderlust intensified. I became a Lufthansa ground hostess at Kastrup, the international airport in Copenhagen, which afforded me the first taste of dealing with the flying public. It was then I learned honesty by far surpasses deception. Grumbling passengers were told frankly why no aircraft was there or when a mechanical problem could be resolved, and that it would be far better for their emotional well-being to joyfully kill time by savoring the exhilarating airport atmosphere than to fly into a rage. It worked like a charm every time.

Talk is sweet, but action is what counts—especially in a marriage—and mine had turned from a dance on roses to one on thorns. After a solitary journey to North America, I informed my husband of my decision to move there to join a major carrier as a flight attendant. He was not amused. Two months later I was gone, separation papers in hand. My marriage was over, but my dream career had begun with the airline I shall refer to as NorAm.[2]

After passing the six week flight attendant training course with flying colors, the airline based me in Montréal, Québec, Canada where for the first years I flew exclusively to Copenhagen. During a layover, I met yet another sailor whom I joined whenever possible to cruise around the world or to steal kisses in his ports of call. But, alas, good things don't last forever and we parted ways when he made no sincere attempt to pursue a life on earth, and I refused to raise our yet to be conceived children on my own.

Though on off-duty days during the summers I was steady racing crew on sailboats, I soon tired of the long east coast winters. I requested a transfer from NorAm and moved to Vancouver, British Columbia, Canada. Taking advantage of the nearby coastal mountains, I learned to ski and spent all my spare time at Whistler until marrying a long-distance trucker who modified my travel interests to cruising the continent in his Peterbilt. Flying and trucking, however, took their toll. And to my great sorrow, when children did not announce their arrival, my trucker and I split—for a while.

Eventually, I bought a house in British Columbia and began attending Simon Fraser University to broaden my intellectual horizons. Trips to Greece, Turkey, Italy, Morocco and even attending school in Spain delightfully augmented my scholarly endeavors. Soon my life was unfolding with all the color, excitement, and delight that I had imagined would accompany a cherished career as a flight attendant. I had the perfect job, the stability of my own home, and life was balanced with a satisfying blend of intellectual, emotional and spiritual growth, travel, fun, and work. My happy, busy world seemed infallible, until a mid-air aircraft engine explosion in 1988 turned my existence and my being upside down.

The explosion triggered a downward spiral of events and consequences that has disrupted dreams and broken wings of flight. Shortly after the incident, I was diagnosed as having Post Traumatic Stress Disorder (PTSD). The journey to recovery has been arduous and lengthy, primarily because PTSD in aircrews is so little understood by the medical establishment and partly, I surmise, because the airline industry has little to gain and much to lose from such understanding.

An ordeal of almost indescribable proportion began, as I was constantly assailed with demands from the Workers' Compensation Board, mental health practitioners, the airline, my union, and the insurance company. Confusion, obfuscation, and senseless political and bureaucratic parlaying created unreasonable turbulence in my life for almost a decade.

A turning point in my journey came when mental health professional number eleven—twenty-four physicians dealt with my case in all—insinuated that I must have been raped, otherwise I could not be PTSD-impaired. His verdict so infuriated me that I began research at the university into PTSD in flight attendants. (I had by this time completed a university degree, graduating in high standing.) I quickly discovered that no research on PTSD in cabin crews existed, and that only three studies had been conducted exclusively on flight attendants—one on menstrual cycles, one on pregnancy, and a third on cabin crews' physical energy expenditure during long haul flights.

Casting a wider net, I extended my research on PTSD to encompass pilots, but was equally unsuccessful. Only one obscure study remotely relating PTSD in military pilots and their passengers existed. My innate curiosity now knew no bounds, and I meticulously searched through volumes of books, journals, periodicals, anything which perhaps would give me insight into aircrew mental and physical health. The peculiar absence of research on commercial airline crews amazed me. It was as if we did not exist.

I did find research concerning psychiatric illness and stress in military and commercial pilots, in wives of commercial pilots, and in people on the ground hit by aircraft. I also found the one and only study conducted on fear of flying in commercial pilots and cabin crew published in the mid-90s.[3] The overall result of this research taught me that my reaction to the explosion, combined with innumerable previous and subsequent incidents, was perfectly normal. I concluded that my PTSD symptoms continued so long after the explosion solely because of the "treatment" I received from the Workers' Compensation Board, which acted on instructions from the airline, the flight attendants' union, and the wage indemnity insurance company.

Convinced I was not impaired by a fear of flying, I jumped on a Boeing 737 stateside heading to Las Vegas. During takeoff, I cried out of pure joy to be doing what was most dear to my life—flying. In Nevada, I tested my hypothesis again as I checked out the Grand Canyon in a Comanche. The flight was as exhilarating as it was affirming. Upon my return to Vancouver I told my psychiatrist about my achievements and he informed the airline. He supported my desire to return to work by gradual reintegration, but NorAm would not or could not make up its mind whether I should be permitted to do so. Instead, it seemed that everyone involved set about rallying forces to rattle my cage in all ways imaginable. But I held my ground, sometimes not too steadily, and I patiently awaited the carrier's verdict.

Remarkably, the decision took nine months. By the time it arrived I had ventured to China, flying as a passenger to and fro all over that country. This was something even a vaguely sane individual rarely undertakes, for it is well-known in flying circles that Chinese air traffic controllers seem to have an aversion to space between aircraft. I wasn't bothered in the least by the Chinese trips—I was just thrilled to be flying. Believing I would die when my time was up, I now knew until that time arrived, the world was once again my playground, a world where distances meant nothing. My broken wings mended, I could now take flight to wherever and whenever the urge compelled me, for work or for pleasure.

From that point on I was far too busy mending my soul to waste much energy on the airline's decision. My lawyer would handle the dispute, while I continued the task of researching, revisiting and putting on paper the traumatic events of the past years that I had suffered the effects of PTSD.

Writing this book became a task of almost indescribable upheaval, though the experience was not altogether negative, because while writing, the awesome events of the last decade became liberally interspersed with joyful remembrances of episodes with my peers in days gone by.

As I wrote, I knew no hours of the day. I walked, dreamed, and talked only about this book—it obsessed me and ruled my existence. Throughout, my closest friend Annemarie, a NorAm flight attendant, spent endless hours on the phone with me, patiently listening to my discourse. And at those times when my expressions and words became too volatile, mirroring my anger, frustration and rage at the hands of my opponents, she gently pried me away from emotional upheaval and led me onto better ways of making my point. My psychiatrist and general practitioner encouraged me, so did two of my previous professors, now dear friends of mine.

Within two months I had a basic manuscript in which only the research concerning PTSD and other threats, afflictions, and dangers to aircrews needed to be integrated with my own story. Determining how to do that became child's play in comparison to the immense catharsis I headed toward while going through my personal files. Even though no end of my catastrophe was in sight, and with my mother's and friends' immense help, compassion, empathy, knowledge, feedback and belief in my capabilities, I overcame the emotional trauma inflicted by my opponents, and was now unstoppable. This book would be published—if I had to do it myself.

In *Broken Wings* I touch upon the struggles and emotional upheavals experienced during my PTSD recovery. Interwoven are descriptions of aircrew's way of life, both on and off duty. This book reflects the joys, frustrations, and "incidents" my colleagues and I shared during my career which spanned March 1973 to October 1990. I understand, through my continued contact with aircrew, that since then, life in the skies has changed dramatically—for the worse—for both flight atten- dants and pilots, albeit for different reasons. However, the anecdotes I have included about hijack threats, aborted takeoffs, inflight electrical failures, oven and engine fires, turbulence, aircrew training, mechanical failures and mishaps, air quality and quantity, and inadequate ventila- tion systems and their implication in illnesses have a currency and rele- vance to the present. The research I have cited and documented in the bibliography is the latest available, however ancient it may seem. All events mentioned in my own story are documented; all anecdotes factual.

I purposely stayed away from the metaphysical aspects of my journey, even though meditation, yoga, dreams, hands-on healing, and numerous other events in that genre helped me to maintain my sanity. I wanted this book about flight to be as down to earth as possible.

I also wanted to be clear that I was not casting any aspersions on "my" airline, since what I have to say reflects how all major North American airlines operate. Therefore, I used the pseudonym "North American Airways" ("NorAm" for short) because the topics I address are generic to most airlines worldwide unless otherwise specified. And aircrew? Well, they feel and act the same regardless of race, color, creed, or employer. Nonetheless, the identities of those mentioned in my book were equally disguised.

I wrote this book because, to my knowledge, all the issues raised in *Broken Wings*—especially the phenomena of PTSD in flight crews—have never been written about in detail for the general public, nor has a flight attendant ever written a book about his or her professional life. Furthermore, except for one recently published study surveying six flight attendants involved in a crash, no research appears to have been conducted concerning how near-miss and aircraft disaster survivors— including aircrew—are treated following an incident. Their stories have never been told. Their certain change in the perception of the world and everything in it has never been the focus of the mass-media nor has it been the source of insider information for the airline industry itself.

The time has come for commercial air carriers to stop increasing their profits while perpetually eroding and ignoring flight attendants' working conditions. They must change their ruthless and indifferent attitudes toward physically and emotionally injured cabin personnel by taking responsibility when such injury or illness occurs because of PTSD disabilities, deplorable air quality and quantity, radiation, fatigue, inflight turbulence, and electrical and mechanical failures.

Research on professional pilots has shown again and again that nothing will keep them on the ground without good reason. Flight attendants are no different. In my view, we are the world's most motivated work force. For us, flying is not a way of life. It is life. Many earthbound industries can doubtlessly make the same claim for the devotion of their workers. There is, therefore, far-reaching relevance in the treatment that I received throughout my journey from NorAm, the Workers' Compensation Board, the union and the insurance corporation—and unfortunately, the issues I raise through my case description are synonymous with what any North American worker injured on the job site can expect.

The traditional mystery, romance and mystique surrounding the business culture of the commercial aircrew seems to fascinate earthbound populations and to interest people from every layer of society. I believe my story has global significance for every air carrier's corporate echelon, for governments, for aircrews of all stripes and flavors, and especially for the flying public. However, my book is dedicated to the world's flight attendants in the hope that *Broken Wings* will prevent any one of them from ever having to live through what I have.

Broken Wings

NorAm's Boeing 727 took off from Ottawa's McDonald-Cartier Airport en route to Calgary and Vancouver with three pilots, four flight attendants and an almost full house. We climbed into the bluest of skies sprinkled with a few puffy clouds and a breeze too soft to cause even the slightest tipping of the wings after liftoff.

Reaching that undetermined and instinctively estimated height at which flight attendants feel the danger for an unwarranted "incident"—airline terminology for mishaps—had passed, I unbuckled my harness, grabbed a cigarette and matches out of the galley drawer, leaned back in my seat, swung my feet on the counter opposite and waited for the non-smoking sign to blink off.

Suddenly a blue flash shot across the churning rotor blades of engine number three. Seconds later, an enormous roar reverberating through the downward swerving aircraft jolted me into Red Alert. "That's it. We're going down," was my only thought. As my entire life began spinning through my mind like a movie in fast-forward, we leveled out.

Time was suspended; time was not. Nothing existed, except dead silence. We kept steady. The rotor blades whirled within the casing. There was no smoke. "*Ergo,*" I thought, "there is no fire." I focused on my surroundings. "Got to look and see how Patsy's doing." Turning the corner into the tail cone, I saw her clinging to the jump seat, white as a ghost.

"Tanya, I'm so scared. I'm so afraid. I'm so scared," she mumbled over and over again.

"That's normal, Patsy. We're all right now. Just stay put. I'm going up front, OK?" Passengers sat as if frozen and no one paid attention to me. People always seem to turn numb when the wings of death brush an aircraft.

The in-charge flight attendant (also called purser; abbreviated to in-charge) sat by the front exit door, her emergency position for takeoff and landing. She greeted me with an almost nonchalant, "Oh, hi Tanya, I think we blew an engine." Her voice was wooden, controlled.

"Tell me about it. I was sitting right beside it. Anybody going to say something to the people?"

"The pilots are in their manuals. They're in contact with the ground. We've got to dump at least 30,000 pounds of fuel. They'll come on the

P.A. as soon as they've got a minute," she responded mechanically, almost like a robot. No one appeared to notice me when I walked slowly toward the back.

After what seemed an eternity, but could actually only have been about twenty minutes, the captain advised over the P.A. that there was absolutely nothing to worry about. We would be going to Montréal where fire trucks and ambulances would be lined up at the runway: a standard procedure in situations like ours. We would land in approximately ninety minutes. What he didn't have to say was that normal flying time between Ottawa and Montreal is twenty-five minutes. All service was suspended and smoking was prohibited. I returned my cigarette to the galley drawer.

Over our internal communication system, the captain privately told us to be prepared for an emergency evacuation upon landing without explaining why or what we might expect to happen. Patsy and I figured the landing gear might collapse during touch down. If that happened, the friction between fuselage and runway would create sparks possibly igniting a fire and possibly causing the aircraft to explode. In a separate call, the pilot bestowed upon me the task of watching the engine like a hawk, and to immediately notify the flight deck of any changes. I did as he asked, clueless as what to watch for. Perhaps the engine would fall off or burst into flames taking all of us into Nirvana.

The leaves on the trees below sparkled in shards of spring colors. I looked for a road. There was none. If we had to descend, there would be nothing but trees to land on. My mind wandered to the past. I knew we would not have as spectacular a crash as the Russian supersonic TU144 at Le Bourget air show in Paris that I witnessed in 1973. After a touch-and-go (where the plane comes in for a simulated landing, touches the runway for a few seconds, and immediately takes off again), the aircraft returned to the sky at an extremely steep angle and, suddenly flipped—its nose headed straight down.

When pieces of wing began to fly off the plane, strangled cries of "Oh, no. Oh, no." rose from thousands of throats in a muted roar. The supersonic crashed into a high-rise building in Goussainville, a hamlet some twenty miles away, killing twenty-eight of its occupants and the aircrew. As the thick column of smoke rose on the horizon, it was time to follow the custom developed during the First World War to prevent survivors and onlookers of air crashes from losing their sense of invulnerability. As many planes as the sky could safely hold immediately took to the air to "salute the dead."[1] My four pilot companions and I saluted the departed souls at the bar of the closest pavilion.

It crossed my mind that no one would grace us with such farewells if we met with an untimely death here in Quebec's northern forests. And if we did, we would undoubtedly present an equally earth-shattering sight as the one I witnessed in March of 1974 when we approached Paris' Orly Airport a few hours after a Turkish Airways DC10's forward cargo loading door accidentally opened. Three hundred and forty six people were hurled into the Ermenonville Forest, their bodies, severed limbs, pieces of clothing, broken suitcases, freight and aircraft parts grotesquely decorating the trees like ghastly and bizarre Christmas ornaments. Yes, I knew what it would look like if the unthinkable happened.

There is really nothing worse than, without distraction, waiting for an accident to happen. Patsy and our passengers were glued to their seats, and my reminiscences soon bored me. So I asked Patsy for her uniform bow and began to change it, with the help of needle and thread, from a drab, unfeminine, ugly flat pile of junk into a lovely sophisticated artifact. As I put in the last stitches, the pilot advised us to prepare for landing, and shortly thereafter we touched the ground as softly as a feather, fire trucks and ambulances trailing us down the runway until we rolled to a stop. I watched firemen and ambulance attendants approach the aircraft, excitedly pointing at the fuselage.

"Patsy, Patsy!" I hollered, knowing it would not disturb passengers now we were safely on the ground, "Come and look! There's more than meets the eye." She refused to budge. The emergency crews climbed back into their vehicles, and a parade of aircraft, fire trucks, and ambulances headed toward the terminal. Airline ground personnel, standing outside their freight offices and hangars, waved at us and held up thumbs, signaling relief. Tears started rolling down my cheeks. "Stop it," I said to myself, "You can't cry now. You must look good for the people." While still in flight, we'd been told an aircraft stood by to carry us to our intended destinations.

The rear air stairs were lowered as soon as we stopped at the gate. Patsy zoomed out the front exit door after passengers equally eager to depart, but I zipped out the tail end to assess the damage. A ground supervisor in hot pursuit shouted to me, "Hurry, hurry! Get to the other plane." I ignored him. When my feet touched the tarmac, I was tempted for a split second to kiss it. I decided otherwise when I spotted our captain. "Hi! I'm Tanya Andersen. May I give you a kiss for that beautiful landing?"

"Hi, Tanya Andersen. I'm Jean-Paul Dubois. Don't kiss me, kiss the First Officer. He landed it on one engine," the pilot responded. Engine number one, opposite the exploded one, had been shut down to avoid spin-out during the reverse thrust which breaks the aircraft's speed upon touchdown. I approached the First, who stood by the damaged engine surrounded by fire fighters, mechanics, ramp supervisors and ramp guys. We bear-hugged and exchanged kisses on the cheek before I looked at the engine. An unspectacular hole the size of two large dinner plates seemed the only damage. However, holes like bullet shots and clusters of holes forward of the engine and all around the galley door and my window punctured the entire fuselage from the tail section up to midship. "You seen the top?" a mechanic asked. "No? Well, come on then. Let's have a look."

We stepped into the empty aircraft, I opened the galley door, stretched up to see the engine top, and discovered that only the rotor blade casing remained. The mechanic took a peek and pointing at the shrapnel holes, he exclaimed, "My, oh my, honey. Were you ever lucky! If one of these had hit the fuel line, you'd surely be in heaven by now!" He explained to me that the main fuel lines to the engines ran about seven inches above the galley door. The area now looked as if machine gun fire had perforated it.

The ground supervisor came charging down the aisle, shouting angrily, "You gotta hurry! We want to board the other aircraft—now!" He was insisting on standard procedure. Cabin crew has to be on board before passenger loading can begin just in case of a ground emergency. In the early 70s, a DC8 at the gate in Toronto was engulfed in flames so rapidly the on-board crew barely escaped with their lives. Their luggage burned with the plane. Only the blackened skeleton of the aircraft's frame remained.

In no mood to be pushed around, cajoled, bullied or hustled, I informed the supervisor in no uncertain terms that coffee and cigarettes at the gate were next on my agenda, and suggested he get accustomed to the idea. He sped off huffing and puffing. I gathered my belongings, thanked the mechanic for his information, picked up a milk carton filled with coffee, and a bag with cups, snack packs and creamers I had prepared inflight, and caught up with my peers who sat smoking in the terminal by the gate. We shared the goodies and vigorously puffed away in silence until we were rudely interrupted by the now extremely frustrated supervisor. "You've got to board now. You're not paid for doing nothing, you know," he bellowed furiously. He got that right! Hanging around airports never earns us a penny. Only the time between "engines on–engines off" does. We packed up however, and boarded the other plane, where our flustered in-charge knew better than to comment on our tardy arrival.

When passenger boarding had been completed, we noticed two of our earlier passengers had decided buses and trains were preferable to playing birds in the sky. The doors closed, and the purser showed up in the back galley to ask, "You OK to continue?"

"Yep," Patsy and I responded in unison. After the purser left we exchanged annoyed glances. "Good timing on her part!" Patsy hissed under her breath. We'd been on the ground at least two hours and hadn't even seen the purser until we boarded. Her question was rhetorical at best, and clearly disinterested. She knew perfectly well we would not walk off now. Departure could be delayed for hours if the airline had to find replacement crew. The passengers would be furious, the cockpit crew would ridicule us and blame us for the delay, and the company would persecute us if we did. A few minutes later we lifted off.

Throughout the flight, passengers were as quiet as Vatican mice, immensely appreciative, undemanding and polite, and they still had no questions. It's the same in all near misses. Passengers freeze and turn numb—contrary to Hollywood portrayals—and they never want to know anything. This ostrich-like syndrome is well-known among aircrew, as is passengers' sudden gratitude which likely stems from their brush with death. Thrilled to be alive, passengers can be jolted back to life's basics, even to manners.

No announcements were made from the flight deck during the six hour trip to Calgary and Vancouver. Neither Patsy nor I visited the flight deck, nor did we talk about the explosion with passengers or among ourselves. Everyone on board appeared to be blissfully enshrouded in complete denial.

When I arrived at home I shed the uniform, took my dog, Jessie Alabama, for a spin, and, comforted by a case of beer, called around the globe to tell friends I was still alive and kicking, and I loved them. I rang everyone, except my mother—I could not possibly tell her how close I had come to dying in the line of duty.

Three days later I kept an appointment made weeks earlier with a tarot card reader, someone I hadn't met before. (Circumventing the globe in an aluminum can as a profession seems to encourage explorations of the metaphysical, a fascination shared by most flight attendants and even some pilots.) As I entered the reader's home she asked me three consecutive times, "How are you?"

Slightly bored and irritated with her insistence, I replied, "Fine."

After I shuffled and dealt the cards into three stacks, she laid them out and said, "Within the next two years you'll have to make up your mind whether you want to live or die. If you decide to die you surely will. Not by committing suicide but by the power of your mind."

Since the thought of death and dying in the line of duty was alien to my psyche, I didn't mention the explosion. Nor did I share with her that I had developed feelings about the futility of life so overwhelming that everything bored me to death.

The excruciating sharp, shooting pains from the base of my neck to the top of my skull started the day before I had to return to work. Stepping into a Boeing 727 for a two-day East Coast trip, my head pounded with such ferocity that I dug a handful of aspirins from the on-board medical kit and began munching them. The pain continued intermittently as if activated by an on–off switch. I hid in my work position in the forward galley as much as I could and refused to communicate above and beyond the call of duty with my peers (none of whom I knew) and passengers. As far as I was concerned they could all go to hell.

During the short layover I tried to get rid of the headache by lying motionless on my bed, but it helped little. The headache continued until I returned home, and reappeared when I dove into the municipal pool. Instead of swimming sixty-four laps, which I had done for years, I left after four. Jessie sulked when I barked back at him that I did not want to be taken for a walk. All I wanted to do was to lie motionless and try to stop the headache. Night after night I woke bathed in perspiration, but was unable to recall any dreams. At 6:00 A.M., before heading out to work for my second trip after the accident, I called my long-time astrologer. She also holds a masters degree in the General Arts with emphasis on psychology. "Linda, there's something terribly wrong with me," I said, "but I don't know what. I'm on my way to the airport. Could I see you when I come back on Friday?"

"Sure can. Come over Saturday morning at nine," she replied.

Upon boarding the aircraft I started eating aspirins like chocolates, but as I already knew, they would not ease the spasmodic pain. People seemingly tugging at me from all directions as if wanting my soul, further aggravated the spasms. "Don't be so freaking impatient. You'll get what you're supposed to in due time. Just sit down, shut up, await your turn, and leave me alone. Just bloody well leave me alone!" I wanted to shout at the demanding business class vultures—while trying to forget where I was.

The eight hour Halifax layover, at a dive near the airport and the local stock car race track, provided unparalleled listening enjoyment of repeatedly revving car engines. Race enthusiasts shouted and screamed late into the night. The whining and knocking sounds created by air-locks in the motel's pipes would be fixed, the night watchman assured, when maintenance arrived at 7:00 A.M. By then, we were en route to Vancouver via Ottawa and Calgary. This time I worked the back galley, and for takeoffs and landings I again sat by the galley loading door. Both tail cone flight attendant seats were occupied, and rather than hike up front to sit beside the chatty in-charge, I wanted to nurse my splitting head.

Of course I was aware that if an emergency occurs, sitting in the galley can be dangerous. Meal and bar trolleys could break loose, and beverage units could fall from their storage compartments burying the flight attendant in a barrage of heavy items. But I figured we were equally vulnerable wherever we sat. For years I had appeased frightened passengers with a gentle, "If it's your day, it's your day, no matter where you are," until one day a lady quipped back, "But what if it's the captain's day?"

"Well, then it's ours as well," I thought buckling her in. Sitting in the galley would neither enhance nor impede my chances of survival, but it afforded me a view of Mother Earth from lofty heights. My dream to have that view whenever I desired had come true fifteen years earlier—many years after I saw "my" first air hostess at the age of five, and decided in an instant I wanted a flying career.

A short stint as stewardess in the Danish merchant marine, beginning at the age of seventeen, and a nine-year marriage preceded the fulfillment of my dream. During the six weeks I spent at flight attendant training school in the spring of 1973, we were sent on a familiarization flight to work as additional crew members. After I completed my trip, the in-charge wrote just two words on my performance evaluation report, "Super Girl!" I was born for the job, and I knew it. And, after my jubilant graduation, the earth became my sandbox.

This day in May 1988, however, the excruciating headache hampered my delight in the job and my viewing enjoyment of Mother Earth. When the pain reached heretofore unknown proportions before landing in Vancouver, my peers suggested that I must have sprained a neck muscle. Galley duty, pushing, pulling, and lifting of heavy, and often stuck equipment, is hard, injury-inducing labor, and sprained muscles are not uncommon. I filled out a report to the effect that I had a neck injury. One of my peers and the captain signed it and, after landing, I took it to the airline's medical office close to the airport.

There, the physician glanced at it, wriggled my head back and forth while ignoring my gasps, knocked full force on top of my skull, then handed me some Robaxacet and shrugged with his appraisal, "Oh, it's nothing. You'll be brand new in a couple of days." I didn't mention the explosion to him, nor had I talked to my crew about it, and he did not inquire whether anything out of the ordinary had recently happened to me.

At home, I hastened to open a bottle of wine and washed down the muscle relaxing medication while crying uncontrollably without knowing why. My friend Annemarie, a flight attendant, a mother of four and a university student, called minutes later, listened to my despair for a short while, and said, "What you're experiencing is directly related to the engine explosion. Trisha (a flight attendant friend of hers) had the same reaction after an engine explosion mid-air on a DC9. No one diagnosed her properly and she quit. Talk to someone at the office—now."

I made the call. When a supervisor came on the line I was, by that time, almost hysterical, awash in tears. Rather incoherently, I explained my predicament to the best of my ability and told her about the appointment with Linda, my long-term astrologer, the following day. I mentioned Linda had a degree focused in psychology. Apparently relieved that a solution was easily at hand, the supervisor enthused, "Sure, go and see her as long as you want. We'll pick up the tab." Without words of consolation, without reference to the explosion, or its relevance to my condition, she released me from flight duties and rang off. It was 4:35 in the afternoon, Friday, May 13, 1988.

Linda had done my annual astrological chart since 1980. I knew that, since obtaining her Master's in 1987, she counseled people in despair. Furthermore, I believed her knowledge of my destiny would enable her to rapidly shed light on the reasons for my emotional disturbance.

When Linda set eyes upon my miserable being and heard my story, she immediately diagnosed Post Traumatic Stress Disorder (PTSD). I felt a great sense of relief to know there was a reason for my state of mind. "The Gods faltered," she responded when I asked why she had not been able to see a major upheaval in my chart, which she had interpreted for me only three weeks earlier. "And don't despair," she added soothingly, "Since it's not an accident created by the heavens, you'll be back to normal in no time flat." She requested I keep a journal and present her with entries at our future sessions. "In the meantime," she demanded, "eliminate the words *would have, should have, if* and *but* from your speech pattern." Thus began her treatment for my PTSD.

Post Traumatic Stress Disorder

According to medical authorities, to qualify for a PTSD diagnosis, an individual must have experienced or witnessed a recognizable and indisputable distressing event outside the range of normal experiences. Such traumatic events include experiences in military combat, violent personal assault (sexual or physical), robbery, mugging, kidnapping, being taken hostage, torture, incarceration as a prisoner of war or as a concentration camp inmate, natural or man-made disasters, and severe automobile accidents. Other less seemly events include being diagnosed with a life-threatening illness, suffering serious injury, awareness of the unnatural death of another person due to violent assault, accident, war, or disaster, or unexpectedly witnessing a dead body or body parts. The traumatizing event is usually experienced with fear, terror, and a feeling of helplessness. The disorder may be especially severe or long lasting in case of torture or rape. The intensity of the event, the physical proximity to the stressor, and any previously experienced trauma may increase the likelihood of developing PTSD.[2]

Notable symptoms of the ailment include phobic avoidance of situations, activities, or people who arouse recollections of the event or resemble or symbolize the original trauma. Other effects are a diminished responsiveness to the external world, also known as psychic numbing or emotional amnesia, a feeling of detachment or estrangement from others, sleep disturbances manifested by recurrent distressing dreams of the event. The person is easily startled, displaying hypervigilance responses, irritability or outbursts of anger, lack of concentration, memory loss, and avoidance of sensitivity activities, such as a total disinterest in sex (or an intensification of sexual sensitivity) after the exposure to potential disaster. Furthermore, a person suffering from PTSD often has a sense of a foreshortened future.

Other side effects of the ailment are a change from the individual's previous personality characteristics. Sufferers may display self-destructive and impulsive behavior, experience social withdrawal, feelings of ineffectiveness, shame, despair, or hopelessness. They may have feelings of being permanently damaged, suffer the loss of previously sustained beliefs, and exhibit hostility and feelings of constantly being threatened. They may engage in deliberate efforts to avoid thoughts, feelings, or conversations about the traumatic event. PTSD sufferers are also at an increased risk of developing phobias such as panic disorder, agoraphobia, obsessive-compulsive disorder, social phobia, as well as major depressive, somatization, and substance-related disorders. It is not known to what extent these disorders precede or follow the onset of Post Traumatic Stress Disorder.[3]

PTSD can occur at any age, including childhood. Symptoms usually begin within the first three months after the trauma, although there may be a delay of months, or even years, before the onset of symptoms. The severity, duration and proximity of an individual's exposure to the traumatic event are the most important factors affecting the development of this disorder. Duration of the symptoms varies, with complete recovery occurring within three months in approximately 50% of the cases, whereas many others have persisting symptoms for longer than twelve months after the trauma.

There is some evidence that variables such as social support, family history, childhood experience, personality, and pre-existing disorders may influence the development of PTSD, though the disorder can develop in individuals without any predisposing conditions, particularly if the stressor is especially extreme.[4] Victim-battering intensifies the symptoms of an ailment particularly noteworthy for its high levels of depression, suicide attempts or gestures, and alcohol abuse. The ailment affects virtually all spheres of life causing clinically significant distress and impairment in social, occupational, or other important areas of functioning, all of which may interfere with interpersonal relationships and lead to marital conflict, divorce, and job loss.[5] Psychosomatic illnesses often manifest the emotional upheaval.[6]

Approximately 1250 PTSD studies on people of all walks of life and occupations have been conducted worldwide. Among the subjects have been Norwegian fire fighters, victims of holdups at gun point, motor vehicle accident and rape victims, crane operators, people rescued at sea, concentration camp survivors, and Vietnam veterans.[7]

Only one 1991 Ph.D. thesis entitled "Post-traumatic Stress Disorder in Canadian Aircraft Accident Survivors," analyses PTSD in military pilots and their passengers.[8] The results of this study, which involved 261 pilots and 69 passengers (305 males and 25 females), who were surveyed by mail, showed an overall PTSD incident rate of 14.5% (males 13.1%, females 32%, pilots 12.3% and passengers 23.2%). These figures suggest military pilots and passengers are susceptible to it, and that passengers are more likely to suffer from the ailment than cockpit crews. The only study available on PTSD in flight attendants was published in March of 1995, after assessing six cabin crew members who survived an airplane crash in which forty-seven passengers were killed, and they themselves physically injured to varying degrees. All flight attendants displayed PTSD symptoms eighteen months after the accident. It is unknown how the seventy-nine passengers who survived fared, seventy-four of whom were suffering from serious physical injuries.[9] Besides, as I've shown in the list of occurrences accepted by the mental health profession as causing PTSD, aircraft accidents and incidents are nowhere to be found.[10]

But in 1988, I knew nothing about Post Traumatic Stress Disorder and its inherent symptoms. Nor was I aware of the absence of research into PTSD in aircrew and the implications that it would present for my case. I trusted NorAm had expertise in the field. And, because the company consented to my astrologer being the treating therapist, I thought myself in capable hands. Besides, I was fully aware of only one thing—I would be in the air again. Flying for me is more than a profession, more than a vocation, or a way of life. It is life.

Grounded

The void I felt within frightened me—so did my overwhelming feelings of futility. Digging up dandelions in my yard, drinking beer and watching televised baseball games became my passions. Nightmares killed my sleep.

The airline requested I see a new company physician at the end of May (the twit prescribing Robaxacet had been fired), who diagnosed a functional depression because my actions and reactions deviated from my usual behavior. I disagreed. He insisted. "Continue with your counselor and see us later," he demanded while ushering me out the door.

When I arrived home exhausted, cranky, and with a pounding headache, I dug out some psychology books, bought at a friend's garage sale years earlier, and discovered that I did not suffer from a depression in the conventional sense. According to the books, I must be perfectly healthy, for none mentioned my symptoms.

Perhaps the exclusion of my symptoms in the textbooks encouraged me to venture out into the world to test my communication abilities, which I thought lost forever, for my foreign language skills had all but disappeared after the explosion. But nothing had changed. People still smiled at me for no apparent reason and I smiled back, wondering why they did so when I was the epitome of misery. Quickly tiring of participating in the merry-go-round—a futile exercise when we were all going to die anyway—I quickly retreated to the sanctuary of my yard and dug up dandelions, staining them with tears.

At the end of May my counselor, the astrologer, whom I visited twice weekly, asked, "Are you happy being miserable?"

"Miserable? What do you mean? I'm not miserable, just *non-feeling...* I feel nothing," I answered, while silently wondering if I would ever laugh, be happy-go-lucky, strong, articulate, and expressive again. If only I could decide whether to live or die! In brighter moments, however, I looked at my despair as a journey, as an adventure which would, I hoped, lead to perpetual serenity, atonement, and awareness.

I cried bitterly throughout all our sessions. Whereas counseling did little to relieve the pains of my soul, talking to two flight attendants did. Their experience, though different from my own, began to shed light on my feelings.

In 1983 both of them had been working on a Boeing 767 en route from Ottawa to Edmonton carrying sixty-one passengers, six cabin crew members, and two pilots when it ran out of fuel about halfway to its destination.

The plane glided onto the runway of an abandoned military air base at Gimli, Manitoba, Canada. No lives were lost, nor were any significant physical injuries reported. Psychological damage arising from life-threatening aircraft incidents were unacknowledged by the Ministry of Transport. Apparently, only broken bones, burned bodies and fountains of blood are considered injuries.[1]

Investigators noted in the accident inquest report, however, that the flight attendants' anxiety levels had increased during the event because they lacked the understanding that aircraft could glide, and perhaps land, without engine power.[2]

Flight attendants *do* know that planes can glide. What they don't know is for how long a plane will do so, because that depends entirely on the type of emergency. In July 1996, after Trans World Airways' Boeing 747 blew in half in mid-air, the aircraft's aft-section reportedly glided for approximately ten seconds, while the front part immediately descended to earth. Theoretically, a structurally sound Boeing 747 could keep aloft if all engines were lost, but for how long would depend on weight, wind and weather. Consequently, the cause for flight attendant anxiety in emergencies becomes specific to the incident. When, where, and how the plane is going to go down is anxiety provoking—not whether or not it can glide. During inflight emergencies, however, flight attendants most often can only guess at the cause of an incident and the possible consequences, because information from the flight deck is minimal.[3] This further heightens cabin crews' anxiety levels. But when things get rough the boys, logically, have more important things to do than chit-chat with those in the back end.

The inquest report also stated that, "Although the evacuation was successful and the cabin crew reacted calmly to the emergency, there is evidence that [the airline's] evacuation procedures and training may not be adequate to deal with a "worse" case evacuation."[4] The cabin crew, the inquest points out, had previously been trained on the Boeing 747, and the only training they received on the Boeing 767 had been through filmed instructions. Flight attendants employed on various aircraft types, they asserted, should receive training on each type. And they are! Annually they receive training through videos, operate a mock-up door and window emergency exit, and write exams on emergency equipment and procedures. Hands-on training occurs when they work the aircraft—and it has an accident. Only once, while in training school at the beginning of their careers, do they experience what an inflated chute looks like and how it feels to slide down one. For many cabin crew members, that experience dates back to an earlier era of the Super Constellation, the Viscount, and the DC8.

The Gimli inquest commissioner decided that the flight attendants' actions and reactions during and after the accident resulted from a lack of company training. He failed to conclude, however, that perhaps the lack of training also contributed to their post-accident reaction. All six of them suffered PTSD. During their illness, they were kept on the company payroll.

The report does not reveal the pilots' post-accident reactions. Presumably, they failed to exhibit adverse emotional reactions because, unlike flight attendants and passengers, they were not sitting ducks in a barrel but could fight. That ability, one could assume, resulted in feelings of elation, a natural high, after they victoriously defied death.

However, Lisa and Carolyn, the two flight attendants on the Gimli flight who had experienced what I was now living, assured me that my emotional despair—the incessant crying, the doubting of the purpose of life, the feelings of futility, the nightmares, the alienation from others—were normal. "Don't worry. You're on the right track. It'll take time. Eight–ten months...perhaps...sometimes two years or more. But you'll be OK. Once you've analyzed, evaluated, and made peace with your previous, life it'll get better. You'll never be as you were before...you'll be much better. So... don't worry. There's nothing wrong with you. You're absolutely normal."

When Carolyn's husband joined us, I related the story of the Montréal supervisor's behavior. "Disgusting," he responded. "To ignore the explosion as if it didn't happen is a company trick to downplay the affair. They have to pay your salary, and everybody else's, for the rest of your life if you never fly again. That's why they don't offer any sympathy or acknowledgment. Who's helping you work through this?"

"My astrologer. The medical office gave me permission to continue with her. They'll pay for it."

Choking, he responded, "Makes sense. It's cheaper for them than paying the Board [WCB] for an accredited mental health professional. Plus she doesn't have a clue what she's dealing with. And therefore they think she'll force you back on the line faster. And then watch out. Better find a good psychiatrist."

"But I don't want to see any strangers!" I cried.

"Well, do what you want. But I warned you," he replied softly.

Hours later I drove away, exhausted, puffy-eyed, yet elated. I needn't worry—improvement would happen with time. But my elation was short-lived. Time crawled by, every day was an eternity to live, with no feelings other than feeling dead from the inside out, the desire for peace, and to be left alone.

Peace and solitude further eluded me when, on June 2nd, 1988, NorAm ordered me to the airport immediately to write another incident report. Because I appeared in the office too upset and unfocused to think coherently, the union's health and safety officer, and a supervisor dictated the incident report to me—based on their imaginings of the event.

On June 8th, I met with a third company physician. She, too sanctioned counseling by my astrologer but, when I asked if I could bid for a flight schedule in July, she responded, "Forget it! Let's take one step at a time. Come and see us in a month." Later that same day, unknown to me, NorAm's claims officer informed the WCB that—"due to emotional problems"—I was seeking treatment from the airline's Employees Assistance Centre. At that time I didn't even know that such a program existed.

The depressingly sunny days dragged on, and I continued to live in my private world in which nothing mattered, except in my dreams where I ran, always ran. Furthermore, my memory lapsed, my 20/20 vision deteriorated, and driving the car became an anxiety-ridden adventure.[5]

One day, crossing the huge Port Mann Bridge, near Vancouver, during rush hour traffic, I almost froze behind the wheel. Disgusted, I mumbled to myself, "How ridiculous. You've sailed the Seven Seas, climbed extinct volcanoes on the Cape Verde Islands, gone to the source of the Congo River, trucked back and forth over the Rocky Mountains in all seasons, driven from the Yukon to Mexico, done camel racing with the Tuaregs in the Sahara desert, traveled to Lebanon, Morocco, Greece and Turkey alone, and now you tremble with fear when crossing a lousy bridge?"

To overcome my phobia, I resolved to pick up Jennifer—a flight attendant friend who commuted between Los Angeles and Vancouver—at the airport whenever she flew into town. When time allowed, we'd "shop 'til we dropped," and wine and dine together. When she was out, I visited with Annemarie or Carolyn, who lived on opposite sides of town. And always when I parted with any of them, I would think, "Will I see her again or will she die in a crash?" That the Workers' Compensation Board had not contacted me was also becoming a burden to my soul.

The Worker's Compensation Board, a brainchild of Germany's chancellor Bismarck, was approved and implemented under Emperor Wilhelm I in 1884. The concept was adopted by Britain in 1897, and ultimately brought to the Canadian provinces around the turn of the twentieth century. Before long, the idea of a workers' compensation board went stateside between 1908 and 1912, replacing the Law of Employers' liability in thirty-one states, and the territories of Alaska and Hawaii, between 1911 and 1915. By 1921, forty-two states had workers' compensation laws.

The implementation of WCB insulated employers from the economic consequences of employees' injuries, and practically eliminated the incentive or necessity to provide safe and hazard-free work places.[6] However, the right of injured employees to sue their employers was abolished in most parts of North America because of the belief that WCB would ostensibly achieve its goals, which included such promises as the compensation of workers without regard to fault as to the cause of injuries, and to provide swift and certain compensation.[7] The U.S. National Safety Council estimates that every year 14,000 workers are killed and 2.2 million disabled in industrial accidents—an estimate considered far too low.[8]

As a flight attendant though, I did not consider myself a blue collar worker, and thought I would never have to deal with the Workers' Compensation Board after a near miss. I had always believed my airline would look after me if I were to be injured in an accident or incident. But NorAm did not. Instead, they delivered me to the WCB, between whose hands—an image which appears on their logo—I would almost be crushed to death.

My first contact with WCB occurred on June 17, 1988, when someone from their psychology department advised me, "We've arranged for an interview with a Board psychologist on July 25th." Three times I verified the date with the caller before it sank in that this was not a cruel joke.

"That's insane," I hollered. "My accident happened on May 1st and you can't see me before July 25th?"

"Well, that's the way it is. If you don't like it, you can go back to work— *now*. Bye," she retorted, hanging up.

A nervous tick appeared under my left eye. Later that afternoon, NorAm demanded I attend a training session on firefighting the following day. I declined.

On June 23rd, I inquired at the WCB about my claim, and was told by an adjudicator that none had been filed and, therefore, nothing could be claimed. "That's nonsense. Numerous reports have been filed. Your psychology department has made an appointment with me. Get with it and contact the airline," I said, and slammed down the phone.

The psychology department rang seconds later. "We want you to come in tomorrow to fill out some forms."

"What kind of forms?"

"Oh, just routine matters. Bring glasses along if you need them, and be prepared to stay for a couple of hours," she curtly responded, and disconnected.

In a major fury I called my astrologer who haughtily reproached me, "You've no reason to be upset. It's just part of their proceedings. Look at it constructively!"

"Constructively!" I yelled at the top of my lungs, "You call this constructive? My ass. I'm being forced to fight for something I should have automatically. I should be kept on payroll until I'm fit to fly. I'm a good worker and always earned my money. And now I'm treated like dirt. I don't want to see anyone from WCB. I want to be on full salary. I've already seen three company doctors, and none of them sent a report to the Board? And you call this constructive? It's unfair and totally unreasonable, that's what it is! It's not my fault the engine blew.

"Our aircraft have had lousy maintenance for years. Everybody knows that! Last summer in London a mechanic told us we need a major disaster to smarten up and get back to standards. We all know we can't fly without duct tape, for heaven's sake. It's pure luck not more accidents happen. Look at all the mishaps I've had in fifteen years.

"And why don't they want to tell me why the engine blew?—cause they're hiding something! I'm going to the press with this. I will!"

My counselor listened with infuriating apathy and offered no feedback. I threw the receiver down, sensing with all my being that nothing was right and something had to be done about it. I phoned the union, but my officers ignored the calls.

At the Board the following day, the routine matter turned out to be the Minnesota Multiphasic Personality Inventory(MMPI) and Beck's Personality Inventory, tests created to evaluate a claimant's basic personality characteristics and state of mind.[9] The MMPI, developed in the early 40s, couched in archaic terminology and using psychiatric patients as criterion groups, is also used as a screening device in industrial and military settings.[10] It can be administered to subjects sixteen years or older with at least six years of schooling, and an IQ of above 80. The test purportedly requires an hour to an hour and a half to finish, but college-level subjects are thought to be able to do it in forty-five minutes.

To assure the subject knows how to respond to the testing situation, the administrator is encouraged to ask a few questions beforehand, so that any obvious lack of comprehension can be detected. Then, the test is to be presented as a serious and important matter conducted for the subject's benefit. The subject must be encouraged to respond to all questions, even when unsure if a statement applies to him or to her. The test participant is advised not to spend time on any item—first impressions are desired. Test administrators are cautioned not to show flippancy or superficiality, or become overly officious, friendly or gossipy, because subjects are said to easily sense such attitudes, and might respond with lightness or an unwillingness to reveal personal feelings or socially unacceptable actions.

If asked by a subject, "Should I answer the items as they apply to me now, or as they did before my trauma?" the administrator circumvents the issue by directing, "Answer *True* if it is 'mostly true'." If, however, the administrator knows that the subject has recently faced a trauma such as a close relative's death, and questions arise whether to express current feelings or feelings before the death, the subject is encouraged to describe the present emotions.[11]

Lapping up the instructions given by the secretary, I dove in to the testing with some enthusiasm. After all, I reasoned, these people were interested in helping me to get better. After responding to the MMPI's 550 statements which included such declarations as:

- It takes a lot of argument to convince most people of the truth
- Once in a while I think of things too bad to talk about
- I hear strange things when I am alone
- Most of the time I wish I were dead

I then went on to the completion of the Beck's Inventory's 21 groups of ideas from which to make a choice, such as:
- I have not noticed any recent change in my interest in sex
- I am less interested in sex than I used to be
- I am much less interested in sex now
- I have lost interest in sex completely

...and:
- I do not feel sad
- I feel sad
- I am sad all the time and I can't snap out of it
- I am so sad or unhappy that I can't stand it.

The tests seemed to be child's play. Two hours after my arrival, I left with a splitting headache and the directive that the Board would call when a psychologist was ready to see me.

The following day, June 26th, an Air France Airbus crashed. I saluted the dead and waited for two more accidents to occur.

Three days later, for the first time since the accident, I consulted my personal physician who had been my GP for the past eleven years. "I didn't come before," I explained to him, "because I thought NorAm's physicians were qualified to deal with this. But now I have my doubts." He diagnosed my condition as PTSD, informed the WCB that there were marked differences in me before and after the May 1st, 1988 incident, and requested a report from my astrologer. When I returned home, a message from the Board's psychology department mandated my presence on their compound the following day, June 30th, at 10 A.M.

A well-dressed, pleasant looking psychologist named Rosaly Cavarro greeted me that morning and escorted me into her office, where teary-eyed I told my story, and said that I wanted to fly again as soon as possible.

"Be patient. It'll take time," she cautioned, "But don't worry. You'll be your usual self again." She, too, gave me permission to continue seeing my astrologer, but stipulated that, if satisfactory progress were not made after a reasonable time, a change of treatment method and therapist would be considered.

I didn't inquire about what constituted a "reasonable time" period or what other methods would be applied. When I left her office 90 minutes later, I was also unaware that I had just left the lion's den, and that everything I said would be manipulated, distorted, and held against me from that point on.

After my interview, Cavarro issued a report to the adjudicator that read like an astrological chart, except, that it was based on the MMPI result instead of the planets at the time of my birth. Loaded with modifiers, and expressing apparent concerns about the validity of her MMPI-guided opinion, the report bordered on the ridiculous.[12]

"This tall, slender, well-groomed, friendly, cooperative, readily-responding-to-questions stewardess," she wrote, "appears to present with features of PTSD. These symptoms appeared to be related to the work incident of May 1st, 1988. The claimant had admitted to feeling somewhat abandoned and upset by what appeared to be a lack of response from NorAm related to this traumatic event. There was insufficient information to determine the presence of pre-morbid factors which affected this disability. The claimant reported no previous history of psychological or psychiatric difficulties. Thus, there did not appear to be pre-morbid factors." In her conclusion Cavarro thanked the adjudicator for the interesting referral.

Cavarro's specific reference to the non-existence of pre-morbid characteristics was prompted by NorAm's claims officer who had requested, on May 18th, 1988, that the Board kindly scrutinize all medical reports in order to ascertain that the engine explosion was indeed the cause of my current disability.[13]

Unaware of the happenings behind the scenes, some of my innate optimism returned because, I figured, the WCB would now accept my claim and leave me in peace to recuperate.

This dream soon blew to pieces. On July 1st, my astrologer demanded that I start thinking about going back to flying. Hardly believing my ears, I asked her to repeat her statement, whereupon she yelled in a shrill, high-pitched voice, "You *must* learn to listen to what's being said. You must start thinking about returning to flying."

I began to cry and begged her not to mention it again for a while, because the thought of flying made me sick to my stomach and gave me a splitting headache. I left her house in a miserable state; the pains soon disappeared by drowning my thoughts in beer and baseball. Two days later she called to remind me to visualize going back to flying.

"Visualize going back to flying?" I shouted. "If I hear 'visualize going back to flying' once more I'm going to scream. The thought alone makes me ill," and I slammed down the receiver.

My sense of helplessness increased, along with my emotional exhaustion. I felt a lack of sparkle in my life; my energy and appetite had all but vanished. My excessive smoking, drinking, and crying worried me, but I did not have the energy to change my behavior. It was fine and dandy for my astrologer to say, "Ignore the past and live in the now," but how could I? My future was at stake—and I had no money coming in, and no clue about what the WCB or NorAm intended to do to me.

My fears became compounded when, at every given opportunity my astrologer mentioned that she was on a first name basis with the Board's adjudicator and psychologist, and how pleased they were with her reports on my splendid progress. I became distrustful of her. I lashed out at her in my journal, but she never addressed anything I wrote in it. Instead, she condescendingly hammered it into me that I had never loved myself—therefore my kindness to others was but an act of hypocrisy. The hopelessness and the fear of never coming out of this disaster sent me to the television, searching for a baseball game. Instead, the news blasted that an American aircraft carrier had shot down an Iranian Air Airbus over the Gulf of Amman.

I reeled as if in a tailspin. There would be retaliation. Where? When? Who? "Stay in the now. Stay in the here and now," I kept repeating. That night, July 3rd, 1988, my most terrifying dream—being kidnapped by terrorists at a terminal while on the aircraft—began. It reoccurred relentlessly, but lunches and shopping sprees with Jennifer, tending the garden, killing dandelions, and walking the dog returned me to some equilibrium after a few days. And in my brighter moments I knew within my heart that I would get through this upheaval with flying colors.

But my nervous system was frayed, and at an African drum concert the unruly behavior, yelling and screaming of some youngsters so infuriated me that I wanted to strangle both parents and kids; the violence of my thoughts frightened me as much as my driving. Even wonderful Jessie Alabama irritated me by following me around like a shadow wherever I ventured. Occasional glimmers of hope presented at low tide, such as a retroactive cheque from WCB on July 11th, 1988. The check heralded their decision to pay me $420 weekly in wage loss benefits, about $1000 less than my monthly flight attendant salary. Busy deciding whether to live or die—with the help of beer, baseball, and dandelions—overrode my sentiments about the injustice of it all.

"One night without nightmares. Just one night without nightmares," I appealed to the heavens after another night of images with terrorists and running, interspersed with Zeus and Apollo foretelling my future at the Oracle of Delphi. I was unable to recall how it would unfold after I woke up. My astrologer interpreted it as coming into my own power again. I grasped at the straw. My headaches became less frequent and cabin fever set in. I inquired about an Alaska cruise. At our July 16th session, however, my enthusiasm to go died with the astrologer's incessant harping about my mandatory and imminent return to flying.

Later that day, two flight attendants shared with me over dinner their most recent extraordinary events in the sky. One was an unscheduled emergency landing and evacuation at Goose Bay, Labrador, because of a bomb scare. Another flight experienced bad engine trouble mid-air, resulting in super high anxiety levels for cabin crew. Still another involved lightning hitting the aircraft at 35,000 feet. Unknown to me at that time, the U.S. National Transportation Safety Board recorded forty lightning-related aircraft accidents between 1963–89, ten involving commercial airplanes. Four of those resulted in 260 fatalities and twenty-eight serious injuries.[14] After listening to these and numerous other incidents of lesser severity for two hours, I excused myself and flew homeward on the Trans-Canada highway at breakneck speed, my own near misses crowding my mind.

I remembered the DC8-Stretch flight in 1974 en route from Halifax to London, England, with Teapot Charlie (a captain who carried his own teapot wherever he ventured), with an all female cabin crew. I had volunteered to work both economy galleys mid-ship, positions normally held by two flight attendants. While picking up plastic glasses in the back cabin, a swarthy looking passenger ordered me to sit down beside him.

"I don't have time now. Maybe later," I replied.

"Better sit down. I've gotta gun." I sat down, and he informed me that five armed Palestinians were in the forward cabin ready to take down the aircraft as soon as he gave the command—but first he wished to see the captain. "Now!"

"I'll ask him," I answered, "But may I have some ID, please?" He produced a card identifying him as a Palestinian medical doctor. Card in hand, I went to the flight deck.

"Don't breathe a word to the others, Charlie instructed. "Watch him like a hawk. And don't let anyone near here. Call as soon as he moves. We'll land in Prestwick in about two and a half hours." I left, asked my colleagues to let no one near the cockpit, and requested they keep on watering the Arabs in row 15 and 16, who were drinking rum and coke. I then returned to my dangerous acquaintance in the back cabin, told him that the captain would see him after the meal service, and handed him a rum and coke.

When I began to stall the service, and use trolleys to block the aisles to make movement difficult, my peers became increasingly distressed with my idiotic performance, so I clued them in. When we finally began serving dinner—90 minutes out of Prestwick my fellow made his way to the galley demanding access to the captain. "Won't be long now," I responded, handing him another rum and coke—spiked with Gravol as the previous one had been. (His companions had received the same tincture). He turned about, and I followed him back to his seat with his meal. When I picked up the remnants, he was fast asleep. So were his companions.

Prestwick police awakened the would-be hijackers and took them into custody. We debriefed at our London hotel without Charlie, who never hung out with his crew. On the homebound run he imparted the information that the Arabs had carried handguns, and that machine guns had been found in their luggage. We heard nothing more about the incident.

Another episode on a DC8-Stretch also came to mind. On a summer evening in the mid-70s on an evening run between Ottawa and Toronto, we were filled to the rafters with businessmen. The captain advised all aboard over the P.A. system that engine number four was on fire, and to prepare for an emergency landing at Toronto's Lester B. Pearson International. Our numb and muted passengers handed us their attaché cases. We piled them up in the washrooms, took our emergency positions, and waited silently for events to unfold. Touchdown was smooth, and the fire trucks and ambulances that had lined up along the runway dispersed immediately afterwards. Wild applause from the passengers broke the tension.

While at the gate awaiting our scheduled deadhead flight—deadheading is when aircrew fly as passengers in the line of duty—on another aircraft to Montréal, our home base, the other flight attendants and I began to tremble. Once aboard, we threw sweaters over our uniforms and launched a survival celebration, which continued until the early morning hours in a Dollard-des-Ormeaux brasserie.

But no incident could top the L-1011-100 near miss I experienced a few days before Christmas of 1980 during takeoff en route from Vancouver to Toronto. Zooming down the runway on a crystal clear Sunday morning, packed to the roof with a Torontonian cockpit crew at the controls, engine power was suddenly cut. Minutes later, the captain announced that a light on the instrument panel indicated a technical malfunctioning. We would taxi back to the start of the runway, where a mechanic would board to investigate the problem.

A short while later we tried again. The scenario repeated itself halfway down the runway. This time the first officer apologized for the inconvenience before announcing the same message as the captain had before him. My colleagues and I smilingly reassured our passengers that there was nothing to worry about. "Happens all the time. Standard procedure. Don't worry. You'll be there soon enough. Jet stream's going to get us there on time," knowing full well that a frown or a worried expression would alarm our charges.

The mechanic apparently insisted that there was nothing wrong, for we took another run at it. Passengers' faces fixed on ours, we knew as soon as the brakes released, upon revving up the engines, that something was terribly wrong; but we did not move a muscle. Instead of roaring forward, the aircraft sluggishly crawled ahead for seconds before suddenly hurling down the runway at tremendous speed. An enormous bang, followed by cracking and groaning noises brought the plane to a shrieking halt. Overhead bins burst open, spilling some of their contents. No one budged. No one made an announcement. Complete silence filled the cabin. I can't remember when we came to life again, nor if anything was said until we reached the gate. I only remember the silence.

By the time the flight attendants deplaned, our captain and first officer had long disappeared to write reports. The fledgling second officer was still around, however, and revealed to us on our way to the crew lounge that engine number three had exploded and caught fire. The water bomb inside the engine had extinguished it. We had been ten knots away from the point of no return, the moment an aircraft has to fly regardless of what happens. If we had taken wing, we would have landed in one of the largest shopping malls in town. Before we could press the Second for further information, the First arrived to haul him away. Three hours later, our contractual on duty time limitation prohibited the airline from sending us anywhere that day. We were free to go home.

Cruising down the Trans-Canada at a high rate of speed I steamed myself into a frenzy reliving these near misses, and called the astrologer the second I stepped into the house. "Why did you push me to return to flying again today when you knew how upset I became?" I asked as soon as she picked up the phone. "You've no idea what it is to be up there. You've never tried it. So for fuck sake drop it, will you, 'cause you don't have a clue what you are talking about."

"Well, I just want to give you an opportunity to prove that you can do it," she answered with infuriating calmness.

"To prove to whom that I can do it? I don't need to prove anything to you or anyone else! I'll go flying when I'm ready. And now is not the time," I replied angrily.

"O.K., Tanya, just calm down," she responded.

"Easy for you to say," I screamed and hung up.

The next day I picked Jennifer up at the airport and told her about the latest development. She had also known the astrologer for years.

"I tell you!—she's not helping you. She's only in it for her own profit. She hiked her fee thirty percent when you walked through the door, didn't she? And now she's trying to establish a reputation with the Board by trying to get you back in record time. So...watch out. Have you seen your GP again?"

"Got an appointment tomorrow."

"Good. Get him to find a psychiatrist for you—now."

"But I don't want to see a stranger!"

"If you don't, you're doomed. I warn you."

The following day my GP insisted that a psychiatrist knowledgeable about PTSD in aircrew had to be found to treat me. He would shop around for one and make the referral.

"My physician is looking for a psychiatrist for me," I said to the astrologer at our next session.

"What on Earth do you think you're doing?" she yelled, outraged. "Don't you know that the first thing he'll do when seeing you in your pitiful state is to give you drugs? And what do you think'll happen with WCB?

They'll cut you off if you switch to someone else! Or they'll force you to see another psychologist at the Board. Your GP only wants you to see a psychiatrist because he thinks you'll have problems with NorAm in the future. But you know they accepted me as counselor—so if you leave me, you'll have nothing but trouble," she screamed, scaring the living daylight out of me.

"But I want to go on seeing you. It's just to have someone better qualified," I wailed.

"Can't do".

"But why not?" I cried out.

"Conflict of interest," she replied coldly and launched into an explanation of how not to give one's power away—a topic which intrigued me.

"Perhaps her treatment is beneficial after all," I thought on my way home, pangs of guilt and disloyalty gnawing at me. The dandelions experienced mass slaughter. A few days later my GP had arranged for an appointment with a psychiatrist who also held a private pilot's license.

"Tell me your story," the psychiatrist asked at our first meeting.

"But you already know what happened," I replied, my heart racing. I knew he had heard the story from my GP.

"Doesn't matter. Tell me anyhow," he kindly persisted. So I did, tears streaming down my cheeks. Our time was up before I knew it.

"Try not to worry. Everything will be fine. Come and see me again in fourteen days," he said while escorting me to the door. He hadn't mentioned either medication or journal writing, and I drove away relieved knowing I was in good hands—finally. At home, the answering machine related the message that the astrologer still wanted to see me on July 29th.

"Brother, did I cry throughout the session," I exclaimed when I stepped into her house.

She replied acidly, "We do that because they're paid to listen to us. That's why we dump everything on them. But you should think very, very carefully about seeing this man again. After all, I know you not only through your astrological chart and your journal writings—I also have a deep spiritual understanding and can read your aura and perceive the radiation coming from your solar plexus. Don't you realize that?"

Scared once more, I thought, "What if she has psychic power? What if her predictions about WCB and NorAm come true? What does she know that I don't?" I sat motionless, silently awaiting the next blow.

Seconds later she screamed, "You've called me about a hangnail in the middle of the night and now you don't trust me with the evaluation of your state of mind even though I know so much about you?"

"But *both* you and he can treat me," I suggested meekly.

"You deaf or something? I've already told you—that's impossible! It would be conflict of interest! Don't you listen?"

"But I want to continue to see you, and where there's a will there's a way," I insisted, trying to maintain peace. I had to. She still had $435 of mine on retainer. I left greatly disturbed and limped home to contemplate the situation while watching baseball and drinking beer.

A few days later, when Jennifer heard the story and learned about my feelings of disloyalty, she could barely contain herself. "For heaven's sake, woman, get with it! She only takes care of one person—herself. Now, let's go get your money and dismiss her!"

Aircrew
and
Cosmic Radiation

My psychiatrist, a Scottish, Santa Claus look-alike, enjoyed sharing episodes about his life and anecdotes about his patients with me. And through his subtle method, I slowly became aware of the complexity of the psyche and drifted back to living life. Dandelions lost their appeal, and the acute stress attacks and tension headaches began to afflict me less frequently. Cabin fever set in again, and I drove to the States to visit with friends.

Hurrying homeward-bound down Interstate 5, an eighteen-wheeler in the passing lane lost a right tire—which missed me by a hair's breadth. Moving at a snail's pace to the next off-ramp, I made it home via country roads and a ferry to avoid the Port Mann Bridge. The following day I became the owner of a 1973 Cadillac Eldorado—armored tanks were nowhere for sale. When hearing about my acquisition, my psychiatrist commented, "You know, when you finished your life during the explosion to find yourself on earth again afterwards, you began to mourn your former self which was no more. Since then, you've spent time like a child in the womb, resolving the old, and creating the new. And now, you're being born again. And like a newborn, you'll start to move your limbs, then you'll crawl and walk and, if you want to, you'll run again. Be patient. It takes time. But you're going to make it. You'll not be as you were before. You'll be much better. Just wait and see."

In September I went on a spiritual quest in an effort to help myself. In the months that followed, I began attending yoga classes, and participated in seminars about kinesiology, reiki, rebirthing, self-hypnosis, and reflexology. I also adopted a ten-month-old black Labrador female so that Jessie would have company when I returned to flying.

Behind the scenes, on September 13th, NorAm requested that WCB provide information about when I would be considered fit to work. They offered to assist by gradually reintegrating me into a suitable employment of their choice. The adjudicator asked Cavarro to evaluate my health; she, in turn, requested an interview with me on October 18th. After that interview, Cavarro advised the NorAm adjudicator that I had made notable improvement, but at this time could not return to my pre-accident employment—nor was she able to estimate when I could do so. The adjudicator blew his stack, barking that he wanted to know *when* I could work, not *what* work I could perform. So she hauled me in for another evaluation on December 12th, which was followed by an interview with a WCB Vocational Rehabilitation Consultant (VRC) named Ray.

Ray reported to the adjudicator that I liked being a flight attendant, but believed in a balanced life where work would allow more freedom, more money, and more time off for leisure activities. Doubting his sanity, I wondered in what other type of employment, other than that of a flight attendant, a woman could earn an annual salary of $40,000, enjoy thousands of dollars in tax-free expenses while flying, have forty-two vacation days (which translated into at least two months off when combined with days off), and work eight to twelve days a month, which allowed for all the leisure activities imaginable. But I knew that he was an absolute ignoramus, when telling him about my practice of Transcendental Meditation (TM) inspired him to supreme ridicule and sarcasm.

What Ray either didn't know or wouldn't acknowledge, is that relaxation training—of which yoga is one type and meditation another—has been reported in the medical literature to have wide clinical application. That Transcendental Meditation positively influences emotional and psychological stability is well documented.[1] For example, Vietnam veterans, after three months of practicing TM, showed significant reductions in depression, anxiety, emotional numbness, alcohol consumption, insomnia, family problems, and other symptoms of PTSD.[2]

When psychotherapy includes meditation, subjects experience greater change in the direction of positive mental health and positive personality change, self-actualization, increased spontaneity, self-regard and inner directness, and a self-perceived increase in the capacity for intimate contact, than control groups who do not use meditation. Furthermore, studies suggest that meditation, "through its capacity to awaken altered states of consciousness, may profoundly reorient an individual's attitude and sense of well-being and purpose in life."[3] In the literature, researchers emphasize that relaxation and meditation should be considered as an adjunct or alternative, non-pharmacological therapy for psychiatric disorders, such as hypertension and flying phobia. This therapy is especially recommended for people in occupations such as aviation, where the side effects from medications cause great concern,[4] and almost always disqualify the patient from flight duties.

Ray also stated in his report that I fully intended to go back to my job. The time frame for that return was uncertain because, he noted, I had been advised by my psychiatrist that improvement would be slow, and therefore, I was the best judge of my own ability to resume my duties. I would know, the psychiatrist said, "when the time comes" to go back. In the report's conclusion, he quipped that "with this worker the period of disability appears to be somewhat open-ended." But he did warn the

adjudicator that cajoling or marshaling me back to work could be premature and counterproductive, and that WCB's involvement, to any significant degree, would be disruptive if not done properly.

At a pre-Christmas team meeting on December 20th, 1988, the adjudicator raged that "the claimant is dictating when she will be returning to
work and under which conditions." He went on to declare that the spo-
radic medical documentation provided insufficient data for him to grasp
the claimant's progress. Despite testimonies of all the mental health professionals, who agreed that I'd made gradual progress but was presently
unable to engage in any gainful employment, the adjudicator aimed at
cutting off my benefits before the holidays. On December 22nd, my
psychiatrist told him that possibly I could return to work in January.

Blissfully unaware about these interactions by the main players, I nevertheless sensed that kicking me back to work, regardless of my psychological condition, topped their agenda. It made me very anxious and,
when just before Christmas, two aircraft collided on a Birmingham
runway, a KLM Royal Dutch Airline crashed during a thunderstorm at
Faro, Portugal, and a Pan American Airways jet fell out of the sky over
Lockerbie, Scotland, I was thrown for a loop. All three kindled long-
forgotten memories.

Flying in and out of Moscow from Copenhagen for months on end in the
mid-70s, I remembered, always sparked excitement because of the language barrier. On these flights, we almost never carried more than ten
passengers, and during descent and approach, I could be in the flight
deck, with headset donned. That's when things always turned dicey,
because the Russian air traffic controllers' English left much to be
desired. "What's he sayin'?" rang out after almost every exchange, and
the crew would take a guess at the message, for requests to repeat were
met by silence. In we would steeple chase, throttle on–throttle off. One
day, having successfully landed in thick fog and instructed to cross the
runway and taxi to the terminal, we had just started following orders.
Three feet onto the runway, a military jet landed right in front of us.
It took us a few minutes before proceeding. The return to Copenhagen
was uneventful, and that evening, after a deadhead to London, we par-
tied at the Heathrow Airport Hotel's disco—subconsciously releasing the
inner tension caused by the close call at Moscow.

I also recalled a couple of hairy approaches and landings during thunderstorms which helped me visualize what those people on the Faro must
have gone through before final disaster hit. I remembered flying over the

Irish Sea en route to London on the morning of June 22, 1985, when British air traffic control asked us to look out for Air India's Boeing 747, which had disappeared from their radar. Nothing could be spotted in the stormy seas below, but we heard on arrival at our hotel that the aircraft had vanished, and that a bomb had most likely brought it down. That night we saluted the dead.

Now, alone two days before Christmas, I saluted those who had died over Lockerbie. While feelings of futility and loss of belonging washed over me, I again questioned whether I would die in the innate struggle to live. By New Year's I had regained my bearings—somewhat. Neither the airline nor the union had contacted me throughout the year.

On January 30, 1989, my psychiatrist called me to advise that NorAm had proposed a fourteen day reintegration into the system, and that they were willing to guarantee the minimum sixty-five hours flying time pay for the month. "If that's their idea of reintegration I'm going back full time or I'm not going back at all ," I responded.

He agreed, telling me that he thought the proposal ludicrous, and suggested, "Fly to Montréal and do your emergency training. If things go well, just dive in. If not, we'll wait for a while. How about that?"

"Fine with me."

"When do you want to try it?"

"At the end of February," I answered, silently hoping that I would be ready then.

WCB hauled me in on February 9, 1989, to complete another MMPI and a Beck's Inventory, and to be interviewed by Cavarro. She later reported to the adjudicator, that my somewhat lowered relative scale elevations suggested an improved level of functioning, but still indicated a propensity for psychological and physical illness if I was exposed to continued emotional stress.

Nineteen days later, I flew to Montréal. An excellent instructor and a congenial atmosphere in and out of the classroom put my mind at ease. After we received our safety qualification cards, and while we waited for the elevator to take us to the ground floor where cabs stood by to drive us to the airport, I asked a mechanic passing by, "Do you recall a 727 engine destroyed by a mid-air explosion last year on May 1st?"

"No, honey. I don't. We get so many of them. Happens all the time." We turned our homebound trip into a party.

No fanfare sounded when I reported at the airport for duty on March 8, 1989, bound for London. When I returned on March 10th, Air Ontario Flight 1363 had crashed in Dryden, Ontario, Canada, killing three crew members and twenty-one passengers. (Three more passengers died of their injuries shortly thereafter.)[5] Three trips later, NorAm ordered me to take thirty-five days of outstanding vacation leave before the end of May. Worn out, I obliged. My psychiatrist, whom I continued to see, advised both the Board and the airline in mid-April that I still had flight phobia, and that I needed systematic reintroduction to duties and monitoring. Otherwise, I would be subject to relapse. But when I returned from a two-week Hawaiian vacation at the end of May, he declared, "You've now reached awareness, atonement, and serenity, and are well on your way to a complete recovery."

In June, I flew domestic because it had given me more days off while on vacation. Because cabin crew tend to fly voluntarily either domestic or overseas, and I preferred to do the latter; it meant that I worked with strangers.

On the first trip of the month an emotionally shaken Vancouver cabin crew greeted us at the Toronto layover hotel's reception. An engine of their L-1011 had exploded shortly after takeoff en route to Vienna. At their debriefing I said, "You were lucky! At least they turned you around right away. They kept us hanging up there for an hour and forty-five minutes."

I launched into my tale and it's aftermath, after which one attendant said to no one in particular, "You know, I believe I had PTSD after a guy held me up in London."

"What! What happened? When? Where?" we all chorused.

She slowly began to speak. "Well, there I am, all dolled up, ready for pick-up [crew gathering in the lobby to be driven to the airport], opening my door, juggling shopping bags, suitcase and all that—you know how it is— and this black guy grabs me. Oh...he's 6'2"–6'3". He turns me around, pushes me back into the room, one hand over my mouth, knife at my throat, wanting my money and rings. I just gave it to him, and he left. Jessus, I was rattled. But my crew was super. Cooled me down somewhat. But you know, when I told Peter about it, he couldn't understand why I was so upset. Thought I was stupid or something. Threw him out that same day. Haven't seen him since.".

"Good for you. Ignorant ass. Pilots! What do you expect!" was the consensus.

"You remember the girl who was raped in Honolulu?" someone asked.

"Two," someone added. "That's why we switched hotels!" We now stayed at one which had security guards on each floor. "Didn't a TWA (Trans World Airways) stew get murdered in Trinidad a few years back?"

"Yeah, and another one in the U.S.—just saw it on *20/20* or *Unsolved Mysteries* the other day! Didn't show up for pickup and they found her murdered in her room. It's getting bad everywhere. Got to travel in packs—and even then.... In Kingston [Jamaica] they didn't want us to leave the hotel—even to walk a 100 yards for a change of scenery, and in New York it's hopeless. Did you know that Mick," [a six-footer with a boxer's build] "got robbed there in broad daylight a block from the hotel? Took his gold Rolex."

"Yeah, and Annemarie was stalked twice near the hotel in London this year."

And on and on it went, until the beverages we carried for just such occasions, were depleted. I returned to overseas flying in July to be with familiar faces in case the proverbial substance should hit the fan.

A couple of hours before liftoff for my first cycle of that month, a DC10 blew an engine, taking the aircraft's hydraulic system with it, and crashed short of the airport in Sioux City, Iowa. Two more mishaps would doubtlessly occur in rapid succession, we predicted, and our L-1011 was similar to the DC10. The full house, however, allowed little time for conscious contemplation, but, on the crew bus carrying us to our London hotel, we decided an immediate visit to the pub was in order.

Among pints of lager, the pilots explained the difference between the two aircraft's hydraulic systems. According to them, a DC10 loses all hydraulics when blowing the top engine, whereas a L-1011 maintains some maneuverability. "It was just short of a miracle they kept that thing afloat for as long as they did. Thought they were in for it when I heard about it. Fantastic piloting. Now you know what to stay away from," our captain exclaimed.

I could only think, "Thank heavens we don't have DC10s in our fleet." Homebound from London a few weeks later the Lockheed's huge engine hanging from the portside wing so mesmerized me, it almost threw me into a stupor.

A few days later, my physician discovered a lump in my breast. "Must be from my collision with a trolley door," I said.

"What'd you mean?"

"Happened when someone opened a meal trolley door when I bent down. They've steel corners, you know. Hit me right here," I explained, pointing to the lump. "I filled out a boob injury report. Gave everyone great joy. The pilots howled with laughter when I asked the skipper to sign it. What do we do now?"

"Send you to a specialist to determine whether it's malignant or not and take it from there," he advised, making an appointment.

In August 1989, approaching Toronto on the first flight leg of a five day cycle—a trip half way around the globe—we witnessed spectacular thunderstorms raging in the area, as tightly packed, mile-high cumulus clouds saturated the skies. The captain, looking like a kid in a candy store, swerved around the huge, threatening, dark clouds, and the Boeing 767 descended rapidly, bouncing, twisting, and turning. Ours was the last flight in before the airport shut down, and we flight attendants breathed a sigh of relief when the wheels touched the ground.

The following afternoon, another violent thunderstorm passing over the region halted air traffic for hours, and when Pearson reopened, only one runway could be used for takeoffs and landings. After we left the gate on time for our European destination and had joined the lineup, the captain announced, "We're number thirty-seven for takeoff and will depart in about two hours. Sit back and enjoy." The passengers moaned and groaned, but we heightened their spirits with spirits and peanuts, served by hand, because trolley movement through the aisles is prohibited during taxiing in case of an emergency. When the fuel-loaded tarmac air had become almost unbreathable, we took off. Our charges—watered, and fed some more—were tucked in for the night. Then we watched one of mother nature's most spectacular displays of lightning in the thunderheads below us, aurora borealis to the north, and a lunar eclipse above.

Late in the afternoon of August 28th, after I was packed and ready to depart for my last five day cycle the following morning, the phone rang. The Inflight Service Personnel Manager on the other end informed me, "We've taken you off your trip. You're overprojected."

"Overprojected? How so? I'm more than legal outbound!" I argued. This was ludicrous. They were drafting left, right and center, and *I* was illegal to go?

"That's just the way it is," Ted insisted. "We've got people on standby with less hours than you. They gotta go first. If the union officers check the records, we're in trouble."

"But Ted—first of all—I *am* legal. And when does the union ever check records? For goodness sake, you know that they fly over ninety hours every month in the summer if it suits them! Are they taking themselves off flights? Of course not! And I'll only have 84 hours when I return."

"Well, can't do anything about it. You're replaced, so don't show up tomorrow," and he hung up. I went ballistic. Throughout the week, no union officers were available to take my calls. Losing the cycle cost me $1200 net.

In September I returned to domestic flying and to the university—where I'd been a part-time student since 1985—to take one Spanish literature course. Working mostly with unfamiliar crew members was trying, and the rough approaches and landings on the East Coast during thunderstorms had put me on edge. Still, I felt much safer when not crossing oceans, and did domestics again in October. Everything was going well until the 27th when my psychiatrist told me of his immediate retirement. "Don't worry," he said, "You don't need to see anyone else. You're well on your way."

I went on vacation in November, and in December resumed overseas flying. I found myself scheduled to spend Christmas in London and New Year's at home. Only the most senior aircrew are able to get both holidays off. On December 11th, the cyst in my breast was removed under local anesthesia, and on December 20th, the surgeon confirmed that it was benign. I had been lucky. Later, my research on cosmic radiation and aircrew would reveal just how lucky I'd been.

Cosmic Radiation and Aircrew

A study conducted on Finnish female and male cabin attendants between 1967 and 1992 revealed that flight attendants are up to four times more likely to suffer from breast cancer than the earthbound female population.[6] Dr. Eero Pukkala (from the Finnish Cancer Registry) and Dr. Anssi Auvinen (from the Finnish Centre for Radiation Nuclear Safety), both participating researchers in the study, asserted in 1996 that "significantly raised risks" of breast and bone cancer had been found in female flight attendants. Another study by the Danish Cancer Society revealed an excess of breast and bone cancers as well as leukemias among both pilots and cabin crew. Preliminary studies by other researchers suggest that female flight attendants are almost twice as likely to suffer breast cancer and fifteen times more likely to have bone cancer than women in the general population.[7]

According to an article published in the 1996 issue of *Aviation, Space, and Environmental Medicine,* pilots appear to have the highest risk of leukemia among workers in any occupation, and are more likely to develop melanoma and cancer of the lower gut.[8] Incidents of cancer in male United States Air Force (USAF) aircrew compared with non-flying Air Force officers indicate that statistically significant excesses in aircrew cancers exist for all sites, including testes, and urinary tract. All other aviator cancer classifications, most notably cancers of the colon and rectum, skin, brain and nervous system, Hodgkin's disease, and leukemia, are said to be not significantly different from the comparison cohort.[9] However, research conducted in British Columbia, Canada, between 1950 and 1984 revealed that pilots suffer elevated mortality rates due to Hodgkin's disease as well as cancers of the colon, brain and nervous system.[10]

Some researchers hypothesize that the excess of brain tumors in pilots might be related, among factors such as number of flying hours, routes and altitude, to the synergistic interaction of cosmic radiation and ozone exposures existing at high altitude.[11] No one seems to have given it a thought, however, that radioactive materials, perpetually released into the atmosphere since Hiroshima and Nagasaki, might have settled at high altitudes forming a nuclear belt which is traversed by aircraft on a regular basis. We could deduce that something is detrimental to health when flying at high altitudes, because we know that for the very large aircraft (VLA) presently on the drawing boards, cabin altitudes as close to sea level as possible are recommended.[12]

Presently, we can be certain that aviators suffer from brain tumors hitherto unknown to specialists, and that breast cancer generally regarded as common among flight attendants is well-known throughout the aircrew community.

Mr. Burgess-Webb, representative for the Canadian Airline Pilot Association, however, asserts that "The whole subject of cancer risk has been the subject of a number of studies in Canada and the U.S., and abroad, but nobody's been able to come up with anything definitive." He has gone so far as to suggest that aircrew may have to wear personal health badges and be *removed from their job* if radiation levels exceed health standard limits.[13] Why, one wonders, does he represent pilots and not the airline corporations?

A large survey to establish if there is any risk to *frequent flyers* is supposedly "underway" in the United States. That excludes aircrew. And *underway* does not mean it is presently being done. *Underway* for North American carriers means that it might be considered if no avenues can be found to avoid it. And who would push for it? Not the North American Airline Pilots Association. Not the North American Fight Attendant unions. Why? They are too fragmented to present a united front and push, or possibly pay, for in-depth investigations. And if the pilots are not pursuing the topic with a vengeance, flight attendants need not bother, because they wouldn't get a foot on the ground. After all, their primarily female ranks are perceived to be prone to ailments linked to their gender alone, giving carriers an enormous leeway to ridicule, downplay, or even misrepresent the health risks associated with flying. Besides, there are no data available on cabin crew health and there are no government regulations covering the reporting or documentation of the health and safety of cabin attendants. Furthermore, more than ten years ago, airlines largely closed their medical clinics to flight attendants.[14] That leaves passengers to pursue the matter, and they will not demand these investigations, for the vast majority of them are entirely unaware of the health risks lurking in the skies.

The growing fear that aircrew face an increased risk of cancer from exposure to cosmic radiation has recently prompted a European Community (EC) directive laying down safety standards for the protection of earthbound workers and the general population that will be extended to include aircrew. The directive, effective in May 2000, requires carriers to monitor and limit the radiation dose received by aircrew. This can only be achieved by either insulating aircraft so that less radiation penetrates the fuselage, or by reducing aircrew duty times. Reinsulating or upgrading the insulation would mean that a few commercial aircraft manufacturers worldwide would have to reconstruct aircraft. Reducing aircrew duty times would mean that carriers would have to hire additional crew. Both options would mean greater corporate expenditures and, therefore, less profit to share-holders—many of whom are management. But no one's panicking yet. A year remains before the directive's implementation in Europe, and by then, the industry will have found a way to get around it. After all, there are thousands of aircrew applicants who would give an arm and a leg to be roasted by the radiation after those who are presently flying have been burned in the line of duty and are permanently incapacitated.

———————✈———————

I nursed my sore breast until Christmas Eve, the day I went to London with an all female crew. Patricia, a jolly Scottish girl, and I worked in the back of the well-packed L-1011. Everything seemed peaceful in the cabin, even though booze consumption was as heavy as it always was on Christmas flights. Suddenly, fists were flying. Two men, one from Ireland and one from England, battled in the aisle. Our attempts to sepa-rate them were entirely unsuccessful, and we appealed to the flight deck for assistance. Our First Officer, a man of impressive stature, emerged, restraining devices in hand. The fighting cocks, stunned into silence, stood still, clinging to each other and staring into his face. "Airport Police will be waiting for you," he growled, which inspired them to let go of each other with a stream of profanities. Five hours remained to touch-down. To prevent further altercations, we transferred the Irish man and his family to First Class. And, because it was Christmas Eve, we did not contact Heathrow Police to arrest the two offenders for disturbing the peace on board a foreign vessel. We were little surprised when neither of them apologized to us for their behavior or thanked us for our leniency.

In Europe, all airports close on Christmas Day, and most cities are ghost towns. London was no exception. Most of my crew members spent the holiday with family in Britain, and the others gathered at the pub which opened for a few hours during the day. But it was dismal, and I retired early. On the 26th, however, there were people on the street, and the mom and pop stores were open. The hotel, after much nagging by air-crew from all corners of the world, made a hospitality suite available to us. A large poster to that effect had been placed in the lobby, and by five o'clock the room was packed to the rafters. Liquor flowed as the air-crews shared sordid and funny stories revolving around life in the fast lane. Time passed, kindred spirits turned melancholic, and when the party broke up in the wee hours of the morning, one pilot, who had flown in from Delhi that morning, navigated toward his room with a magnum of Grand Marnier glued to his lips. The strong and silent type, he'd barely uttered a word throughout the evening.

PILOT PERSONALITY TRAITS

Little is known about the personality traits of commercial, military, and trainee pilots because, after all, a pilot's highest recommendation is based on his or her flying experience. Nevertheless, the excess of applicants over demand places airlines in the position of making selections from a large pool of pilots—some of whom undoubtedly have interpersonal skills as well as impressive flight records. Other applicants have neither, but nonetheless are hired when acquainted with influential individuals able to pull strings.[15]

According to the latest survey dated 1974, however, there appear to be distinctive personality traits both in general and U.S. Navy aviation personnel when they have been compared to the earthbound American male population. Both aviator groups tested significantly higher than "normal" U.S. male adults in categories concerning autonomy, achievement, exhibition, dominance and change, and they tested significantly lower in factors such as deference, order, affiliation, succorrance, abasement, nurturance, and endurance.

From a psychoanalytical point of view, pilots portray profiles of courageousness, romance, and masculinity. Their orientation is to demonstrating strength and competency; they find pleasure in mastering complex tasks, and thrive on adventure. Decidedly heterosexual, whether male or female, the stereotype of myth, folklore, and motion pictures pervades this group.[16] It is also noteworthy that military combat pilots entering airline employment potentially manifest a "macho" personality which could pose training problems.[17]

I found only two studies on female aviator personality types: one on female military pilots and one on general aviation pilots.[18] Both indicate that women are just as capable of competently commanding an aircraft as their strong and silent macho counterparts. Interestingly, the pilots' statistical interactions, when evaluated by passengers, showed that the level of passenger concern was not entirely based on pilot performance, but rather on gender. When a female pilot performed well, her rating scored higher than that of an equally performing male, but when she performed poorly, her rating dropped lower than his.[19]

Men by far outnumber women aviators in military, general and commercial aviation, and this fact is often attributed to the assumption that various attempts to attract women into the industry have failed.[20] But this is not so. It is well known within the industry, that the management of major airlines—who usually perceive women as emotionally unstable and psychologically fickle—assume that passengers resent having female pilots in command. Once again, this is indeed not the case.[21] Yet, to this day, commercial carriers appear only to employ enough female pilots as they deem necessary to protect the airline against charges of gender discrimination.[22]

For those few women admitted into the hallowed male domain of pilots, life isn't exactly a dance on roses. The behavior of male military pilots towards women pursuing a flying career has been reported to be, at times, prejudicial, exploitive, patronizing, and, often, frankly sexual. Most likely, commercial pilots display similar attitudes.

Female flight attendants are accustomed to such antics. Taunting about body shapes, racial and ethnic backgrounds, age and looks are common, heavy-duty jokes and sexual innuendoes the norm. A mature female crew member's requests to change cabin temperature inevitably leads to the response: "It's that time of life, is it?" If the request comes from a younger woman, the forthcoming response is usually: "That time of the month?" When complaining about lack of air, the same cracks are uttered, or the men tell the women that more oxygen will only generate headaches, to which women are prone as far as they know. That's average pilot behavior, and it has been grudgingly tolerated by female cabin crew since the dawn of flying. What then, might one ask, would persuade women to fly as pilots? The answer is simple and eloquently expressed by an anonymous aviator:

> ...people are in it because it's their way of life.
> They are in it because they want to be;
> they don't want to be in anything else
> and would probably be happy to fly,
> even if they were not getting paid for it—well, almost!
> It's not really a job, it's a part of one's life.[23]

Anyone without this inexplicable and deep rooted love for flying, and the extraordinary lifestyle it represents—particularly for commercial aircrew—is incapable of coping with the inherent and inevitable stressors it provides. And one of those stressors is passenger combativeness. But our homeward bound flight from London on December 27th, went uneventfully, and on New Year's Eve I again thought, as I had the previous year, that neither NorAm nor the union gave a hoot about how I was doing.

In January 1990, I returned to domestic, hopping from the continent's extreme west to the extreme east and back again on Boeing 727s.

During the second cycle of the month we hit such severe turbulence during a descent into Halifax, that passengers and flight attendants in the back were paralyzed with fear. Working business class up front when the bad weather hit, I distanced myself from the distressing situation by focusing on NorAm's logo—attached to a galley unit across from my seat—until we landed. After we stopped at the loading bridge, our captain took the entirely extraordinary step of actually walking through the aircraft before the doors were opened, presumably to check that everyone aboard was uninjured. Ironically, he and his mates declined to participate in our St. John's Newfoundland debriefing, claiming their extremely short layover disallowed extracurricular activities. We, however, had forty-two hours to regain our bearings.

Cruising into St. John's fourteen days later, wind gusts and rain beating the aircraft, the fuselage moved at unreasonable angles, creaking, moaning and groaning, the wings popping up and down, seemingly ready to detach any minute. Flight attendants and passengers listened in dead silence, the cabin crew individually thinking we'd never make it this time. The only solace in the tension was that last week's pilots were in command. While everyone waited suspended for the wheels to touch the ground, the aircraft suddenly crashed onto the runway from a great height and careened from side to side until it screeched to a brief halt before veering onto the taxi way toward the terminal. Even the hearty and seasoned Newfoundlanders, who were used to rough weather landings, had lost their buoyancy. Many journeying with us every Friday night departed stunned and mute, their normally boisterous farewells sadly missing after the wings of death had brushed the aircraft.

This time, our pilots joined us in the pub, where the First Officer, at the controls during approach and downfall, freely admitted, "I almost pissed my pants trying to keep it on the ground." Whereas our pilots reluctantly removed themselves from the watering hole an hour or so later, we closed down the place at 3 A.M., and continued in my room until 6 A.M., when my phone ringing made us aware of the hour. I put a pillow over the telephone, kindly shuffled my companions out of the door, tucked myself into bed, and slept. As soon as I awoke, late in the afternoon, I removed the pillow and noticed the blinking red light which signaled that a message awaited. I contacted the hotel operator who told me that crew scheduling had tried to draft me for a flight early that morning. "Brother. Now they haul us out of bed at 3 A.M. Pacific Standard Time, after a fourteen-hour day hopping from coast to coast. That's downright exploitive," I thought, and went to the pub, where all of my peers were celebrating happy hour. No one had tried to draft them.

Mid-Air Turbulence

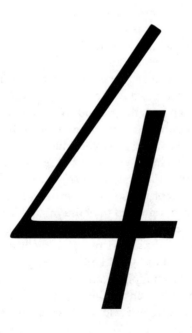

Many large corporations work like machines, rather than the human institutions that they are, with little or no regard for their workers' well-being. They relegate this responsibility to the jurisdiction of labor laws. While employees of most earthly industries and even commercial airline pilots come under the protection of these laws, flight attendants do not.[1] Neither the Federal Aviation Administration (FAA) nor the Occupational Safety and Health Administration (OSHA) accept U.S. flight attendants as their responsibility; a similar state of affairs exists in Canada.[2]

This is all the more alarming because, since 1980, governments and the industry have been well aware of the fact that cabin crew perform in an increasingly hostile environment that is characterized by exposure to a host of dangerous forces: inflight acceleration, circadian rhythm desynchronosis, lack of oxygen, lack of humidity, excessively high ozone and excessive carbon dioxide quantities, exposure to increasingly higher cosmic radiation levels (due to higher altitudes flown by newer aircraft and the depletion of the ozone layer), fatigue induced risk of anemia, onboard electrical shocks, and risk of infections caused by airborne viruses and microbes.

More than a dozen American flight attendants die or receive severe injuries each year primarily because of crash deceleration forces, fire and pyrolytic toxic products, emergency evacuations, decompressions, galley burns, falls, lacerations, drownings, injuries received from combative passengers, and turbulence.[3] Both airlines and governmental agencies, through acts of omission or commission, have either ignored or complacently stood by in the knowledge of these hostile working environments and the serious consequences they produce. Instead of striving to better the working conditions of flight attendants, they have turned away from their moral obligations to examine the issues and provide solutions. A good start in the process of protecting flight attendants would be to establish industry standards based on legislated laws to prohibit cabin crew from working while the seat belt sign is illuminated.

A month after the St. John's incident a man approached me at Ottawa's airport. "You were on board that awful flight into St. John's the other day, weren't you?"

"Yes?" I replied, knowing that he must have been on that particular flight, even though I did not recall his face. I waited for his next comment.

"A friend of mine was in the [air traffic control] tower when we came in. You know we hit a sixty mile 'n hour wind sheer fifty feet above the ground?"

"You sure about that?" I was taken slightly aback. After the flight, the pilots hadn't mentioned anything to us about wind sheers.

"Yeah, of course—he's been there for years and knows what he's talking about."

"Thanks for letting me know. We were surely lucky, then."

"Sure were. Hope I won't have to live through that again," the tall, husky man sighed.

"Makes two of us. Got to run. Have a flight to catch. Might see you on my next trip. Enjoy."

Hesitantly he said, "Yeah, you too...have a safe one," looking at me as if I were out of my mind to fly for a living. As I continued on to my gate, I wondered why the pilots hadn't told us what could have happened that night.

Wind sheers are caused by micro bursts of energy in storms. They happen in the blink of an eye, frequently occurring in areas where summer thunder and lightning storms erupt within minutes, swirl violently, and evaporate. Storms build in circular patterns and create pockets of downdraft winds. A plane flying along on a head wind can suddenly get sucked into a downdraft that hammers it toward the ground in a nano second.[4] If the plane is on approach, therefore rotating slowly and close to the ground, there is little hope of recovery. When they hit during take-offs or landings, all aboard have been strapped in far in advance, and passengers and cabin crew usually walk off board physically unharmed.[5] But when turbulence hits mid-air—either unexpectedly or even when it is expected—the outcome can be drastically different, as was the case when an Airbus 320 transited the Gulf of Mexico en route from Toronto to Cancun, Mexico, on October 9, 1993. Aboard were two pilots and four flight attendants scheduled for a turnaround, and 132 passengers.

Cruising at 35.000 feet, the aircraft suddenly experienced a severe downdraft followed by an equally severe updraft, propelling the plane to 37,000 feet before the pilots were able to return it to its scheduled altitude. When the turbulence hit, the in-charge, who was on her way to the rear galley, was thrown about the cabin. Her body rose to the ceiling and fell back to the floor twice. Two flight attendants, sitting unsecured in their aft-galley jump seats, experienced the same motions. One struck her back on the upper galley control panel, and the other's head struck the metal first aid kit in the headrest portion of her seat, which had opened during the turbulence. Despite their injuries, all three immediately resumed their duties. The forward flight attendant was jostled about the cabin, but she had been able to remain on her feet uninjured. One passenger was slightly injured when she struck her head on an overhead bin. The event had lasted for about thirty seconds. The *Fasten Seat Belt* sign had been illuminated throughout the incident.

When the purser reported the flight attendants' injuries to the captain, the exalted one ordered the two back end flight attendants to report to the flight deck, so he could personally ascertain if they were, indeed, hurt. After landing in Cancun, a physician examined the one injured passenger and reported that she had not sustained significant injuries. The flight attendants did not ask for medical attention, however, the in-charge and one flight attendant informed the captain of their inability to perform their duties on the return flight because of the injuries they had sustained. He argued that by curtailing the service and by operating in a *restricted emergency capacity*, they would be able to work the flight home. The flight attendants refused on the grounds that they would be incapable of complying with emergency procedures if one should arise. The aircraft returned to Toronto without passengers.

Physicians later determined that one flight attendant fractured a vertebra, and her arm, shoulder, back, and lower limb muscles had received minor strains. The other one had sustained minor strains and minor multiple contusions on her neck, back and shoulder area.

The carrier's flight operations manual (FOM) states that inflight illumination of the seat belt sign because of anticipated turbulence will apply to all passengers—but will *only* be considered a precautionary warning as far as flight attendants are concerned. Cabin service may continue unless otherwise advised by the captain. Obviously, had the two injured flight attendants been seated with their seat belts fastened, their injuries would most likely have been prevented. The aircraft fuselage had not sustained any damage during the violent 2000 foot upward motion. No evidence of airframe damage or system malfunctioning could be detected on the aircraft. [6]

When clear air turbulence hit a Canadian Regional Airline's De Haviland en route from Cranbrook, British Columbia, to Calgary, Alberta, on

October 22, 1993, with two pilots, two flight attendants, and twenty-one passengers on board, the flight deck had advised passengers at 11,500 feet, that turbulence was anticipated during the descent into Calgary, therefore, the seat belt sign would be left on throughout the flight. Suddenly, two sharp jolts of turbulence hit the aircraft within six seconds, and with such force the landing gear door jarred open. Both flight attendants were serving passengers near the rear galley when the event occurred. During the first strike, they crashed against the ceiling and fell back onto the floor. During the second jolt they were thrown to the ceiling again, but this time one of them was seriously injured when she struck the passenger seats before landing on the floor. The other sustained injuries when striking the mixing table enforced with metal edgings.

The Transportation Safety Board of Canada (TSB) investigators asserted that one passenger sustained her minor injuries because she refrained from fastening her seat belt, having been lulled into a false sense of security perhaps by observing the flight attendants walking about while preparing for inflight service. The nature of all the injuries sustained in the incident was undisclosed, but an ambulance met the aircraft in Calgary—presumably to pick up the flight attendants.

This carrier's flight operations manual (FOM) states that, even when the "Fasten Seat Belt sign" is on, and even when the flight deck crew briefs cabin attendants on anticipated turbulence, inflight service *must be provided* to passengers. Only in the event of severe turbulence is cabin crew to take the nearest seat and buckle up. If no seat is available in the vicinity, they are to sit on the floor or hang on to the nearest armrest while advising passengers to fasten their seat belts—and to shout if necessary. And if a serving cart should be around, they are to instruct a passenger to hang on to it, if that is safe and possible.[7]

The FOM directives from these two particular airlines—demanding that cabin crew work when the seat belt sign is illuminated unless otherwise advised by the captain—is consistent with those of the majority, if not all, North American air carriers.

One of the most remarkable turbulence incidents which could not be hidden from the public happened to a United Airlines flight en route from Tokyo to Honolulu on December 28, 1997 with 393 passengers and nineteen crew members aboard. First reports stated that fifty-three passengers and nine flight attendants had been injured. Upon returning to Tokyo, the media announced that 100 passengers had been injured, one thirty-two-year-old Japanese woman had been killed, and the pilots were unhurt. Nothing was said about the injured flight attendants. By December 29th, it was reported that ten of the injured had been released from hospital. We were not told whether they belonged to the passenger or flight attendant category. The report revealed that between 1981 and 1991 the FAA had received 252 turbulence injury reports of which sixty-three were deemed serious. Two deaths occurred. No occupational backgrounds for the deceased were mentioned.[8]

On April 17th, 1998, the media claimed that eighty-three people were injured on the United Airlines flight, with one dead. Through simple arithmetic we can deduce that seven of the original ninety that were hospitalized must have been flight attendants, however, nothing was said about them. We only know that on April 17th, 1998, Air Canada announced that as of that day, passengers would be required to keep their seat belts fastened for the duration of all flights. Transportation Safety Board of Canada spokesperson, Jim Harris, eloquently defended the new policy by stating: "The more we learn about flying, the more we can do to insure passenger safety."[9] And what about flight attendants' safety?

Thus, when turbulence hits and they have nothing to hang onto, flight attendants might experience the doubtful joy of weightlessness, and risk breaking bones or having their faces slashed open when they come crashing down on seats or trolleys. Presumably the captain knows when it is safe for them to perform their duties. The reasoning behind these directives is obscure to say the least. Is it that captains know when turbulence will hit because of the fact that the cockpit is ahead of the cabins, or perhaps because of their psychic abilities?

This inspires one to wonder if the commander is invested with powers to heal those cabin crew members who are injured in mid-air turbulence, or if he or she is willing to financially compensate them for their suffering while the attendants lie in hospital beds with internal injuries, broken limbs and ruined faces? And I wonder if captains are prepared to financially carry the victims of their failed psychic abilities and healing powers throughout the attendants' lives should they become unable to return to their careers? Obviously, the pilots, even with up to $250,000 in annual salaries, wouldn't be expected to cover these costs, but the fact is, neither will the airlines or the WCB. But most flight attendants are ignorant of that fact—until it is too late. Thus, cabin crews continue to stumble about during turbulence to perform the airline's precious service, unaware that their health, their livelihood, and all their worldly possessions are at stake.

———————————✈———————————

Winter storms continued in February and, when leaving Ottawa one evening en route to Vancouver, it got bumpy the second we lifted off and continued to hit at five to ten minute intervals. The pilot, safely buckled in, and concerned about wining and dining the passengers, turned the seat belt sign off and on at his leisure. The purser, suffering from verbal diarrhea, apologized for wind and weather in her whining voice every time he did. I could have strangled her. Not only did her nauseating discourse annoy me, it also helped to further delay the business class service, which had turned into a supreme farce. It didn't make me any happier when a heavy-set, puffy-faced woman stopped by my galley on her way to the toilet to complain about the lack of mayonnaise on her lobster main course—which she had yet to see. Focusing on her bulging waistline, I unsympathetically commented, "Be glad you're getting something to eat. Forty thousand children on this Earth starve to death every day."

"That's not my problem," she chirped, when the purser, rounding the corner at that very minute, took matters out of my hands by inquiring if she could help the lady, and wasted further precious time in order to appease her.

So the service proceeded—literally—in leaps and bounds. And in between, when the sign was on, I fed the pilots. When swaying around preparing meals for the back end cabin crew, an elderly gentleman in the last row of business class furiously rang the bell while shouting, "Where's my cake? I *want* my cake. She's got hers," pointing at a large woman seated in the row ahead.

I stumbled towards him saying, "You'll get your cake as soon as it's a bit smoother."

"Didn't you hear what I said? She's eating hers, and I want mine. Now!" he yelled for all to hear.

"You must have noticed that it's rough. I'll get it for you as soon as the sign is off," I tried once more.

"You just don't care!" he continued petulantly at the top of his voice. "That's why things are the way they are. You just take care of your own. You've just served the pilots, and everyone else," he screamed, red-faced. "I think that you think..."

At the end of my endurance, I interrupted him midstream, "That's enough. You'll not tell me what I think. Is that understood?" He shut up. When I brought him his cake the minute that the sign extinguished, he pouted and pushed it away. Fifteen minutes later we made an unscheduled landing in Winnipeg, because of a snowstorm on the West Coast that had clogged up traffic and hotels east of the Rocky Mountains. As I prepared to walk off board, I noticed that my uniform cardigan had disappeared from the jump seat at the exit door.

When contacting crew scheduling upon our arrival at the hotel at midnight, we were told that we would be shipped out in the morning on the first available flight. But, alas, my phone rang at 6 A.M. "You're drafted for flight 224 departing at 14:00 hours," the scheduler said matter of factly.

"Couldn't you have waited to tell me that until later?" I quipped, clearly annoyed.

"No. I wanted it done," he responded gruffly.

My crew members deadheaded home during the morning. It was my last flight of the month of February. For three weeks in March, as I sat as a juror on a rape-at-knifepoint trial, the new base manager checked flight attendants' performance records.

Aircrew Interpersonal Relationships and The "Need-to-Know" Concept

At the end of March, during the first of my two remaining cycles, we were standing at the loading bridge in Ottawa awaiting a Boeing 727, which we were to work to Montréal, when a DC9 appeared instead. None of us had seen one in years. Since only three flight attendants are scheduled to work this type of aircraft, the two junior ones deadheaded. Full to the rafters, three of us leapt into action seconds after liftoff and were halfway through the cabin with bar carts when all cabin lights went out. The Montréal-based captain announced that electrical problems necessitated an emergency landing at Dorval Airport. He gave us ten minutes to touch down, and initiated descent.

We packed away equipment in a wild dash, prepared the cabin with the help of our two deadheads, and strapped ourselves in seconds before landing. No fire fighters or ambulances awaited our arrival, and the pilots rushed off minutes after stopping the engines. During our debriefing in Winnipeg later that night, we decided that our commander had staged the event to get home in a hurry, for just that evening, Montréal had been heavily congested because of a snowstorm in Toronto. How flight operations regards such escapades is unknown, but probably not kindly. Such behavior could develop into a trend whenever someone in command suffers separation anxiety from a significant other.

AIRCREW'S INTERPERSONAL RELATIONSHIPS

We could assume that aircrew experience the same kind of interpersonal relationship problems as earthbound folk, but we do not know that, since no research on the topic is available. Therefore, we must look to the 282 wives of British commercial airline pilots who were interviewed on the topic[1] to obtain a vague idea about the co-habital attitudes and domestic lifestyles of these men who have been characterized as being autonomic, macho, and self-sufficient.

What these spouses complained about most bitterly was the lack of glamour in their lives.[2] And reasonably so. An aircrew's *glamorous* lifestyle rarely rubs off on the significant other, but is all ours, if it is there at all. The significant *other* is left at home to cope with the often lackluster burden of domestic chores, troubles and responsibilities. And if those become overly difficult or cumbersome to handle, the significant other shouldn't expect the flyer to give up the job to take over. That won't happen until retirement.

The marital union seems to be further disrupted because of pilots' wives view that the aircrew job is extremely conducive to promiscuity.[3] Of course it is. And so are many other occupations. However, it is not part of either flight attendants' or pilots' job descriptions to provide stress relief for each other through indiscriminate sex therapy. That does not mean that we do not fall in lust or love occasionally, but it rarely happens with one of our own. After all, who wants to be talked about when the cockpit turns into a locker room? Earthy folks' assumption that aircrew stage wild orgies or have lovers and mistresses stashed away in every port of call is equally ludicrous. As a matter of fact, I discovered when I rented my basement suite to a lovely bank clerk—who turned out to be a part-time hooker—that compared to earthlings, aircrew live like virgins and saints.

That we socialize with each other while hanging out in foreign ports, and seldom when in residence, comes with the territory. After all, flight attendants are in the job partly because of their congenial natures. But, whereas we prefer to shop till we drop, visit museums and art galleries, or go sightseeing, pilots most often prefer to indulge in *rah-rah* pilot talk over pitchers of beer. We do all get together at happy hour and for dinner, to talk about the world at large. Every topic is fair game, except for politics, which seems of little interest to our universal minds.

Because of our social interactions while on the road, we neither want nor need an extensive social life at home base, which appears to drive pilots' wives to distraction with feelings of social isolation.[4] And any attempt to involve the precious husband into anything he missed while he's been away is as futile an exercise as dragging him to a party with the Joneses. He really could not care less about what happened on the home front yesterday while he was hanging out in Swaziland. In his mind, he hasn't missed anything unless he's missed a scheduled flight. And if his wife should feel rejected because of his fatigue, his lack of sexual prowess, and his general disinterest in her and their surroundings when in residence,[5] that's her problem. Jet lag, social activities while away, and lack of sleep come with the job. Any nagging and sulking on her part won't change that. Just adjusting to the fact that when at home he wants to do one thing, namely *his* thing, may help to promote a harmonious co-existence.

Wives, furthermore, resent it when their flyer refuses to share his work experiences with her and when he, dominant by nature, denies that the effect of the stress he experienced affects him. If bugged about it, he turns into the strong and silent type.[6] But pilots really can't go home and tell their significant others about incidents and near misses they experienced in the line of duty, can they? Would it not scare the wits out of her? We do not know, since the question whether or not a wife ever thinks about, or fears losing their husband in a crash, or having him return badly injured, was not posed in the British survey.

If a woman dreams of having an influence on her husband's career or to be an asset to him,[7] she better not marry a pilot, since she is entirely immaterial to his advancement. If she needs recognition for her good deeds while he has been away,[8] she need not look for that, either. Isn't she there to tend home and hearth while he is gallivanting around the globe? Isn't he supporting her, and the kids—often in a very affluent fashion—for just that reason? But the worst that she can expect is criticism for things she proudly accomplished by being told crankily upon his return that she did it all wrong, because he is, often, a perfectionist at heart.[9] It's of course a Catch 22 situation, especially when knowing that many pilots probably feel just the same as three pilots who, responded this way to flight attendants queries about how they liked to be on fourteen day cycles: "It's tough. They (the company) tear us away from our loved ones and send us back to wife and kids."

Being married to a pilot is a difficult task for an earthbound other. Pilots are not easy to live with at the best of times, gregarious when out, often cantankerous, seemingly always in a different time zone, and suffering energy deficiency only to return to "normal" merely hours before taking flight again. Therefore, we can assume that aircrew marriages fall apart just as easily and regularly as those of earthlings. And aviators' wives have been known to take off for good during hubby's journey to foreign or domestic shores—without announcing such intentions before his departure. Suspicion that she will planning such a move is stressful in a profession acknowledged to be loaded with stress. Perhaps such suspicions enticed the commander of our Ottawa-Montréal DC9 flight to declare an emergency so close to home port.

We found out, when arriving at the airport for the last trip of the month, that our Boeing 727 had been replaced with an Airbus 320. None of us had ever seen one before. But, our sense of curiosity surpassed our apprehensions, and we conquered the inevitable with some enthusiasm—only to discover immediately that the aircraft had been designed with total disregard to flight attendant ergonomics. After liftoff with a full house, I spent most of the morning in the diminutive forward galley, repeatedly standing and bending like a yo-yo, preparing business class meal trays on the floor because of the lack of counter space. Halfway through the flight, stars appeared in front of my eyes whenever I rose to my feet, and I felt dizzy. Upon landing in Montréal, all of us were so exhausted that we broke with the tradition of chatting during our one hour waiting time; instead we spent the time in splendid solitude—far apart from each other—before picking up the last leg to Winnipeg.

When boarding the 727, a ballroom compared to the Airbus, our giggles and bounciness so astounded the familiar pilots that they inquired, "What've you been up to?"

"Flew the Airbus in this morning."

"Anything extraordinary happen?" they asked.

"Nothing. Except—the First came to the back to ask how we were doing. We complained about the noise from the air vents, and he promised to fix that," one flight attendant remarked.

"Oh. That explains it. You've been asphyxiated," the captain said.

"How?" we chorused.

"Well, the noise from the air vents can only be lowered by cutting back on oxygen. You got asphyxiated in the process." He paused for a moment, then inquired, "How long had they [the pilots] been on the Airbus?"

"Captain said he had thirty-five hours, the First, seven," the in-charge replied.

"Well, there's your answer: lack of training," the captain responded before returning to his duties.

The "Need-to-Know" Concept

These days pilots receive training based on the "need to know" principle, meaning that the aircraft manufacturer provides a manual in which it is specified what pilots need to know to operate, and preferably control, the aircraft. Whereas in the early days they were also trained to know how the engines, various gadgets, and mechanical parts inside the aircraft worked, the need to know method gradually evolved as a consequence of the increasing complexity of aircraft. The concept began with the introduction of the Boeing 747 in the early seventies. Then, with the introduction of the 767, came the "crew performance objective," which referred to front-end crews working together rather than the captain running the show more or less individually. The reasoning was that no one could reasonably expect pilots to acquire all the intrinsic knowledge of how these increasingly complex aircraft work. Instead, the *operation* of the aircraft is now their specialty.

But there is just one problem, as Captain Steve Last, principal Vice-President of the International Federation of Air Line Pilots Association (IFALPA), and a captain with British Airways, stated at the Gimli inquest in 1985:

> I think the fundamental problem is nobody will dispute a basic statement that you only need to know what you need to know. The problem we are faced with right now, and it is not by any means exclusive to Boeing or to any other individual manufacturer, is the total trend of the air transport system [which] is generated by one thing alone, and that is money. The fact of the matter is that the major manufacturers have no interest in being in the business of building airplanes other than to make money; the more they can sell, the better off they are. And the easier they can sell them to operators, the better off they are. The operators are in the business of reducing their costs to the maximum extent. Training is a cost which does not show up as having any positive benefit on the balance sheets. It does not produce revenue unless you can sell your training to someone else, and you will sell it to someone else if you can sell a five-day course instead of an eight day course.[10]

Captain Last also pointed to the fact that with the older planes and the previous kind of pilot training, if something went wrong with the aircraft, the margin of safety did not drop drastically. On the other hand, with modern complex airplanes 99% of the time there are no problems, but when problems *do* occur, the drop in the overall level of safety is much more severe. In his opinion,

> The designs [of aircraft] are being pushed closer and closer to the limits in many cases because they [carriers] want to squeeze the last ounce of performance, weight payload, et cetera, out of it. The knowledge given to the crews [pilots] to deal with the edges of the envelope is that much less...either it is all going fine and stays going fine for weeks on end and suddenly it all falls totally apart...the adjustment that has to be made from everything being wonderful to everything being absolutely terrible is much more severe than when the thing was, you know, a bit ropey all the time and it got a bit ropier, but you could handle it.

> And we have also—in order to achieve that, we have removed a crew member out of the whole system on the basis that none of the things around the edges would ever go wrong. But they do still go wrong.[11]

Captain Farrell, a Boeing 757 pilot with British Airways, commented on the need-to-know philosophy's detrimental effect on the training of maintenance engineers:

> Now it worries me that not only are the pilots not being told, but the ground engineers are being told: Just interrogate the BITE; it will tell you which piece of equipment to pull and slot in a new one. You do not need to know how the system works."[12]

Many pilots' perspective on the quality of training on new aircraft can be summed up by the response of an Airbus 340 captain to a flight attendant admiring the cockpit layout. "Yeah, it's quite all right. But I tell you, if anything goes wrong we're in for it."

He seems to have a point. The observation that Airbus' have a will of their own has been demonstrated far too frequently in recent years, not only by a significant number of crashes, but also by stories circulating through the grapevine, such as an Air Canada A320 that supposedly took its pilots for a ride when it suddenly initiated a go-around and entered a holding pattern. Rumor also has it that an A320 pulled the same stunt over New York City for over two hours before the problem could be rectified. The aircraft landed minutes before running out of fuel.

Airbus Industry, however, maintains that the A320 computers cannot override the pilots or initiate maneuvers. When a group of Canadian Airline International pilots, trained on DC10 and Boeing aircraft, visited the manufacturer's training facilities in Toulouse, France, for three days, they appeared to be very skeptical and to have preconceived ideas—particularly about the A320. The manufacturer, however, felt that by the end of the sessions their fears had been put to rest.

No need to harp away about Airbus. Boeing uses the same operational principles and is no better or worse. One of their 757s went into the Pacific Ocean after takeoff from Lima, Peru, in October 1996. The pilot was at a total loss, because the on-board computer had apparently lost it. When interviewed about this issue, the manufacturer's third 757 crash in ten months, a Boeing spokesperson arrogantly stated that *of course* the aircraft could be flown without a computer. That might well be. But only if pilots are taught how to!

So, pilots—many of them macho men—appear to be afraid. And do they have reason? Apparently they do, because studies show that, as aircraft systems become more and more automated and complex, the more they become prone to human error. And that problem can be eliminated or reduced only if good human principles are incorporated in the implementation of the systems to guarantee a good man/machine interface. This can only be achieved with extensive—and therefore cost deficient—training.

Returning to the story of our Airbus 320 pilots illustrates my point. They knew enough to get the thing back on the ground; however, the question remains whether or not they were taught during their *need-to-know* training how much oxygen had to be administered to cabin crew to avoid asphyxiating them. But perhaps the aircraft manufacturer considered this unnecessary knowledge for aviators' overburdened brains. Especially since the pilots themselves need not care—they have their own, separate, 100% fresh air supply. Furthermore to enhance the equilibrium of those traveling in the line of duty in the back of an Airbus is the fact that at least one North American carrier has an Airbus 320 simulator so sophisticated that pilots can complete their *need-to-know* training without ever setting foot on the aircraft until their first flight in command of one. Their on-board practice will teach them about the necessary mid-air cabin oxygen supply—when flight attendants begin to crawl instead of walk through the aisle.

The Role
of
Cabin Personnel

An utterly peculiar incident occurred when I deadheaded back from Vancouver to Toronto on the last day of April. The moment the "Fasten Seat Belt" sign went out following takeoff, the in-charge, a former supervisor I hadn't seen in years, rushed down the aisle, planted herself across my armrests and inquired, "You remarried? Got a lover? You tired of men? Want to get together to talk about your problems?" When I did not answer, she beat a fast retreat.

Turning to a colleague sitting beside me, I asked in disbelief, "Has what I think happened just happened?"

"Sure," she said, "she's just made a pass at you."

"But why?"

"Don't know. Don't let it bother you. Happened to me, too."

But it did bother me, and I discussed it with a couple of "straight" colleagues during an Ottawa layover. "Look at it this way," they suggested, "Men adore you and women like you. What more do you want?"

"Are you saying I should ignore passes from lesbians instead of getting upset about them?" I asked.

"You got it, hon. Their persuasion is their problem, not yours!"

As in any profession, flight attendants come from a variety of backgrounds and represent a vast range of personality types. Nowadays airlines employ cabin crew of both genders and of all sizes, shapes and ethnic backgrounds. It has not always been that way. When Ellen Church became the first "sky girl" for Boeing Air Transport in 1930, and until W.W. II, only registered nurses were hired for the job. During the war, North American carriers began to employ outside the nursing field, and with a decided preference for young, single, pretty, slender, peppy, perky, charming, tactful, refined and intelligent Caucasian women willing to please from a variety of educational backgrounds. Their job title was *Stewardess* or *Air Hostess*.

In 1964 Title VII of the U.S. Civil Rights Act and the Age Discrimination Act provided flight attendants with the basis to legally challenge airlines' regulations concerning age, appearance, weight, marital status, and maternity. Carriers' restrictive policies fell one by one. And in 1971, after Pan American Airways' refusal to hire a man as cabin attendant was ruled a violation of Title VII (Diaz vs. Pan American Airways), males were employed as cabin crew, and the job title was changed to *Flight Attendant*. Currently, the female/male cabin crew ratio is unknown, though females constitute the vast majority of flight attendants.

In 1994, 31% of the approximately 50,000 members of the Association of Flight Attendants (AFA) union held college degrees, 60% were married, and of those 38% had young children. Flight attendants are permitted to fly up to two months before delivery, or to take maternity leave throughout the entire term. In Canada, flight attendants must speak at least French and English to be interviewed for the job. But without at least a third language—preferably Japanese, Mandarin, Punjabi, or Korean—their chances to be hired are slim. Applicants number in the thousands, and the resignation rate in 1978, the latest statistic available, was approximately 3%.[1] American flight attendants can stay "on the line" to the age of seventy, whereas Canadians can fly until age sixty-five—and many will do just that.

With a minimum hiring age ranging between eighteen and nineteen years of age, our careers can span fifty-two years (statistics are unavailable). And since we rarely, if ever, switch airlines during employment, and therefore will work with each other occasionally, and because our survival in a crash or in an on the ground emergency can depend on peers' actions or inactions, we are practically always civilized towards each other. But on rare occasions, temperaments and personalities clash unpleasantly. My first flight in July 1990 was a classic example.

The first leg, from Vancouver to Toronto, began with a colleague's announcement that he was HIV-positive. His revelation was met by deafening silence on the crew's part and followed by a lecture on HIV by "Mr. Aids." During his rhetoric, the purser stuck his head into the galley and listened for a few seconds before lifting his middle finger behind the lecturer's back and taking off to first class. This did not bode well, especially since I was scheduled to work the galley, where battles resulting from differences in personality types, opinions and work ethics most often occur. I braced myself for the inevitable.

Tio, our in-charge on that flight, was a good tempered but conceited and condescending individual whom I knew from long hauls. Unfortunately, he disliked Mr. Aids so passionately that it affected his reasoning and led him to insist on ludicrous and hitherto unheard of ways to provide service to the people. Ironically, if we argued against Tio's ideas, he would insist; if we agreed with him, he would do an about-face and have us return to the well-worn path of normal procedures. Having figured out how to handle him, we then worried about Mr. Aids' possible actions.

Throughout the flight he roamed around, with purple lesions on his arms and face, acting like a powder keg ready to explode. He did whatever he pleased whenever he pleased, stuffing his face with every edible in sight while we performed his duties. Tio, red with fury, threatened to advise passengers that, "Your lunch will now be served by an HIV-infected flight attendant." We stared at him aghast, greatly relieved when he changed his mind and didn't carry through with his threat.

Unable to take even a one minute break throughout the flight, we dimmed the galley lights during the approach into Toronto to create an illusion of tranquillity, knowing that preparation for the next flight leg—and the entire trip—would be hectic. When Mr. Aids stepped into this soothingly dim atmosphere, he flew into a rage and turned the lights up full force. I turned them down. And so it went, lights dimming and bright, until he threatened to call in a supervisor upon landing. That won him the battle. His victorious smirk invited a kick in the shins, but I resisted the temptation, thinking, "We crash, you can burn in hell." At that time I didn't realize that because of his disease Mr. Aids could not change his behavior.[2]

Whereas crew conflict is infrequent, fights with passengers are easy to pick if one wants to waste energy on them. And, at times, one has no choice but to voice one's opinion. So it was when a woman of immense proportions saw fit to stampede through my galley on her way to a washroom, pushing me away from the trolleys that I was preparing as if I were a piece of luggage. I made the mistake of quipping, *"Excuse me* works miracles. You might want to try it one day."

That did it. She exploded. 'Who did I think I was to give her etiquette lessons? I should be glad to have a job and should behave accordingly. Didn't I know the airline had just announced it was laying off another 500 employees?' This water buffalo finished her sermon with, "You obviously don't give a hoot about the airline and couldn't care less about passengers. It's me who pays your salary, you know. Your role is to be subservient at all times so I'll fly with you again. Remember that in the future."

I looked her up and down, while she eagerly anticipated my response, and then replied quietly, but coolly, "You know, you are truly blessed today. I will not give you my opinion of you." Forgetting about her bodily needs she stormed off, not to be seen again in my vicinity.

Another incident occurred shortly before landing, when another woman, waiting in line for the washrooms, asked me, "How'd you like your job?"

"Love it," I answered with my typical enthusiasm, as I stowed stuff away.

"How can you possibly? You're nothing but a *glorified waitress!*"

I stopped in my tracks and turned to face her, eye to eye. "First of all, we're all servants to someone or something. And secondly, my colleagues and I are here to risk our lives to save yours in case of an emergency. The rest of the service is provided so that you won't die of sheer boredom. Therefore, a plane is not a restaurant, and flight attendants aren't waitresses. Is that understood? And, by the way, accidents do happen at the most unexpected times." I left her standing there, her mouth wide open, as I resumed my duties, too busy to waste more time before touchdown. I wondered whether or not it was a full moon.

Both of these incidents on my flight that day typically demonstrate how completely the public has lost sight of the flight attendant's role to care for and assist passengers who suffer from inflight illness or who need help in crash evacuations. What is the source of such misconstrued attitudes?

In the 1970s, the advertising campaigns of several North American airlines, including National's "Fly me" campaign and Continental's "We move our tails for you," contributed to disguising, misrepresenting, and denigrating the role of cabin personnel on-board aircraft. Dress codes of the time didn't help, either. Female flight attendants wore uniforms that left little to the imagination. Whichever way you bent, butts or boobs would show. When male flight attendants were hired, airline managements had to modify flight attendants' attire. It would look rather peculiar to have these men roaming around in scant mini skirts or designer gold lamé—even though some fellows in the industry may not have minded in the least. Despite the airlines change to less sexually enticing uniforms, and their move to advertising campaigns that had less demeaning implications for flight attendants, there appears to have been little corresponding shift in the public's conception of the "air hostess" image created in that era. Many passengers still view flight attendants as sexually available, promiscuous, or believe that we are mentally challenged.

Many others see us as indentured servants, there to answer their every beck and call. In their view, aren't we there to water, feed, and clean them? To pick up their garbage? To soothe them and put them to sleep? Aren't we there to be blamed for flight delays caused by weather or mechanicals, or the lack of food selection, blankets, pillows, toys, aspirins, crossword puzzles, or newspapers? "If you're miserable, blame the flight attendants—that's what they are getting paid for," seems to be the motto of many experienced and inexperienced flyers alike.

On the other hand, those passengers petrified of flying, the sick, the elderly, and the very young, often see us as angels—an appropriate image of our role in the sky. Who else would possibly attempt to fish your dentures out of the toilet, lost during a vomiting spell caused by overindulgence and, if unsuccessful, arrange for the "honey wagon" to retrieve your precious belonging? Who would treat you civilly when, drunk and in urgent need of the occupied washroom, you urinate in the galley corner? Who else would get you into shape when you wet yourself after downing massive quantities of beer following six weeks spent in Muslim Libya? Who else would wrap you in blankets, and arrange your pillows, so you can pleasantly snooze while your pants dry in the galley oven, and rescue you from the intense sexual overtures of a fellow passenger? Who would be tolerant and cheerful when you mistake the aircraft for a tabernacle, as you roam through the cabins attempting to convert crew and passengers to your beliefs? Who else would sympathetically mourn the death of your escaped green snake an ignorant galley slave drowned in the lavatory? Who else would provide psychological counseling, free of charge, throughout the night when you despair over some earthly misfortune? Who else, but flight attendants—and, perhaps, your mothers. And we do these things not because we are paid to do them, but because it is inherent in our personalities.

Even though the rare passenger will express appreciation for a good trip, "Thank you's" from customers for extended courtesies from flight attendants are viewed by many as unnecessary. Moreover, apologies for inappropriate on-board behavior are generally avoided at all costs, because, in the eyes of the public and airline management alike, we are only doing our duty.

How Flight Attendants See Passengers

Each month, as flight attendants deal with an average of 4000 people of every stripe and flavor, and while responding to the good, the bad, and the ugly with tolerance, and goodwill, our consensus on passengers is,

"They check their brains with their luggage." Our good humored responses, such as, "Hay is what you feed horses," after the umpteenth time being called *Hey you*, or "Want my dress?" when being pulled excessively by all parts of our uniform by attention seeking passengers, do not register. When a passenger reviewing his supper protests, "This meal isn't fit for a pig," he usually remains oblivious to the jollying retort, "One moment, sir, I'll find you one that is." Most people's thinking capabilities just become too impaired to grasp subtleties when flying.

Some airborne mothers are a particularly special breed. Many mistakenly assume that we can supply everything required by their precious young ones during the journey. "What! No baby food? And no more diapers, either? You must wash these, then!" are not uncommon demands. Sorry, flight attendants won't do that any more than they will accept dirty diapers in the seat pocket or garbage bin. "Why not?" a mother will often reply before issuing another order. "Well, take them to the washroom, then!" Sorry, ma'am. That's *your* responsibility. I've actually heard mothers exclaim, "What? No baby sitting service?" No, generally we're not in the nursery business, though exceptions are made if baby's howling disturbs the peace for prolonged periods. Some mothers have requested a few drops of cognac be added to the formula, in a humanitarian effort to allow rest and relaxation for all; it has been known to solve the problem.

Mothers also have an inexplicable desire to let infants dine when everyone else does, demanding bottles or food be heated in the middle of a meal service when boiling water is needed for brewing tea for the multitudes. But try to explain this to mothers! And, if mummy forgot to bring baby food altogether or, in her infinite wisdom, checked the formula with the suitcase, I've known some flight attendants that have volunteered to wet nurse starving infants. Mind you, the mothers I've portrayed here are most often "first time with infant" flyers. Once they've learned the ropes—and we do everything in our power to subtly teach them—they do just fine. But until they have learned the on-board *do's* and *don'ts*, mothers either love or despise us depending on their inflight experiences.

Some passengers seem to have only one thing firmly anchored in their minds: "I bought my $99 around the world discount ticket. That means I bought the plane, the flight attendants, and everything else, and can behave however I please, and have whatever I want at all times. Right?" No. It does not. Making flight attendants race up and down aisles to fulfill your every whim is not included in the airfare. Neither is the right to use bad manners. Cabin crew members pay for your discount fare by doing their jobs with fewer flight attendants to assure shareholder profit. In reality, the customary on-board announcement, *"Sit back, relax, and enjoy your flight,"* used by major airlines worldwide, should be replaced on North American airlines with *"Sit down, shut up, and await your turn,"* in an effort to knock some sense into passengers. Perhaps this shock treatment would heighten passengers' awareness that flying is not the same as dining at the Ritz-Carlton, where wait staff depend on tips to make a decent living.

The True Role of the Flight Attendant

The role flight attendants play in accidents and incidents is never referred to by airline corporations. You are not likely to see advertisements proclaiming "Our Flight Attendants are the best trained in the industry, and there are enough of them on-board to assist you in the unlikely event of an accident," or "Our superior air quality and quantity will ensure that you and your cabin crew are mentally alert and physically ready to leave the aircraft should an emergency occur." Mentioning the possibility of dying while flying does not contribute to their bottom line.

A police officer, who was asked how she felt about going to work after one of her colleagues had been shot and killed, said, "We don't go to work saying, 'Today I'm going to be killed.' If we did, we could not do our job."[3] Cabin crew, however, are required by government aviation regulations and their employers to face the possibility of being killed or maimed in the line of duty whenever they take to the skies by doing a two minute "Silent Review"—a mental rehearsal of evacuation procedures—just before takeoffs or touchdowns.

This awareness of the possibility of disaster, and knowing exactly what to do if it occurs, is flight attendants' primary responsibility. But my two discourteous female passengers would never know it.

During our return flight, crew scheduling drafted me mid-air for a London trip departing the following afternoon. I arrived back at the airport disenchanted. But when I saw the familiar faces with whom I would work, my mood brightened. Four of us shared the mid-ship L-1011-500 galley. I was responsible for passengers in the forward section of the economy cabin. Many of them were elderly and undemanding, wanting nothing from the bar. I crossed the invisible line to continue with the service in the rear flight attendant's territory.

Three women, cozily cuddled up to each other, came to life when I approached. They greeted me as if I were their long-lost buddy, and started to touch my hands, my arms, my hip, while seeking long-winded advice about what to drink. "Lesbians for sure," I thought, recommending beer. The ladies sniffled. Wine would be more to their liking, they said then asked what I had to offer? "*Andre's Speciaux*–red or white," I said politely. Silently it crossed my mind that "They probably think I'm of their persuasion." After, they decided on the white, I supplied them with generous portions, and split to my assigned area in the forward section, not talking to them again throughout the flight.

Shortly before arrival in London these same middle-aged women addressed the in-charge, requesting his name and mine. "You mind?" he asked me, and wanted to know what it might be about.

"Couldn't tell you. Probably gonna write a commendation," I answered dead seriously.

"Get a life, Tanya," the Italian said, "They've been looking for something to complain about all flight. Haven't you noticed? Everyone else has!"

"No, I haven't. And it doesn't matter, anyhow, Paolo. Whatever they scribble will get back to us one way or another. Who cares! Just give them our names."

"OK, but I'm going to put in a report to cover our asses."

"Fine with me," I answered. When the trio walked off board, ignoring our farewells with disgruntled scorn, my peers, filled with premonitions, promised to back me up if I was called into the office. During the return trip an odd anxiety hit me half way through the flight and stayed with me until touch down.

In August I continued the usual East Coast runs working the galley, surrounded by mostly unfamiliar crews. When mid-air, I turned into a situational escape artist. Unknown to me, my behavior–especially my withdrawal from the public by exclusively working the galley–signaled recurrent PTSD. I only knew that I had to remain detached and calm at all times. Otherwise I could not fly.

"Break-off" Syndrome

These sentiments and my reaction to mid-air aircraft stimuli, which are nothing unusual in aircrew, are referred to as the "break-off phenomenon." This term originated with an early report from a pilot who described that he felt as if he had "broken off from reality." The term has come to refer to a syndrome that has been exclusively researched in military pilots. The "Break-off" syndrome manifests itself by inflight sensations of separation from the ground, the environment, and the aircraft, and can precipitate acute anxiety attacks with phobic manifestations that lead to a "fear of flying" reaction. Association between "break-off phenomenon" and positive psychiatric findings in aviators is well documented.[4]

Modern psychiatric nomenclature would classify symptoms of "break-off" in the category of anxiety disorders such as agoraphobia without panic disorder or dissociative disorders. The long-term prognosis for such cases has not been defined. Even benign presentations, however, may cause military pilots to lose their flying confidence, thereby affecting their operational availability and safety.[5]

Data about commercial aircrews' fear of flying symptoms are scarce. In 1978, a researcher—sponsored by Malaysia and China to explore treatments for flight phobia in trained military aircrew, commercial flight crew, and civilian air travelers—wrote that, "Comparable figures for the United States commercial aircrews are conspicuous by their absence in the literature, at least during the years reviewed (approximately 1960 to 1978). Similarly, no studies reporting the use of behavioral techniques [to treat] commercial aircrews were found."[6]

And none are available today. Evidently, however, from the sheer percentage of psychiatric illness reported in commercial airline pilots, we know that the complex *man-machine-environment* interaction present in modern aviation generates intense psychological stress.

Psychiatric Illness
in Pilots

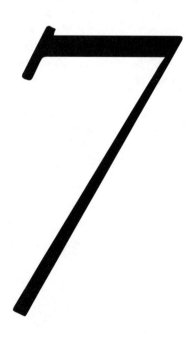

A flight attendant visiting the cockpit for a mid-air visit and a breath of fresh air, or to obtain permission to bring up passengers, or to inquire, "How much longer?" will immediately pick up on the flight deck atmosphere. If the captain is a well-balanced, happy-go-lucky type, heads will turn to see who has entered, and the reception will be cordial. If, however, "the boys" are not enjoying each other's company, their bodies will remain motionless, and eyes will stay fixed on the nothingness ahead in space. The response to any request will be a bovine grunt quickly translated by the flight attendant as, "Don't bother us." The all-pervasive tension will inspire a fast retreat to inform the rest of the cabin crew, "Don't bother to go up. The captain is an ass." In his exalted position, he sets the tone, and his psychological characteristics rule the cockpit.

Usually, aviators get along with each other just fine. After all, they are mostly boys playing with their favorite toy, an aircraft. And when the plane is humming away on auto pilot, the flight deck becomes a locker room, a place where tall tales and gossip help maintain alertness during the hours of sheer boredom that are only rarely interrupted by some unforeseen incident that jolts the nervous system and sends the adrenaline soaring. How are pilots, individuals capable of changing within split seconds from a vegetative state to high alert, chosen by the airlines? And how are their psychological characteristics, tendencies, and aptitude for the job measured before and during their employment with a commercial carrier or the military?

When selecting airline pilots, commercial carriers search, more or less, for air "bus drivers," while the military establishment looks for highly gifted and brilliant "race car drivers."[1] Psychologists, who design tests for the selection of pilots, want potential aviators in both categories to be stable introverts. This will ensure that rookie pilots will sweat over manuals, rather than spend time in local watering holes, and that they'll pass training with flying colors. Fledgling pilots are then expected to emerge from their cocoons of studiousness and become stable, extroverted butterflies. In other words, the ideal pilot is the strong, silent type who is capable of occasional flashes of congeniality and intelligence. After all, pilots are known to fly "by the seats of the pants" and not by intellect.

Aptitude and motivation are perceived as much more important than IQ for a successful aviator career. Because intelligence, however, to some extent seems to positively influence adaptation to novel situations and the ability to cope with the deleterious effects of stress, some brain activity is an asset.[2] The fact that commercial aviation pilots rarely pursue intellectual activities beyond the field of aviation is inconsequential, when we consider that their job description demands that they are not only capable of coping adequately with the responsibility for a multi-million dollar machine and innumerable lives, but that they maintain their equilibrium under adverse conditions.

PILOTS' HEALTH

Because of the high stress inherent in aviators' professional lives—stress which in uniformed personnel is second only to that of police officers—and because of physical problems created by altitude, speed, and motion, the standards for the physical health of pilots have been set by the International Civil Aviation Organization (ICAO). Practically every country in the world abides by those standards. In addition, pilots must meet physical health standards promulgated by government agencies responsible for issuing licenses to cockpit personnel.[3] Pilot's *mental* health, however, is not governed by anyone other than an individual carrier's medical department.

It was estimated in the mid-70s that, of the more than 600 fatal aircraft accidents each year occurring in the U.S., 80 to 90% were caused by bio-medical factors, including the use of drugs and alcohol which pilots may have taken to cope with stress, anxiety, or frustration on-board aircraft.[4] One could assume that these facts would have encouraged carriers to investigate pilots' long-term physical and psychological reactions to their work environment, but the lack of empirical data suggests otherwise.

In 1973, the latest data publicly available, only five airlines in the U.S. had full-time, in-house, medical departments staffed by personnel pre-sumably familiar with aspects of aviation medicine. And each of these facilities, which were instrumental in the selection and supervision of flying personnel, had varying standards and rules for hiring pilots and for determining their ability to control aircraft during their piloting careers. Furthermore, whereas a pilot's pre-employment physical exam-ination might have been thorough, his or her psychiatric evaluation appears to be limited to short interviews, or superficial summaries of the results of a series of psychological tests, or entirely omitted.[5]

The renowned American psychologist Joy P. Guilford insists that, to make valid statements concerning an individual's present and short-term health status, at least as much time should be spent on examining the psyche as is spent on evaluating the physical body. Airlines' medical departments seem to differ with this view. Whereas pilots' mandatory, and often trimestral physiological examination during their careers may be thorough, their mental health status is generally ignored under the pretense that the classification "suitable and fit for flying" had to have been established prior to flight training.[6] Consequently, we can infer that in the view of these medical departments, a pilot's psyche is reduced to a self-regulated, low-maintenance computer inessential to the individual's overall well-being.

Whereas anxiety disorders, cardiovascular diseases, and sudden heart attacks in previously healthy and well-functioning earthbound individuals are often stress-related regardless of their profession, such ailments in professional aircrew are believed to be directly linked to the job. Incapacitating or distracting physiological phenomena may have psychological origins and be the underlying cause for many obscure crashes.[7] Therefore, many aircrew health problems, projected by industry and governments to be of purely operational or physiological origin are, in fact, related to flying.[8]

In the mid-60s, after United Airlines' Medical Department in Denver established a daily relationship with their flight training and flight operations department, they discovered within a five year span that ten of their pilots suffered psychiatric disorders, three had cerebral-cortical atrophy, two had brain tumors, and ten had hypoglycemia. Fourteen out of twenty of those aviators were thought to have operational or proficiency difficulties, because, initially, no medical issues were suspected. All of them constituted potentially serious accident hazards, and seven were in the process of being terminated as incompetent pilots.[9]

Again, one might reasonably assume that these results would have alerted carriers to take an interest in aircrews' psychological and physical health. But the airlines have more than enough reasons not to, because it saves them millions annually to ignore the fact that cruising the skies for a living can have severe physical and psychological repercussions. However, when a carrier's medical staff finds it impossible to ignore an individual's psychological deficiencies, the medical staff is empowered to ground the aircrew member. For pilots, that means loss of license and, if grounded permanently, loss of livelihood.

How often do pilots get grounded because of psychiatric illnesses? A 1980 study in the U.K. revealed that 21.4% pilots lost their license because of psychiatric disorders, including alcoholism, and 39.8% because of cardiovascular diseases. According to British aircrew license insurance files, psychiatric disorders rank *second* only to cardiovascular disease as a reason for permanent grounding.[10] Though no exact figures were given from the insurance files, Dr. Kornelis Vaandranger, KLM's Chief Medical Officer in 1972, asserts that pilots known to have cardio-vascular abnormalities such as hypertension or episodes of substernal discomfort, for which medication is being administered, are often permitted to continue their career.[11] The incidence of psychiatric illness in female aviators is unknown, except for a six year period (1976–82), following the U.S. Air Force's initiation of female pilot training, during which seventeen women were referred to psychiatric evaluation out of a total of 2701. Of those seventeen, 53% returned to flying duty, compared to 64% of their male counterparts.[12]

In 1975, forced to consider that psychiatric disorders produce impaired performance in such vital components of flying as concentration, judgment, and attention, the industry had to heed appeals to monitor aviators' psychological well-being. European aviation medicine health professionals had discovered that the number of pilots they examined demonstrating symptoms of flying fear and of being psychologically conspicuous had more than doubled within a five year period. Therefore, the aviation medicine specialists alerted the airlines and encouraged them to monitor aviator's psychological well-being.[13] But most airlines (if any) paid no heed because it is infinitely cheaper for them to haul disintegrating flyers into the office when at the cracking point and push them for early retirement, or depending on their seniority, fire them. If a pilot's psychological disequilibrium causes a crash, who cares? It'll just be broadcast as yet another "human error" accident.[14]

Such a calamity was narrowly avoided on January 17, 1995, shortly after the earth ceased to shake in and around Kobe, Japan, which had begun at 5:46 A.M. local time, killing 5000 people. Severe tremors were felt in Osaka, jolting a laying-over NorAm crew into an abrupt awakening—or interrupting the nail painting, soak in the bathtub, umpteenth trip to the bathroom, crossword puzzle, TV viewing, reading, knitting, needle pointing, studying, eating, or whatever else crew members do when coping with drastic time changes. After the initial shocks subsided, the earthquake-seasoned Mexican purser and some Japanese flight attendants ascertained that their shaken crew members were physically intact, and then ventured to help wherever they could during the more than twelve hours remaining before flight departure at 1900 hours. The others huddled together, scared out of their wits, as threats of further major quakes loomed too alarmingly for comfort and relaxation. Aftershocks persistently throbbed throughout the region during the day, and exhausted the crew members' inner resources. When midday approached, the captain requested that flight operations send out relief pilots. They refused. No eyes closed before departure time.

Crossing the Pacific, prohibited from snoozing on duty, the aircraft's approach and landing in Vancouver the following morning at approximately 10 A.M. was uneventful. Cabin crew proceeded to the solace of their homes to recuperate from the earth shattering experience. The pilots, meanwhile, laid over at a downtown hotel, then worked to their Toronto base the following morning, where they eventually drove to their respective residences by mid-afternoon.

The captain briefly shared his earthquake adventure with his wife, showered, dove into civvies, and they both went to their son's birthday party. Minutes after their arrival, he collapsed with a massive heart attack. He was three months short of mandatory retirement at age sixty. If he had suffered the heart attack during the approach into either Vancouver or Toronto and a crash resulted, would the blame have been laid squarely upon his unblemished shoulders by calling it "human error?"[15] And had the heart attack occurred at the steering wheel while on his way home from the airport, to what would it have been ascribed if he had accidentally killed a few people?

The captain survived, but would never be able to control an aircraft again. Even if he had been fifty years of age, his health was ruined forever simply because the carrier failed to acknowledge the severe psychological trauma of the earthquake on his psyche. One shudders when thinking about the compounded psychological affects on these pilots and flight attendants had they faced an aircraft emergency during the approach into Vancouver that same day.

Psychiatric disturbances such as depression and anxiety in private pilots are commonly attributed to business and personal stressors. In professional aircrew, however, they are believed to be mainly caused by flying, where the inherent stresses involved virtually ascertain that a significant number of pilots continue to control aircraft while suffering psychiatric instability to a greater or lesser degree.[16] Mental health professionals assert, however, that it is difficult to define the boundaries between psychiatric ailments and normality in aircrew, because the profession tends to attract eccentrics.[17]

Doubtlessly, all humans cross the border between "normality" and eccentricity occasionally but, perhaps, aircrew does so more frequently than earthbound folks. After all, much of our lives are spent flying and figuratively speaking we live in "the twilight zone," a state induced by the nature of our job and rapid time zone changes. Skinny dipping off Honolulu's Ala Moana Beach at 3:00 A.M. on star-studded nights became one of our trends for a while, driving police to distraction. We've also been known to launch happy hours at swimming pools around the world, while other hotel guests were having breakfast. What both mental health professionals and the general public view as unconventional, eccentric, or downright lunatic behavior when observing or hearing about some of our jet-lagged antics, we simply call enjoying ourselves.

One such escapade found us drinking wine out of brown paper bags in front of a very reputable London hotel around 9:00 A.M. one sunny summer morning. Our unconventional activity so aroused the curiosity of two New York journalists that they approached us, bedazzlement on their faces. After sending the journalists to Marks and Sparks to augment our quaint outing with appropriate beverages, the ten of us promptly took them along to our Hyde Park picnic.

At 4:00 P.M., booze all gone and feeling no pain, the five of us that remained, including the First Officer, stood at the curb at Oxford Circle. While hailing a cab, the cotton scarf which I wore as a bodice slipped to my waist. A taxi came to a screeching halt seconds later, a wildly protesting passenger tumbled out, we happily climbed in, told the driver where to go, and entertained him with exotically truthful tales throughout the journey. Generously tipped upon arrival at the hotel, we also rewarded him with our classy picnic utensils. The First Officer, wanting to sober up before happy hour, fell asleep in the tub while running his cold bath, flooding seven floors beneath. The hotel, used to aircrew antics, bore the event with fortitude.

To eliminate any risk of boredom while spending time away from home in the line of duty, aircrews carry along gym gear and, if a layover is long enough, they undertake excursions by plane, bus, train, or boat on the spur of the moment. If the mundaneness of earthly life drags down the spirit during a longer stretch at home, the possibility of curing the malady by hopping on a plane is always there. And if in doubt as to where to go for a change of scenery, there's always the "Paris quickie" for a champagne and Crepe Suzette luncheon for those based on the East Coast, or popping over to Hawaii for the West Coasters. And—according to our yard stick—these activities are all so perfectly normal.

Extremely free spirits, unbound by distances and locations, we are exotic, colorful and unusual, perceiving the entire globe, not our place of birth or domicile, as a playground created for our pleasure. We're at home wherever the wind blows us—willing and able to entertain ourselves anywhere, any time, and with an unbounded curiosity about our surroundings and its inhabitants. Wherever we go, be it for a few hours or days, we live life the way it is meant to be—with fun, enjoyment, and with kindness to our fellow humans. Adding rays of sunshine and rainbow colors to the world, we have given many a soul good reason to burst out laughing about our "overt and unusual behavior" when off duty—and sometimes even when on duty. Naturally, our psyche gives the mental health profession cause to wonder. We do not fit in their molds, nor into anyone else's. If that earns us the reputation for eccentricity, so be it. Within our souls we know that we are the epitome of normality. This perception we doubtlessly share with the Wright brothers of Kitty Hawk, Charles Lindbergh, and Amelia Earhart.

Because aircrew are aware of the perception of "oddity" they inspire in the earthbound population, 442 British commercial airline pilots participating in the most recent study on stress in aviators (published in 1986) most likely did what they are accused of when asked about their mental health and smoking and drinking habits—downrated and modified their answers.[18] However, despite the boys' efforts, the researchers still judged 28% of them as mentally handicapped, a percentage greater than that expected in a male industrial population. After the researchers developed a cut-off point by dividing pilots considered "normal," but at the upper end of the average distribution, from those that were clinically "ill," just over 12% of pilots showed mental health scores above that point. And 2.2% had scores higher than those expected in psychiatric outpatients. Of course, those participating in the survey had all passed their mandatory airline check ups in recent months with flying colors.

Puzzled almost beyond belief, and looking for explanations, the researchers discovered that pilots with difficulties relaxing and winding down, and those avoiding stress level reduction by socializing with colleagues and friends, generally reported higher ill-health scores than those demonstrating proficiency with our forte—to mix and mingle. Socializing with our own is one of the most cherished and perfected activities of the flyers' trade, and many of our innermost secrets are shared with peers on such occasions. Often we know each other's life stories more intimately than do our closest and dearest family members. Unless in severe physical discomfort, nothing will stop us from seeking each other's company during layovers, and anyone crying the blues—despairing loneliness—does so of their own volition. A perpetually anti-social crew member is viewed as a very sick puppy.

One of our captains exhibited such a personality, causing everyone flying with him to moan and groan. His reputation as a pilot was excellent, but he ran his domain with an iron fist—no locker room talk or laughter on his flight deck. Cabin crew shunned the cockpit, passenger visits were prohibited, and long haul journeys turned into an eternity for co-pilots, while the commander cherished his solitude in a crowd of three. He was never seen in England's pubs or Germany's Weinstuben, routes he preferred to fly, and no one missed him. His unflattering reputation was further enhanced when it simmered through the grapevine that the barking of his neighbor's German shepherd had driven him into such a frenzy that he shot and killed the beast. Henceforth, he became known as "Mad-dog McCarthy."

Thus, he startled me, as I dined in splendid solitude, when he stopped at my well-hidden table in the farthest corner of our hotel's Weinstube, where I was studying for a mid-term exam. He was eager to engage me in conversation. Because it was almost midnight—but far too early to retire—I, out of politeness and expecting no for an answer, invited him to join me. He sat down.

At closing time, and a few beers later, we shifted to the lobby to watch people meander to and fro as we talked some more. I became the commander's father confessor throughout the evening. Our presence there was not unusual, for more than 250 crew members from around the world laid over at this hotel, providing around the clock entertainment in the reception area. By the time we bid each other good night in the lobby at 3:00 A.M., my perception of the skipper considerably changed, none of our crew had rolled in. The nearby disco closed at 5:00 A.M., almost within the mandatory twelve hour "bottle-to-throttle" rule. Our departure time was set at 16:00 hours.

From that evening onward, I made it a point to visit the flight deck whenever McCarthy was in command, and he always made me feel welcome. However, he continued to cherish his solitude on layovers, and we had no further private conversations. But one September McCarthy flew us into Frankfurt and we, on our way to the hotel, discovered that the Wine Festival, the carousels, the beer tents, the um-pah-pa, awaited our enjoyment. The layover's shortness did not deter anyone from diving into civvies and participating in the festivities for as long as our feet could carry us—except for McCarthy that is. Since time doesn't count when having fun, some of us rolled in very, very late.

A few hours later, one of the revelers climbed on the crew bus taking us to the airport looking like death warmed over. Once aboard the aircraft, we forced her to eat a dry bun, which only made her sicker. The tea we imposed upon her as a health remedy sent her to the washroom with lightning speed. A heart-wrenching and sorrowful sight to behold during takeoff, she required but one resolution to ease her misery. Into the cockpit I went, and with unheard of formality, inquired, "Captain, one of our flight attendants is really ill. Would you mind if she came up to get some oxygen? She's useless to us."

Turning around inquisitively, and looking at me with sparkling eyes, he asked, "This wouldn't have anything to do with the Wein Festival, would it, Tanya?"

"No, not to my knowledge, sir," I replied, a smirky little grin on my face, knowing full well he knew the truth, but preferred not to hear it because of rules and regulations.

"Send her up, then," he responded, turning back to his instruments.

Marianne, too incapacitated to protest about spending time in Mad-dog McCarthy's company, fell asleep in the cockpit while imbibing copious amounts of bottled oxygen. She alighted in the back five hours later, as fresh and energetic as a healthy newborn. Meanwhile, the rest of us were fading fast.

"How did you do it?" she asked me.

"Oh, no big deal. He's been there too, I guess," I responded nonchalantly, but overjoyed within my soul. McCarthy had a heart, as I had expected all along. And whereas McCarthy's earthly stressors did not affect his piloting skills, it appears to have been a different story for a Japanese Boeing 747 captain who, in the mid-80s, told his co-pilots of his dismal marriage minutes before the aircraft hit Mount Fujiyama.

In order to detect any form of psychiatric disturbance, some aviation medical professionals suggest openly questioning pilots during their mandatory check ups about whether they suffer from anxiety, irritability, depression, headache, impaired concentration, or insomnia, and if they abuse alcohol.[19] This suggestion is ludicrous, because the chances of receiving honest answers from the boys to such a line of questioning are infinitesimal. It's just too unbecoming for the strong, silent, macho ones to confess fragile mental health. Drinking is a different matter, and must always be admitted to, because it is well-known that liquor, the only drug officially sanctioned by commercial airlines, is as much part of aircrew existence as is milk to babies. It helps many of us to simmer down after performing our duties for—most often—extremely long hours.

Furthermore, research also suggests that, if company physicians suspect that a pilot is psychologically unstable, observations made about his behavior—as well as observations relayed by family, colleagues, and the employer—should be carefully analyzed.[20] That suggestion is not only a trifle naive, but also rather difficult to carry out. The wife or significant other, already knowing she has an oddball on her hands, will hesitate to jeopardize her harmonious relationship and monetarily lucrative lifestyle by reporting his occasionally bizarre demeanor to the airline. His colleagues will decline to pass judgment on possibly overt behavior, or repeat drunkenness, knowing full well they themselves might go over the brink if the proverbial substance hits the fan once too often. And the employer doesn't have a clue, because he is seldom present when exotic and eccentric behavior (as measured by earthly norms) takes place. Unless there's a check-pilot around. (Check-pilots are pilots, in management positions, who conduct occasional line checks, meaning they check out a pilot while he or she is actively flying an aircraft rather than a simulator.) And if that's the case, the entire crew is forewarned and behaves accordingly.

The only way carriers could detect something amiss with a pilot is through an increase in his or her book offs, but book offs can be due to a trillion reasons other than psychological fragility. That leaves check-performances in the simulator to detect a potential mental health issue. In the simulator testing, pilots are subjected to a wide range of potential mid-air crises, and it is widely believed that mental ill-health and intellectual deterioration are interconnected. There is a flaw in this reasoning as well, for simulator-check dates are known to pilots for months in advance, and therefore allow the pilot advance physical and mental preparations—such as laying off the booze a couple of weeks before the tests.

Perhaps the airlines should supervise pilots' psychological states according to their age, since seniority apparently enhances aviators' chances of developing psychiatric disturbances. Whereas in younger ones, ill mental health is purportedly caused by unspecified factors unrelated to aviation—only lack of money springs to my mind—the most common precipitating factor in middle-aged pilots is said to be domestic stress arising out of the way of life and frequent absences from home in the company of young females.[21] This sounds utterly absurd, because by then a pilot's lifestyle ought to be familiar to his wife (if he's still married to his first spouse), and his colleagues have changed little since the beginning of his commercial piloting career. If it's his second wife, she's probably a flight attendant, and is thus unfazed by his way of life.

A transition to a new type of aircraft is reported to be another factor teasing that age group's psychiatric equilibrium, because, apparently, change challenges pilots' rigid thinking.[22] If aircrew were, they would perpetually be in colossal turmoil. The "new-type-of-aircraft" theory, however, has more validity than one might wish to acknowledge, especially when "need-to-know" training methods force the boys to command aircraft without knowing intrinsically how the machines work. Surely that method is a far greater threat to pilots' psychiatric stability than marital squabbles.

Real or imaginary signs and symptoms of declining performance associated with the natural aging process are also assumed to distress middle-aged aviators' psyche.[23] One could discuss at length what types of performance the no longer golden-locked and rarely trim middle-aged pilot is worried about. But the experts fear that, if he perceives his assets and abilities as fading, then anxiety, depression, and boredom could set in. That, in turn—given the amount of social drinking and easy access to alcohol inherent in the life style—could lead to alcoholism.[24] That appears to be pure hogwash.

Pilots are only bored on layovers when they want to be. Alcohol is available everywhere and is an aircrew staple. Drinking is age independent. And alcohol abuse over a series of years can, but not necessarily does, evolve into alcoholism. And, except for the few Alcoholics Anonymous members in our midst, we are very much in control over our liquor intake, have no intention of losing home and hearth because of it, and are disinclined to hide our affinity for it as so many earthlings do. Vulnerability to psychiatric disturbances in middle-aged pilots, therefore, has nothing to do with mid-life crisis, but is related to accumulated mid-air stress, augmented by constant threat of potential malfunctioning of super-sophisticated aircraft.

This view seems to be substantiated by the fact that a major reason for psychiatric ailments in pilots of all ages is anxiety caused by a phobic fear of flying which may, insidiously, develop in response to stress and conflict or, more dramatically, in response to a single overwhelming stressor[25] such as a near miss, or a potentially disastrous mistake in the flight deck. Aviation medicine experts suggest that, if the recollections of fear following the event are repressed, it can lead to the development of phobic symptoms. That most often happens, however, when no peers are available to discuss the incident immediately after it occurred.

Therefore it is the case that pilots worldwide—much more frequently exposed to undesirable events than one wants to know—maintain their equilibrium by sharing mid-air exploits over pitchers of beer during the customary sessions at brewery holes around the globe. It enables them to shake off any creeping phobia and to maintain the sense of invulnerability without which flying becomes an intolerable burden. Mental health professionals and airline medical officers, unless they themselves are or were commercial pilots, lack the intimate experience of joyfully living with the ever present possibility of mishap and disaster. Hearing or reading about it doesn't cut it. Only walking in a professional flyer's moccasins imparts true understanding and the ability to assist when psyches reach the breaking point.

COPING WITH STRESS

How flight crew cope with the insidious stress of flying is said to greatly depend on their home lives, their significant others, and their resting capabilities while in residence and abroad. Of 272 British commercial airline pilots surveyed in the mid-80s—which is the only study available to us—the majority judged their stress and arousal levels to be significantly higher when away from home. That does not seem at all surprising when we consider that commercial aircrew on domestic runs work up to six days in a row for up to fourteen hours daily, interrupted only by luxurious ten to twelve hours layovers that are insufficient to allow for abreaction—the chance to gear down and relax even though the brain continues to react to the adrenaline search. It is understandable that the accumulated stress, and consequent adrenaline flow combined with fatigue, prohibits appropriate resting upon collapsing at a hotel. On long hauls, however, the lack of recuperation might be influenced by other factors. If the port of call is exotic, fatigue and jet-lag may be ignored in lieu of explorative activities which, occasionally, deplete the energy resources to a bare minimum. It is for those reasons that rest away from home is perceived as inferior to that in the home, the oasis of tranquillity and quiet, a place to reload the batteries and let the world go by without participating in its movement.

But frequently the aviator's nomadic existence is perceived as disruptive to residential harmony, because aircrews' desynchronization with time and their physical and psychological fatigue generates a need for relaxation. This can become hampered if the wife and/or kids impose demands. In fact, aviators' psyches are said to be burdened and troubled by a number of domestic issues: complying with household timetables; getting out of synchronization with normal home routines; sleep disturbances caused by noisy children; awareness of placing restrictions on other family members while relaxing; getting up too early or retiring too late; and being attracted by social activities that tempt him to cut rest to a minimum for fear of a broken social life.

Those who maintain the home hearths may have failed to notice that for aircrew sleeping in leaps and bounds, at home and on layovers, is the norm. "Normal domestic routines" are an unknown concept for them, and earthly social activities hold little attraction. But there might be a valid reason for this, because those pilots surveyed limply conceded that they accepted traveling the world as part of the job, but failed, neglected, or chickened out in mentioning that cruising the globe in the line of duty—liberated from earthlings' humdrum existence—is what they love and cherish just as much as flying itself. It is, however, not impossible that their significant others looked on while aviators completed the survey, thereby forcing pilots to misrepresent their actual sentiments. The desire for unlimited movement across time and space, and a longing for freedom from socio-cultural and industrial norms and boundaries might well have subconsciously propelled us into pursuing a flying career to begin with. Nevertheless, the "Do not disturb" signs swinging from all door knobs should remind co-habitants to tread lightly when an aviator is in residence wanting to do but one thing—relax, vegetate, phase out. And so it goes until retirement.

However, as much as pilots enjoy leaving the home, they seem to be greatly distressed when doing so because of the worries about administrative hassles when they arrive at the Sheratons and Hiltons of the globe. When safely settled in there, the environment feels restrictive and artificial to them, and the normal hotel routines apparently also disrupt their sleep patterns, thus depriving them of their beauty rest and disallowing optimal post-and pre-flight recuperation. Simultaneously, they struggle to adjust to local time. While whiling away the hours in hotel rooms feeling sorry for themselves, perceiving time spent as dead and wasted, their discomfort increases because of separation anxiety from their loved ones, the impotence to act if anything goes wrong in the home, and the events missed while tragically imprisoned on foreign shores. While in ports of call, such stressors to pilots' tormented psyches, combined with the after-effects of a long and exhaustive flight, encourages them to silently lament their ill-fortune while teetering on the brink of a psychological abyss.

If away from home more often than desired, a pilot's stress level is said to further increase significantly. Understandably so. Anyone who is where he or she doesn't want to be is an unhappy trooper. Book offs are designed to avoid such conflicts of interest. But that recourse will only be taken as a last resource, and most likely only if a loved one is in mortal danger, or if the aviator is physically and/or psychologically too fatigued—because of excessively demanding, computer-designed, flight schedules that ignore punishment thresholds for body and psyche—to command aircraft or to cope with the flying public.

When viewed from a psychological perspective, a dismal picture emerges when combining all of the calamities aviators purportedly face when attempting to rest away from home and at home: 20% of them were judged to be at the edge of psychiatric ailment. But, because appropriate normative data for the analyses of flight crew moods' were, and still are, unavailable, the findings have no statistical significance.

Be that as it may, aircrew are largely less judgmental, more tolerant, more filled with *bonhomie*, more understanding, and psychologically better adjusted than many earthbound folk who often drown themselves in mind-altering chemicals or drugs to escape their true personality traits. With aircrew, on the contrary, what you see is what we are. So take your next flight without hesitation. Whoever is in control, is probably just as sane if not more so, than the majority of people on the face of the earth.

Flight Phobia
in Aircrew

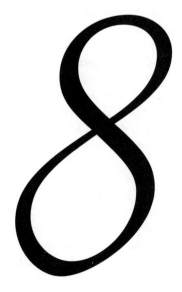

Unaware of the natural dynamic of long-term psychological stress, I kept on flying. Having no symptoms when off duty, meditation and yoga kept my pre-flight anxiety in check. When airborne, I controlled my anticipatory anxiety by imagining a white cloud around me as a buffer zone against possible emotionally disturbing events. To further protect my equilibrium I, by nature an outgoing and fun loving person, shunned all conversational or social activities with my crew, both onboard and during layovers.

My almost supernatural calmness must have been very trying for my colleagues, for I did not share my apprehensions about flying with them, and domestic flights were far too short to generate sufficient physical and emotional exhaustion to erode my psychological barriers. Short hauls left no time to initiate those peer-therapy sessions that often spontaneously occur between flight attendants during long hauls when, due to physical and emotional exhaustion, barriers and pretenses frequently fall away, and cabin crew exchange their most secret life stories and feelings with each other. Thus, I looked forward to my six-week vacation starting in early November, rationalizing that my inflight anxiety would fade away with rest and recuperation. Quitting flying was out of the question—the thought of living what I considered the mundane and boring lifestyle of earthlings was more petrifying than flying itself. I would just have to learn to live with the fears.

It's unknown what exactly motivates aircrew to choose flying as a career. For individuals to incorporate flying as a normal activity in their lives depends on the degree to which flying compensates them for the potential risks and dangers. Entrusting oneself to another human operating a machine places profound restrictions on the "flight or fight" response in the event of an incident or disaster. The process of weighing such inherent risks versus personal satisfaction takes place within each individual, and is manifested by controlling basic fears to levels that allow flying with psychological ease.[1]

Commercial aircrew balance the natural instinct for self-preservation with control over the fear of flying. Typically, professional flyers reach a level of perceived invulnerability so their equilibrium is preserved even under adverse conditions. If their control over the basic fear instinct weakens, they develop anxiety based on an instinctive anticipation of injury or death. Even though the development of flight phobia in individuals as accustomed to flying as aircrew might seem abnormal, it is actually nothing but a temporary predominance of the instinct of self-preservation. As such, flight phobia in pilots and cabin crew ought not to be mistaken for the psycho-pathological or phobic neurotic reaction of airline passengers with flight phobia. Flight crew psychologically accept as normal the inherent dangers of flying.[2] Therefore, my "break-off " reactions—detachment from the public, sensations of separation from the environment, and anxiety[3]—signaled nothing other than a subconscious development of flight phobia, the basic fear of death set in motion by the instinct for self-preservation.

Later I learned that the only empirical study on aircrew flight phobia surveyed 393 male cockpit crew and 184 male and 563 female cabin crew.[4] The researchers found that male aircrew showed a tendency toward denial of flight anxiety when the survey questions were answered outside flight situations. This could reflect a general reluctance in men to admit emotional reactions, however, rather than a gender difference in encountering tricky situations while on duty. Whereas the earthbound population of men and women differs in reporting emotional reactions—with women typically relating more anxiety, phobia, depression, and other emotional reactions or problems—the researchers noted no such gender differences among those aircrew who had flown more than ten times during a two-year time span. This psychological difference in emotional tendencies between flying personnel and earthly folk seems to be attributable to self-selection, meaning that flight personnel choose to work in a dangerous environment instead of being exposed to it involuntarily.

According to this study, anxiety and fear of flying appears to be almost exclusive to cabin personnel. Only 20% of the pilots surveyed, all of them male, admitted to occasional feelings of flight phobia and apprehension. The researchers found that 43% of female and 24% of male flight attendants reported having felt occasionally, often, or periodically anxious or afraid, whereas only 18.8% of female and 40.8% of male cabin attendants claimed they never felt this way onboard aircraft. Anxiety and flight phobia levels in female flight attendants were higher if cohabiting or married, and of those women, mothers with pre-school children showed significantly higher anxiety levels than those without. No significant differences were found in levels of anxiety between married and non-married male aircrew. The researchers also noted that cabin crew members suffering from flight phobia appeared to be significantly more anxious about safety procedures than those free of fear. The percentage of flight phobia in aircrew is considered to be a conservative estimate, since denial is a known mental defense mechanism characteristically associated with aircrew.[5]

As a professional, I already knew what the researchers disclosed as the most common reasons for cabin crew anxiety: turbulence and bad weather were, by far, causes cited most frequently, mostly because cabin crew members did not know how much movement an aircraft can tolerate before it disintegrates. General bad weather conditions, incidents or emergencies, fear of hijacking, and bomb threats ranked next in causing trepidation. Aggressive behavior from intoxicated passengers as well as medical emergencies, especially those occurring during long hauls, were also reported to heighten flight attendants' anxiety levels. Reports of aircraft crashes–anywhere in the world–were perceived as stress-provoking to both the cabin crews and their loved ones. Whereas air disasters have a certain, but limited, psychological impact on the earthly population, major crashes universally and deeply affect aircrew communities. For them, the saying that disasters come in threes too often moves from prophesy to reality. "Missed me this time," most of us will sigh, while nervously waiting for two more planes to go down.

The researchers also found that cabin crews' trust in pilots' professional expertise presented an important factor in stress levels–lack of experience in an aviator being considered a grave stress factor. Cabin crews' assessment of cockpit crew was also greatly influenced by pilots' layover behavior, where cabin crew could observe their fatigue, unstable temperaments, and conflicts between aviators.

Recently when my colleague and friend, Annemarie, worked on a two engine Boeing 767 flight to Hawaii, one engine failed half an hour after takeoff, only to restart a few minutes later. Then the other one gave up its spirit, but also kicked in again. Flight attendants began to worry, knowing that the Captain and his First, both known to have bizarre personality traits, were new on the aircraft. Cabin crew made a quick count of deadheading pilots, just in case they might be needed to assist the commander should the streak of incidents continue. Finding several experienced and well-respected off-duty pilots among their passengers somewhat eased the back end cabin crew's tension. They made it safely to Honolulu; however, the flight attendants were hypervigilant and relieved when the eagle hit the ground. The Captain held no debriefing upon arrival.

The lack of debriefings–and more often the complete lack of communication between front end and back end crew during and after critical situations–adds to cabin crews' tension and anxiety. Research suggests that because of the lack of operational control in the cabin, flight attendants should receive the same factual information as pilots about the cause of an incident. Cabin crew should also be told how the cockpit crew managed the situation, and then be provided with the opportunity to talk about technical and psychological aspects of an event. Such debriefings would enable flight attendants to get a better cognitive grip on what exactly happened which, in turn, would lessen their anxiety and facilitate a return to the sense of invulnerability.[6]

But the study showed that adequate information about why an event occurred was commonly absent, and the carrier had established no follow-up nor formal routine to provide group and individual support. However, the researchers did note that aircrew who received an adequate work-through after a close call were less anxious than those who had not.[7] Details about these debriefings—what they consisted of, and where and how they were conducted—were not stated in the survey, but one could safely assume those debriefings were crew-initiated rather than initiated by management.

Debriefings for pilots seem to be of lesser importance to their mental health and their reasons for anxiety differ distinctly from those of flight attendants. Fatigue, lack of experience in the co-pilot, difficult landings, and making errors, as well as concerns about the lack of a sterile cockpit due to passenger visits provoke cockpit crew's anxiety. Aviators' general fearlessness, however, might be the result of their limited awareness of the hazards and risks associated with the job. Or their low level of flight phobias and anxieties could be attributed to an increase in the feeling of personal invulnerability, which heightens with pilot experience.

This is not a factor that we should take lightly. Increase of personal invulnerability has been commonly associated with general aviation accidents. Research has shown that among private pilots, males are more than twice as likely to be involved in pilot error accidents than females. We could, therefore, conclude women's perceptions of risk factors are more realistic than those of men. This conclusion, combined with the dearth of debriefings after aircraft incidents, would explain the higher levels of anxiety and fear of flying noted in female flight attendants.

Aircrew members who had been exposed to critical events one or more times, report significantly more anxiety when flying and attested to greater percentages of fatigue, irritability, and sleep problems than those with no such experiences.[9] One would expect, and thus we can infer, that pilots should fare much better than flight attendants after such incidents, because the successful handling of an event not only increases their sense of invulnerability, but also provides them with a natural high after managing a dangerous situation. For the sitting ducks in the aluminum barrel, however, the opposite effect most likely occurs.

No major carriers appear to have a program in place to assist aircrew personnel after incidents, events or crashes.[10] The most cabin crew can expect from management after a critical occurrence, if acknowledgment is forthcoming at all, is to be greeted at the gate with a, "You OK?" "Yeah, we're fine," will be the answer. Management, unions, and cabin crew alike choose to ignore the fact that the psychological consequences of life-threatening incidents seldom manifest until days, weeks, or even years later.

Overall, the paucity of research into flight phobia and anxiety experienced by commercial aircrew is conspicuous. Why is that? It makes perfect sense when we consider that the absence of research data in this area protects airlines from lawsuits by passengers who suffer psychological injuries sustained in life-threatening incidents—especially if it can be proven that such injury-causing incidents was the result of an existing aircraft defect before engine start-up. Air carriers or the aircraft manufacturers would be left culpable for negligence because they failed to provide the highest standards of air travel safety.

The fact is, flying is not as safe as North American airlines would like the public to believe. This can be deduced from a recent Canadian federal court judge's decision that the confidential results of Transport Canada safety surveys, conducted through the voluntary participation of commercial airlines since 1985, will not be made public out of fear the airlines would reject continued participation if the guarantee of secrecy were removed. Transport Canada argues the surveys provide an opportunity to review human performance elements of aviation management and operation, which are not measured in its mandatory safety audits. Those mandatory audits, in turn, have been criticized by the Canadian Transportation Safety Board for their lack of thoroughness and limited consequences. But the audits, unlike the safety surveys, are accessible to the public via Canada's Access To Information Act.[11]

Making such information public would not be conducive to lowering the anxiety levels of either aircrews or passengers. Knowing that Boeing has asked its corporate customers to check the new 747s for rudder problems,[12] and all Boeing 767s for engine problems, and that the FAA recently recommended a recall of all Boeing 737s due to possible rudder problems should be sufficient to enhance apprehension about flying those planes. Nor is it in industry interests to focus on the history of flight disasters such as the three Boeing 757s that crashed during the first ten months of 1996.[13] The numerous calamities experienced by Airbus' 320s since the first one crashed during its inaugural flight at the

Paris airshow in the mid-80s does not add to the equilibrium of those working or frequently journeying on that type of aircraft either. It is this knowledge, combined with a series of close calls, which can cause a professional flyer's psychological coping mechanisms and sense of invulnerability to weaken or to fail. This is especially true of flight attendants, though we can only speculate that passengers too are far from immune in developing similar ailments. If the speculation were true, however, the airlines would have us believe that the psychological derailment is linked to pre-morbid characteristics, or, if found in females, attributable to emotional fragility or menopause.

If you think any treatment strategies have been developed for anyone experiencing an aircraft emergency, think again. Whereas an abundance of response plans representing the best in emergency medical technology and expertise exist at major airports worldwide, no services are offered in terms of meeting the psychological needs of those who are part of a disaster scene—not for cockpit and cabin crew, nor passengers, nor victims' families, nor emergency and investigative personnel, nor cleanup crews.[14] Neither government authorities nor airlines have an apparent interest in providing appropriate mental health services in moments of crisis and disaster. They refuse to acknowledge that these services can be of critical importance in reducing panic and hysteria, and in minimizing the long-term psychological and psychosomatic impact of such events. Why? Because to supply such services would be harmful to the bottom line.

Fully 75% of individuals experiencing a life-threatening incident show some degree of disaster syndrome, with behavioral reactions of being stunned, unresponsive, bewildered or docile. The lack of extended concern for those individuals after the accident or incident reveals the airlines' chilling disinterest in the latent development of psychological disturbances such as anxiety, restlessness and irritability, or in physical symptoms such as tension headaches, and in behavioral changes such as the exhibition of extremely constricted and guarded personality traits. If this disinterest is expressed in terms of denial at the point of the accident, individuals are even less prepared to cope later with stress and psychological impacts. The lack of mental health treatment to survivors, aircrew, ground personnel and their families, and to the investigative personnel themselves, leaves open the possibility of these people developing long-term psychological dysfunction due to prolonged and unresolved stress.[15]

———————————✈———————————

The string of peculiar incidents cursing me since the summer of 1989 continued. The impression that I was jinxed had spread through the ranks. "You coming with us? What's gonna happen?" became a familiar remark when I faced a new crew at the beginning of each month. I also began to deeply resent both the inflight management of our small base who never bothered to ask me how I was getting along, and NorAm in general, who categorically denied me an explanation of why the engine had exploded in 1988. Therefore, I took every opportunity to vent my anger and frustration by lashing out at the company.

One early August morning, the new base manager took the unheard of initiative of visiting the 767's back galley before our departure to give us an unsolicited lecture on the generosity of the company's latest contract proposal. I snapped, "You've got guts trying to persuade us to accept a proposal which clearly only benefits one party—management! You should learn to appreciate the danger and psychological pressures we face every time we go up, and pay us accordingly. Instead, you are offering a 5% wage cut, longer working days, more monthly flying hours, and a cut in crew."

"Yeah but, it benefits all of us when the airline prospers. You'll all keep your jobs," he counteracted.

"Oh, yeah? As far as I know, you're working to get government permission to increase our workload from fifty to sixty passengers each. And you tell me we're all going to keep our jobs? A blind person can see something doesn't jive!" I responded while continuing to prepare the galley, unassisted. My co-workers, too mesmerized by the verbal battle, had stopped dead in their tracks.

"Yeah, but..."

"No yeah but," I interrupted, "The company's proposal is unethical and unconscionable. The only ones who profit from it, if it is accepted, may God forbid, are you, your cohorts, the union officers negotiating for us, and their fellow in-charges. They get some perks in every contract, whereas we get shafted. But let me remind you, what you try to stuff down our throats will surely affect you sooner or later, because what goes around comes around. That's a universal law."

After a vague "If that's how you see it," he beat a hasty retreat, weaving in and out of the boarded passengers whose entry had been ignored by all during our exchange. My peers looked at me in awe, while I grinned happily, exhilarated I had let off steam.

That same month our regular purser, a jovial fellow, was taken off our flight for reasons unknown and replaced by Miss Bunio, an Italian woman without the vivacious and lighthearted spirit often associated with that nationality. An Italian newspaper was attached full length to her suitcase, and remained there, neat and straight, throughout our two-day journey. That she disliked me on sight became quite apparent during our pre-flight briefing, where contemptuous behavior characterized her first interaction with me. I ignored her rudeness even when things became dicey minutes after we took wing.

Apparently unfamiliar with the timing and sequence of service on this early morning Toronto run, Bunio insisted I turn the meals ON right after takeoff. "Far too early," I offered. "Once we've finished buns, coffee and tea," I said, as my colleagues presently performed that service, "we do bar, and two hours out of Toronto, meals with wine and beer *et cetera* on top of the trolleys. At least that's how we've been doing it for the past four months."

Bunio, disinclined to listen, ordered, "Just do as I tell you!"

"Fine. As you please," I said, turning on the ovens, silently attributing her need for control to an inferiority complex. My peers, when returning to the galley, glared at the cooking meals in disbelief and demanded answers. "Go ask our amiable purser," I suggested, unwilling to spend energy on explanations. They did, and the meals stayed on. Half way through the cooking cycle, black clouds belched out of one oven. I turned it off and advised the flight deck, as required.

Bunio exploded into the galley minutes later, immediately noticed the dead oven, and demanded explanations. "There was lots of smoke coming out," I said. She turned the timer back to ON. "Imbecile," I mumbled under my breath, as thick black smoke instantaneously billowed out of the oven. Other flight attendants watched in shock as the purser took no action to end the spectacle. I had moved away to the bathroom door when Annette screeched around the corner. Seeing Bunio mesmerized by the clouds of smoke, Annette turned purple before shouting furiously at the stunned woman, "Turn off that oven, you f...ing bitch! What the hell are you trying to do to us? You out of your mind?" Her astounding language took me by surprise. Always a lady, Annette in the six months I had flown with her had never sworn or lost her temper. Shocked out of her reverie, Bunio reacted immediately to the command. The rest is history.

The entire service on the flight was a tragic comedy charged with hostility and questions from the cabin crew about Bunio's sanity and competence. The mechanic repairing the oven during the station stop nonchalantly volunteered that the problem with the oven was "Just a misconnection."

"Yeah, just a misconnection," I thought. "And that's what caused twenty-three out of forty-one passengers to die in the skies over Cincinnati. And afterwards, the flight attendants were crucified in the media—accused of not having done all they could for the survival of their charges." The inquest showed people died as a result of the toxic fumes generated by the polyvinyl chloride plastics used for cabin fixtures and furnishings, which generate hydrogen chloride and cyanide gases when burned. Deaths were not due to cabin personnel's incompetence, though this fact was not made explicit to the public. The cabin crew were also accused of not giving passengers explicit emergency evacuation instructions.[16] That the toxic fumes probably affected flight attendants' vocal cords and restricted their ability to yell evacuation commands went equally unmentioned during the inquest.

"Easy for you to say," was all I remarked after the mechanic's statement, since I was too busy preparing for the next flight leg, the Toronto –Halifax mad dash. As soon as he left the galley we worked with lightning speed, tossing beer cans and white wine bottles (always boarded lukewarm) into ice-filled garbage bins, transferring meals from trolleys into ovens and turning them on, and preparing bar trolleys while passengers boarded. We closed the last security latches on galley units during the takeoff roll.

According to Transport Canada regulations, once an aircraft either pushes away from the gate or rolls toward the terminal after landing, only safety-related duties are permitted—such as checking passengers' seat belts and arming doors for departure by attaching the escape slides, or disarming them before arrival at the terminal. If cabin crew perform service-related functions, such as distributing newspapers, attending to galley duties, or passing out pillows, aspirins, writing paper, headsets, toys, or drinks while taxiing, they can be fined if caught by an inspector. But there are never any inspectors around, and on short hauls with full houses, violations of those rules occur on a perpetual basis to provide customers with service designed by airline management. Neither the airlines nor government officials acknowledge that the rule requiring personnel to be at assigned emergency positions during taxiing is routinely being violated in order to provide top service to passengers.

And why should they? Once in a blue moon, the flight attendants' union publishes a statement to the membership that the cabin crew have to be at their emergency positions at all times while aircraft are rolling.

Not adhering to the governmental regulations can have dire consequences for cabin crew, who make the best scapegoats in the event of an accident. May the heavens have mercy on flight attendants not at their assigned stations during any on-board, on the ground emergency while the aircraft is taxiing to or from the terminal. If they die, and others with them, it will be blamed on their incompetence and unavailability at their assigned emergency position. And if they survive, but lives are lost, they will be accused of negligence, unavailability at their assigned exits, and possibly incompetence. Prohibited by the airlines from publicly stating their version of an event, flight attendants deflect media attention away from the pilots, who might be directly or indirectly responsible for the accident.[17] The worst of it, however, is that those flight attendants psychologically and/or physically injured in any aircraft incident will most likely end up in the hands of the Worker's Compensation Board, which is more punishment than anyone deserves.

And so it was that we buckled ourselves in seconds before liftoff from Toronto to head for Halifax. The service went without a hitch; Señorita Bunio, ever vigilant for a husband-to-be, kept out of sight, catering to the exclusively male First Class crowd.

Upon touchdown in Halifax, and pleased with our one hour and twenty-five minute whirlwind performance, we headed to the hotel for a seventeen hour layover.

Flying Etiquette and The Minimum Equipment List

At the pre-flight briefing the following day, Bunio focused her attention on one person and one topic only, namely me and my incompetence. She portrayed the smoke-billowing oven as a figment of my imagination. It was I, she said, who instigated the improper timing for the meal turn on, and I who threw wine bottles on ice causing the labels to detach. "Passengers have a right to see what they are offered," the Italian declared.

"My arse! As if they care to know when the choice is to take or leave *Andre's Speciaux*. They drink anything wet, cold, and potent," I thought, while one of my colleagues piped up: "But it's the only way to cool things down in a hurry." Bunio told her to shut up. I was the one she was after, and no one was going to spoil her vendetta. Staring motionless and silently at the Italian while intermittently turning ghostly white and beet red, I felt her unwillingness to take responsibility for her actions and the onslaught on my integrity. I had a desire to strangle her. The energy I exerted on controlling my fury, as I resisted leaping into a lecture of my own, was enormous, and I only succeeded because I suspected an ulterior motive. If she ignited my fuse and I engaged in battle with her, a visit to the office would inevitably follow.

After half an hour, the verbal manure session ended. Remaining composed and quiet had nonetheless driven me to the point of exhaustion, and on my way to the back galley I began to cry. My colleagues, equally upset and as stunned as I was about the purser's behavior, consoled me. The dangerous consequences that the insane scene could have had were we to face an emergency lingered in our minds as we journeyed homewards.

As I noted earlier, crew conflict is rare, but how well flight attendants work together depends on their interpersonal dynamics. When they enjoy each other's company, passengers walk off board deeming the airline to be the best in the world. If a crew from hell is at work, however, passengers turn into miserable little creatures, and dissatisfaction is all-pervasive for no apparent reason. On the other hand, passenger behavior also greatly influences the on-board atmosphere.

FLYING ETIQUETTE

Pleasant manners and a civilized attitude are of the essence in the confined aircraft environment with nowhere to run or hide. It's worthwhile to keep in mind that rudeness doesn't get anyone anywhere, and that kindness, patience, and consideration are assets, not a curse, especially when in the twilight zone. So do yourself a favor and smile at your neighbor when settling in; he or she suffers just as much from the limited space as you do. Besides, your life may depend on it later. If an emergency strikes, it's too late to atone for unpleasantness. Be appreciative and kind to your flight attendants as well. It's not their fault that the world treats you unfairly and tests you beyond tolerance, or that your wife is a nuisance and your boss a pest, or that you're overweight but unable to diet, or that the flight is five hours late because someone left a screwdriver or a pop can in the engine, or because an earthquake, tornado, or a snowstorm has caused havoc somewhere, delaying your departure.

Please do understand that it is an absolute No-No to ring the call button, unless, as was the original intention, you are alerting cabin crew that someone is incapacitated. It was not installed, as believed by some passengers, to startle flight attendants into a sprint to bring you another round of booze. Remember, flight attendants regularly patrol the cabins for you to ask them for a refill or to express other concerns or wishes.

Those souls in need of mid-air attention, be it because of an approaching epileptic seizure, a severe nosebleed, a heart attack, air sickness or fainting spells, to name just a few incidents which can occur mid-air, often choose to collapse close to the galleys or the lavatories where immediate assistance is available to them. If they are in their seats when the impairment occurs, their neighbors, if experienced travelers, prefer to alert us personally instead of going through the call button routine.

And just one more thing. Never ever ask more than one cabin crew member for whatever it is you want. Yes, the attendant may have forgotten your request. But chances are that a hundred other passengers are clamoring for the same attention you desire. So, when you have patiently waited for a while, but nothing has been delivered, catch the flight attendant's attention by using eye contact. You'll be surprised how often he or she lights up when catching your gaze, and your perseverance will be rewarded with an extra stiff drink (free of charge if venturing in economy) in appreciation of your patience. That's about the only reward we can give you.

Like many other cabin crew members, over the course of years I became an expert in delivering one-liners to jolt some of my deserving charges into the awareness that their very temporary servant was, indeed, a human being who believed in goodwill among people. Even though my preferred position as the galley slave through most of 1990 largely sheltered me from contact with the public, occasionally I did switch positions and practiced what I preached. On one of those days, a gentleman who had watched me working in the big 767 economy cabin, handed me his calling card saying,

"I'm a promoter for stand-up comics and you're a born one. If you want to switch careers, call me—you'd be perfect." Grinning from ear to ear, I pocketed the card.

In September, I was doing the same runs with a purser equally as unimpressive in demeanor, charm, and personality as Bunio. Jerky in her movements and nervous in her manner, Missy was under foot far too often for comfort, disturbing our well-practiced routines and unnecessarily interfering wherever and whenever she could. Therefore, when time rolled around for my voluntary "beer-run"—the passing out of complementary beer between Toronto and Halifax—my colleagues, noticing my unpreparedness for the task, asked, "Aren't you going to do it?" All summer long, during sweltering days of heat and humidity, we had extended this gesture of goodwill, and our regulars had come to appreciate it very much.

"No, no. Not with this one," I answered.

"Oh, come on! She won't say anything."

Going ahead against my better judgment, I had just begun to distribute the goodies from front to back when Missy entered the economy cabin. It propelled her into a fit. "You out of your mind? This kind of service is unacceptable! Stop immediately. And don't dare do such a thing ever again!" she yelled.

"Fine with me," I answered, turned about, and walked back to my galley handing out beers to happy passengers on my way.

But Missy had a point. Besides orchestrating the show in the event of an emergency, her job was to ensure that the cabin crew performed service-related tasks according to company regulations for the purpose of consistency. And a complementary beer-run was definitely not in the books.

Mountains of papers are issued to all flight attendants to study so they become familiar with the sequence and timing of service on any given route, at any given time, and to acquaint them with how food and beverages are to be presented to passengers. Fair enough. Otherwise every inflight service, if conducted according to cabin crews' desires, or their individual moods of the day, could turn into a fine circus. The need for these regulations becomes abundantly clear when you remember that we thrive on what most earthlings abhor—variety of action.

Whereas the in-charge's job is to assure the implementation of the service plan by guiding and directing crew activities, it is also expected that flight attendants will innovate when situations warrant it. The extent of such innovation depends, of course, on the purser's personality. The larger the ego and the greater the need for power, control and authority, the less willingness the in-charge has to listen to crew suggestions. Mind you, the majority of pursers, especially on long hauls, are superb at "guiding and directing," though they are unenthusiastic about dirtying their clammy little hands with manual labor. They leave it up to their cabin crew in the back of the bus to swing the service according to their time frame, in particular when flying with senior crew.

But, Missy liked to mix and mingle. One could be inspired in believing in her happiness, especially when the airport manager, her lover, always escorted her on-board, and they longingly waved good-bye to each other during aircraft push back. She was, however, a miserable individual. Stern in speech and unsmiling in demeanor, an expression of constant dissatisfaction marred her features throughout our trips. Endlessly rear-ranging empty trays in empty food trolleys for no purpose during her company-regulated meal distribution duty in economy class in a full house, she became a silently tolerated aggravation.

Sneaking up behind me when paying an unexpected visit to the back galley on the homebound leg of our third trip, she forcefully knocked me on the shoulder and announced, "What's the excuse this time?"

I controlled my reaction to hit her back before uttering my favorite line, "*Excuse me*, works miracles. And may I ask what you are referring to?"

With fury in her eyes she fired back, "What? You should know better! Why aren't the meals on?"

Perplexed, I consulted my watch and replied calmly, "We've still got ten minutes, Missy."

"That's not so. You've turned them on late all month," she argued.

"No, I haven't," I responded fiercely, "But if all month you felt that they should have been turned on earlier, why didn't you say so until now?" She stormed off without dignifying me with an answer. I began to wonder how it could possibly be that, after flying conflict-free for fifteen years, I was suddenly encountering nothing but, in one way or another, month after month, since I had returned to the line in March 1989.

Later that evening, a Catholic priest offered me an English teaching position at a missionary college in Macao. Even though declining the offer, I took his card, beaming with joy. There was a life available in exotic places if I ever wanted to quit flying.

Homebound on our fourth cycle, we left Halifax late, due to a mechanical problem. When we arrived in Toronto and wanted to board our next plane, which was to carry us to Vancouver, we were told that crew scheduling had put a new crew on it. This was against contract rules, but no union officers were available to argue the point, and management did not listen to us. We were refused boarding unless we produced proper deadhead tickets waiting for us at the inflight communication center—which was miles away. Thus, missing the last west-bound flight of the night, we were forced to stay over, and would not receive remuneration for this lost trip. The peculiar incidents were now beginning to interfere with my private life, for I had an exam the following day. Signing a pink slip became a very tempting proposition.

Exam writing immediately after a flight is a sure recipe for disaster. Only the body is present upon return to earth, while the mind still lingers in the upper hemisphere. Hoping to catch some sleep at home before venturing to do the unavoidable, I hopped on the first flight of the morning, an Airbus 320. During our descent into Vancouver, my eardrum punctured, and the airline's physician booked me off duty for two cycles. Joyously kissing Missy bye-bye in spirit, while diving into civvies at the medical clinic, I rushed to the university, where my brain refused to kick into gear. After a spectacular job of bombing the exam, quitting life in the skies became ever more tempting.

But I showed up at the airport for the first cycle of October more buoyant than I had been all summer. Fourteen days off duty had worked miracles. When I saw Erika in the briefing room, my spirit soared. "You coming with us?" I asked. She nodded. "But why didn't you tell me the other day?" I questioned, ecstatic to be flying with my buddy again. We'd worked together for years of overseas flying, and had spoken on the phone frequently.

"Wanted to surprise you. It's the only one I'm doing, besides *Londons*," she replied. I didn't pause to wonder why the company suddenly paired overseas schedules with a crummy domestic trip. "Oh, this's Eileen, our purser. She's union. Just moved in from Halifax. I know her from Toronto," Erika introduced me to a homely, butch-looking granny. After the emergency briefing, work positions were distributed. Erika and Kaye, a Toronto-based flight attendant, would be working with me in the back.

Whereas Kaye worked like a horse, Erika, who said that she had never before been on a Boeing 767 when not doing the cabin service, leisurely hung around the rear exit door. Instead of showing her the ropes, which included assisting the galley slave, I answered the trillion questions she bombarded me with while trying to maintain order in the developing chaos with Kaye's help. Shortly before landing in Toronto, the galley resembled a disaster area which the in-charge perused with disgust on a brief visit before disappearing in a hurry. We locked in the last trolley seconds before landing, and were lucky at that. The performance between Toronto and Halifax, without Kaye, went much better. Even Erika suddenly pitched in to avoid the humiliation of asking the pilots for a delay in landing.

In Halifax, Erika and I did what we had practiced so many times when flying long hauls—we dove into civvies and checked out the local watering holes. The homebound flight legs with half full houses went smoothly. So did the next three cycles. And, as luck would have it, I missed the fourth, a late night Vancouver–Las Vegas turnaround.

The flight attendants stepping aboard the Boeing 767 that evening were greeted by the random flickering of emergency, cabin and galley lights; ovens and hot-cups worked as if they had a life of their own; and the intercom, as well as the public address system, embraced the same mysterious code, all of which created a rather spooky atmosphere. The captain, however, unconcerned about the weird phenomena, happily took off with a full house. His cockiness was temporary. Bernie, a flight attendant with a private pilot's license, was hauled into the cockpit half an hour into the roughly two-hour flight to push malfunctioning circuit breakers back into their casings until the aircraft, during the final landing phase, fell onto the runway from approximately thirty feet. The weather was calm, and no clouds obscured the star-studded sky.

The pilots checked the plane for structural damage and kicked the tires, while the cabin crew spent a few dollars at the slot machines, before again venturing into the skies on the same aircraft. Minutes after takeoff, a distraught passenger waved a flight attendant over to his window seat and with great agitation explained that pieces had flown off the wing. "Bah," the cheerful soul bravely responded, "Nothing to worry about. Happens all the time."

The electrical scenario of the down trip repeated itself, with Bernie again on "push-in-circuit-breakers" duty, until the eagle landed uneventfully in Vancouver. Anxiety levels among cabin crew members skyrocketed during the flight.

At the airport the following day, a supervisor rushed up to me and breathlessly inquired, "Tanya, you went to Vegas last night?"

"No—made a flight switch."

"Thank heavens—pieces flying off the wings punctured the fuselage," she informed me, and stomped off without further explanation. The half-cocked story left me puzzled, until, during our next cycle together, my colleagues did not want to talk about anything else but their experience. Becoming aware that others were just as psychologically vulnerable to unusual on-board occurrences as I was, I cherished listening to their stories. What I found amusing was that they were much less indignant about the fall-down landing and the pieces flying off the wing than what they described as "the Captain's irresponsible behavior." But had he really demonstrated that?

THE MINIMUM EQUIPMENT LIST

The Minimum Equipment List (MEL) is the document detailing which equipment malfunctions—under what specific conditions—can be disregarded in order to allow aircraft to still be dispatched for flight. In the United States, the MEL became obligatory in the 1960s. In Canada, it was made obligatory by virtue of an air navigation order in 1977. Some Canadian airlines, however, incorporated the MEL as early as 1970, introducing it as the "Minimum Equipment Guide (MEG)," which became part of the Aircraft Operating Manual. However, relief from the MEL has apparently been authorized by one carrier's main maintenance department who was said to possess an expanded MEL called the Master Minimum Equipment List.[1] Consequently, if the electrical malfunctioning on the Vegas aircraft was listed in the MEL or MEG as a "GO item," the captain *had* to fly the aircraft. And if he contacted the main maintenance department and received a go-ahead, he had to take the aircraft up. Only if he failed to contact anyone, and acted entirely on his own accord and gut feelings, did he act irresponsibly.

Because flight attendants are not taught how, and by whom, decisions on whether to fly an aircraft or not are authorized, they jump to the conclusion that the captain has the final word. He does not. He appears not to even have an iota of influence in the decision-making process. If maintenance declares an aircraft is airworthy, the pilot must take it up or risk disciplinary action. To educate cabin crew about the rules and regulations governing the decision-making process when mechanical problems arise would not be cost efficient. Moreover, it would also jeopardize the carriers' desire to keep both flight attendants and passengers under the illusion of being in safe hands and "on safe ground" when on-board aircraft. After all, the assumption that a captain will only fly an aircraft when he knows that it is safe to do so, because his life is at stake as well, soothes all those in the back of the bus.

For my last cycle before my vacation, I happily trooped into the airport, but smelled a rat the second I entered the aircraft. Patty, a flight attendant supervisor whose permanent facial expression of stupidity and ignorance never ceased to amaze me, glared at me angrily with piggish eyes, her waistline bulging. She responded to my cheerful greeting with a "You are eight minutes late boarding." If I was, we all were, since I entered in the middle of the pack. I decided not to argue because of my previous experiences with her.

Once, eight years earlier, she had gone ballistic over my cute, dark blue patent leather shoes because policy only permitted plain leather ones. By that time I had worn them for three years, and they were so divinely chic with the uniform, that even my personal supervisor had ignored the crime. On another occasion, I, in my infinite wisdom, had shown off my Leonardo da Vinci idea of inserting an elastic into the bottom of my uniform blouse, to prevent it from sliding out from under my skirt. I had demonstrated this to some of my colleagues in front of a management gofer. She had immediately reported it to the on-duty supervisor, who happened to be Miss Patty.

Going bonkers, claiming that my creative idea ruined the look of the uniform, Miss Patty nevertheless intoned that, if I promised to restore the precious outfit to its original state upon my return from the three days overseas trip, she would take no further action. I did. Therefore, it surprised me to find her two-page dissertation detailing the violation in my company mail folder when I set out on my next cycle a week later. Ever since then, I dove out of her sight whenever possible, which was easy to do—until this day.

"She coming with us?" I asked my colleagues when I reached the back galley.

"Yeah, but only to Toronto."

"Why?"

"To check up on us."

My intuition said otherwise. The only consolation in the approaching dilemma was that I, for once, would have adequate crew support in the galley from others besides just Kaye. A supervisor on board—a once-in-a-blue-moon occurrence—always has that effect. The aircraft packed solid, Patty took a passenger seat immediately forward of the galley instead of, as was customary, in a spare flight attendant jump seat. Obviously, NorAm had spared no expense to make her journey a joyous one.

Throughout the flight, she played hide and seek. Whenever I was out of my spotless galley, she galloped into it. And whenever I returned, she was gone. Loss of separation was avoided by split seconds. Patty's behavior moved me from silent laughter to despair. Shortly before landing, Kaye gave me her telephone number saying, "Something vile's brewing here. I think she's after you. If you need anyone to back you up, call me." I was grateful for her gesture, even though I knew that there was nothing Patty could criticize on this flight because everything had run like clockwork.

Patty lingered after the landing, seated in the last row of the back of the bus and chatted amiably with my colleagues, while the Halifax galley was boarded and the aircraft was superficially groomed. I went to Business Class to meditate and to await the unfolding of events. Just before galley boarding had been completed, Patty showed up, chanting, "Tanya, we've gotta talk!"

"Yes, Patty?"

"You're to meet me in the office on October 31st, at 1:00 P.M."

"Yes, Patty. What kind of a day is that?"

"Never mind. Just be there. And better bring a union rep with you," she quipped, and headed off towards the rear, while I got up and went to see Eileen, the union-affiliated in-charge.

"Ask her why she wants to see you at the office—and why you haven't been notified before leaving home base, and by the way, you know you can book off here?"

"I don't want to," I replied, and headed towards economy where I confronted Patty. "Why are you telling me this when I'm on my way to a layover? Aren't you aware what that does to me psychologically?"

"I'm going to Calgary over the weekend, and you're on vacation in November. And I want to *cater* you before then." I had no idea what she meant by that, but before I could ask, she snapped, "And right now, you should be putting meals in the ovens."

"As you can see, that's being done already." My colleagues were busy performing the task. "I want to know what this is all about."

"Well, I can't tell you. I've nothing with me. But someone will meet you in Vancouver tomorrow night. I've got a flight to catch now and you'd better get busy," whereupon she dispatched herself from the aircraft.

During the Halifax run, Eileen suggested that she and I should wine, dine and chat together when we reached our destination. "Forget it. She's union," my colleagues warned when I told them about it. I heeded their warning, but because none of them wanted to go out after we arrived, I ventured into the Halifax rain alone to cool my head.

Returning to the hotel an hour later, I tried to get in touch with the union's Vancouver president, Harry, and his vice-president, Tobias, but they were at a convention in Toronto. Neither of their wives would divulge the conference's exact location; however, they expected their husbands to return home the following evening. The Toronto hotels I contacted refused information about whether or not they were hosting a flight attendants' union convention. After laboring to Vancouver the following day, a supervisor handed me an envelope the second I stepped off the aircraft. It was Saturday, October 27, 1990.

WCB
and
the Injured Worker

I drove home in a daze, shed the uniform, grabbed a bottle of wine, and sat down to study Patty's missive. The three maidens of the London flight had indeed raised their ugly heads, and according to the letter, accused me of "splashing, slashing and spilling food" over their precious beings and belongings without apology, refusing them access to the toilet facilities, and being extremely "rude, sharp, and impolite" to them—as well as to other passengers. They went on to note the other passengers would most likely refrain from expressing their disgust with my unprofessional demeanor in writing.

Because, they continued, the senior steward had failed to sense from the "tense and quiet atmosphere" of my cabin that something was amiss, they had found it necessary to inform him about my atrocious behavior shortly before landing in London. My manner had not improved, they claimed, up to their departure from the plane. Their complaint concluded with the statement that I had inflicted such "irreparable harm" on them, that neither they, their friends, acquaintances, dogs, cats, or travel agents would ever journey with us again. A peculiar note at the bottom of the letter, written by the same pen, "NorAm, 7/8 Conduct Suit, London WIA I7G," escaped my attention. Later I realized this notation indicated that the maidens worked for NorAm, British Division.

Infuriated by their accusations, I failed to see both the humor and the insanity of it all. "Slashing, splashing, and spilling" are rarely a flight attendant's forte unless they are due to retire soon. On those occasions, bowls full of Caesar Salad and entire Black Forest cakes have been known to land upside down on irate passengers' heads. Their claim that I was rude astonished me. Whereas I am lucid and quick-witted, rudeness is alien to my nature, and I had yet to join that elite group of flight attendants who mumbled "s.f.s."—so fucking stupid—under their breath when setting eyes upon a customer. Accused of denying the lovely maidens access to the washroom, however, struck me as so bizarre and demented that I temporarily doubted management's sanity in dignifying this complaint with an iota of attention. "Can't use the facilities today, hon," must be one of the few remarks as yet unuttered by cabin crew on aircraft in-flight, for cabin crew definitely prefer that passengers use the toilet rather than having to clean up the mess from seats, trolleys, and floors—even though that, too, has been done on occasion.

Their inane claim brought back the vivid memory of the early morning scene by the washroom on that fateful flight. As usual, a multitude of passengers stood in line half an hour before landing, desperately squeezing their thighs together after having pushed their bladders to the limit after indulging in the rarely delicious morning snack. One of my charges, a tiny East Indian centenarian who had been boarded by wheelchair and had not moved all flight, faced the same urgency at that unfortunate hour. Practically carrying her to the facilities, I did what every flight attendant does in a similar situation, and what any remotely intelligent passenger would understand—I informed those waiting in line that the next available washroom was ours.

After accompanying her into the lavatory to ensure her familiarity with the environment, I asked one of the waiting passengers to tell me when she reappeared, so that I could take her back to her seat. I was far too busy with pre-landing preparations to hang around. Throughout all this, the middle-aged maidens must have been standing in the lineup, but they had been smart enough to remain silent, possibly aware that more understanding, compassionate, and equally anxious bystanders would have scorned them if they had launched a protest.

Continuing to turn the pages of Patty's voluminous letter, a note from a Mr. Kallendo caught my attention making both the lavatory and the "splashing, slashing and spilling" indictments pale by comparison. In it, Kallendo whined bitterly about my "extreme rudeness and incompetence" when he traveled in economy with his wife to Toronto, in September 1990. Coffee and tea pots had been waved in their faces, he claimed, but the precious contents denied them, and moreover, I had refused them a badly-needed paper containing a crossword puzzle to while away the hours. "Therefore," he pronounced, conveniently forgetting that I lent them my own *Toronto Globe and Mail*, "their journey had been ruined." Kallendo's letter went on to suggest I be given a refresher course in dealing with the general public to get me in line. He concluded with the statement that he and his wife considered my abusive attitude so grave that future travels with the airline were out of the question.

How well I remembered these two middle-aged, well-dressed people purporting to be experienced travelers, because Mr. Kallendo had mentioned to the in-charge, Missy (the airport manager's lover), that he normally flew Business Class, but on that particular day journeyed in economy on accumulated air mile point tickets. His importance as a repeat customer had filtered down to me, and I remember thinking it odd that he, of all people, would board without crossword puzzles. After all, if he was a frequent flyer, he would have known that newsstands had yet to make their appearance aboard aircraft. His claim about "waving around coffee and teapots" also baffled me. It had never been my style.

I detested that habit and always used eye contact to get passengers to tell me what they wanted from pots in hand, and for me, that always worked like a charm.

Important facts in Patty's letter—and their implications—eluded me the first time I read it. For example, it didn't strike me as peculiar that neither the maidens' nor the Kallendo letters indicated the addresses where they could be reached—nor that there was an astounding similarity in the letter writers' choice of syntax, punctuation, and spelling. That these letters of complaint, the first in my career, only reached me months after the company had received them, instead of after a week as was customary, also escaped my attention. Also, at the time, it didn't strike me as odd that the supposedly attached, yet missing, copy of an apology letter to the Kallendo's had been extended by a NorAm president who had long-ago retired. Nor did it register that no similar letter of apology had been extended to the maidens. I wasn't puzzled by the fact that for all the accusations of performance deficiencies apparently made by my crew members between May and October of 1990, none were substantiated in writing. It didn't even register that Patty lied when stating that the base manager had reprimanded me on October 12th, 1990 for being late in boarding, when I had not seen the man since our discussion on board aircraft in August.

All of these critical points faded into the background. Only one thing registered clearly: the conclusion to Patty's litany of complaints stated that disciplinary action for my offenses against the public at large, and my crew members in particular, were being contemplated, and that I should seek help from the union.

Knowing that both officers should be home from the Toronto convention, I called Harry. His machine answered, but Tobias picked up the phone. "Ah...yeah...got your message. Wanted to call you tomorrow. I'm trying to set up a meeting with you and Cecile McLair. I'll let you know tomorrow."

"Who's that?" I asked.

"Oh, she's been with the union for years. Started flying with us about ten years ago. Came over from Pacific[Airlines]."

"Never heard of her. Can't you do this with me?" I inquired.

"No. Got to fly tomorrow...but I'll call you before I leave," he said and hung up. When I rang his house at 9 P.M. the following day he remarked,

"Oh, yeah...forgot all about you...call Cecile and see if she wants to do your case," and gave me her number. I contacted her, and she did not object.

On October 31st, 1990, I stepped into the airport practically catatonic. My physician had given me Ativan an hour earlier so that I could control my jitters. Cecile didn't show at our agreed rendezvous spot, but I found her chatting amiably with Patty in the office of the inquisition. While the pills' magical powers increased, I listened stone-faced to the presentation of charges against me, regarding the whole performance as an utterly disgusting farce. Patty questioned me in an increasingly aggressive manner, peppering her charges with statements such as, "You're guilty of this, aren't you?" She cut me off whenever I opened my mouth by saying, "The evidence presented speaks clearly against you. You're guilty. Why can't you just admit it?" I wondered when she would propose throwing me on the rack to secure an admission of guilt.

Cecile, meanwhile, observed in silence, but when I returned from puffing my first cigarette in six months during the ten minute break called by the supervisor, she blasted me. "You gotta show some emotions. Your career's at stake here, you know!" This unexpected piece of information had the marvelous effect of snapping my emotional barrier, and when Patty entered the room, I began to howl and sobbingly confessed that the engine explosion of 1988 still haunted me.

Upon that revelation, Patty left, only to return minutes later and announce, "In view of circumstances, and your meritorious record deserving an Award of Excellence—had it not been for the latest events— I'll limit my action to a one-day suspension without pay. I've also made an appointment with Dr. Norsk (the company's medical officer) for November 5th." Her unexpected tender loving care so overwhelmed me, that I hugged and thanked her for her heart-warming compassion.

I departed in tears, Cecile in tow. When we were out of earshot, she exclaimed with a sigh of relief, "Wow. That was close. They intended to fire you, you know."

"And so you say. What's gonna happen now?" I answered.

"That's it. You can go on with your merry life," she quipped. She declined to go for a coffee because she had business to attend to with management. Believing that NorAm would help me to regain my sense of invulnerability, I skipped home quite happily, and buried myself in neglected school work. Little did I know that the attitude of assistance and cooperation prevailing among those working in the skies is not always applicable when we're on earth.

I kept the appointment with the company's medical officer, and Dr. Norsk diagnosed recurrent PTSD, without explaining why it had happened. Up to that point, I had no idea that the ailment can re-develop after a latency of months or years if similar incidents to the one which caused it in the first place occur, or if the illness is unhealed when returning to the scene of action.

Perhaps more importantly, though, I was unaware that most, if not all, corporate medical physicians are engaged to protect employer's productivity rather than to advocate for the health of workers, before, during, and after an injury.[1] Therefore, I saw Norsk's order to visit a psychiatrist, a Dr. Oliver, the following day as a gesture of goodwill. I didn't know then that 9.4% of workers' on-the-job-site impairments are caused by mental disorders, and only 8.8% due to physical injuries and poisonings. Instead, I believed that the medical officer of one of world's ten largest airlines would be thoroughly acquainted with PTSD symptoms and cures, so I happily introduced myself at the psychiatrist's office on November 6th at the appointed hour.[2]

"You're too early," the secretary chastised me.

"No, I'm not. NorAm told me to be here at 1 P.M."

"No. *You're* wrong. They told you to be here at 1:30 P.M.," she snarled.

"Fine with me," I said and left, unimpressed by the surroundings and the waiting patients. I returned thirty minutes later, when the psychiatrist beckoned me into his Italian leather furnished office, and asked me to sit in a low armchair, far below his eye level and at a considerable distance from him, with sunshine glaring into my eyes. He inquired about what presumably led to my present disposition, and I related the well-known story. It occupied the slotted thirty minutes.

The only words spoken by his eminence throughout our session were, "I want to see you again soon. Please arrange two more appointments with my secretary." After she arranged for the future encounters, I started to leave the office but, confusing the doors, opened one which lead to what appeared to be a linen closet. Behind this door, however, was Dr. Oliver—plunging an enormous needle into a fragile woman's forearm.

"So that's the way he cures his patients," I thought aghast, and stormed out as fast as my legs would go. Seconds later I alighted two flights below in my GP's office, distressed, confused, upset, anxiety-ridden, and crying, "I'm not going to see that man again. I will not be treated with drugs."

"Take those two sessions and we'll find someone to treat you afterwards," Sammy counseled soothingly.

On December 10th, 1990, my next appointment with Oliver, I knew that the whole exercise had little to do with my return to flying. The week before, a registered letter from Patty had arrived, asserting that I had been unable to satisfactorily explain the customers' complaints and my verbal abuse of passengers. Furthermore, the letter went on, there were numerous reports received from operating crew members, and those—combined with my poor organizational skills and inappropriate interpersonal dealings with my peers—proved that I had demonstrated a total disregard for my job responsibilities. Despite that, according to her, I had admitted that personal problems were the reason for my behavior, a repeat performance of my disgusting demeanor would mean company discharge.

I checked with Norsk, and he confirmed that Patty was aware of his diagnosis of recurrent PTSD when writing her Fact Finding Interview report.

"If I get Patty to rewrite the letter, will you let it go without a grievance?" Cecile asked when I called her.

"Fine with me," I responded, believing without a doubt that she would carry out her promise.

When I contacted her again in mid-December, she said that Tobias was now handling my case. She had briefed him "on everything," she said and he was presently working on the appeal. "Don't worry, you'll hear from him," she assured me, and wished me a very happy holiday.

Hunting down Tobias proved to be a futile exercise; his wife and the union office were ever ready with a multitude of plausible excuses for his absence. On December 22nd, I gave up, trusting Cecile's continued assurances that "things were being done according to rules and regulations." Had I known that unions are legally obligated by labor laws to thoroughly investigate the nature of a grievance, discuss the merits of the grievance with the member and, if accepting the grievance, are legally responsible to process it according to the steps and time limits specified in the collective agreement, I would have been more concerned about Tobias' unavailability.[3] But all I knew was that he (an in-charge flight attendant) had handled employee-management conflicts for the past twenty-five years. Therefore, I was confident that he knew what steps had to be taken.

Meanwhile, at the end of November 1990, the Workers' Compensation Board adjudicator noted that the reopening of my case ought to be conducted very cautiously because it appeared utterly ridiculous that I, two years after a return to flying, claimed to be unable to work because of PTSD. The mystery enshrouding my illness so disturbed and puzzled him that he requested that my file be immediately assessed by the Board's medical advisor, and he arranged for a WCB mental health specialist to interview me. Until that had been accomplished, he said, not a dime would be paid to me.

Because an injured worker must prove the work-relatedness of the injury, the Board's objective now was to gather evidence that I had been psychologically defective *before* the 1988 incident, and that my present state of mind was directly related to those deficiencies. The Board deemed two important facts inconsequential to their position: first, psychiatric disturbances are unnecessary antecedents of post-trauma psychopathology,[4] and secondly, empirical data on flight attendants and pilots on the topic were absent. And as for me? Well, if I starved, lost home and hearth, and ended on skid row in the process, desolate and silenced, the WCB's objective would be achieved.

In my third interview with the stony Dr. Oliver, who made me feel like a mouse caged with a rattlesnake, I was not petrified enough to refrain from expressing my opinions about his drug-pushing therapy. I obstinately refused him permission to shuffle medications into my body—orally or otherwise—unaware about possible repercussions for my stance. Had I known that many privately practicing physicians and mental health professionals make handsome livings by examining workers for WCB or for employers with the sole purpose of discrediting the injured, I would have been better prepared for his evaluation report of my psyche.[5]

In it, Oliver pronounced that unsatisfactory dealings with men in my life was the underlying cause of my PTSD, and that I suffered from an anxiety-related PTSD combined with a personality with histrionic traits.

According to Webster's Dictionary, *histrionic* means having theatrical tendencies. After reading this I thought with some amusement that perhaps histrionics might be a valuable asset for flight attendants, allowing them to display appropriate expressions in the line of duty to a wildly differing populace under a large variety of circumstances. However, *histrionic personality traits* in the world of psychiatry means that an individual constantly seeks or demands reassurance, approval or praise; is inappropriately sexually seductive in appearance or behavior; is overly concerned with physical attractiveness; expresses emotions with inappropriate exaggeration, (e.g. embraces casual acquaintances with excessive ardor); uncontrollably sobs on minor sentimental occasions; exhibits temper tantrums; finds situations in which he or she is not the center of attention uncomfortable; displays rapidly shifting and shallow expressions and emotions; is self centered; requires immediate satisfaction; has no tolerance for the frustration of delayed gratification; and has a style of speech that is excessively impressionistic and lacking in detail.[6]

All of these were surely undesirable flight attendant attributes—I agreed—but how could these disastrous personality deficiencies go undetected throughout my career? This fact was inconsequential and Dr. Oliver's verdict opened a door for the Board to attack my psychological integrity.

How successful workers compensation boards and corporations are in disavowing workers is documented in a United States Department of Labor report issued in the early 80s. Of almost 2 million workers disabled by job-related diseases, only 5% receive WCB pensions. This fact is attributed to the difficulties involved in establishing the work-relatedness of disabling diseases, and the defensive litigation adopted by some insurers.[7] WCB's success rate is further enhanced by the fact that some compensation statutes still require that a work-related disability must be the result of an on-the-job "accident," meaning visible physical injuries where blood flows. Using this definition, they exclude non-visible injuries, or occupational diseases caused by toxins, hormones, asbestos, cotton dust, radiation, and oxygen deprivation—all of which are creeping and crippling diseases which have lengthy incubation periods.[8] Because of the difficulty in proving that such diseases are effectively caused by an unsafe work environment, 95% cent of employees injured on the job are forced to survive on social assistance. And those receiving WCB benefits are paid less than one-quarter of their total income loss.[9] Healthy taxpayers, through their payment of social insurance, pay for employer negligence.

The Board's impressive success rate of discrediting workers is partly attributable to WCB personnel's expertise in victim bashing. Their favorite game is played according to mutually understood rules. First, employers and the WCB alike operate from the basis that the employer is not responsible for the worker's safety. It is the worker's responsibility, because he or she knows the risks and has the freedom to choose whether to accept or refuse hazardous or potentially dangerous work. Furthermore, working people are thought of as being responsible for their occupational disease or death because of their carelessness on the job and their lack of concern over job safety and health issues.

Secondly, employers and the WCB argue that disease and death among employees is not really due to their work, but rather attributable to workers' lifestyle choices—choices such as smoking, drinking, poor diet, lack of exercise, marital arrangements or the absence thereof. Attributing illness to a worker's "lifestyle," regardless of social class and educational background, has become one of the "victimizing the victim" techniques applied by WCB and employers. The ultimate purpose for this tactic is to distract attention from the basic causes of the injury even though it is documented that the vast majority of workplace accidents are caused exclusively because of unsafe working conditions.[10]

The major strike against me, however, was not my "lifestyle" but that I am a woman. Therefore I am judged to be anxiety prone, hysterical, deviant, unpredictable, unreliable, and manipulative on one hand, and weak, receptive, passive, responsive, consolidating, and cooperative on the other. Those dealing with my case, except for Cavarro, the Board psychologist, were all males, the majority of whom viewed themselves as active, creative, level-headed, and aggressive in competition. They had a singular purpose in mind for this case—to win—especially when they regarded the opponent as an insubordinate female. My fight against their assumptions faced almost insurmountable odds. The fight, I knew, could prove deadly.

The prejudice in our patriarchal culture that views women as the lesser of the species had never rung true for me, and I had never been taught the role of subservience well enough to suffer from an inferiority complex in the presence of males. Generally, I disregarded their rules of perceived superiority, power and influence. Not eager now, as always, to project an image of a passive, receptive, cooperative, docile, weak, and unintelligent woman, I dismissed the idea that I posed a threat to the ego of those men intending to decide my destiny for me. Furthermore, at this point in time, I thought that they were all on my side—all working towards the goal of my return to flying.

Clueless about the witches brew in the making, I trooped up to the Board on January 14th, 1991, for an assessment interview with Dr. Plauski, another psychiatrist. He later described me as an alert and oriented woman with preserved memory and a wide-range of affect, who presented herself as an honest and straightforward person, not suspicious or defensive toward himself or the Board. He detected no pre-morbid characteristics. His diagnosis: PTSD related to the explosion of 1988 and five potentially disastrous incidents between 1989–90. Oliver's and Plauski's opposing perceptions of my psyche infuriated the adjudicator to such a degree that he ordered Cavarro to see me on February 20, 1991.

Ignorant about these behind-the-scene events, and knowing only that I would return to flying once this breather from duty had cured my apprehensions, I began two upper level Spanish literature courses while awaiting a consultation with an independent psychiatrist, at the end of February. The psychiatrist was an Irishman and a frequent NorAm flyer. He had been discovered and enlisted by flight attendants and had counseled many of them including Jennifer, my California friend. The fact that neither WCB nor my employer had offered financial assistance during the past months held little concern for me. My mortgage was a low $300 monthly payment, and my mother's generosity, as well as the rent generated by my basement suite, assured that wolves would not howl at my door.

Aircrew
and
Mid-Life Crisis

The Board accepted my claim on March 20th, 1991, and advised that my progress would be reviewed at the April 25th staff meeting. Dr. O'Doherty, the Irish psychiatrist, had given me hope that my emotional stability would return with peace and tranquillity and, therefore, I assumed that WCB would allow me time to achieve this objective. On April 12th, I awakened from this illusion. Ray, the WCB vocational rehabilitation consultant (VRC), demanded to see me for a vocational assessment.

"I don't think so. I've got a vocation," I quipped.

"Doesn't matter. Want to see you on the 18th, OK," he replied and hung up.

Quickly learning that once in the Board's clutches, it was jump and slide whenever they dictated, I showed up at the security guard loaded lobby where Ray greeted me with the question, "So, you witnessed an engine explosion?"

"No, I sat five feet away from it when it blew up mid-air," I answered, controlling an impulse to punch him when the vacant look in his eyes spelled, "What do I care?" Instead, I explained while we walked toward his office.

"There are several ways of losing an engine. One is when it literally falls off, as happened at Chicago's O'Hare Airport in the 80s because the mechanics forgot to bolt it on properly. Then there's feathering an engine. That's when an engine dies silently, just as when a car gives up the spirit without a sputter. And then there is an engine explosion, which is enormously noisy and poses a multitude of threats. Shrapnel can hit a fuel line and cause the aircraft to explode, or the pressurization system is destroyed. If that happens, the pilots initiate a nose-dive to get down to breathable air in a hurry.

"Now—*any* of those events are emotionally disturbing to flight attendants and to passengers if they participate in it, and not just witness the event from the ground. You understand the difference?"

He stared at me blankly. I refrained from asking him whether he would think of it as "witnessing an event," if he lay with a broken body and mind in the wreck of his car after an accident. After I had answered his numerous questions—with answers he knew already from the report issued by the Board's psychologist which lay in front of him—I told him of my intention to return to flying as soon as possible.

"You gotta job to return to?" he asked, surprised.

"Of course I have," I retorted, perplexed.

"You sure about that?"

"Of course I am."

"Fine, then," he said, getting up, "I'll call you after the team meeting to let you know what other plans have to be made."

Eager to escape, I failed to inquire what he meant about those "other plans." Unemployment Insurance information from NorAm awaited when I returned home. I phoned to inquire why NorAm had sent unemployment information when I was still employed, but payroll said that mailing them out was standard procedure. The following day, WCB ordered me to attend yet another interview with Cavarro, on April 22, 1991, after which she again declared me unfit for any employment because of PTSD and a non-pre-morbid depression considered a side effect of the ailment. She also noted my inability to tolerate mind-altering drug therapy because I had allergic reactions to Prozac. She did not mention, however, that I did depend on Ativan and liquor to control my anxiety arising from the feeling that the Board planned a sinister future for me while I could only stand by helplessly.

Substance abuse, a well known side effect of PTSD, I could cope with, since I did not indulge unless induced to do so by the Board's actions. But at this time, I did not realize that PTSD could lead to serious social and occupational disturbances such as depression, a sense of loss of control, overwhelming anxiety, psychomotor retardation, psychological decompensation, confusion, and paranoid reactions. Unaware, I was gradually slipping into an abyss of immense proportions.

Despite my excesses and nightmares, I passed the spring semester with flying colors, and registered for only one course for the summer, because I expected to be up and flying by then. Unversed in WCB–employer interactions, I silently thanked NorAm's management for their disinterest in me, believing that they had accepted my therapeutic treatment and did not wish to disturb my psyche or my healing. Completely misinterpreting their actions as extended goodwill, it never occurred to me that I had entered a system reminiscent of the Dark Ages.[1]

The Workers' Compensation system is so well-orchestrated to under-mine the injured that workers have little chance of success when fighting the Board. As United States Congressman Miller, Chairman of the House Labor Standards Subcommittee, so eloquently expressed in the early 80s,

> Workers' compensation keeps the workers from organizing. Each one's treated as an individual case so that each worker goes into a system that's inadequate and has his personal experience and by the time it's all resolved he's out, he's out of the union, he's inactive or he's out of a job, he's not seeing his friends anymore, and he's not going to organize. The belief of each worker is that in fact the system does work, until they engage in the system. It's like inadequate payments of welfare. They sort of keep the people quiet. That's all that's going on. People aren't getting compensated for their loss. [2]

The Board, with its amazing expertise in traumatizing the trauma-tized, now prepared to target me with their devious tactics. Blissfully oblivious to their intentions, I dreamt about my return to life in the skies. However, if the WCB had counted on O'Doherty to substan-tiate their pre-morbid ammunition against me, they were out of luck. Unfortunately, though, he did tell them that my PTSD symptoms could be even more incapacitating because I was in *the involutional period,* also called *mid-life crisis.*

I almost choked as he wrote that in my presence. The gap in his logic became instantly apparent to me, and I had argued, "Over 50% of flight attendants and pilots are presently in the involutionary period. Don't you think it's rather ludicrous to assume they're *all* susceptible to PTSD because of *that?*" But it was to no avail. He had been taught that menopause causes volatile psychological reactions in females, and was not about to change his mind because an incapacitated flight attendant told him otherwise.

Aircrew Pains of Mid-Life Crisis

Mid-life crisis in earthlings is assumed to be synonymous with a con-frontation of the psyche with the self that concerns the following issues: an evaluation of intimate relationships; a reappraisal of one's career and of one's self-concept with regard to lost youth; altered body image, and physical prowess; onset of physical illness, menopause or loss of sexual potency; one's perception of time–either feeling an urgency for time running away or a fear of limited time remaining; a reappraisal of the meaning of one's life and one's past; pressure to come to terms with unresolved trauma and losses before it is too late; and a preoccupation with existential concerns such as death anxiety.[3]

The lifestyle and general *joie de vivre* enjoyed by flight attendants and pilots leave little room to dwell on such a mundane topic as "time running away." How can it, since we live outside of earthly time frames most of our lives? And death anxiety? Most unlikely. Because, on a regular basis we are mandated to prepare for the possibility of disaster, death anxiety is not a dominating issue for professional flyers. Are intimate relationships an issue? Hardly, when we have numerous colleagues who are our friends. Career reappraisal? Why should we, having the best of them all? Lost youth and physical prowess? Most of us are in superb shape, and our appearance and grooming almost always exceeds that of the earthly population. And our physical prowess? It is impaired only by jet lag which, in flight attendants, is compounded by deficient air quantity and an overload of carbon dioxide in aircraft cabins. Is resolving conflicts of the past and present before it is too late an issue? Why would it be? We are leading, and have led, charmed lives with little residue of conflict, since we regularly engage sounding boards, namely our peers with whom we have shared our lives—often for decades—to help us resolve our personal problems. No, it surely was not *involution* that prolonged my PTSD symptoms.

On May 4th, 1991, Tobias, the union's local vice-president, remembered my existence and advised that, because I had agreed to not proceed with an appeal of the Fact Finding interview decision, no grievance had been submitted. He would now close my file. I hit the roof, and responded to his impertinence with an eight-page letter demanding that he file a grievance immediately. Drained to the point of collapse, but beaming with satisfaction, I mailed him the essay. He not only ignored it, but forwarded copies to the Board and NorAm. It did not dawn on me that I could now file a complaint with the Labor Relations Board because Tobias had acted arbitrarily by not filing a grievance on my behalf, handling my request superficially, capriciously, indifferently, and in reckless disregard of my interests. Kept expertly off balance and in constant turmoil, my cognitive capabilities were woefully impaired when it concerned anything to do with my predicament. As my energy further decreased, my anxiety level skyrocketed—and there was nothing unusual or unexpected about that.

Pierre Janet (1859–1947), the first researcher to systematically study dissociation as the crucial psychological process with which the human organism reacts to overwhelming experiences, noticed that many traumatized patients, after struggling to master their traumatic memories, become caught in a descending spiral of increasing emotionality, followed by the loss of will to act and the development of psychosomatic symptoms. Trauma-related impressions, which have bypassed consciousness, continue to plague the individual as internalized—but unrecognized—memories, which causes a further narrowing of consciousness and a consecutive decline in their capacity to deal with current reality. In turn, progressively more severe pathological symptoms are created. Eventually, only a pervasive desire to get away from it all remains. In the end, the capacity to adapt breaks down and these patients end up in a state of chronic helplessness expressed through both psychological and psychosomatic symptoms. I was being expertly forced into this same downward spiral.[4]

In June 1991 it became apparent that WCB had not the slightest inclination to assist me in returning to flying. Ray advised me by phone, "I've put you on active rehabilitation benefits, and now you must consider other types of employment with NorAm. Take tickets or something which doesn't involve flying. Some time in the future your claim will be considered plateaued, and that means you'll be cut off all benefits if you're not participating in a rehab program."

"Such as Toilet Attendant training," I thought, listening to his incantation, unable to get a word in edgewise.

"We should be planning for that time, since it may come sooner than you think," he added menacingly before pausing.

"But my psychiatrist wrote you that it'll be a while before I can return to flying," I argued.

"Oh, that doesn't mean anything. When do you think you can start in some job?"

"I'll return to flying when my psychiatrist thinks that I am ready."

"Very well. But I want to see you in the near future."

I threw the phone onto the cradle and flew into a rage, unable to cope with the implied threat of cutting off my benefits despite the fact that six reports from four different mental health professionals stated that at present I was too ill to engage in "any and every gainful employment," as WCB called it. The Board's adjudicator, meanwhile, ranted with equal vehemence about my stubbornness in not accepting alternative employment, and in insisting that I would return to flying without providing the Board with an accurate time frame as to when I would do so. The fact that there are no set recovery periods for earthly PTSD sufferers had escaped him, and so had the knowledge about aircrew motivation. [5]

He was also ignorant of the fact that aircrew's prior exposure to traumatic incidents might make them susceptible to the re-emergence of reactions to traumatic events, in particular, if such incidents had not been satisfactorily resolved. However, in most cases flight crew will master the trauma and return to flying.[6]

My unwillingness to even consider alternate employment, however, gave the adjudicator a new weapon to deploy—that of accusing me of malingering. The airline's claims officer happily participated in this demolition derby by demanding that the Board find out exactly what kept me from an immediate return to work. So the VRC hauled me into his office on July 29th, 1991, where I patiently explained once again that, at the present time, I could not fly due to PTSD, and that WCB's constant harassment interfered with my recuperation.

"You must be prepared to do alternate work outside the airport when you are declared medically fit to do so," he intoned, ignoring my comment.

"I'm afraid that's not possible," I said with saintly patience, "Union conflict, you know. Besides, I have no other job qualifications but flying— and that is what I'll return to in due time."

"What do you do with your time," he now wanted to know.

"Well, school keeps me busy, and I take care of my garden."

"Oh, you like gardening, do you?" I felt that already he was planning a new career for me as groundskeeper.

"No, not really. But I like things neat," I countered.

"And what else do you do?" he pressured, and I saw his ears prick up when I told him that I had sanded out and painted the trunk of my 66 Thunderbird. The thought "Would she qualify as a sheet metal worker or painter?" conspicuously crossed his mind. When mentioning visits with friends, I surely did myself a disservice, contravening the view that, if treated properly by the Board, injured workers have no social contacts. When he saw my face light up when he asked how my summer course was going, I revealed that studying "Literacy, Education and Culture" was giving me great joy. No sooner had the words escaped my lips that I knew that I was in for it. A woman capable of attending university and enjoying it was definitely capable of engaging in some type of work.

If I'd only known then of Pierre Janet, who used directive techniques to help traumatized patients overcome the legacy of helplessness and feelings of inability affecting their lives by involving them in meaningful activities of increasingly prolonged and complex tasks.[7] Of course, if I'd shared that knowledge of Janet's therapy with the VRC, he would have welcomed it as much as a school of piranhas in his bathwater.

And, sure enough, Ray told the adjudicator that I appeared to be in perfect health, but that he would share his precious observation with Cavarro before deciding whether or not I could immediately enter some form of employment or return to flight attendant work. Thereupon, Cavarro looked me over in August and again in September, and observed a worsening of my PTSD symptoms and my depression. With that news, the Board must have taken a sigh of relief. Things were going according to plan. The claimant was weakening. To speed up the process, a more intensive treatment intervention was now called for, and I was ordered to attend a mental health facility's eight-week outpatient program.

On October 8th, 1991, I, together with seven prospective clients, assembled in the reception area of the mental health facility for an introductory meeting. We were met by a woman dressed a in tight sweater, leotards, and three inch high heels, who reminded me of the ladies of the night. We obediently followed her, and entered a room with bars across the windows. There we were introduced to a psychiatric nurse, who requested that we give a brief history of our professional lives. I hastened to oblige.

"Why do you feel you should be allowed into the program," the icy-eyed nurse inquired after my synopsis.

"It has nothing to do with being allowed or not allowed," I responded, "It's WCB who demands my presence."

"But do you think it'll help you get back to work?" she pushed on.

"I've no idea, since I don't know what your program consists of. And even if I did, I would not know if it would help me." Just by looking at the surroundings, the staff, and my companions, I began doubting the venture, but nonetheless continued with a positive tone. "And besides, it's really inconsequential, since I don't have a choice. When can I begin?"

"That depends," she replied and I, eager to escape the nerve-wracking gathering, excused myself without inquiring about what it depended upon, and left to attend my university classes. After my psychiatrist informed them that the mental health facility treatment had to be postponed until January 1992 because of my emotionally fragile disposition, the Board demanded yet another assessment with Cavarro on December 18th, 1991. At that meeting the psychologist revealed several interesting perspectives. She pointed out that I was costing WCB and the airline a lot of money. She inquired whether my mother was wealthy, and if I would visit her in Europe over the holidays. Then she tossed in the tidbit that I could not be considered as totally disabled since I had recently painted my living room.

After being summarily released by her without so much as "Season's Greetings," I contacted the mental day care facility about my enrollment, only to be told, "Don't know yet. We don't have vacancies, and there's no waiting list. We'll call you a week before you can come in."

"That's nice," I grumbled, "keep people guessing and in suspense so everyone has ample opportunity to put their life on hold for the big event to happen," and slammed down the receiver. The news meant that I could not attend university in the spring.

On January 10, 1992, the facility administration advised me to report for treatment on January 13th at 9.00 A.M. On the appointed day, trotting calmly alongside a guy who had met me in the reception area without bothering to introduce himself, I shocked him out of his aloof silence by asking, "And who are you?"

"Oh...mmhh...I'm Roge."

"And *what* are you?"

"A psychiatric nurse. I'll be asking you some questions."

Settling into his disorderly office scattered with second-hand furnishings and dirty coffee cups, he began the inquisition with a multitude of ambiguously-phrased inquiries about my personal and medical history.

I responded to almost everyone of them with "Would you be more specific?" or "Could you reformulate your question?" or "What do you mean by that? What do you want to know exactly?" My love life held extraordinary interest for him.

"Have you known a person for five years?"

"Of course. I've known many people for five years," I replied.

"Well, I mean, have you known any man for five years?"

"Of course. I've known many men for five years."

Slightly exasperated he tried again. "Well, have you lived with someone for five years?"

"Yes, I was once married for nine years, and for the past thirteen I've had a relationship with a trucker."

"Well, have you lived with him for five years?"

"That's hard to say, since he's out of town a lot."

"You planning to marry?"

Pointedly staring at the ring on his left hand, I quipped, "Apparently you're married. I don't know if it's your first, second, or fifth time. I've been married twice and had one common law. You might be able to understand that I'm not in a rush to repeat the performance."

Relentlessly pursuing enlightenment about my erotic endeavors and aspirations he tried once more to get to the bottom of the conundrum. "Well, are you common law, then?"

"If that's what you want to call it," I fired back.

Perhaps it was my obvious disgust with his silly persistence that encouraged him to change the subject. "How do you feel about PTSD?"

"That's hard to explain to someone who hasn't lived it. Have you?"

"No, but how do you feel about it?"

"The futility of life seemed overwhelming," I reported.

"Well, were you depressed afterwards?" he continued. I wasn't sure if he appeared more bored with me or with my ailment.

"Listen, it took me some four months to decide whether I wanted to live or die. And, as you might know, we don't have to lay hands on ourselves to achieve that objective," I answered slightly irritated, momentarily forgetting the importance of staying calm, cool, and collected.

"Well, what do you mean?" he asked.

"If we decide to die we surely will by the power of our mind."

"Oh, so you decided to live?"

"Obviously."

"Well, what symptoms did you have?"

"What do you mean?"

"Well, what kind of symptoms? In your profession you should know what symptoms relate to PTSD."

"No, I don't," I answered truthfully.

"Were you angry about the accident?"

"No. It was the revelation of my life. Pure enlightenment."

"What do you mean?"

"You might have heard that people who've had a life-threatening experience must make peace with their pre-accident existence in order to live fulfilling lives afterwards. This means soul-searching at the deepest level. And when peace is made with the previous life, building of the new one can begin."

Now he had definitely heard enough, for he swiftly moved to my level of education, anxious to know when I would graduate.

"That depends."

"Well, you're in your fourth year now. How much longer do you think it'll take?"

"That depends on flying."

"Well, how was your last semester?"

"Stressful."

"Why?"

"Because of my hassles with WCB, and because I took something I didn't like."

"But how did you do?"

"Very well, thank you."

After he scrutinized my finances and living accommodations, and after I had established that survival on WCB's handout was indeed possible, he asked, "Which airline did you use to work for?"

"I'm *still* working for that airline."

"Well, with whom did you use to work?"

Hitting him became exceedingly tempting with each newly-uttered "Well,..." and his rigid use of the past tense.

"As you know, I am a flight attendant with NorAm—and to that I shall return. I am here solely on WCB's request because I am ill with PTSD due to the engine explosion," I challenged, getting testy.

"But why aren't you flying *now*?" he inquired.

Exasperated, I responded, "Because I am booked off with PTSD, and therefore have little tolerance for people at the moment."

"And when that happens you feel frustrated and angry...and then you think...."

"No, I don't—what about yourself?" I spat, incensed by his impertinence in telling me what I thought.

"Well, How do you feel?"

"I love people. I just can't handle them right now."

Apparently tired of sparring, he sent me off to see the secretary. Greeted with the same inquisitive look Roge had given me when first setting eyes upon me—as if I were from another species declared mentally deranged unless able to prove otherwise—she asked that I give permission for blood tests and examinations.[8] I declined. The head nurse would have to be informed about my indolence, she threatened. I still declined. She gave up. Handing me a questionnaire, she directed me to the "Project Room," where an occupational therapist began her inquisition aimed at establishing a career-oriented project for me to fiddle around with while at the center. "What was your last employment?"

"I'm a flight attendant—still employed."

"What do you want to be?"

"A flight attendant."

"Yeah, but if you can't do that?"

"A writer or editor."

"What would you change about your body if you could?"

"Nothing."

Her questions flooded over me: "What do you like best about where you live?" "What does an employer look for in an employee? How much do you drink and where? How do you handle your household chores? Do you cook nutritious food for yourself? What sports activities did you participate in? What creative things could you do?" Question upon question came phrased as if I were a vegetable—my answers received a skeptical notation, as if spoken by a pathological liar.

The exercise completed, I announced, "I'd like to learn how to make picture frames."

"I'll tell you what to do when we've analyzed the survey," she answered curtly.

"But that's all I want to do," I insisted, having noticed inmates fiddling with kindergarten needlepoint, scarf knitting, and clay duck creations. I had knitted socks with heels at the age of seven, and am an expert in petit point needlework. Designing and baking clay duckies somehow left me uninspired.

"No," the therapist barked. "We'll discuss it when we've gone over the survey. It has to be career-oriented," and she released me. Fifteen minutes remained to lunch time. I wandered off to the cafeteria, where I asked the Chinese cook, "Tell me, please. Do you use monosodium glutamate (MSG) in your cooking?"

"Of course we do," he cheerfully piped up. "Don't everybody?"

"Nutritious sustenance," I thought to myself and decided not to indulge in the hot cuisine during my incarceration. Green salad and a banana would do just fine, thank you. Observing the dining habits of my fellow inmates encouraged me to rapidly depart to a distant garden swing. There I sat, gathering my thoughts until joining the "Total Group Meeting," where I was formally introduced to fourteen inmates and staff of five, and assigned to "Billy"—my "buddy" for three days who would assist in my familiarization with the institution.

After that, it was time for a confession of sins and uttering of pet peeves, to be forgiven or punished by the wardens. Scathing criticisms for tardiness and rudeness towards each other and staff successfully completed, left some souls in tears. Orders to stay away from the swing were handed down to me. They rationalized this restriction by telling me I needed to acquire interpersonal communication skills through constant socialization with my peers.

We were then divided into three groups. With five inmates and two psychiatric nurses (one of each gender) in my group, we moved to a different locale after a brief coffee break. We were to begin "commitments" which, as the only newcomer, I was told specifically would build up my confidence and self-esteem, teach me assertiveness, and help me acquire discipline, freedom from procrastination, and the ability to structure my life for a week in advance. "You got that?" one of the nurses asked me. I nodded obediently. Then it was time to find a topic to commit to and to present in the total group meeting on Wednesday. On Friday we would be graded on our topics by ourselves and our fellow patients.

My commitment idea—to research PTSD at the university—was vetoed as too difficult. Someone suggested that instead, I should socialize with two of my comrades-in-arms to build up my confidence. Unable to contain myself, I retorted, "But I *am* confident."

"Well," the kid persisted, practically cringing, "It's just so you don't feel the stress of the program."

"I don't feel any stress here," I replied truthfully, since astonishment and curiosity about the place numbed my senses. My buddy Billy got the brainstorm that it would be an ideal exercise for me to remember the names of patients and staff.

"No, that's too much. Five are sufficient," the nurses intervened.

"Well, you want to do that then?," Billy asked.

"Yes, sure. I obey your wishes," I mockingly replied.

An hour later, we were encouraged to partake in yet another lovely cup of strong coffee before herding together with everyone else to discuss how to while away the remainder of the afternoon. Our exquisite choices ranged from work on occupational therapy projects or homework assignments, and socialization in the game room which contained snooker and table tennis equipment, a shuffle board and a dart board. Desiring to start my picture frame production, I was told coldly of the impossibility of doing that, and left standing to contemplate how to occupy myself. When rebuffed by an inmate for wanting to show her how to divinely start a needlepoint—"I'm not making a career out of this, you know!"—I went in search for better ways to kill time.

Seeing two guys at the table tennis desperately trying to make the ball jump, I suggested a different hold on the racket might do the trick. This earned me a gruff, "No, no, we'll manage." This inspired me to question whether the inmates of this weird place were so insecure as to view acceptance of assistance as synonymous with admission of failure. However, the rejections were gifts from the heavens, since with them came the awareness that silence was a virtue while involuntarily imprisoned here.

Rushing out of the building at 4 P.M., greatly disturbed, I struggled to comprehend how anyone could possibly thrive or survive in that environment which vibrated with power struggles, manipulation, harshness, lack of love and empathy, and where those leading the blind resembled surrealistic creatures wearing masks of superiority and behaved like emotionless robots. I drove home mentally exhausted and at a loss.

The Nuthouse

The next seventy-two hours were pure hell. During the day, when I entered the mental health facility, a feeling of suffocation engulfed me, and during the nights, I suffered through agonizing dreams. When Annemarie called on Thursday (she had been out of town since Monday), I told her, "I'm getting ill. I took three Ativans when I got in, and nitroglycerin for my chest pain. And I think I'm getting an ulcer—my stomach burns." I started to cry.

"Get out of there as fast as you can," she urged.

"But WCB's gonna cut me off."

"Doesn't matter. Your life's worth more than money. That'll all fall into place. Just get out of there!"

"But I can't. O'Doherty is in the States and doesn't come back before Sunday."

"Leave a message on his machine that you've quit the program. Just in case they (the Mental Health facility staff) get a hold on him before you do. And don't bother going back!"

"I've got to. I've some clothes in a locker."

"OK, then. But remember, they can't take your power away. And don't breathe a word about leaving. They'll destroy you if you do. You all right now?" I was.

I hoped that O'Doherty would understand—and agree—that I did not need to be taught the value of conversation, how to pursue meaningful exchanges of thoughts and viewpoints at bus stops, supermarkets, night schools, and night clubs, or in theater lines, political rallies, banks, PTA meetings, churches, and libraries. I hoped that he could see that any suggestions to encourage conversational exchanges at those places with "Hello, my name is...," or to request help by saying, "I can't find this law case. Can you help me, please?" had thrown me into revulsion. Other miraculous ways we were being taught to engage in meaningful communication with strangers were self-disclosure and exposure statements such as, "Hi there. I've got something to share with you," or "I'm not sure what I'm doing here. I'm really quite shy," or "I just got divorced and feel a bit shaky." Those kinds of statements, we were told, would endear the message receiver to self for evermore. Almost propelled into hysterical laughter with their suggested openers, I caught myself in time. Staff were crowding in on me; I had to be careful.

As a remedy for shyness, they recommended eye contact, and to overcome our inhibitions, they ordered us to greet every passing stranger we met while beating the streets with a joy-filled smile and a cheery, "Hello. Nice day," which, they assured us, would earn us an equally cheerful response. Pleasantly exiting from a conversation was the skill they viewed to be of utmost importance. The speaker must convey three messages when doing so—"I'll be leaving soon; I enjoyed the conversation; I hope that we can continue the conversation in the future." To achieve this objective, they instructed us to break eye contact, move our feet in the direction that we wanted to go, and use non-verbal behavior to indicate that we were shipping out—or onto the bus. Hysteria once again overwhelmed me, but self-control won out.

Drug treatment ruled equally high on the facility's agenda. "You've all been in psychotherapy. Otherwise you wouldn't be here. And because you're here, you're sick, no matter how you behave. And because you're severely ill you must take your medication. The more of it you take, the better you'll feel. The benefits by far outweigh the side effects. And mind-altering drugs are not addictive," the staff ground into us. I wanted to protest, but kept quiet.

Next came sessions on family relationships. Staff—positive that we all emerged from dysfunctional family backgrounds—explained the essence of trust to us. "It means that a family member or another person, whoever it is, doesn't willfully abuse your feelings. Nor you theirs," the lecturer droned on, adding that humans have a well-developed denial system by age nine at which we, the inmates, according to the lecturer, operated at present. They then asked us to complete a diagram depicting our original and present family, and to define the role of each individual member, including ourselves—as persecutor, victim or rescuer—and to answer questions such as, "What important reason does my partner have for being the way he is?" "What part do I play in his problem?" and "If you find out that I am not perfect, will you abandon me?"

Not intrigued by what I heard, I escaped the plagiarized and patronizing psycho-babble by blissfully receding into my own world and reminiscing on my interview with the resident psychiatrist the previous day. After having heard my story, and after having posed the same questions already heard *ad nauseam* from all other mental health professionals, the kind soul had said, "I really don't think this program is right for you. We aim to teach assertiveness, self-esteem, and social skills. You *have* all that. What you need is time. Only time will heal. It always does. But try it out, and we'll see in fourteen days." I had awakened from my reverie by the call for games designed to hone our concentration abilities.

The staff demonstrated the first game: slapping thighs, clapping hands, snapping fingers, calling out someone's name, who then picked up the beat—and so it continued for an eternity until all had taken their turn. Eventually the word "picnic" was introduced. One person chanted "I went to a picnic and took along something," beginning with the first letter of the individual's first name, before calling out another person's name—who then continued the spiel. And around it went until everyone, with staff vigorously participating, had taken a turn.

For the next game, we were ordered to form lines of an equal number of participants on each side of the ping-pong table. The first person at the front of the line had to send the ball over the net and, before the one on the other side could return it, put down the racket and run to the end of the line. The second individual picked up the paddle and played one shot. And so it went on. Those who failed to bounce the ball over the net were out. I had speedily removed myself from the contest and moved to the sidelines. Immediately a watch dog approached me.

"You disappointed?"

"No," I said, and turned away.

The staff won the competition, and congratulated each other, oozing with pride. I observed the obsequious interaction, doubting the sanity of it all.

When ordered to play a game based on the premise of completing the phrase, "If I were you–then I would do..." I declined participation on the grounds that I really didn't know what I would do when walking in someone else's moccasins. This drew weird looks from staff. Next, "feeling sheets" were handed out to assist us in explaining our emotions throughout the games. Had we felt "caring, exited, comforted, happy, confident, angry, defensive, degraded, fearful, guilty, hopeless, rejected, sad or sorrowful?" Or did we have emotions such as "apathy, anxiety, confusion, ridicule, or surprise?" Each of the definitions were detailed with ten approximations to our possible sentiments. Upon turning the sheets in (I had marked mine with an X), we were allowed to depart for lunch.

The Greasy Spoon served the daily diet of yesterday's peas, broccoli, gravy, some animal parts, and sponge cake. Staff honored us with their presence at the table. The fear of the all-powerful hawks, looking for their pigeon prey permeated the mental health facility and now spread to the lunch pavilion. It had reached my ears and eyes that some of the inmates acted as informers which, I knew, was a common occurrence in settings like these.[1]

Twice reprimanded for wandering off on the grounds during lunch time, I stuck around those puffing away outside and, on the third day, asked two women standing with me, "Do you meditate?"

"No," they answered.

"You might want to try it one day. I've meditated since 1985, and I think it saved my life. It's marvelous for emotional balance," I continued as if it were the most natural topic in the world to discuss.

My companions reacted with agitation and aggression, "Yeah, it shows in you—you a journalist or something? You writing on this place?"

Briefly I told them my story, but they did not believe me. As far as they were concerned, I did not belong there. Then Roge approached me, as he did daily, to demand that I sign the form which would permit the institution to take non-specified tests. "It doesn't mean anything," he coaxed, "It's just like signing a consent form at the hospital. And you can change it any time."

"My arse," I mumbled, and declined. Left to my own devices during the occupational therapy sessions, picture frame production activity having been denied me, I wandered around, lost in a strange world whose rules and ways I could not adopt. The staff had asked me to complete a stress survey—which I noticed came from an unknown source and dated back to 1980. On my last day at the institution, after an assertiveness and stress management session, my ridiculously low score inspired staff to deeper inquisition.

"You don't have any debts? You've not divorced lately? You've not moved within the last year? You've not had a death in the family?" they asked incredulously.

"No, I've only had numerous near misses while flying, and that's not asked anywhere in your survey," I said, stoically refusing to be intimidated or manipulated into admitting any untruths. They backed off. Displaying my memory skills by remembering ten of the names assigned to me on Wednesday earned me just short of a standing ovation later that afternoon.

"How did you like your performance?" staff asked.

"I liked it. Therefore it's perfect," I answered. That shut them up.

At 4 P.M. I sped out of the facility, knowing that, even if my psychiatrist would not agree that I did not need to learn how to express my opinions; or be taught to read movie and book reviews; or to familiarize myself with cultural, political, and social topics so as to turn into an interesting person; or to come up with five exciting episodes that had recently occurred in my life and turn them into brief stories by practicing in front of a mirror and with a tape recorder; or to jot down jokes if I felt comfortable telling them (but only if I had no trouble remembering the punch line); or to not make assumptions about people's motives and inner states without checking with them by asking, "It seems to me that you are really hurt because you were not invited to the party," I would adamantly refuse to set foot into that place again.

It was Friday, January 17, 1992. That evening, in the company of friends watching the movie *One Flew Over the Cuckoo's Nest,* I could barely contain myself from pointing out every second minute, "That's it. That's *it.* That's exactly it."

When O'Doherty called Sunday night and agreed to the termination of the program, I began to cry. The next morning when I informed Cavarro, the WCB psychologist, about the decision, she asked, "But why? Did the center give you the same feeling as NorAm?"

"No, not at all. They're like fire and water."

An hour later the Board invited me to a psychological assessment interview scheduled for February 13th, 1992. It would be the eighth such assessment in fifteen months.

The evening news reported that an Airbus 320 had crashed near Lyon, France, killing eighty-four of the ninety-six people aboard. A couple of days later, O'Doherty greeted me with a, "Isn't it gruesome what people do to each other in such places?" and he accepted my decision to take flight from the nuthouse over fight for my emotional survival within it, without even so much as asking what had motivated me to terminate the program. He seemed to know why.

The Union and I

On the morning of February 13th, 1992, I was so eager to get the assessment interview over with that I arrived early at the Board's compound. While sipping a cup of coffee on a bench outside, a stranger joined me. "An evil place this is," he said, and began to tell me his sordid story. When he mentioned the Workers' Assistance office, a government agency aiding injured workers in their fights against the Board, I took note, scribbling down the phone number. I wished him good luck, and ventured inside, where Cavarro introduced me to Dr. Zagreb, the director of psychology, who would conduct the interview.

The usual questions about me, my mother's finances, my social life, and my love life were posed before Cavarro asked, "And what do you think of the mental health facility?"

"That's hard to say. The best thing for you would be to enroll there as pseudo patients for a week or so. That would give you an idea."

They stared at me, looked at each other, and Zagreb then said, "Mmmh, that's interesting. But tell us something else. What kind of work would you like to do in the future?"

"Why—flight attendant, of course," I chirped.

"But that's impossible. We don't want you to fly again."

"That's your problem," I felt like spitting back, but instead inquired, "And why not, may I ask?"

"You're too high a risk factor."

"And why's that?"

"Well, people's lives could be lost if you're not functioning properly."

"I don't think so. I think I'll be able to function much better than those who've not lived through a life-threatening experience. It takes away the fear of death, you know."

"Well, that could be. But if you had to choose another vocation what would it be?" he insisted.

"Psychologist," I answered.

"But why?" they chorused, aghast.

"Because I have a fabulous idea for a Ph.D. thesis."

"Yeah? What?"

"I would like to do a follow-up study on those people completing the program I've just skipped out of to see how they're coping."

Thundering silence followed, and my vocational aspirations were discussed no further. Shortly thereafter, they released me. The interview had lasted two hours—during which both had feverishly taken notes.

Then the Board enshrouded itself in eerie silence, because Zagreb's attempts to unveil a previous personality disturbance in me must have been timeconsuming. By the beginning of June—four months after the interview—he had been unsuccessful in detecting anything pre-morbid other than my withdrawn lifestyle. Of course, he missed or ignored the fact that before the accident, roughly a thousand people trucked through my life at weekly intervals, and that I had regularly attended university since the spring of 1985. Instead, he decided that I was perfectly capable of immediately engaging in any job on earth. If I refused, the disability department would figure out whether or not I had pensionable status, and if so, he decreed, a 5% permanent functional impairment pension (PFI) would be adequate. Permanent functional impairment awards are made when a worker is left with a permanent residual disability after an industrial injury—and no further improvement is anticipated. In my case, however, the exact percentage would be accurately defined after the psychology department had contrasted my pre-morbid condition with my condition after the accident.

On July 27th, 1992, a team meeting was called, attended by a multitude of adjudicators, psychologists, and rehab consultants. In this meeting, Ray (the VRC) declared that I would never be able to return to work as a flight attendant or work at an airport because of my "agoraphobic state," The psychologists agreed, failing to mention that agoraphobia can be a direct result of PTSD.[1]

Unanimously assessing that I had plateaued, they laid plans to put me through the wringer until I was emotionally and physically too exhausted to continue to fight and would silently join the ranks of welfare recipients. That would be the most cost-efficient for both WCB and NorAm. On August 4th, I was informed that my wage-loss benefits had been cutoff, and that I was to meet with a rehab consultant on the 6th. After that, all hell broke loose.

The ax fell the minute I entered Ray's cubicle. "As you know, we've decided that you've plateaued, and therefore we've cut off your wage-loss benefits. Before I can put you on rehab assistance, your return to work must be addressed. If you still feel as completely disabled as your doctors say you are, you'll get no money. You still taking courses at university?"

"Yeah. Just finished two, and am thinking about taking Psychology to do a Ph.D. later. If you'll sponsor me." I was determined that they would not turn me into a baker, as they had done with another flight attendant who had sustained serious back injuries because of a midair turbulence incident.

While awaiting Ray's response, the phone rang. NorAm's WCB claims officer was on the line offering me a job as either a clerk in an airport hangar, or performing flight attendant duties on board aircraft, but leaving the plane before it took flight. "But you absolutely must be cleared by their medical department if you take the onground flight attendant position," Ray specified after hanging up.

"How charming," I thought. "My physicians declare me unfit for any employment. The Board cuts me off regardless whether I work or not— and what happens if the company doctor vetoes my return to inflight?" I kept the thought to myself and quipped, "I'm *not* a clerk. I'm a flight attendant. And to that I'll return in due time." Ordered to make a decision right there and then I, biding for time, agreed to try out the onground flight attendant position.

"Fine. NorAm will contact you and arrange for the medical and a gradual return-to-work program," he said smiling broadly, and let me go.

Heading straight for the union's office, I found that the local's WCB committee chairman, Teddie Wong, an in-charge flight attendant with another airline, happened to be in. After explaining my predicament to him, and finding his ignorance about PTSD bothersome, he pompously announced, "I will appeal the Board's cut-off if your case has sufficient merit. In the meantime, you'll be on wage indemnity. I'll call you when I've made up my mind."

I zipped over to the Workers' Assistance office, where a lawyer confidently informed me, "But there's nothing to appeal. You've rights to rehab benefits. I'll get right on it." The following week the benefits were reinstated, but the lawyer advised that, if I insisted on returning to flying, they would be in jeopardy. She also conveyed to me that NorAm was willing to permit WCB to "buy" a position for me as a ticket agent at a downtown office, and that I should go for that.

Disenchanted with her career plans for me, I faxed her letter to Wong on August 9th, 1992, and turned my attentions to my mother, who was in town for three weeks. On August 31st, Wong denied receiving of the fax, so I delivered it to him personally. After perusing it briefly, he chirped, "Can not trust the lawyer. She's dangerous. She writes like an adjudicator. I don't think she's good for you. But don't worry. Here, sign the release form for your WCB file, and I'll help you in the future—and make an appointment with the company doctor as soon as possible."

I did, and on September 9th trucked to the airport and met with Dr. Norsk, who inquired about my finances, my living accommodation, my love life, and my interpersonal relationships, before cruising on to the topic of my return to inflight.

"I know that I'll be able to fly if I can just get some peace. But what happens if you decide that I cannot go back now?"

"Oh, then you can take a leave of absence without pay for one to three years, and after that we'll re-evaluate. Right now, you're too ill to fly— or to do anything else. Let's get together again in a couple of months."

"Would you give me that in writing, please?"

"No, I'm not putting anything down unless I've got your psychiatrist's position. To get that, you must sign this form."

I declined and instead proposed, "Can't you just call him?"

Terminating the interview, he said, "Well, I'll see."

And he must have, because Dr. O'Doherty informed NorAm on September 12th, 1992 that I suffered from chronic PTSD and was presently unable to perform any gainful employment. Norsk, in turn, wrote to the union that I was incapable of engaging in any work for the next two to three months. But when the VRC asked me over the phone on September 25th how my case was doing, I didn't know more than he did. When I tried to contact Wong about my case, I learned that he would not return from vacation until the end of October at the earliest, and that he'd left strict orders—with my file under lock and key—that no one was to get involved with me or my case.

Four days later, NorAm requested for the third time in ten days that I show up to have an I.D. picture taken, and for the third time I declined, too ill to drive downtown. "It's your last chance. If you can't do it now you'll have to go to Montréal," the caller threatened.

"So be it," I answered, close to hysterics. The next day, Norsk rang and demanded that I arrange a meeting with their rehabilitation consultant within a week. My union officers were unavailable for comment.

On October 1st, an odd message appeared on my answering machine: "I've heard you're looking for a career change if the money is right. I've something which'll suit you. Please call 525-8841." But when Annemarie contacted the number, a male voice refused to disclose the nature of his business to a caller unwilling to give her name. Later that afternoon, Ray from the WCB left a cryptic message on the machine: "Do you understand your situation?" When I tried to reach him, I was told that he had left on vacation.

The constant aggravation and my consequent feelings of uncertainty about which way to turn left me bewildered and distraught. But nitroglycerin relieved my chest pain, and I dropped one of my two university courses to better cope with the strain of the personal onslaught.

On October 2nd, my union brother Harry called to inform me that he had been unable to reach management to discuss a clause in our contract stipulating that cabin crew suffering from PTSD after an aircraft incident must be kept on the payroll. "Thanks, Harry. I didn't know such a clause existed. But can you find out how others have been paid?" I asked.

"Yeah, I've requested info from Toronto. I'll look into it again."

"And what about WCB? Wong's out of town."

"That's Tobias's area, then."

"And what am I to do about NorAm's rehab consultant?"

"Oh, don't worry about that. I'll talk to them and call you Monday," he promised.

I left numerous messages for Tobias, but when I finally reached his wife, she said that he was busy. And when catching Harry on October 7th, he could only say, "Sorry. Still haven't got a hold of the base manager.

You should never've been taken off the payroll 'cause of the characteristics of your case. I'll work on it when I get back from Hawaii."

"And when might that be?" I inquired.

"Oh, I'll be gone until about the 18th—at least."

Then out of the blue, Helen, a flight attendant well-versed in union affairs whom I had not seen in years, called. Briefing her on my situation she started laughing. "For heaven's sake! Don't fiddle around with those guys any longer. They won't do anything for you. Write a letter to Nolton, (the union's national president)." So I did. And when Helen scrutinized the letter, she was certain that he would have to appoint a lawyer to fight WCB on my behalf. But brother Nolton ignored my scribbles.

So, I contacted the union on October 9th and spoke with brother Maynor, the local national representative. "Never heard of you," he said, "But give me a brief history of your case, if you want to."

"There's no brief history."

"Tell me anyhow," he growled, then gruffly remarked when I finished, "You're obviously a very distraught woman. I'll take a look at your file and call you back."

"When?" I asked.

"As soon as I've looked at your file," he spat.

When I had heard nothing from him for four days, I rang to demand a meeting. "He's in Calgary, but will be back tomorrow. I'll make a tentative appointment for 11 A.M. and confirm it as soon as I've talked to him," his secretary offered. She rang back minutes later. "He would prefer you call him at 11 A.M. before coming to the office."

I did phone, and received the news that he was unavailable. "Wonderful! He couldn't call me before leaving, could he?"

"Well, you know how men are," his secretary answered limply.

I ignored her attempts to placate, and bellowed, "Is he in the building?"

"Ummh...ah...oh yeah, he's in the office," she said.

I slammed down the receiver, swallowed three Ativans, jumped into the car, and burst into Maynor's office forty-five minutes later to see a fat slob doodling on a blank piece of paper, his feet parked on his desk.

"I am Tanya Andersen. Why didn't you have the courtesy to call me before attending your 11 o'clock meeting when it was you who asked me to call you at that time in the first place?" I was livid.

"I never asked you to call me. Why're you here, anyway? To vent your spleen or get assistance? I've other things to do, you know."

"You know I need help," I answered.

"Nothing can be done until Wong returns," he exclaimed, feet still on the desk.

"You know anything about PTSD and the anxiety it causes?"

"I tell you," he casually tossed back at me, "*lots* of people have stress."

"You don't understand, do you?"

He went into a lengthy tirade about his wife's wheelchair confinement. Once he finished, I charged, "Do you know anything about WCB's rehab procedures?"

"Oh, once you've been through that mill, you'll be dropped like a hot potato."

"Oh, yeah? Watch me. I assure you that's not going to happen to me!" He continued to doodle in silence, as if I were invisible. "What do you think? Should I go public with my case? My member of Parliament says there's ample evidence of mistreatment to make interesting news," I tried again.

The doodling stopped as his feet hit the floor. He shouted, "You can do what the hell you want to. But I warn you. Once you're out of the system it'll be very, very hard to get you back in."

"Should I hire a lawyer, then?"

"Well. One could be appointed to represent you...under certain circumstances."

"What kind of circumstances?" I challenged.

"Oh, I'd have to inquire about that."

"Well, Mr. Maynor. Would you please do that. And have you called the number I ask your secretary to give you?"

"Which number?"

"The one that accompanied the message about my desire for a career change—if the money was right?" I pushed the number across the desk to him.

"Oh, yeah. I can do that right now," he said, as he picked up the phone, and dialed. After a brief, monosyllabic conversation he hung up saying, "That's nothing. Somebody's just farmed something out." Seconds later, the receptionist entered and advised him of a long-distance call. Hand still on the phone, he looked across the desk at me. "I'll try to arrange a meeting between Wong, Harry, Tobias, me and yourself so we can discuss your situation. But I warn you, it's gonna be difficult. We all have very heavy schedules, you know," and, with his feet again propped up on the desk, dismissed me as if I were a dog. Upset, confused, and shaking, I drove home.

On Friday the 16th, VRC Ray left a message on my answering machine that the airline had no work for me, and to call him on Monday. Maynor was in a meeting, but would be in touch on Monday; Harry and Tobias were nowhere to be found. I fired off another letter to Nolton, who had yet to respond to the first one. When Ray returned my calls three days later, he confirmed that NorAm had no position for me, inquired about my health, and informed me, "I now can't pay you any longer."

"Well, since my physical and emotional deterioration is directly related to PTSD caused inflight, there has to be another avenue for compensation," I fired back.

"If you think so, we should perhaps meet," he suggested.

"Fine—when?"

"October 29th, at 1:00 P.M."

"O.K. See you *then*," I snarled and hung up.

Harry rang during the evening. A tentative meeting with him, Wong, Maynor, and Tobias, had been set up for October 26th, 1992. While I awaited the day, occasionally distracted by school, I took nitroglycerine and Ativan on a regular basis. Suffering from constant tension headaches, I had no appetite, found myself too anxiety-ridden to sleep for more than a few hours each night, and felt close to a nervous breakdown.

When Annemarie and I stepped into the union office on the 26th, only Maynor and Harry were present. After they had perused my factual report of the 1988 accident, and the list of near-misses I had experienced during my career, Maynor piped up with the comment, "It breaks my heart that someone who's been going through so much should go through this. It's a very complex case, but worthwhile fighting for. To make it easier for you, Harry here and Wong—he's back tomorrow—will come with you to the WCB rehab meeting. If you can change it to the 28th."

"I'll try and let you know." My union brothers kept my WCB disclosure file, which I had picked up at the Board earlier that morning, so as to familiarize themselves with my claim. As soon as I came home I called Ray, but he could not change the meeting date. Later that afternoon, however, Maynor advised me that it would take place on the 28th, and my union brothers would meet me outside the WCB building. Because of the date change, I knew I had to go alone; Annemarie would be flying.

That day Harry, Wong, and I were introduced by Ray to a Miss Katts, who would be taking over my case. After they reviewed my history, Wong asked me, "What do you want to do workwise?"

"Return to flying, of course. When my health has improved."

"But you must retrain to stay on rehab benefits," he argued.

"No, I must not. Once I get some peace, I'll return to flying."

"But you *can not* return to flying, and NorAm does not have a job for you. And if you *do not* look at other options your benefits will be cut off," Wong squeaked again.

"We want you to look for work as a Spanish translator," Ray suddenly kicked in.

"As a Spanish translator? But why? I'm not qualified," I responded.

"Sure you are, once you've got your degree..." he insisted.

Wong chimed in "You must face this change."

Katts and Harry followed the action without expression.

"No, I mustn't," I exclaimed. I've done nothing to cause my situation."

"Well, that's the same with a guy who gets his arm blown of. He hasn't done anything to cause it, either," Ray carped.

"Now, you just stop a minute. We're not talking physical disability here. We are talking about PTSD caused by a midair engine explosion, and constantly exacerbated by your so-called *treatment*. I've not been allowed a moment of peace since this whole thing started—thanks to you guys. But as long as I'm not better, I can't be expected to deal with the public or do anything else."

"But you must at least job search," Ray said, failing to keep the exasperation out of his voice.

"But how?" I countered.

"Well," he began, "you could call five companies and embassies a week and ask if they need any Spanish translators. And then you report your contacts to me or Miss Katts biweekly. And you should finish your B.A. and get your ESL (English as a Second Language) teaching certificate in the meantime. And when you do a job search, you can ask at different schools if they'll hire you when you get your degree." He then inquired, "How many courses do you have left?"

"Two—after this semester," I answered.

"It doesn't matter." Wong jumped in aggressively, "If you are not compliant, you will be cut off."

"But I'm far too ill to job search. My doctors will attest to that," I protested.

Harry asked for a recess; the VRCs left the room.

"Now you know, if you do not comply—you are *cut off*," Wong chastised me once more. Harry excused himself and went outside.

"What about wage indemnity?" I asked.

"Oh, no! *No way*. I'd be in deep trouble now that I'm executive of that," Wong protested. He was referring to his position as the union's executive of the flight attendant wage indemnity insurance plan. At the time, I didn't know enough to question this apparent conflict of interest.

"Then I have to live with the job search strategy," I sighed, biding for time. When the VRCs returned with Harry in tow, Wong proudly announced my compliance.

"We'll write to you about what you must do to qualify for benefits," Ray said, and left with Katts, whereupon Wong smugly handed me copies of my letters to Nolton.

"How on Earth...? Those were sent *private and confidential*," I gasped.

"Yeah, but you wrote you wanted acknowledgment of receipt from his staff. *I'm* his staff. What you write to him for, anyway? He doesn't have time for you! You now choose between me and Maynor to represent you. We're the union reps, and no one else will do it for you. Think about it and write me when you've made your choice," and he left without another word.

Harry, silent throughout the entire meeting, declined my invitation for coffee. "Can't do. Got a meeting with management. Call me at 5:00 P.M." When I did, he announced, "Got good news for you. Management is 90% sure you'll go on NorAm's insurance if WCB cuts you off. I'll speak to Tobias about it."

"What about wage indemnity?" I inquired.

"I've no idea."

"Listen, Harry! Wong doesn't have the knowledge to handle my case. Can't you get it through to Nolton that this is precedent-setting and that I need a lawyer. After all, you've known each other for thirtysome odd years?"

"I'll see what I can do. Call me on the 30th, at noon." I reached him on November 2nd, but he purportedly had nothing to report, conveniently forgetting that the union, NorAm, and WCB had met at the Board that very same day.

A week later, Dr. O'Doherty and my family doctor made a joint statement to the WCB and my union brothers that, at present, I was unfit for any and all remunerative work. NorAm's president, meanwhile, through my encouragement, had reviewed my case with the airline's Vancouver management, its director of medical services, the employee benefits program, and the labor relations department. He concluded that my situation was intricate and involved many details, which were best explained to me by the local claims department—a one man show. Also, he had advised local management to monitor my situation so that I would be provided with all possible assistance.

He failed, however, to offer any comment on the airline's mysterious insurance policy, though I had it on authority from two Toronto union officers that the insurance for flight attendants injured in an accident was kept top secret. They also informed me that Wong had requested help with my case. Assistance would depend on how much money the union felt like spending. "And yes, of course you'll be on wage indemnity if WCB cuts you off," they had each assured me. Both promised to discuss my case with Nolton and to call me back later that same day. I did not hear from them again—ever.

I had also contacted the local union's health and safety officer, a NorAm flight attendant, and asked if she could get me the 1988 accident report from the Federal Ministry of Transport (MoT). No, she had responded. Such reports were inaccessible unless very specific questions were being asked. Three days later, however, she had checked with Wong and Harry, and would now mail a letter to Ottawa. On November 6th, she instead sent a request for information to a Mr. Lee at the Vancouver office of Aviation Occupational Health and Safety.

That same day a letter from Wong, copied to nine unknown union brothers and sisters, arrived in lieu of a response from Nolton. Because Wong portrayed my predicament in ambiguous, inaccurate and misleading terms, and omitted any mention of the reason for my misfortune, I found it necessary to pen another essay to Nolton and copy it to the nine others. No one responded.

On November 19th, 1992, the VRCs demanded that I make ten job contacts every week, and submit to them in writing the names, phone numbers, addresses, and any comments made by the prospective employers, so that Miss Katts could follow up on possible on-the-job site training options. Additionally, they informed me that because I had only one university course to complete before graduation, it would be impossible to pay me full rehab benefits. However, NorAm had now indicated that there might be a slim possibility for my *re-employment* with their Toronto Linguistic Services Department—if I were competitive in that position.

Ready to kill or die, and beginning to doubt my capacities for verbal expression and mental comprehension, I fired another letter off to Nolton and proceeded to track down Harry, which took until November 23rd.

"No, no. You're not mistaken. The rehab consultants changed their minds. If you don't like it, write them a letter. And ask them to copy me."

"Tell me, Harry, who's actually dealing with my case?" Dead silence.

"I guess I'll have to wait for a reply from Nolton?"

"Yes." he said.

"And Harry, what about NorAm's insurance?"

"Well, someone bungled your case in '88. Stay on WCB as long as you can. If they cut you off, you'll go on their insurance."

"Thank you, Harry, you've been *most* helpful," I said, slammed down the phone, and wept.

On November 25th, Nolton informed me that the union was now prepared to hire legal counsel of my choice with the understanding that they would only cover the costs for the initial consultation, and that Wong would retain overall responsibility for my case until I had acquired permanent counsel.

"Tidbits for a pauper. 'Til donkey's fly," I thought, and called Toronto and got my union brother on the phone.

"Your offer is an insult. One consultation with a lawyer doesn't get me anywhere, and afterwards I'm stuck with Wong again—and he doesn't know his arse from a hole in the ground. I think you can do better. *Much* better. Get help from the big guys. That's why we joined them, isn't it."

But he hummed and hawed, and intoned how wonderfully well-qualified Wong was for the job, and how many wonderful things he had done for the union.

"That might all be true. But he isn't qualified for *this* job. You should know that."

"All right, all right. I'll try to get someone for you. I'll call you back later." And he disappeared into the woodwork. His promise kept me filled with hope until, numerous long-distance calls and many sleepless nights later, shaking like a leaf from nervous tension, I contacted the Workers' Assistance lawyer and begged her for help.

"Fax me your doctors' reports, and try not to worry. I'll get you back on wage-loss benefits." Shortly thereafter, the union health and safety officer called to express her sympathy and disbelief in the handling of my case and asserted, "I'm going to request information on all PTSD cases in the East and let you know as soon as I get something." She added, "And trust Harry. He's on your side and will fight for you."

I would not hear from her again for fifteen months

On December 1st, 1992, a special delivery letter arrived from Wong announcing that he had been directed by Nolton to be in charge of my WCB case—*if* I decided to have union representation. Therefore, it was essential that I forward to him all pertinent correspondence and that I maintain open communication with him. Nolton had also requested that a meeting with one of the legal counsels (I could choose from the five listed on a separate sheet), Wong, and me be arranged to assist Wong in researching my case. I must understand, the letter directed, that all costs subsequent to this initial meeting would be borne by me, and that Wong would continue to have the overall responsibility of my WCB case until I had decided whom I wanted to represent me.

"Swine," I thought, "These swine." If these morsels were all they were willing to throw my way, I'd slap them with a lawsuit. The Labor Relations Board had told me that I could sue them for lack of representation, but that thought did nothing to calm me down. Calling Toronto to protest against Wong's participation in my case might have had the desired effect, but when I reached that office, no one "with authority" was available. When I tried phoning again the following day, December 2nd, someone promised to get in touch with Nolton and ask him to call me. But he never did.

Harry rang the next day, his voice filled with tenderness. "Just came back from a trip. How're you making out?" he asked brightly. I filled him in on recent events. "Why don't you make an appointment with one of the lawyers and take it from there?" he suggested.

"Oh, no, Harry! Until I know that Wong is out of the picture, I'm not doing anything. He's not competent—and you know it! The union ought to appoint a lawyer for my entire case. This is not run-of-the-mill stuff. This is precedent-setting. What's happened to me has happened—and will happen—to many other flight attendants. And you guys know that but choose to ignore it and let us go to the dogs. If this had happened to you the fiddle would be playing a different tune," I raged.

"Oh, well. Don't get upset now. I'll look into it."

"Great," I answered, "You do that. Call me when you have," trusting that I would never hear from him again. I sought Helen's advice once again, and she suggested that I write a letter to the president of the Canadian branch of an international union, which we had joined years earlier. I completed the task the following day, and began to wait. Union officers haunted me in my nightmares.

On December 8th, the Workers' Assistance lawyer addressed WCB's adjudicator and noted that my psychological condition had deteriorated significantly since August and, therefore, I was unable to carry out a rehabilitation plan. The following day, an order arrived for me to present myself to the Board on December 18th for a pension assessment interview with Cavarro. Next came a call from Miss Katts.

"Have you followed up on your job search?" she asked.

"Both my doctors and the Workers' Assistance lawyer sent you information confirming that I'm far too ill to do anything right now," I said.

"Did you finish school?" she inquired.

"Yes. But with great difficulty," I replied on the verge of tears.

"Have you signed up for courses in the spring?" she probed.

"Yes, but only tentatively. It all depends on my health."

"Well, you better hurry. It'll help you get a job!"

Too exhausted and weak to engage in an argument, I instead asked her, "Did you speak with the Assistance lawyer?"

"No, I haven't. And I really wonder whether you should not be on wage-loss benefits. I'll have to talk to my supervisor about it before I can issue a cheque. And, by the way, I'm on vacation until January 4, 1993. Bye, bye."

Killing time, I studied my WCB file that I recovered from the union and discovered that discrepancies, lies, untruths, and ambiguities were rampant, which added to my aggravation. However, it afforded me insight into how WCB, employers, and unions dealt with injured workers.

Harry called on December 13th. "Just want to see how you're making out."

"My psychiatrist has put me under strict rest because of the anxiety and stress caused by you guys and WCB...and my rehab benefits will probably be cut off...and I've a meeting with the Board's psychologist on the 18th, and my overall health is lousy and deteriorating. Make you feel good?" I said bitterly.

"Oh, don't worry," he chirped.

"Easy for you to say, but thanks for calling."

"I've tried numerous times but you're never home," he protested weakly.

"Bull, Harry. I'm always in. Try again if you feel like it," I said and hung up.

When I arrived at the Board psychologist's office on the appointed day, Cavarro greeted me with a cheery "How *are* you?"

Skipping nonsensical verbal foreplay, and knowing that I looked like a skeleton, I replied, "As you can see, my health has deteriorated steadily since we last saw each other. Because everything is misportrayed in the disclosure, I've taken copies of my own accident report and near-misses to set things straight. Since I've problems concentrating, I've made notes about what provoked my health deterioration. Please bear with me," and then I began to rattle off the occurrences of recent months.

Halfway through my recital she interrupted. "I don't have much more time."

"Oh...but this is far from all," I said, and continued to read from my list, beginning again with the peculiar "you want a career change if the money is right," incident. "You know it's against the Privacy Act to disclose information on my dispute with the Board and NorAm, and *that* I can take..."

"Your condition hasn't improved over the past four years, has it?" she interrupted me again in midstream.

"No, that's not so. It has deteriorated steadily since November of 1990 because of the way I'm treated, and that has little to do with me or the accident at this point," I retorted.

"You feel yourself a victim, then?" she questioned.

"No. I'm just saying that the way I'm treated is unconscionable."

"Yeah, but do you see yourself as a victim?" she prodded more intensely.

"No. I just think that the treatment I receive from the Board borders on mental cruelty. After all, we don't want to forget that I'm ill with PTSD," I maintained, suspicious about her line of questioning.

"So you *don't* think you're a victim, then," she repeated again, sounding like a broken record.

"No," I grumbled, growing weary of the question.

"Mmmh," she hummed, as if dissatisfied with my response, and then asked, "You going to school next semester?"

"Depending on my health," I replied.

"How do you picture your life?"

"Going back to flying."

"Yeah, but if you can't do that?"

"I will."

"Yeah, but let's say you can't. What would you do, then?"

"Continue school and become a psychologist."

"You cannot live off your pension, you know," she said pointedly, then added when I did not respond, "You're so much better off than most people coming through here." My face held its blank expression. She opted for a different tack. "How're you going to go about your job search?" she asked.

"I've no idea. Besides, I find the whole thing awkward, since I'm morally obligated to let my prospective employers know about my PTSD and how it happened—and also that I'm too ill to accept a job at this time. That, of course, could ruin my chances of ever getting a job, if I wanted to work on the ground."

"Oh...but how are you coping?"

"Not well, as you can see. My psychiatrist wants me hospitalized, but I think I'm better of at home with my dogs. My mother's willing to come over any time."

"Well, Tanya, you had problems at the mental health facility—you would have problems in the hospital as well," she remarked sourly. I let it go unchallenged. "Just once more. You *sure* you don't feel victimized?" she harped.

And once more I responded, "No."

And then Cavarro declared without malice, "Now that WCB and the airline have caused you so much stress, why don't you get off your arse and take the reins into your own hands and forget all about us? You're financially secure. You told me so!"

"Pardon me?" I questioned, doubting my ears.

"Well, I choose to be honest and straightforward with you," she asserted.

I graciously thanked her for the advice and did not breathe another word, almost strangling myself in the process.

Encouraged by my silence she seized the opportunity and proposed, "You've got time to fill out the MMPI, haven't you?"

"Sorry. Can't. Got an appointment with my GP at 12:30." As she glanced sideways at me, I could almost sense the accusations of non-compliance crossing her mind, and pre-emptively I volunteered to adhere to the command on December 22nd, 1992. Content with that, she sent me on my merry way.

DEFINITION OF VICTIMIZATION

I found out later that Cavarro so doggedly pursued my admission of feeling victimized because feelings of victimization apparently have a powerful and long-lasting effect on an individual's beliefs about their self-worth and self-esteem. That, in turn, leads to a great deal of self-questioning and selfdoubt. Victims, purportedly seeing themselves as weak, frightened, out-of-control and powerless, as well as lacking in autonomy, feel singled out by misfortune. Furthermore, they are apt to perceive themselves as deviant, thus reinforcing their negative self-image. To cope after being victimized, the afflicted must rebuild and re-establish a conceptual system that can account for and incorporate the victimization, a process often taking years—during which they will have to live with all the negative connotations associated with feeling victimized.[2] If I had admitted to such feelings, the Board would have asserted that they were the primary reason for my PTSD.

On December 21st, 1992, Miss Katts informed me that I had been cut off from benefits since December 4th. The Workers Assistance lawyer had gone on Christmas vacation, and so had everyone else who might have one iota of a chance to do something about it. I canceled my MMPI appointment, but was pressured into accepting one for December 28th.

Harry rang on Christmas Day, late at night, and wished me a Happy Holiday. "Many people have been in your predicament," he consoled, "Don't despair. I'll help you. Yours is a very special case—very intricate. You're not giving up, are you?"

"No. Not yet," I said.

"Good...don't cave in. Fight this to the end," he encouraged.

By December 28th the city was buried in snow, and I again canceled the WCB appointment, and again—as I had done for days—I tried to reach a Workers' Assistance lawyer before continuing to study volumes of books explaining the function and purpose of MMPI testing.

On New Year's Eve, a lawyer returned my calls, pronouncing, "This is *appalling*. We're 100% behind you. Don't dignify them with being so upset over this. And try to see your psychiatrist to get the Board off your back." But Dr. O'Doherty was in Ireland, and the office of his replacement was closed until January 4th. Before ringing in the New Year, I called Ma Bell and arranged for an unlisted telephone number, because WCB had taken to harassing me several times a day to commit to a MMPI test date.

Friends dropped off some groceries, because I was too weak to leave the house. A DC10 and a Boeing 727 crashed somewhere. And so began 1993.

The Hired Assassin

The New Year began as the old one had ended. On January 5th, 1993, when I told Harry about my unlisted phone number, he blasted back at me, "What on earth did you do that for?"

"I need peace, Harry. Peace. And to get that, I need help. You know that the Board has cut me off, and our wage indemnity insurance says my benefits expire on March 2nd, and then I must go on unemployment. You've got any idea what I'm to do when that runs out?"

"No, that's Wong's domain."

"OK. And did you get any info on PTSD from Toronto?"

"No, there's none available. But I'm getting together with management tomorrow about outstanding 1992 cases. Perhaps they know something," he answered.

"Don't bother. Tell them I'm willing to sign a statement that I will keep silent about the treatment I've received, providing that I can return to inflight when I'm ready, and that I get some money from WCB until then."

"Giving up fighting, are you?"

"Yeah. I've had it."

"Oh, good. I've already heard that somewhere."

"So you'll find out if that's possible?"

"Sure. I'll see what I can do. Call me tomorrow at 7 P.M.," he said and we disconnected.

The following day, I showed up at the Board, and handed the secretary who was waiting with the MMPI and Beck's Inventory tests in hand, a statement demanding that the results of these two tests, as well as the previous ones, be mailed to Dr. O'Doherty. I asked her to sign it.

"But that's absolutely not necessary! Your psychiatrist can get those any time!"

"Could be. But I'm not taking anything until someone's signed this," I insisted.

"I've no authority to do that," she said defensively.

"Get Dr. Cavarro, then."

She did, and after more arguments, the psychologist signed, while I went into a stress attack, trembling from top to toe, with chest pains and breathing difficulties convulsing my body. When I had cooled down somewhat, I proceeded with the tests, carefully counting so as to leave at least thirty statements of the MMPI blank, which should render it invalid. To be on the safe side, I left fifty unanswered. For the Beck's Inventory, I figured five should do the trick. The analysis of both tests would be impossible.

Back at home, the big mother union's boss advised that a brother Kevin had been appointed to investigate my case, and that he would be in touch. Harry called on January 11th, to tell me that no meeting with management had taken place because he thought it wiser to take brother Tobias along as a witness. It would now be held on the 14th. Next, the wage indemnity brokers told me that they were still investigating my claim. Exhausted in mind and body, I dropped the two courses I needed to graduate. On the 13th, brother Kevin phoned at 7 A.M. to inquire about my case history. I gave him the most outstanding details, weeping all the while.

"Thanks. I'll call you back later," he promised.

"That's what they all say," I grumbled hanging up. But at 1:30 P.M. he did phone back, and instructed me to contact one Andrew McCormick, a lawyer, who would review my file. Before heading to McCormick's office the following day, I rang the wage indemnity insurance company, whose representative said that the Unemployment Insurance notice had been sent in error, and that I would be paid another fifty weeks of benefits, after which a lesser amount of long-term disability would kick in.

McCormick struck me as a condescending ass, but his apparent expertise in WCB issues made up for it. Reporting to the union on January 22nd, in a letter copied to me, he asserted that the Board would have to put me back on wage loss or temporary total disability benefits because of my PTSD "flare-up." And because there was no such thing as an identifiable and immediately available job for flight attendants on the face of this earth, and because I could not return to flying, a 100% loss of earning pension should be paid by WCB.

He advised me that it was extremely important to be wary of the Board's talk about "proportionate entitlement," which meant that if WCB decided I had pre-accident personality deficiencies, part of the pension would be hived off because of it. Since the early medical diagnosis and the claim file expressly stated that no pre-morbid characteristics existed, WCB or the Review Board (if my case went for an appeal), should be counterattacked if they attempted such a move. Suspecting that my symptoms would be exacerbated if I were represented by someone I distrusted, he recommended that Joanne, the Workers' Assistance lawyer, continue to look after my interests, especially since it was free of charge.

I broke into a jig. Union WCB chairperson Wong had been effectively sidelined. And Joanne, upon her return from vacation on January 13th, immediately told the Board that they had done me untold psychological damage over recent months. By January 20th, I was back on wageloss benefits.

"Cavarro thinks that you should be on it for at least six months. If you've improved by then, they'll hire an outside vocational rehabilitation consultant to evaluate your skills," she said when telling me about her communication with WCB.

"That won't be necessary," I responded jubilantly. "I'll be ready to go back to flying by then. I know I'll be."

But my dreams were shattered again when Cavarro's December 18th, 1992, assessment report arrived on February 23rd, 1993, confirming I had blown the MMPI. Ignoring the possibility that I purposely invalidated the tests, she attributed the failure to successfully complete the test to several possibilities: either I had reading difficulties (clients should be able to read the test at a sixth grade level); or I was suspicious about how the test results would be used; or I had been rebellious and uncooperative; or I was confused and disorganized; or severe depression and lack of energy had prevented me from answering all questions; or I was extremely obsessive or overly intellectual, and therefore had found difficulties deciding on the answers.

Regardless of the invalid test results, Cavarro continued to view my case as particularly challenging from a rehabilitation perspective, and she now proposed a short-term, intensive behavioral treatment program which would target my chronic PTSD symptoms and provide a strategy to reduce the risk of exacerbating the symptoms. A pension assessment, she noted, should be deferred for five months to allow for treatment.

But if I were to refuse it, she indicated, the Board could justify the cessation of my wage loss benefits and immediately proceed with a pension assessment. The following day an adjudicator, probably inspired by Cavarro's suggestion, advised me that a desensitization specialist would be appointed to treat me in the future.

"Do what they suggest. If you don't, it'll influence your pension because you rejected treatment," Joanne counseled, adding, "Oh, by the way, I've been appointed to the WCB Review Board. Your file has been transferred to Shirley. She helped you over Christmas, didn't she?"

"She tried to," I remarked, not amused.

On March 30th, 1993, Cavarro notified me that an appointment with a psychologist, Dr. Bernstein, had been set for April 22nd. Subsequent treatment sessions were to be arranged between me and the therapist. Meanwhile, NorAm's claims officer told the Board that my fear of flying could not possibly preclude me from other types of employment, especially since I had continued my university studies—which in itself proved that I was fit as a fiddle. According to him, my susceptibility to relapses, therefore, was doubtlessly related to pre-accident defects harboring in my psyche.

That same day, a congratulatory letter arrived from NorAm's In-Flight Service Vice President. Dated February 17th, 1993, his letter thanked me profusely for my commitment and dedication to customer service over the past twenty years, and solicited my continued dedication and support in "our" efforts to keep "our" company strong and profitable. The letter had me spitting fire.

When the local management demanded my attendance for French language testing on February 26th, I was fit to be tied. Since copies of the summons had been issued to everybody and his dog in upper management on the East coast, who never before had been receiving copies when employees were language tested, I wanted to ask Harry what management was up to. But he appeared to have vanished since January 19th, when he had informed me that the meeting between him, Tobias, and management had been rescheduled for January 25th. So, I entrusted brother Kevin, who professed to have neither knowledge nor influence over company–employee issues, with the job of tracking Harry down.

But instead of receiving a return call from my union brother Kevin, NorAm management phoned on April 6th to mandate my attendance for a meeting at the Airport Inn on April 22th, 1993. "Can't make it, Sandra. I have an interview with a psychologist that day—ordered by WCB. Can you change the date?"

"No. Impossible," she snapped curtly .

"OK then. I'll see what I can do. Has Harry been invited?"

"Yeah. He'll be there."

I rang Harry and left a message to please confirm receipt of NorAm's invitation, then rang Cavarro, who authorized changing my appointment with Bernstein—if I would see him within one week. I then called the therapist's office, where the receptionist put me through an inquisition about the reasons for my cancellation before slotting me in for April 29th. Never-home-Harry buzzed the second I hung up. "I haven't heard a word about that meeting. I've got to fly on the 22nd."

"What to do now, Harry?"

"I've already raised hell at the office. They're trying to change it."

"What's it about, anyway?" I asked.

"Oh, just a fact-finding interview."

"A fact-finding interview? Aren't there enough facts already?" I hollered, feeling my blood pressure rise to hitherto unheard of levels.

"Don't get upset now. There's nothing to worry about. Got to run. Sandra's changing the date. Give her a call."

To hear that the 28th—or 29th—was now being considered did upset me.

"Sandra, can't you confirm the 28th? I've just changed my appointment with the psychologist to the 29th?" I begged her.

"No. You of all people should know how difficult that is. Why don't you just get your old appointment back," she snapped and hung up.

I tried, but Bernstein's secretary, after querying in detail my reasons for requesting a return to the original date, announced, "There's no vacancy on the 22nd." I stuck with the 29th.

The following day NorAm had still not made up its mind, except that the meeting would now be held at the union office or at WCB. The hotel had been ruled out because of budget considerations.

"O.K. Sandra. Once you've made up your mind, please inform me in writing about the objective of this meeting, and where and when it is to take place—exactly. Thank you." Trembling from anger, tension and fury, I threw down the receiver.

When I finally reached Harry on April 14th, he panted, "I'm on my way out the door, but the meeting is on the 28th at the Airport Inn and you're number seven. And don't worry. Everything has worked out so far, hasn't it? Got to run now. I'm leaving for Arizona. But I'll be back on the 27th. I'll call you then. Bye," and hung up before I could get a word in edgewise.

Of course, he did not ring before the 28th, and when he did call, he promised to meet me at the Inn at 3:45 P.M. so that we could discuss matters. He showed up at 4:20. We drove over to NorAm's medical building right away, where Annemarie waited for us. At 4:30, we entered the conference room, where anybody who thought that they were somebody in local management—except for the base manager—awaited us. There were ten people in all, all silently staring at me as if they were mesmerized. Someone extended greetings, a few platitudes were exchanged, the reason for the meeting acknowledged as "we just want to keep in touch," and the gathering adjourned. It had lasted for about ten minutes. During the whole affair, Harry had sat in silence.

On our way back to the Inn (Annemarie had rushed back home), I was shaking badly, not knowing if it was out of rage, indignity, or relief.

"Well, that wasn't bad, was it?" Harry asked brightly.

"No. It was an insult," I haughtily replied. I then invited him for a coffee at the Inn.

"Sorry. Don't have time," he mumbled, and I didn't push it. He probably was in a rush to meet with his management buddies at the nearby strip joint for booze and bullshit. After all, they had all known each other since Christ was a cadet. And what did I care? Annemarie had witnessed the event. That was all that mattered. But when I merged into rush hour traffic I didn't know whether to laugh or cry hysterically. At home, a six pack and a few more Ativans put me into a nightmarish sleep that left me bathed in perspiration.

The following morning, during the drive downtown in rush hour traffic, I chanted "Amazing Grace," set to my own lyrics, because to me the meeting with Bernstein was synonymous with being thrown into a crocodile-infested river. Annemarie and I entered his office at precisely 9:30 A.M. Shortly thereafter, the therapist, a tall, immaculately groomed, and Armani-dressed man approached, a questioning look on his face.

"I'm Tanya Andersen and this is Annemarie Bjerg," I said.

"You sisters?" he inquired.

"No—friends,"

"I'll be joining Tanya for the interview, if you don't mind," Annemarie explained. "She's very anxious,"

"No...that's fine," he replied, and began firing questions at her: "Are you a flight attendant? For how many years? Twenty-four? How long have you known each other?" He finished the inquisition with, "Coffee?"

"Sure. Love some." We followed him into a diminutive pantry to prepare it. Carrying our cups into his office, Annemarie and I plunged down on the love seat facing the window. He seated himself at his desk opposite the door and inquired, "Why didn't you come in on the 22nd?"

"Didn't your secretary tell you?"

"She might have. But I've forgotten."

So, I explained.

"Fine then. Because you know you better co-operate with me. If you don't, the Board will cut off your benefits. You realize that, don't you? And where would you be then? Must be hard to get along on the money you get from them and the airline as it is...isn't it?"

"No," I replied, without bothering to correct him by revealing that my employer offered no financial assistance. Instead, I handed him my 1988 accident report and the list of near misses.

Perusing the papers for a second, he asked in disbelief, "What do you want me to do with these?"

"Read them if you like."

"Oh...but I'm not interested in this. Unless you want me to read it," he quipped holding them out to me.

"Doesn't matter," I replied, taking them back, my suspicions mounting. But they faded away quickly, because Bernstein's exotic appearance—neither Caucasian nor black—combined with his charismatic, charming manner and his gregariousness, lulled me into letting my guard down.

"How do you feel about the meeting with NorAm?" he inquired.

"OK. Haven't had much time to think about it yet. But I find their ignorance about PTSD astounding. It's because of that that I'm in the situation I'm in. I was perfectly healthy and well-adjusted before the '88 explosion," I answered, omitting any mention of my feelings about the unfairness of it all.

"How was she functioning on the job before the accident," he turned to ask Annemarie.

"Very well—indeed she loved it. She's a very adventurous person, you know," she responded while smiling at me.

"How so?" he asked.

"Oh, she's been all over the world on freighters with one husband, and trucked all over North America with another, and traveled extensively on her own." Annemarie went on to relate her perception of the treatment I had received from NorAm and WCB, including the mental health day catastrophe and Cavarro's "get off your arse and do your own thing" statement.

Occasionally, Bernstein, who had pulled his chair in front of us, looked down at me for validation. "Tanya's healing process has never been allowed to start," Annemarie concluded matter-of-factly.

"Are you angry about that?" Bernstein demanded, facing me. "You've a right to be angry, you know!" he asserted.

"Anger doesn't get me anywhere. Love and Light works much better," I demurred.

"Oh. You also believe in heart and soul knowledge?" he inquired.

"Of course I do." We dwelt on the topic of intuition for a while, the interview now resembling a gathering of friends rather than a meeting with a mental health professional whose perception of my psyche might determine my future. Not being a moron, unlike many of his cohorts, he joked about histrionics being related to hysterectomies (an operation I underwent in 1979), while watching my reactions like a hawk.

"What do you think of the MMPI?" he asked me when Annemarie and I returned from refilling our coffee mugs.

"First of all it's totally subjective. And secondly, it's only 44% accurate in detecting PTSD."[1] He didn't comment.

"How do you feel about your situation in general?" he continued.

"The way I've been treated since November 1990 is why I'm still sick. It borders on the traumatization of the traumatized—and must come to an end, so that I can go back flying."

"Good. Then you'll co-operate with me?"

"Of course I will," I answered, thinking the objective, desensitization for the purpose of reintegration into inflight service, would be easy to reach with the help of such a delightful being.

I agreed to see him for intensive treatments on a weekly basis for two months, beginning in seven days. "Annemarie doesn't need to come along. We'll do just fine." He beamed at me, hand outstretched to bid me farewell. When I took his hand, he said, "Now that I've asked you so many things, let me pose you another question. What do you think of me?"

"I'll answer that another time," I chirped, enthralled.

Annemarie was equally enchanted with the man, whom we discussed with great joy over lunch at a nearby pub. Later I drove home elated, yet puzzled by only one thing: Bernstein had not asked if I took any medications. "Must have slipped his mind," I thought. And did it really matter? He knew what he was doing, and I would not need to depend on Ativan to calm me down once he helped me mend my broken wings and fly. But then the dreams began.

Psychosomatic Illness

"You have no reason to feel guilty. NorAm purposely neglected to monitor you in 1989 and 1990 because they intend to fire you. It's cheaper for them to hire new staff for half your salary. And be wary of Bernstein. He's the hired gun of the airline and WCB. He'll kill you if you're not careful."

This was how I interpreted a dream I had in early May. In the dream—a nightmare—I sat paralyzed by fear in Bernstein's ninth floor office as he grabbed my chair to throw me out of the window after I had caught him recording a conversation between Annemarie and me in his reception area. Just as he lifted my chair, I awoke, petrified and bathed in perspiration. The dream gave me food for thought. During the following night, I had another dream in which I saw myself buried alive, with NorAm's management, WCB psychologists, and Bernstein all dancing on my grave. In this dream, the soil beneath their feet cracked and shifted as I struggled to break free. In the morning, I jumped out of bed and rushed to my physicians; because of cancellations in their schedules, they were available to see me.

Independently of each other, both of them decided that future visits with Bernstein would be unconscionable, because this therapist had instilled such intense emotions in me. O'Doherty, furthermore, intended to advise the American Association of Psychiatrists of Bernstein's purported capabilities, exclaiming, "This is wonderful. The man has found a cure for PTSD in flight attendants, aircrew in general, not to mention passengers, when the rest of psychiatry has failed. I am absolutely delighted. His discovery is so immense that others must share in it," he said sarcastically before counseling me. "Get your lawyer to draft a letter stating that, if he decides to treat you, he'll take full responsibility for your well-being during and after his treatment. If he says that you are able to work as a flight attendant, legally oblige him to monitor you and include that you will hold him responsible if your PTSD reoccurs due to an onboard incident on NorAm, or any other airline. And also write that you will legally hold him accountable if he fails to cure you, and that you will pursue the matter in a court of law." That night I slept peacefully knowing that both my doctors accepted my adverse reactions to Bernstein. The following day I began the summer semester.

Before heading to the university, I phoned Shirley, my new Workers' Assistance lawyer, who listened attentively to my portrayal of the newest development. When she received the validations from my physicians, she told WCB a few days later that it was O'Doherty's firm view that for me to attend sessions with a doctor who provoked such strong reactions of distrust and hostility in me was very threatening to my psyche and would be harmful to my health, because of my extremely vulnerable and fragile emotional condition. Furthermore, she queried the exact objective of Bernstein's treatment, knowing he had shown no interest at all in my flying career. She further requested his credentials for counseling PTSD sufferers, and concluded the letter by quoting paragraph 74.50 of the Workers' Compensation Board's Rehabilitation and Services Manual:

"A Board Medical Advisor or Rehabilitation Centre Physician may arrange for the claimant to be referred to a specialist, however, the worker is not forced to accept treatment from a doctor against whom he has some objection."

The letter reached the Board on May 11th, 1993. After that, an eerie silence prevailed. Anticipating turmoil to engulf me once again, I methodically distracted myself with school and homework. A few weeks later, it arrived. On June 7th, Cavarro responded to Shirley's letter by noting that the specific purpose for desensitization treatment was to assist me with the anxiety-related symptoms arising from the May 1988 incident. Desensitization, she maintained, was an established and highly effective treatment for aspects of the symptoms I experienced. Thus, she insisted, it would be most beneficial and effective for me to follow up on the Board's treatment recommendation, and I should select a mental health professional specializing in treatment of PTSD symptoms from the attached list. It included the Board's acting director of psychology, a Dr. Iliana Kowal, who had emigrated from Romania with a degree from the University of Bucharest in 1991.

But in what type of PTSD cases had the people on this list specialized? And did those include aircrew in particular? I had yet to begin researching the topic, but quickly discovered when I did, that, while considerable research has been devoted to understand the etiology and dynamics of a basic fear of flying in earthbound individuals, the ailment itself is generally discarded as refractory to treatment, since physical and psychotherapeutic methods have proven minimally effective.[1] With regard to aircrew, some aviation medicine specialists asserted that a strengthening of repression, denial, and counterphobic defenses worked just as well as conventional therapy in flight phobia reduction.[2] This principle, of course, is alien to most mental health professionals, even though it is acknowledged that aircrew differ from earthlings in all ways imaginable, including their psychological reactions to danger. The luxury of repression had certainly not been afforded me by WCB and NorAm.

Once again I saw myself being railroaded; my weight dropped and my consumption of Ativan and alcohol increased. However, I crafted the statement suggested by Dr. O'Doherty and had it verified by a lawyer. "Nobody's ever going to sign that," O'Doherty chuckled. On June 18th he issued a statement in response to Cavarro's letter questioning the effectiveness of intensive desensitization, seeing it as tool to recovery only if applied with the objective of returning me to inflight. If the intent of the treatment was merely to facilitate a better opportunity to re-establish me in the workforce at another vocation, it would be a futile exercise, O'Doherty pointed out, because studies had shown that high levels of general anxiety impede or even prevent progress in treating phobias with desensitization.[3]

I took O'Doherty's note over to Shirley, since the correspondence between the two had a tendency to disappear en route. I also showed her my document, just so that she knew that I was serious about not exposing myself to further abuse by WCB's hired assassins without a fight. She, in turn, fearing a standoff, hastened to propose to the Board that they quickly assess me for a permanent partial disability pension in order to enable me to plan for the future I had already charted out for myself—to regain my wings. To me, journeying by mule, donkey, box-carts, trucks, boats, buses and trains for the rest of my life was a bizarre and grotesque thought. On June 13th, 1993, I paid out my mortgage.

No idleness prevailed on the other fronts. In an astonishing develop-ment, the international union closed my file because, according to them, my peeves with the WCB, the flight attendants' union and NorAm had been settled to my satisfaction. NorAm's claims officer pressured the Board to consider a "relief of cost" because, they claimed, evidence in my file clearly showed that my pre-existing psychological condition and propensities—and not the 1988 incident—were responsible for my PTSD development. Mid-July, the Board cordially invited me to a July 22nd pension assessment party to be hosted by the newly appointed director of WCB's psychology department—Dr. Kowal. To finish my studies in relative peace I was able to change their proposed date to August 5th.

In the meantime, however, Bernstein's evaluation report arrived, abort-ing the intended peace and sending me into a fury of hitherto unknown proportions. In his report, declaring that he had purposely remained neutral during the interview to lower his threat-value, he regretted to say that his recollection of events were impaired, "because Miss Andersen had refused to communicate whenever he had begun to take notes." This was a curious statement because Annemarie and I knew that he was not in need of notes, for we saw him activate the tape recorder underneath his desk when we returned more quickly than he had anticipated from our coffee refill. The report continued with his statement that I had responded to his various requests for information with "inappropriate giggles, jokes, and sarcasm."

Everyone acquainted with me will attest that "giggling" is not part of my personality and, whereas my arsenal of humorous life experiences is massive, my repertoire of jokes is limited to two.

The first one is: "A filthy rich Arab asks one of his sons what he wants for Christmas. 'A Mickey Mouse outfit,' sonny quipped, whereupon daddy ventured out to buy NorAm."

And the second, "What's a cockpit with women pilots?" "A pussypit!"

I told neither one at Bernstein's.

My opposition to jokes stems partly from my dislike of vulgarity, and partly from my frequent failure to get the punch line. Years ago, when colloquial English vocabulary was still foreign to me, one of our pilots told a joke—one of the pilot's favorite "give-me-attention" screamers when bored to death on the flight deck—expecting roaring laughter after delivering the punch line: "A blow job!"

"What's that?" I asked in all innocence. All three, unsure where to look and blushing, probably wished they could vanish into thin air. One of them built up enough courage to suggest that I consult my boyfriend. Having none at the time, I was left to wonder about this blowing business for a while. Some years later, when an in-charge asked one of our male passengers during a station stop, "Aren't we wonderful? We dine and wine you and allow for blow jobs," I knew exactly what it was all about. While the guy blushed from head to toe, I hurried away—killing myself with laughter.

The episode leading up to that finale had began in London on a very hot summer day, when a half-naked young man covered with scabs on all visible parts of his body handed me his boarding pass. Shuddering with disgust, wondering about the health of cabin crew and passengers, I watched him sit down in my cabin. Shortly thereafter, a middle-aged woman seated herself in his vicinity. Cupid must have struck as she passed him, because, less than half an hour after takeoff, they were drinking together and intimately conversing side-by-side in an empty row of seats on the half full 747, their infatuation with each other steadily progressing. Watching with eagle eyes, we passed out blankets to hasten the evolution of events for our entertainment of the day.

Busy in the galley after supper, I soon returned to the cabin after completing my chores. The lovebirds were nowhere in sight, but three irate nuns, sitting at the overwing exit by the center washrooms, clamored for my immediate attention. Wildly gesturing toward the lavatories, their arms flaying the air, they exclaimed loudly, "They're in there! They're in there! Both of them together! Can't you see?" They pointed at the bulkhead rhythmically heaving to and fro.

"Yes. And what would you like me to do about it?" I inquired unperturbed, finding their outrage amusing.

"This is *totally* unacceptable. You must do something," they demanded.

"Well, what do you suggest? Want me to open the door?"

"*Oh, no,*" they exclaimed aghast, "But you *must* talk to them when they get out."

"OK., I'll do that." Of course, I graciously forgot to.

Using the washroom for a tryst shows a consideration for fellow travelers which is not always present. Once, on a 747 long haul Paris flight, we had turned off the lights in the empty back cabin, but nevertheless patrolled the area occasionally. During one such mission, one of my peers discovered a naked couple buoyantly fornicating on a row of seats. As the news spread like wildfire among the crew; one by one we wandered by to observe the gymnastics. The in-charge, intrigued by our unusual roaming behavior and the chuckles whenever someone returned from a jaunt to the back, did his own trip to check out the state of affairs. When he reappeared, he grumbled, "You guys are brutal. You could've at least thrown them a blanket!" He then took a few and left to tuck the lovebirds in. Experiences like that are funny. Jokes most often are not, since they make fun of people or their defects, which I detest.

Bernstein's reference to my sarcasm was equally ludicrous. Any hint of sarcasm in his presence would have been suicidal, for I was aware at the time that it would have given him leeway to portray me as a pre-morbidly embittered and hostile individual. The psychologist also asserted that, because I seemed to be quite anxious about flying and wanted to be free of the Board, he had suggested helping me plan a career which would enable me to not have to fly again. At that time, he asserted, I had appeared to be interested and had agreed to return for treatment on May 7th. My subsequent refusal to appear in his charismatic presence was incomprehensible to him. Reviewing my overall behavior as having been quite inappropriate for someone disabled by anxiety, he claimed that my "histrionic style" and the theme of mismanagement of my case which had run through the interview, portrayed the posture of a "victim." Given my current state, he went on in the report, and suspecting that an underlying mental illness he was at a loss to diagnose was the root of all my problems, he concluded that he felt incapable of helping me with my phobia, my PTSD, and my career planning.

Livid, I wanted Bernstein's head on a platter and his body in a meat grinder, I barely stopped short of arranging for the accomplishment of my desires with a motorcycle gang. Annemarie helped me control my anger. Professional help, on the other hand, was harder to come by. O'Doherty was in Ireland, and Shirley had transferred my file to someone else because of "internal office reorganization." To find an outlet for my frustration, I inquired all over the continent until I found out that Bernstein had graduated from a theological, evangelic, and non-denominational college in San Jose with a Master of Arts degree (1974) preceding his Ph.D. in clinical psychology (1975). And no, they were not a mail order institution, the registrar's office assured me. He had practiced in Canada since 1985.

Revealing these facts to O'Doherty upon his return, he mumbled disgruntledly, "Bloody Americans judging Canadian mental health. Why don't they practice on their own citizens. God knows they need it more than we do," While checking for Bernstein's expertise in a book listing all mental professionals in the greater Vancouver area, he discovered that Bernstein specialized in career counseling, consultation and training, pain control, psychotherapy, marital relationships, stress management, rehabilitation counseling, employee health and assistance programs and workplace wellness. This listing conflicted with the Board's assertion that Bernstein frequently treated WCB PTSD referrals in an effective and therapeutic manner.

Bernstein's evaluation and the impending pension assessment threw me into enormous emotional turmoil, which manifested itself in terrific nightmares and teeth grinding so violent that I was in perpetual pain during the last week of classes. Handing in my final assignments on July 29th, I felt a sigh of relief, but then the back pain began. Within a few days,

I resembled the contorted figure of the wicked witch in Hansel and Gretel. My GP agreed my misery stemmed from psychosomatic causes. Declining his offer to arrange for medication as well as postponement of the pension assessment interview, I hobbled out of his office bent over at a 90 degree angle, maneuvered myself into the car, and ventured home on the Trans-Canada highway at around 2 P.M.

Traveling at a snail's pace behind a tractor trailer at a mere 65 M.P.H., I put the pedal to the metal when I saw a break in traffic and swung into the outer lane. As I did, I heard a hissing sound, which I assumed came from the big rig now beside me. But when he exited onto the off-ramp, the noise persisted and a voice in my head yelled, "Get to the side! Get to the side." Without any cars impeding my movement and without touching the brakes, I rolled to a stop on the shoulder seconds later. Limping up front to examine why the car leaned so precariously to the right, I stared at the flat tire. Finding the nearest lamp post for shade and support, I sat against it and stared motionless into the oncoming traffic. Time was not. Nothing mattered.

A biker stopped. "What happened?"

"Blew a tire."

"I'll change it for you."

"No, thank you. But could you please call BCAA (British Columbia Automobile Association)."

"Sure," he said and took off. I continued to stare into nothingness. A while later he returned with a Coke and a paper for me. "It'll be awhile before they can get here," he said. "You sure you don't want me to change that tire?"

"Yes, I'm positive. But thank you so much," and he drove off again. A car pulled up, same make as mine.

The driver exclaimed after seeing me, "Gee wiz. Thought it was my ex and wondered what the f—- she'd done now. What happened?"

"Blew a tire."

"Wow. You were lucky. Let's change it, then."

"No, no. Thank you. BCAA's on its way," I protested. But the biker pulled up again and said, "I just called again. It'll be a while yet."

"Don't worry. I know how to do it," the second driver said, taking the keys out of my hand. He opened the trunk, and took out the spare tire. A few minutes later I drove off on the shoulder without any intention of merging with the now volatile zoo beside me.

Proceeding at the manageable speed of fifteen miles per hour, I turned off at the nearest ramp and made it to a self-serve gas station where the cashier put air in the tire for me, and refused the $5 I offered him. After another ten miles at the same neck-breaking velocity, during which nobody honked their horn, gave me the finger, blinked their lights, or shouted obscenities, I parked the car in the garage, determined that I would never drive again as long as I lived.

My resolve was short-lived, however, for on August 5th, I dressed myself in a colorful Italian outfit, folded my pain-riddled body into the car, and drove in the morning rush hour traffic—knowing that I was not going to die.

I had now survived two extremely life-threatening incidents. A flight attendant's nineteen-year-old daughter had been killed in a tire blowout just weeks earlier when she applied the brakes when the tire blew, causing her car to spin out of control and into the ocean, where she drowned. In my case, I and others would most likely have been mangled in a heap of cars hurdling down the highway. Because I had been spared such a fate against all odds, I concluded that my life took its own path beyond my control. Realizing that there was something larger than life controlling my destiny, I understood that the same force would decide when I would pass on to another dimension, but that I would never die. Therefore, death was not, and there was nothing to fear.

Monetary considerations further encouraged me to take the wheel again. It would cost $120 for the round trip taxi to WCB's compound and a similar amount to visit with my psychiatrist who lived on the other side of town. In addition, I recognized that if I refused to drive, I would be further isolating myself from the outside world; agoraphobia vividly sprang to my mind. That tire blowout compounded the engine explosion's effect on my health, and that my reaction to both was "normal" became evident in my later research.[4]

The traffic that morning, with thoroughfares looking like parking lots, suited my desire for slow motion. Annemarie waited at WCB and gave me two Tylenol 3s and some herbal remedy to swallow. Union Harry, who had promised to be there, was nowhere in sight. Alighting at the receptionist's desk a few minutes later, we were told that Cavarro's office had been moved downstairs. Unable to take another step, I refused to budge without a wheelchair; one was reluctantly provided.

We made a spectacular entrance. Kowal and Cavarro exchanged glances and exclaimed in unison, "What happened?"

"It's psychosomatic," I said, and Annemarie added, "I've given her a couple of Tylenols." Before introductions could be made and the interview started, Dr. Kowal engaged Annemarie in a Bernsteinian conversation, discovering, as had the previous therapist, that she was my close friend and a flight attendant. She then decided to bestow her attention on me. She probed for details about my education and asked what I wanted to do with a Spanish literature degree.

"Hold prime flying once we begin routes into South America and the Philippines, because there are few Spanish-speaking flight attendants in Vancouver, and I could pick and choose my schedule," I answered, my face a ray of sunshine. No comments. Instead, Kowal suggested that I change psychiatrists. "And may I ask *why*?" I said, unperturbed on the surface.

"Because it will be beneficial for your health," the psychologist answered obliquely.

"Beneficial to my health?" I questioned. "Really, Dr. Kowal, that would be the first time the Board ever considered what is *beneficial* to my health. I don't need a new psychiatrist. I have an immensely qualified one. What I need is peace. Just peace," I said calmly, although spitting fury inside. "The treatment that I have received from the Board is the reason why I am as sick as I am, and nothing more."

Annemarie added her statement about how my "healing process had never been allowed to begin." Ignoring her, Kowal hurried to inquire about my Ativan consumption. I replied that I took up to eight tablets a day, depending on what rocked my boat. Before concluding the interview, she requested the completion of yet another MMPI and Beck's Inventory. I declined. Cavarro's participation throughout the interview had been limited to a compliment on my outfit.

When Annemarie wheeled me to the elevator, Cavarro walked with us, escorting us all the way to the exit, where I struggled out of the wheelchair, having been prohibited from taking it outside. Conversing throughout the trip to the door, I then asked her, "Don't you think it's peculiar that roughly 1250 studies on PTSD have been done on subjects ranging from Norwegian fire fighters, to crane operators, concentration camp survivors, to Vietnam Vets, but there is absolutely none done on air crew?" No response. "I assure you. I'm going to write a thesis on it once I get through this mess," I tried again.

"Do that, and let me know," she said and, before we split, promised to issue her pension assessment report within fourteen days.

Five weeks later, on September 13th, I had heard nothing from Cavarro and asked Shirley—who had been reinstated to deal with my case—to investigate why the Board delayed its decision. On September 23rd, an Amtrak train left the tracks and plunged into a bayou in Alabama. For those involved, the accident spelled tragedy, but it turned into a miracle for me. One man, who had rescued passengers and crew from the alligator-infested swamp throughout the night, surveyed the scene at dawn and exclaimed, "Brother, if I had known about the danger and how close I came to dying I could never have done it."

Reflecting on his experience, I had my answer why I—and none of my crew members—had developed PTSD after the May 1, 1988 accident. My curiosity had been my downfall. Seeing the evidence of how narrowly we had escaped death, and hearing it from the mechanic, had been the cause of my psychological derailment, and the plunge into PTSD.

Knowing *why* I had this affliction lifted my spirits, and buoyantly I trooped to university on October 1st, a glorious Indian summer day. The world-class SFU pipe band led me and my fellow graduates, dressed in caps and gowns, into the ceremonial hall. After I received my degree, my friends handed me a beautiful bouquet of roses, and beaming with delight I took them all to lunch. The only shadow in my life that day came from the regret that my mother lay in a European hospital with a fractured hip. But I told her all about the wonderful day over the phone and continued to glow whenever I looked at my degree. When Shirley advised me on October 7th, that the Board had labeled me 35% disabled, but that, due to my unemployability, I would receive a 100% loss of earning pension for the rest of my life, I smiled even broader. But the following day, my elation was crushed when Kowal's and Cavarro's joint pension assessment report arrived at my house.

The report was brutal in its distortions. I had faked the necessity for a wheelchair entrance, Dr. Kowal's report claimed, and I had exited the interview by slowly walking to the elevator without assistance. According to her, only a residue of my PTSD condition remained. She continued, claiming that my occupational functioning—which had been evaluated as grossly impaired and too disabling to return to flight attendant duties—and my overall level of adaptive functioning, considered "poor to very poor," were both attributable, she insinuated, to my pre-morbid characteristics which were conducive to my development of PTSD.

If I would only seek appropriate counseling, she ventured, I would improve sufficiently so as to be employable in a low stress and supportive environment. She went on to suggest that moving my residence to where I would be unable to see aircraft would benefit my health. Rehabilitation consultant, Miss Katts, had been instructed to search for a job, any job, she deemed I would be capable of performing.

After I made Shirley aware of the fallacy of the "pre-morbid characteristics" assumption, she said to just wait and see. And so it was that at a WCB team meeting in November, Katts proposed the job as Spanish document translator. This was to be conducted out of my home, and would be a desirable, fulfilling, and readily-available career choice for me if I were motivated to receive appropriate psychotherapy. Her suggestion was accepted unanimously.

I was informed of my new career on December 18th, 1993, and hit the roof. O'Doherty was in Ireland.

Asking Shirley if I had to be a vegetable before I would receive adequate compensation for my employer's inadequate aircraft maintenance, and furious about the issue of appropriate counseling (reminding her that O'Doherty had practiced psychiatry for more than twenty-five years and presently taught at the University of British Columbia), I was told that there really was no urgency to do anything, because my loss of earning benefit was guaranteed for the time being.

Unhappy with such a meager response to my frustrations, I gave big union brother Kevin a dingle. My local brothers had been unreachable for months, but Kevin offered little more. "I'd like to help you," he whined, "but I really don't know if I can. Give it until January, OK?" Then he wished me a Merry Christmas with a "God Bless" and murmured how sad it was that I had to celebrate the holiday under such circumstances.

I rushed to the airport to pick up my mother. Over the holidays, the choice between severing my ties with my psychiatrist, or living without a WCB pension—and without a job, if I refused to obey their orders—weighed heavily on my mind.

Loss of Separation
and
Air Traffic Control

As soon as the western business world resumed functioning after New Year's Day 1994, I instructed Shirley to demand that the Board clarify why they deemed my psychiatrist to be unacceptable, and what exactly they thought was achievable for me in terms of employment. Meanwhile, a WCB disability awards claim adjudicator noted, on January 5th, that I was "overly stubborn" in my refusal to engage in other than flight attendant employment, and that I had an excessive desire for control over my life. Evidence of this, he claimed, was clearly demonstrated by my perception that various WCB professionals were considered by me to be as distrustful, hostile and threatening.

His distaste for my intention to be in charge of my life may have arisen from his supposition that individuals who believe that they are in control of their lives can withstand enormous amounts of psychological pressures and will continue to fight for what they regard as their right. Those who view their circumstances as uncontrollable, on the other hand, will be overtaken by helplessness, decreased motivation, and depression, and finally cave in to the demands of others.[1]

Regardless, there was no doubt in his enlightened mind that appropriate counseling and proper claimant motivation would return me to top shape. Miss Katts was therefore instructed to establish a figure representing the maximum I could earn as a Spanish translator.

Furthermore, the adjudicator decreed that, because the May 1988 incident might have been a precipitating factor to the PTSD onset, but my restrictive employability and the psychological information on file supported the view that pre-existing personality traits and pre-morbid characteristics played an equal part in its development, NorAm would be granted a 50% relief of cost to the tune of $175,184.74. Meanwhile, aware that events beyond my control had taken place behind the scenes, I hovered in a chronic state of fight-or-flight readiness.[2]

On March 4th, I was informed that a Permanent Partial Disability pension of $770.68 in 1993 dollars had been awarded to me retroactive to November 22, 1993, and the adjudicator had reserved the Board's right to conduct health reviews whenever they desired.

The adjudicator arrived at this figure by determining that I was capable of working fifteen hours a week as a translator, if I sought appropriate counseling, which should earn me $1,630 a month. Because my pre-1988 earnings were said to have averaged $2,446.26 a month, a figure issued by my employer and deviating from my actual income by $500 monthly (a fact I had fought for years to rectify), it left WCB to pay $624.26 expressed in 1988 dollars.

Not amused, I called Shirley. She sorrowfully expressed powerlessness unless I consented to the WCB proposed psychotherapy, because the Board held to the position that therapy would enhance my employability.

I rang brother Kevin and asked, "The Workers' Assistance and the WCB are both government agencies. Can you tell me if my lawyer has the same firing power as the Board?" He assumed she had. "Tell me, then, is it part of my job to instruct and motivate her into action when I have no knowledge about legal procedures in general, and WCB procedures in particular?" He did not know. "But Kevin, nothing is being done unless I explicitly express the course of action I want her to pursue—and to do that constantly drains me of the little energy I have."

"That is regrettable."

"And what about NorAm profiting from my misfortune to the tune of $175,000?"

"Well. Those must be the rules," he said.

"Kevin, I need help with this. I want McCormick to fight the Board for me. Can you please, please, get him back for me?"

"No, I can't. You must contact the local national rep," he quipped, then wished me a "God Bless" and hung up.

My mother shook her head, a worried expression marring her features, and I said, "Don't worry, Mum. I know that sooner or later things will turn my way," and collapsed on the chesterfield, hoping that my health would last until that time dawned.

Later that day I instructed Shirley to demand that the Board clarify the basis from which they formulated enhanced employability if I sought alternate therapy. She, in turn, requested that I set out in writing—within one week—all errors and omissions in letters issued by Dr. Kowal and the disability adjudicator. Furthermore she wanted clarification about my school attendance, and in particular the justification why I felt incapable of engaging in a career as a translator .

"Why do you want that? It's a gargantuan undertaking!" I questioned.

"To prepare your appeal," she responded flippantly .

I did as she asked.

Dr. Kowal responded two weeks later. No focused, goal-oriented, cognitive-behavioral therapy with systematic desensitization or adequate psychotherapeutic treatment had been afforded me, and therefore I still suffered from PTSD. I concluded that she had lost her marbles. By stating that PTSD was a treatable condition in flight attendants when conventional mental health therapies were administered, Kowal, with an astounding flourish, declared ten Board (or Board-appointed), five NorAm (or NorAm-appointed), and three independent mental health professionals who had dealt with my case so far, to be incompetent charlatans.

However, it worked to her credit that my adamant refusal to participate in appropriate psychotherapeutic counseling was seen by this angel of mercy as a cause for mourning. If I but would participate in this counseling, she thought that my performance of a productive activity, at my own pace in the sanctuary of my low-stress and supportive home environment, would know no bounds—if I moved away from aircraft flight paths, of course. (I only lived twenty-five miles away from the airport.)

Admiring Kowal for her unwavering gracious intentions to save my troubled and distraught soul, I felt relieved to hear her announce that it was premature to declare "Miss Andersen unemployable for life without having her exhaust all existing treatment options, because Tanya was such a bright and educated woman." That Miss Andersen did not display the slightest inclination to watch the world go by while idly awaiting the call to kick the bucket appeared to have escaped her Eminence. That Miss Andersen had seldom been idle throughout her existence had also gone unnoticed. That Miss Andersen knew precisely how to productively engage herself in the future, however, did not merit valor, since Miss Andersen intended to return to her flight attendant profession. It was her birthright. Or at least that's how she saw it.

Those events coincided with a NorAm 747 engine exploding in mid-air, catching fire, and a DC9 engine exploding mid-air without erupting into flames. I knew crew on both planes. A mid-air collision between a US FC 103 and a transport plane—which resulted in an on-ground collision with a fully-loaded military transport plane—further threw me for a loop, since I had narrowly escaped such an occurrence in the spring of 1990.

LOSS OF SEPARATION

Early one evening in the Spring of 1990, we were heading to Orlando, Florida from St. John's, Newfoundland, more than ready for the customary crew get-together when returning to our point of origin at 2:00 A.M. To reach Orlando from the extreme east coast, one inevitably flies in the vicinity of Cape Canaveral, the U.S. launching facility, and Pensacola Air Force Base. Just after our Boeing 727 started to descend through a cloud cover, I heard a loud bang. I rushed from the front galley into the cabin to ask, "What was that?"

Some of the passengers on the left, noses glued to their windows, answered, "Jet just passed us." Other passengers could only stare at me too numb to move. I raced into the cockpit, where the pilots confirmed that an ascending fighter plane had zipped by us with less than 100 feet to spare. Such occurrences, termed "loss of separation," (incidents in which aircraft had collisions with objects, vehicles or aircraft or incidents in which separation criteria between aircraft were breached[3]) are frightfully frequent over the Atlantic Ocean and in North American skies.

Traffic over the North Atlantic, which is controlled by Gander Oceanic Control, has increased by over 30% in a very short period of time, escalating from 157,884 flights in 1988 to 223,992 in 1993. In that time, eighty-two "Risks of Collision" occurred, as did many other losses of separation that did not result in collision risks.[4] The annual average loss of separation incidents in Canadian skies between 1992 and 1996 was 158.[5] In 1996, there were 189 *reported* losses of separation, a 32% increase over 1995 and a 25% increase over the previous five year average.[6] A further increase was noted in 1997, where 224 loss of separation incidents were reported.[7] These incidents appear to occur because of air traffic controllers' increasingly heavy workloads—workloads that impede them from simultaneously and effectively monitoring traffic and verifying their work.[8]

After an Air Canada jet and a United Airlines plane experienced a near collision at La Guardia Airport in April 1998—only five to ten meters separation between the aircraft prevented a disaster—President Clinton decreed that air traffic controllers (ATCs) were to have two hours of refresher training to prevent future occurrences.[9]

To avoid near misses in the air and on the ground, it might be more appropriate and more effective to evaluate, and perhaps change, the ATCs' rapid rotation shift schedules used by most civilian and military air traffic facilities in the United states. These schedules have been designed to allow ATCs a decent social life, but are nonetheless taxing on their rest and recuperation abilities.

Apparently the rapid rotation shift system results in ATCs frequently carrying an acute sleep debt into the night shift, where they have little active work other than to sit in the dark at the nadir of their circadian rhythm. This could, researchers assert, jeopardize aircraft safety.[10] Falling asleep on duty, combined with increased confusion and fatigue levels, seems to be the consequence for military ATCs.[11] One could assume they differ little from their civilian colleagues. Indirect evidence that air traffic control errors are highest on the night shift appear to exist, but whether or not these errors are associated with controllers' shift work is as yet unclear.[12]

Perhaps substantially increased overall workloads for ATCs that have evolved during the recent decade, combined with rapid rotation shift schedules that never allows them to completely relax off duty, is the root of the problem. Within a very short period, these workplace factors would tax controllers' stress levels and attention spans to the limit, and create situations that can precipitate loss of separation disasters.

In non-radar-monitored environments, controllers maintain separation between aircraft by relying on position estimates provided by pilots, other controllers, and the Northern Airspace Display System (NADS), which uses computerized wind information. Controllers adjust these estimates as necessary to reflect the actual ground speed of aircraft. However, if the track of one aircraft is affected by a localized area of unusually strong upper level winds (or unusually slow ones), and another aircraft in the vicinity is not affected by either, and the NADS has not been updated to reflect the information but continues to calculate ground speed predictions on inaccurate forecast winds, aircraft end up on a collision course.[13]

Fortunately, the Traffic Alert and Collision Avoidance System (TCAS), installed in some jet liners, can alert pilots to conflicting traffic in their path. In 1994, thirty-five cases of TCAS alerts were reported in Canadian airspace alone. In ten out of twenty of those cases, a potential mid-air collision was avoided because pilots took evasive action. We can assume that air traffic controllers alerted the pilots in the other cases.

To avoid such situations to begin with, hiring and training additional ATCs would seem to be an obvious solution. Passengers and aircrew alike would find it soothing to know there are enough well rested and competent ATCs on the ground to assure safety in the heavens. I regret to say, however, that to employ more controllers is out of the question.

Why? It would be *cost inefficient* for the privately operated air navigation services, privately operated airports, and their shareholders.[15]

Because loss of separation in fully radarized surroundings appears to be just as frequent as in non-radarized areas, air traffic control, or the lack of it, was one of the aspects that pilots at a meeting of the International Federation of Air Line Pilots Associations in Montréal in April 1998, considered before publishing a list of the world's worst airports—Hong Kong and San Francisco among them.[16]

At larger airports such as these, loss of separation seems to occur more often during takeoff when overworked and fatigued controllers accidentally assign converging tracks to aircraft. Luckily, these too-close-for-comfort situations are often detected by vigilant aviators during their departure climbs.[17] But what happens when highly computerized aircraft takeoff and land in zero visibility or, as in our Orlando experience, clouds prohibit a clear view?

With the report of the loss of separation between the two military aircraft came the simultaneous news that one of our 747 captains had slipped off a tree branch, while taking photographs of a rock concert in London's Regent Park, and had impaled himself on the iron picket fence below. He had been found hanging there at 3 A.M. the following day. The compounding effect of these two incidents and WCB's "care giving" was severe enough for O'Doherty to open his practice for me on Saturday, March 26th, to help me regain some emotional equilibrium.

After another consultation with him two days later, I told Shirley that I had changed my mind and would now like her to inform the Board that alternate treatment with a mental health professional of their choice, who specialized in PTSD counseling and desensitization techniques, for the purpose of returning me to inflight duty had now become my choice. "And please," I asked her, "emphasize that O'Doherty unequivocally rejects seeing me while such treatment is ongoing. And also get their written assurance that when I've completed the full course of therapy, I have no further obligation to the Board, except to reassess for a pension. Please also tell them that I want full wage loss benefits during treatment." Shirley, appearing very disoriented and discontented, complied. I then waited with apprehension.

While I did so, I was entertained by a command from NorAm on April 11th to attend a meeting with management on the 13th. Far too ill and weak to pull myself together on short notice, I declined, suggesting that they again extend their cordial invitation the following week. They did—for April 29th.

Brother Tobias would be present, because brother Harry was on vacation. Too sick and worried to care, too weak to walk more than 300 yards to the closest ravine with the dogs, and my suspicions about my physical health overwhelming, I demanded to see *The Compendium of Pharmaceuticals* when I visited my GP on April 14th. Under the listing for *Ativan*, which is in the family of *lorazepam*, a *benzodiazepine*, I found:

> Adverse Effects: Drowsiness is the most frequently reported adverse effect. Other reported adverse effects are dizziness, weakness, fatigue and lethargy, disorientation, ataxia, anterograde amnesia, nausea, change in appetite, change in weight, depression, blurred vision and diplopia, psychomotor agitation, sleep disturbance, vomiting, sexual disturbance, headache, skin rashes, gastrointestinal, ear nose and throat, musculoskeletal and respiratory disturbances.
>
> Release of hostility and other paradoxical effects, such as irritability and excitability have occurred with benzodiazepines. In addition, hypotension, mental confusion, slurred speech, oversedation and abnormal liver and kidney function tests and hematocrit values have been reported with these drugs.... Dosage must be individualized and carefully titrated in order to avoid excessive sedation or mental and motor impairment.[18]

After reading this description, I decided to wean myself off it immediately. "But that'll give you the shakes," my GP warned.[19]

"So be it. Better that than dying a slow and gruesome death," I responded annoyed, went home and continued reading about Ativan's side effects from the photocopy I had made:

> Ativan, of the family of Lorazepam, a benzodiazepine with a short elimination half-life, has produced withdrawal symptoms after a brief period of administration as short as seven days. The most frequently reported symptoms in benzodiazepine withdrawal are rebound insomnia, anxiety, and tension. Others include muscle pain, tremors, agitation, restlessness, sweating, nausea, decreased performance, metallic taste, photophobia, hyperacuisis, and rarely, delusions. High sensitivity to sounds and visual stimuli can occur, as well as increased irritability and suspiciousness, alternating with a sense of elation.[20]

These were the bright prospects for my immediate future—but if that would be all, I could be grateful. Mother and I zipped to the liquor store and picked up two liters of port, and to the bookstore for a novel, and I went to bed, and stayed there reading, imbibing, and sleeping.

On Sunday, April 17th, I arose newborn. Taking Mother to the airport that afternoon for her return to Europe, we both knew that I was well on my way. The withdrawal symptoms never manifested, and I turned to herbal remedies to calm my senses.

The following day, after making just one phone call, I picked up the May 1988 accident report at the Canadian Aviation Safety Board office, and took it over to Annemarie's where we read it together. By the time my mother checked in that evening to announce her safe arrival, I was able to tell her about the 1988 accident and that the Boeing 727 engine had been defective before start-up. The explosion had been so volatile the debris had violently punctured the fuselage and ruined the aircraft's pressurization system.

News that WCB had raised its head on April 6th had reached me that same day by way of a copy of a letter from Dr. Kowal and an attached response from the Workers' Assistance lawyer. The psychologist, jubilant about my submission, invited me to choose between two mental health practitioners, one of each gender, and both, purportedly, knowledgeable "in the area" of PTSD.

Pointing out that "Ms. Andersen's motivation to actively participate in therapy would be a big factor in predicting the treatment outcome," the actual therapy goal had now been narrowed to reduce my anxiety-related problems since there certainly were many short term and intermediate goals which had to be accomplished before the flight issue could be approached in a therapeutic manner.

Shirley had responded in a "Slam-bang-thank-you-Ma'am—I'll-inform-my-client" fashion, which propelled me into an unprecedented fury. Lucky to reach her right away, I issued her the essential instructions: "First of all, I want you to find out if those two therapists are knowledgeable about PTSD *in flight attendants*, since every psychology student and his dog knows about general PTSD after the first semester. And then I want a statement from them—in writing—that I will be able to return to flying when I complete their treatment. I want that before I commit myself to anything.

Secondly, get Dr. Kowal's clarification for *Miss Andersen's motivation*. If treatment fails, she'll say I haven't been *motivated*, and I've lived through another trauma for nothing.

That detail, Shirley admitted, had escaped her attention.

"Then, thirdly, I want to know why there's a change of heart about the purpose of the exercise? Bernstein's intensive desensitization was for my return to flying, wasn't it? And see how gloriously screwed I was by that one!"

That had not crossed her mind, either.

"Next, I also want to know what Kowal means by short-term and intermediate goals, and how and why she thinks they developed in the first place!" I snarled, on the verge of a nervous breakdown. "And I want to know about my post-therapy obligation to the Board if therapy fails, and I want it in writing that they'll pay me full wage loss benefits during treatment," I raged. "I want all these points clarified—in writing—before I proceed any further!" I shouted, oblivious to phone etiquette.

"You can't do that! That's unreasonable!"

"Unreasonable?" I screamed in disbelief, "You say unreasonable? To hell it is! *They're* unreasonable, and I've had it. I want answers to my questions, and in writing!" I yelled.

"You'll never get that," she countered aggressively.

"Watch me. You willing to try?" She was.

Buzzing brother Kevin next, he only referred me to the local national rep—again. But, learning that the written word leads to less deception than the spoken one, I composed a lovely letter for this new representative, sister Fiona (Maynor had been fired on New Year's Eve). In it I outlined my situation and appealed for her to engage lawyer McCormick to battle against the Board in this precedent setting case—not only for my sake, but for the benefit of all other flight attendants who might end up in WCB's clutches for similar reasons.

Saluting her with a sentimental "In solidarity forever," and a postscript inquiring at what time the April 29th management meeting might take place, I sped the treasure to the union office on April 23rd, and forwarded copies of my epistle to the big union's president, and to brother Kevin. I then bought appropriate liquor to calm my nervous system and to celebrate a job well done, and called it a day.

On April 29th, Dr. Kowal responded to Shirley's inadequate composition. She said that the proposed therapy would be aimed at the alleviation of my emotional problems, and that "its effectiveness rested entirely on Miss Andersen's motivation, commitment, and honest effort." Expressing her heartfelt opinion that effective treatment was an overwhelmingly rewarding experience for the participant she cautioned, however, that "some initial uneasiness, discomfort, or anxiety might occur before inception." Asserting that the delightful expedition would afford me "short-term pain" with respect to the initiation of therapy, and "long-term-gain," Dr. Kowal appealed to Shirley to apply her persuasion and power to persuade me into "accepting this unique opportunity for professional assistance with my long standing problems so as to reduce my suffering." The Board, she said, would be awaiting notification of my readiness for the sublime initiation.

Meanwhile, the union conveyed to its membership that, on average, over one million cases of occupational injuries had been reported by Canadian Workers' Compensation Boards annually for the past ten years, and that the latest 1990 national statistics showed there were 1,127 work related deaths recognized by the Board. These statistics had inspired the Canadian Labor Congress to declare April 28th, as a national day of mourning in memory of those killed or injured on the job and those whose health had been undermined by work related illnesses.

The union missive proclaimed that because unfortunately so many flight attendants were incapacitated, and because we all knew someone in that situation, we were encouraged to participate in the day of mourning. I learned that the internationally recognized symbol for the day was a canary in a cage, an image derived from the 19th century coal miners' practice of carrying these little birds down the shafts because canaries would die when exposed to minute traces of gases or other airborne hazards, and give miners a chance to retreat before suffocating, I shed a few tears.

I had never been exposed to such moving rhetoric, so applicable to the flight attendant profession. An idea crossed my feeble mind. Why not take canaries along on duty, especially on long hauls? Then we could measure how long the little creatures lasted before kicking the bucket—which would probably be before the midway point. That there is something very much amiss with the air up there has been known to aircrew, aircraft manufacturers, and commercial carriers for a long time. And with canaries, flight attendants could prove it.

The only problem would be to figure out what to do when the creatures croaked. Force the captain to land?

Air Rage,
Air Quantity
and Quality

In 1990, Transport Canada, conducted a study "to determine the extent to which poor air quality exists [in aircraft], and to what extent it would affect cabin crews' ability to perform their safety-related duties." The study was initiated because the Confidential Aviation Safety Reporting Program (CASRP) had received several letters from flight attendants concerned about poor cabin air quality. After Transport Canada sampled the cabin air on one type of aircraft, the ministry reported that there were "potentially significant problems." Further tests would be conducted. But, alas, in February of 1992, the Transportation Safety Board of Canada (TSBC) was informed that, unfortunately, studies could not be conducted as originally planned.

Instead, Transport Canada, in concert with Labour Canada, would investigate specific air quality complaints only when a reported problem could not be resolved by the air carrier, their employees, and their safety and health committee.[1] And the Airline Division of CUPE (Canadian Union of Public Employees) asserted an investigation would only be launched "to confirm compliance with published air quality standards." But these standards, protested the flight attendants union, were inadequate because limits for exposure to toxins were too high, and ventilation standards too low for an aircraft environment.[2] Meanwhile, I discovered that no government air quality or quantity standards exist for cabin crew in North America—and therefore, there are no such standards for passengers either.

Because the atmosphere at 35,000 feet and minus 60⁰ Celsius does not sustain human life, aircraft must be pressurized, supplied with artificial oxygen, and employ air ventilation and filtration systems. These systems are normally operating at approximately 6000–8000 feet above sea level, depending on aircraft type and altitude. Until the early 80s, airplane systems supplied a 100% fresh air circulation to the cabins at about three minute intervals by pumping outside air through the engines' compressors into the aircraft and back outside through exhaust valves.[3]

Then the fuel crisis hit and fuel prices skyrocketed. Because compressed air diverted for ventilation was no longer necessary to provide engine thrust, and therefore engines were burning additional fuel to provide cabin air, aircraft engineers devised an air-intake system for all planes designed during and after that period, where up to 53% of cabin air passes through filters to blend with fresh outside air before it is re-injected into the cabins. This modification affected Boeing's 757, 767, newer versions of 737s and the 747, as well as McDonnell Douglas's MD80s and MDIIs, and the Airbus aircraft.[4]

The filters used to purify the air on most aircraft purportedly are capable of removing 90 to 95% of dust, bacteria, and viruses—but not gases and odors.[5] Newer filters, which are presently only installed on Boeing 777s and 747-400s, are said to remove up to 99.99% of airborne contaminants 0.5 microns or larger. How often these filters are changed is unknown. Manufactures' guidelines exist but, since the task of changing the filters is time consuming and therefore not cost-efficient, carriers appear to replace them at their convenience.[6]

The air provided to the cabins runs through ventilation loops called power packs. Most aircraft have two or more power packs, which can be individually turned on and adjusted by the pilots. In the aircraft, the configuration of the loop outlets depends on manufacturers' designs. In Airbus, for example, air conditioning divisions roughly correspond to the different class compartments. This configuration, according to the company, "is not a matter of ensuring first class air for first class passengers while providing third class air to the economy class, but is rather due to the fact that seat density varies."[7]

Pilots can adjust the air flow rate traveling from the power packs to the cabins. However, the cabin air circulation rate is also heavily influenced by aircraft type and speed. Because many planes slow down during longer flights to take advantage of jet streams which save fuel, cabin air intake is lower, and slower air circulation rates are the result.[8] The amount of oxygen provided to cabin occupants—low, medium, or high— depends entirely on an airline's generosity. In 1995 one carrier instructed its Airbus pilots to select HIGH only if flight attendants reported to the flight deck to complain about air deficiency.[9]

Boeing's chief spokesperson, Jack Gamble, clarified the issue in 1994: "Ventilation systems are driven by air that comes off the engines. If you cut back on the engine system, cut back on the speed, and therefore burn less fuel, you're going to cut back on the amount of air circulation in the cabin."[10] Consequently, whereas 100% fresh cabin air circulates about every three minutes through older aircraft manufactured before the 80s, newer aircraft provide half-fresh and half-recirculated air every six or seven minutes.[11] Farrol S. Kahn, the founder of the Aviation Health Institute, Oxford, England, estimated the rate of air exchange to reduce the cost of cooling the air to be every twelve minutes.[12] Needless to say, the less air circulation, the greater the reduction of oxygen to flight attendants and passengers.

In regulation JAR 25, the Joint European Aviation Authority requires that each crew compartment must be ventilated and have enough fresh air—no less than 10 cubic feet per minute (cfm) per crew member—to enable them to perform their duties without undue discomfort or fatigue. The US Federal Aviation Administration (FAA), on the other hand, in air worthiness regulation FAR 25.831 (November 1994) only stipulates that a minimum of 10 cfm of fresh air must be supplied to *cockpit crew*.[13] Because of FAA regulations, pilots have completely separate ventilation systems, which administer much higher volumes of 100% fresh air than that received by cabin crew and passengers. For them, the FAA *recommends* the luxurious amount of 5 cfm as "a minimum comfortable level under single [power] pack operation."[14] And research has proven that when calculating fresh air-intake, recycling, air circulation, and human carbon dioxide (CO_2) generation on-board, the cabin air provided inflight translates to *less* than 5 cfm per person.[15]

The Washington-based Academy of Sciences National Research Council measured less than 7 cfm in the high-density economy sections of full Boeing 747s during domestic runs. First and Business class passengers, however, received 30 to 50 cfm, and pilots inhaled the extravagant amount of about 150 cfm of 100% fresh air from their private system on the same trips. The American Society of Heating, Refrigeration and Air conditioning Engineers (ASHRAE), recommended fresh air changes of 20 cfm in enclosed spaces, though this was without specific reference to aircraft.[16] So, now you know. It's not your constitution unduly acting up when you leave the aircraft with a pounding headache and you're pooped for days and weeks after longer or shorter flights. Those ailments are graciously extended, invisible gifts from your courteous North American airline. Count yourself blessed if exhaustion and fatigue are all you suffer.

With its recommendation for a 5 cfm oxygen supply in aircraft cabins, the FAA has officially sanctioned airlines to limit the oxygen intake to the exact point where cabin crew and their charges in the back of the bus are barely coherent and conscious. Pilots, meanwhile, are frequently remunerated by employers for fuel efficiency.[17] Fresh as roses, but bored stiff during autopilot operation, they amuse themselves by calculating their financial gains derived from the sport of depriving flight attendants and customers of the air to breathe. In 1980, figures on how lucrative cabin air deprivation could be were provided by McDonnell Douglas to the major American airlines—American, Braniff, Continental, Delta, Northwest, Pan Am, Trans World, United—when the manufacturer reported that, by halving the fresh air intake and by using recycled air on its DC10s, around 62,000 gallons of fuel on that type of aircraft could be saved annually.[18] The industry embraced the concept with open arms.

Obviously there are drawbacks associated with oxygen deprivation—drawbacks with severe consequences. Passengers and cabin crew turn anoxic and/or hypoxic. With anoxemia, there is an abnormal decline in the oxygen content of the blood, and passengers become combative, hostile, and aggressive. With hypoxia, there is a deficiency in the amount of blood reaching body tissues, and people become apathetic or comatose. I believe it is for that reason the FAA recently implemented a policy that, on flights of four or more hours, emergency exits and evacuation procedures must be repeated to passengers before landing.

Both hypoxia and anoxia cause irreversible damage to body tissue, including the neurological system. In other words, on-board air deficiency and the lack of air quality causes permanent brain damage. How much impairment it causes can be gauged from the fact that psychologists, who have investigated ways to enhance mental functioning, found inhaling pure oxygen for a mere sixty seconds can double the number of words individuals can remember in test situations.[19] Obviously, the opposite effect takes place in aircraft cabins during flight. While most passengers will become subdued with hypoxia, there are those who, in an anoxic state, become dangerous for all those around them.

Unruly passenger behavior has reached such proportions that British airlines have urged parliamentarians to back a bill introduced in the upper house which would enable British police to prosecute travelers who attack fellow passengers (and often cabin crew) or get offensively drunk while on flights to Britain on foreign carriers. Presently, prosecutions are possible only when passengers enter the United Kingdom on a British registered airline.[20]

Carriers in other countries are also voicing their concern. Canadian Airlines International and Air Canada have broadened their definition of unruly passenger behavior to include sexually harassing attendants, causing disturbances, or violating anti-smoking rules. Both airlines have correlated this behavior to an increase in passenger loads over the past ten years—citing that, in most cases, alcohol is a contributing factor. As most professional flyers know, one drink at high altitudes has the impact of two or three on earth, but there is another factor that needs to be acknowledged. That factor is oxygen deprivation. Rather than exploring the possibility of increasing oxygen flow to passengers, the Canadian carriers' response has been to permit their cabin crews to literally handcuff their hostile charges.[21]

Japan Airlines (JAL) has followed suit. JAL recorded forty disturbances in 1996, up from fifteen in 1995. Between January and July 1997, fifteen violent incidents were reported. Their response? A recently introduced policy allows JAL's flight attendants to literally hog-tie passengers—and even to tape their mouths shut if they refuse to be quiet.[22]

American Airlines' cabin crews' complaints about passenger abuse rose from 30 in 1994 to almost 900 in 1995. On a non-stop flight from Paris to Miami in April 1996, one of their aircraft made an unscheduled landing in Boston, because of an on-board passenger–aircrew altercation. Two passengers were charged. The same airline sued another passenger on a Rio–US flight for misconduct based on the almost unthinkable act of defecating and urinating on a trolley.[23] Of course, these charges are unjustifiable, because it appears to be the carrier's air supply policy that caused passengers to act irrationally.

Nonetheless, sometimes charges are brought and fines are levied. For example, on a Los Angeles–New York flight, television evangelist Rev. Robert Schuller felt his needs were not being sufficiently met by flight attendants. Exploding into a rage, he violently shook a cabin crew member. The court fined him $1500, and required a courtroom apology. In another case, a flight attendant on a Paris–Boston run was choked and scratched by an out-of-control female passenger. The woman was fined $650.[24]

These cases, however, are the exceptions rather than the rule—most offenders are let off and court cases are all too rare. "Why is that?" one wonders. After all, when such draconian measures as gagging and hog-tying have been applied to subdue an individual, one should think the airlines would easily defend subsequent assault charges. Jerry McCann, Health and Safety chairperson of the Canadian Union of Public Employees' Airline Division, asserts international judicial systems do not view unruly passenger behavior as a serious crime.[25]

If that's the case, something better be done about it fast, because *air rage* incidents worldwide have increased 400% over the past three years. Flight attendants have been bitten, kicked, choked, scratched, slashed with broken bottles, threatened with having their hands cutoff, battered, punched, pushed, and otherwise assaulted while at work.[26] Physical assaults not withstanding, they also suffer verbal abuse commonly accompanying such incidents and they sustain emotional injuries when forced to deal with violent behavior, threats, and battering in the line of duty.

British Airways, the world's largest carrier, recorded 260 disruptive incidents in twelve months (ending April 1998). The carrier has encouraged that country' s parliamentarians to pass a law allowing the airline to ban unruly passengers from its flights (in addition to fines in British Courts of up to £5,000 or two years imprisonment, or both) for placing an aircraft at risk.[27]

North American carriers appear to be in an equally *encouraging* mode. Cliff Mackay, the Air Transport Association of Canada's president representing Canadian airlines stated that his association is trying to *encourage* the federal government to put an appropriate legal framework in place after having announced, "...whereas there are clearly defined international protocols for dealing with terrorism, there is no clearly defined convention [covering air rage]."[28]

Will any assistance to create such laws be forthcoming from North American flight attendants' unions? Not if we consider a comment made in a recent press interview by Denise Hill, president of the Airline Division of the Canadian Union of Public Employees (CUPE), representing Canada' s approximately 9000 flight attendants. "The [air rage] situation is frightening," she meekly squeaked.[29]

And really, are air rage laws a matter of some urgency? Not according to Mr. Mackay who purports, "Airlines move about one billion people a year, and such [air rage] incidents are an infinitesimally small proportion of that. At most, there are about half a dozen a year on Canadian airlines."[30] Mind you, Air Canada alone reported 41 disruptive incidents in eight months ending August 31, 1998. (The airline began tracking air rage incidents in November of 1997).[31]

Frankly, the industry would be entirely disinterested in air rage altercations, were it not for the fact that unscheduled or emergency landings often associated with such incidents reflect negatively on shareholders profits. Air rage incidents are not cost-efficient. Lobbying for laws protecting flight attendants from violent passenger outbursts is really not conducive to the bottom line. However, air crew and the flying public ought to be grateful that airlines are *encouraging* governments to take steps to punish on-board offenders. If such laws are passed, flyers in whatever capacity can rest more assuredly that neither their travel nor their off-duty plans will be unduly disrupted by delays incurred due to unforeseen violent human interactions in the sky.

Airlines steadfastly blame their non-smoking policy and passengers' excessive alcohol consumption for the increase in irrational and violent on-board behavior.[32] This is, however, most peculiar. It is particularly puzzling when we all know that smoking on aircraft has been banned on most carriers worldwide for at least the past five years and that, for many customers, drinking has always been a favorite preoccupation when journeying in the twilight zone. In past decades, drinking and smoking has rarely resulted in violent and irrational passenger outbursts.

This, then, begs the question: Has the public's psychological makeup changed so dramatically over the last three years as to provoke a 400% increase in irrational, violent and erratic behavior manifesting itself on-board aircraft? (Comparative studies are unavailable) Or is the air rage problem more insidious?

Ask yourself these questions. Is it possible that carriers know mid-air altercations blossom under deplorable air quantity and quality conditions and are unwilling to alter the inflight environment? Have they accepted the likelihood that under these conditions some individuals will slowly and surely lose it (especially when under the influence of alcohol)? How high is the probability that, given sufficient knowledge of the effects of oxygen deprivation, some of those passengers will sue, and the courts will find the airlines culpable? Are legislators on the side of the airlines? Has the airline industry shifted the responsibility and consequences of selected oxygen deprivation to passengers and cabin crews? The answers seem inexorably obvious.

For passengers, the impact of oxygen deficiency might not be of great significance because they are not exposed to this condition regularly. For flight attendants, however, who annually spend between 900 to a 1000 hours in an oxygen-deficient and polluted work environment for a period of years, the repercussions could be devastating. Whereas passengers can sue an airline for damaging their health—*if* they can prove it—flight attendants cannot. They cannot complain either, since labor laws across the land stipulate an employee can refuse to work in hazardous conditions, but also that the employer can fire the employee refusing to labor under those conditions if the conditions arise "from a situation where the risk is inherent in the employee's work or is a normal condition of work."[33]

Air carriers will do nothing to improve the inflight cabin air quality and quantity situation, unless passengers volunteer to pay higher ticket prices. Thus far, the issue has not arisen simply because customers are unaware of on-board oxygen deprivation and, when they are told, the paying public refuses to believe that North American airlines starve them of the air to breathe. But it's a fact. Dr. Andrew Horne of the FAA's Office of Aviation Medicine, acknowledged this fact in June 1993, when he so succinctly stated, "It's a trade-off. If you want to spend more money for fuel, then you get more outside air."[34]

In other words, if passengers agree to share the cost of fuel—in effect paying an "oxygen tax"—then carriers might consider allowing their pilots to increase oxygen flow rates. But don't bet on it, since air deprivation is such a simple and foolproof way to magnificently enhance the airlines' bottom line. Presently, it appears all possibilities for milking hidden profits from the aircraft oxygen supply and circulation system have been exploited—after all, some cabin ventilation has to occur.

This has never been demonstrated better than in April 1995 when South African Airways(SAA), cruising the skies en route to Johannesburg with 300 passengers and seventy-two flatulent pigs aboard a Boeing 747, was forced to return to London, England and make an emergency landing. [35] Livestock was carried in passenger compartments in the rear of this Combi aircraft. The little Babes had farted, urinated, and defecated with such jubilant efficiency they rendered the aircraft ventilation system unserviceable. The collective odor and body heat activated the aircraft cargo's halon fire extinguishers. Though the crew had access to the live-stock compartments and knew that they did not have an on-board fire, fifteen prize stud boars were asphyxiated. To my knowledge, discomfort for cabin crew and passengers on this flight has never been reported.

What happens to pigs will happen to humans if insufficient cabin ventilation takes place. People in the back of the plane will succumb to carbon dioxide (CO_2) poisoning, just one of the inflight contaminants greatly influencing flight attendants' and passengers' health and well-being on-board aircraft. Too many people and too little air lead to an excess of carbon dioxide. Carbon dioxide, a colorless and odorless gas, is a central nervous system depressant which slows responses and reduces alertness. Elevated CO_2 levels can cause feelings of stuffiness, drowsiness or claustrophobia and, with higher levels, lead to headache and depression. At extremely high levels, CO_2 results in loss of consciousness and death.[36]

In a study commissioned by the U.S. Department of Transportation, eighty-seven out of ninety-two flights showed carbon dioxide levels consistently jumping the acceptable boundaries of 1000 parts per million (ppm) set by the American Society of Heating, Refrigeration and Air Conditioning Engineers (ASHRAE), which considers air quality an indicator of *indoor* air quality. However, some researchers argue levels may need to be kept below 600 ppm to minimize sleepiness, fatigue, poor concentration, and stuffiness.[37]

In 1993, when Airbus and Air Canada jointly conducted a carbon dioxide study on Airbus' 320, carbon dioxide levels of 800 to 2300 ppm were measured front to back in the cabin areas, to reach the dazzling height of between 5200 and 9000 ppm in the aft galley.[38] Despite such findings, which are probably not unique in the industry, the FAA proposes a ceiling of 5000 ppm, since the airlines maintain "average CO_2 levels were below the federal occupational standard, which requires that workers, on earth, be exposed to an average of no more than 5000 ppm over the course of a work week."[39] That means 1000 ppm per work day for earthbound employees. For flight attendants, it means up to 9000 ppm for up to seventeen or more hours in one setting.

The 747s, L-1011s and 767s inaugurated the airlines' cost-efficient trend of passenger and cabin crew oxygen deprivation. They let the paying and working people deal with the fluctuating carbon dioxide level increases, depending on where they work or slumber, McDonnell Douglas' MD80 series, the newest addition of environmentally "sick" planes, appears to be an exceptional wonder bred to industry's money making adventures.

After hundreds of Alaska Air cabin personnel bitterly complained about the on-board breathing conditions, the US National Institute of Occupational Health and Safety finally consented to study the inflight air quality in February 1992. Carbon dioxide levels of 4882 ppm were found, but the data was declared invalid and the causes of flight attendants' complaints that CO_2 exposure was responsible for their light-headedness, dizziness, headaches and nausea were deemed "undetermined." Thus the underlying theme of the study trivialized the complaints and insinuated it was all in cabin crews' airy, feeble little heads.[40]

What about passengers, one might ask? An Airbus spokesperson pipes up, "Whatever the passenger wants, he gets—sooner or later, [and] stale air, at least, has offered no cause for passenger complaint for a long time."[41] That, of course, is purely due to the fact that the human psyche refuses to fathom that airlines knowingly and willfully expose both their customers and flight attendants to such unconscionable mid-air conditions.

Ozone is another commodity to be reckoned with on aircraft inflight. Since cabin ventilation derives from the compression section of the plane's engines, in which the air is raised to extremely high temperatures, the ozone molecules would normally decompose. Depending on the aircraft type, however, the length of time the air remains at such high temperatures is usually too short to complete the ozone decomposition process, and a relatively high concentration finds its way into aircraft cabins.[42]

To my knowledge, the only ozone study publicly available was conducted on the March 24–25th, 1977 Toronto–Amsterdam DC10-30 KLM Royal Dutch Airline flight. Researchers measured cabin air ozone levels during the journey and the readings revealed 70% of the ambient ozone concentration entered the cabin through the ventilation system, and about 50% of this concentration hovered around 1.20m (or approximately four feet) above the cabin floor. For about half of the total flying time, the ozone level exceeded 200 parts per billion (ppb) by volume, with peak concentrations of about 600 ppb. Levels of 80–100 ppb are acceptable in most International Aviation Transportation Association (IATA) countries. Whereas the ozone levels on the KLM flight might be considered unfavorable, the researchers asserted that concentrations on other routes, particularly routes across the North Pole during spring and autumn, are probably even higher.[43]

Research into the ozone levels was conducted in cooperation with KLM's Medical Department. Both KLM and the researchers asked the aviation industry to heed warnings of high ozone levels, and to demand aircraft manufacturers construct ventilation systems which could ensure the cabin air ozone concentration would not exceed levels of between 80–100 ppb. Furthermore, air carriers were asked to use aircrew medical files to obtain a deeper insight into the effects of ozone on health.[44] Nothing has been heard on the topic since. What is certain is the perpetual depletion of the earth's ozone layer, and the extended exposure to dangerous levels of ozone concentrations within aircraft inflight, affects the health of the sky's workers. Like coal miners toiling miles below the earth, flight attendants, toiling miles above it, not only depend on the integrity of an artificial air supply system, they have a right to it!

Carbon monoxide and radiation levels are also considered substantial health risks when circumventing the globe in a sardine can. Carbon monoxide, a colorless, odorless, and tasteless gas, is a by-product of incomplete combustion. It is present in high concentrations in the exhaust gas of reciprocating engines, and is absorbed exclusively through the lungs. Hemoglobin, the component of blood that carries oxygen, absorbs carbon monoxide 210 times more readily than oxygen. Carbon monoxide in the blood can cause severe hypoxia. Symptoms are fatigue, nausea, disorientation, irritability, poor motor skills, reduced peripheral vision, and erratic decision making. Death occurs at 60% blood saturation, but levels between 30% to 50% can also be fatal.[45]

Add to that a few loads of plutonium and radioactive material, which is regularly shipped in cargo worldwide, and it doesn't seem far fetched that flight attendants themselves believe they receive radiation doses equivalent to one x-ray on every long haul. Of course, no empirical evidence has been gathered on human exposure to these invisible and silent threats, and governmental agencies consistently refuse to take regulatory action concerning on-board aircraft radiation, ozone, carbon monoxide or carbon dioxide issues.[46] And why should they, when it is hard for the average layperson to understand, let alone to prove, the presence of these dangerous substances?

When bells and whistles go off in the flight deck due to carbon dioxide-activated fire extinguishers, as in the SAA swine affair, we know something is amiss. But to gather evidence that nausea, eye and nose irritation, dizziness, headaches, shortness of breath, tightness in the chest, sudden fatigue, ringing in ears, loss of equilibrium, sinus pain, heart palpitations, blurred vision, dizziness, prolonged nose congestion, nose bleeds and emotional irritability are directly related to quantity and quality of air within the aircraft is not easy. Proving the circulation rate of carbon dioxide and carbon monoxide—both microbiological aerosols—and the ozone-laden cabin air is the cause for such impairments and overall discomfort is another problem. But Transport Canada's Consolidated Regulation, Aviation Occupational Health and Safety Department, after giving it sincere thought, provided the following guidelines on how to accomplish the task:

> Where there is a likelihood that the safety or health of an employee on an aircraft is or may be endangered by exposure to a hazardous substance, the employer shall, without delay, appoint a qualified person to carry out the investigation and notify the safety and health committee or the safety and health representative, if either exists, of the proposed investigation and of the name of the qualified person appointed to carry out that investigation and the following criteria shall be taken into consideration: the chemical, biological and physical properties of the hazardous substance; the routes of exposure to the hazardous substance; the effects on health and safety of the hazardous substance; the state, concentration and quantity of the hazardous substance handled; the manner in which the hazardous substance is handled; the contra methods used to eliminate or reduce exposure; and the value, percentage or level of the hazardous substance to which an employee is likely to be exposed.[47]

Now let's analyze this piece of prose in detail by applying it to a hypothetical situation. We are onboard aircraft flying at between 35,000 and 42,000 feet, most likely the higher altitude since it is cheaper. Flight attendants have reached the suffering stage. Most passengers are blessedly comatose. The anoxics have been handcuffed. Then the smoker on the crew, deprived of the habit in the air, but used to oxygen deprivation and therefore more coherent than the rest,[48] says "I've had it. Let's test the air." The pilots, after much argument with the flight attendant, establish satellite communication with company management, and permission to proceed with the air testing procedure is reluctantly granted. Then the flight attendant notifies the union's health and safety representative, who happens to be vacationing in Timbuktu. In our wondrous world of technology, this minor inconvenience is successfully overcome with a satellite link. Thereafter, our dedicated crew member hunts for, and finds, a qualified person, a biochemist or the like, among the vaguely alert, who is willing to conduct the analysis. Then the crew member searches and finds a container, and catches some cabin air. After it has been analyzed for its chemical, biological, and physical properties, and after having reported the data to the health and safety representative by satellite communication, the crew member transcribes the required report as it is dictated by the scientist—while both combat hypoxia.

But the story doesn't end there. After the eagle has landed, the container with the offensive and hazardous substance, together with the report, are presented to the appropriate government authorities and airline management waiting on the loading bridge. Both are gleeful, knowing there is absolutely nothing in the container to prove that toxins contaminated the aircraft cabin air. All that remains is the kerosene-loaded tarmac air.

It is this impossibility to transport inflight air from planes to the ground which enables airlines to provide seriously substandard air to flight attendants and the traveling public, and the record proves that neither the FAA nor Transport Canada intend to change this. Officially, the FAA has conducted only one air quality–quantity study, and the aviation regulation directorate of Transport Canada intends to implement a policy of carrier self-policing because, they claim, "resource constraints that are being exacerbated by the effects of inflation" have kept the government from legislating and enforcing laws governing air quality and quantity.[49]

Even if an inspection were scheduled by either of those agencies to monitor the breathing comfort of creatures traveling in the back of the plane, carriers would receive ample notice to enable them to instruct pilots to run all power packs on full capacity and to fly at increased speed.

Airflow would circulate at the highest velocity, and create as delightful an air quality as the top of Whistler mountain on a sunny April morning. Afterward, the glowing report issued by the appointed government official would prove flight attendants' health concerns are trivial, caused by an innate impairment of their minds. Because passengers are largely ignorant about the symptoms of air deprivation and unlikely to demand such testing, the issue would not arise from that quarter and the airline would be safe from another inspection for the next twenty years. The carrier's profit bonanza would continue undisturbed.

To imagine an employer is starving his employees of the air to breathe, and that co-workers participate in this duplicity, appears too irrational, illogical, ludicrous and quixotic for anyone to harbor. It is, therefore, not surprising that the FAA admits to only receiving about sixteen complaints annually on health issues related to air travel. Equally unsurprising is the April, 1994 statement by Robert Greenslade, spokesperson for the National Transportation Agency, confirming written complaints concerning health were "few and far between," and were all related to smoking.[50] Mr. Greenslade failed to acknowledge that the measurement of Environmental Tobacco Smoke (ETS) in aircraft cabins is not high enough to result in the kinds of health complaints most frequently made by flight attendants. Such symptoms are much more likely to result from elevated ozone levels, abnormally low relative humidity, and possibly due to factors such as kerosene, fuel vapors, aldehydes, or polynuclear aromatics, bacteria, fungi, and viruses.[51]

Therefore, if you thought you had to abstain from smoking because of carriers' benevolent concern for your health, and because flight attendants complained bitterly about the threat to their precious constitution because you puffed away with a vengeance, think again. First of all, cabin crew, rather than the carrier, could be blamed for the no smoking policy when you grumbled about being forced to skip the habit while on-board. Second, the employer—for once listening to staff demands—could rationalize hiking their profit margin to wondrous levels, since ceasing smoke production allowed them to decrease the oxygen supply to a preposterous amount hitherto imagined only in their most joyous dreams.

The airlines recently settled a $5 billion class action suit based on the effects of second-hand smoke and filed by 60,000 current and former American flight attendants, most of whom suffering from respiratory problems or lung cancer. The case went to trial in Miami in 1997,[52] and was settled out of court for $300 million payable over three years. [53]

Peanuts!—when we consider what consequences a thorough investigation of mid-air quality and quantity, and their attendant physical and psychological effects on humans, would have for the industry.

Joseph Hopkins of United Airlines asserted, just as had Greenslade, that a "statistically insignificant" number of its 430 million passengers filed formal complaints in June 1993. And USAir's David Shipley happily joined the chorus: "We have worked with the FAA over the years to improve air cabin quality, and do not think we have any problems specific to USAir or the type of aircraft we fly."[54] He got that right. The problem is generic for all North American carriers. And one of them, Air Canada, reported on-board medical incidents skyrocketed from a meager 221 in 1982, to 784 in 1992, (down from a whopping 924 in 1984 and 929 in 1988).[55] These figures exclude flight attendants and the two to eleven annual inflight deaths. Knowing that it takes one very ill passenger before cabin crew will fill out a time-consuming report, the numbers give pause to wonder. Overall airline load figures—the numbers of passengers carried—are not mentioned in relation to the on-board medical incident reports, but it can reasonably be assumed they have not increased by over 350% during the past ten years.

Without doubt, these numbers are similar to those experienced by all other North American carriers, and I believe their increase is directly attributable to the on-board environment. But neither the FAA nor the Air Transportation Association (ATA), which represents the major airlines, compile data on passenger complaints related to air quality and quantity in aircraft cabins.[56] Moreover, the vast majority of passengers never consider dismal on-board air conditions are the culprit for their inflight and post-flight ailments.

Air Canada's spokesperson, Ronald White, and American Airline's medical director, Jeffrey R. Davis, both jubilantly proclaim, that the air is generally better on an inflight aircraft than in North American office buildings.[57] Such a comforting thought when stuck at 40,000 feet in an aluminum tube for a ten to seventeen hour flight with a population density that makes high-rises look like a supermarket crowd at midnight. Still, it doesn't take a rocket scientist to recognize that the peculiar ill-health symptoms office workers complain about are remarkably similar to those experienced by flight attendants and passengers. Recent studies have shown office staff's impairments are frequently attributable to insufficient air changes in the buildings, insufficient makeup air from the outside, and poorly maintained filtration and humidification systems.[58]

"But what happens to flight attendants? They are up there so often," you might wonder. Save your breath. The airlines don't worry about them, so why should you? "The pilots?" you ask. Oh, don't worry about them, either. Except if you're concerned about their consciences. As you know, they have their own, separately oxygen-drenched kennel and most of them could care less about passengers and flight attendants' well-being. It must, in all fairness, however, be acknowledged that, even if a captain were to be moved with such compassion for the oxygen-deprived creatures in third class and turned on all power packs to HIGH, it would be feeble-minded of him or her. Not only would this act of humanity cost the bonus, he or she would be hauled in front of superiors at such lightning speed, one would only see a shadow flying by.

In our society, it is a criminal offense to willfully and knowingly endanger another person's life and health. It is a law ignominiously and routinely ignored by carriers and cockpit crews alike. To the cockpit crew, the word AIR is like a red flag to a bull. Even at happy hour, when the word is mentioned, they squirm like worms in grass on a warm rainy day, and no information about air quality or quantity can be pried out of them. If cabin crew complain mid-air to the pilots about feeling ill, the pilots respond by quickly narrowing the reasons for flight attendants' discomfort down to a short, but snappy list, a litany they often repeat: it's our vivid imaginations, our menstrual flow, menopause, party habits, marital or love problems, female hypersensitivity, briefly flying through ozone layers, the onset of food poisoning, the flu, and everything else imaginable—except the lack of oxygen and massive air pollution in the cabins.

When I broached the topic with an Airbus 320 captain hanging out in my gym, he arrogantly quipped, "Well, we need more air than you guys, 'cause we gotta think, you know," and then launched into a complaint about having made four trips after a six-week vacation resulting in his suffering a 40% performance deficiency. I refrained from inquiring what kind of performance he referred to, but wondered what a cabin crew's deficiency level would be after just one trip. But, I thought at the time, better not find out. Denial is still the best armor.

When the Airline Division of CUPE (Canadian Union of Public Employees) surveyed 291 flight attendants—a ridiculously low proportion of the approximately 9000 employed by Canadian carriers—they found 70%, of participants complained about problems associated with cabin air quality. In January 1994, the union submitted "summary results" of this survey to the then Minister of Transport, Doug Young.[59] It barely received a shrug of his shoulders, and the Air Transport

Association of Canada, representing the industry, rejected it with a snide though courteous, "Pure garbage."[60]

When Mr. Sinclair from the industry association was approached by the press about the union's assertions that the air quality problems were caused partly by aircraft flying at higher altitudes and partly by pilots turning off the air circulation equipment to save fuel costs, he enthusiastically countered: "Turning off the air circulation equipment would result in 'negligible savings'." He supported this statement by adding Canadian Transport Department officials dropped plans for an air quality study in 1992 after the industry referred them to several exhaustive US studies that purportedly found no such problems. (In fact, I discovered no published studies, other than those mentioned in this chapter.) Then Mr. Sinclair asserted without malice and apparently without forethought, that flight attendants suffered from jet lag due to changes in their eating, drinking and sleeping habits, and not because of the quantity and quality of air onboard aircraft. He finished with aplomb, "Sometimes you come to work and you don't feel that great!"[61] Once again, people like Sinclair weren't listening or chose not to listen to flight attendants such as Fidel Gonzales, from United Airlines, who publicly contended cabin crew are so affected by on-board air quality and quantity that "Some have been so sick they could not take the next flight."[62]

An investigative study on hygienic conditions for crew and passengers aboard Boeing 737s, 757s, 767s and McDonnell Douglas MD82 aircraft conducted by the Chinese Institute of Civil Aeromedicine in Beijing demonstrated there is absolutely no physical rationalization for our despicable working conditions, or for passengers who are paying to suffer. The Chinese researchers found the fleet had average on-board temperatures of 22.7^0 Celsius with a relative humidity of 28.1%. Contrast this with the average humidity on-board North American carriers which hovers between zero and 11% even though ASHRAE recommends 25–60%. In the Chinese study, carbon dioxide levels were 1326 mg/m 3, or approximately 400 ppm, and lower on the flight deck. You will recall, of course, the FAA proposed a ceiling of 5000 ppm.[63]

These results prove it is not the aircraft which cannot supply adequate air quality, quantity, and humidity to provide for a healthy work environment for flight attendants. It is only airlines motivated by their greed for profits that prevent it.

In January 1997, the Aerospace Medical Association begs to differ with such an assertion, stating fair and square that the "so-called" cabin air problem was most likely related to "hypoxia, decreased barometric pressure, crowding, inactivity, temperature control, jet lag, noise, three dimensional motion, fear, stress, individual health, alcohol, etc." That symptoms such as headaches, light headedness, fatigue, etc. were nonspecific, purportedly further complicates the situation. *All* possible causes needed to be looked at before discarding any, the writer soothingly assures. [64] That's comforting to know, because it might mean that passengers' and cabin crews' inflight health problems are, perhaps, unrelated to their individual psychological instability and fragile physical condition, as is presently being asserted.

While industry looks at *all possible causes* (which will take them eons), it might be a good idea for flight attendants to intermittently and throughout every single flight, don oxygen masks and tanks for breathing comfort, using the on-board equipment which, according to government regulations, has to be refilled and the masks sterilized when partially depleted. By doing so, cabin crew would not only protect their own health but, by raising customers' awareness about the abysmal cabin air, provide an immense service to the flying public. Such *modus operandi* should entice North American carriers to increase cabin air quantity, if not quality, with lightning speed.

But there is an even better solution. Legislate and implement government regulations for aircraft monitoring devices to provide readings on oxygen content, ozone levels, levels of microbiological aerosols, carbon dioxide, carbon monoxide, and radiation levels, as well as cabin temperature and humidity. The monitors must be installed on all commercial aircraft and sealed so as not be tampered with. Such devices already exist and are widely used in galleries, museums and other environmentally sensitive industries. This technology is not particularly expensive and, at the very least, the monitors would be a cheap way to ascertain that flight attendants and passengers are at least alert if the unthinkable should happen.

To accuse carriers of knowingly and willfully endangering customers and flight attendants' health and well-being by consistently denying them sufficient quantities of oxygen might seem preposterous. But it has a long history. The air-deprivation bonanza actually began with the DC8s in the 1960s and 70s, when usually only two of the three power packs were turned on. With the introduction of Boeing's 747-200s in the early 70s, the airline industry turned a blind eye to a corresponding era of passenger and cabin crew complaints about chest pains, breathing difficulties, eye irritation, and coughing spells. With the inauguration of Lockheed's 1011-100, the elderly and frail fell ill by the dozens during long hauls. Upon the introduction of Boeing's 767, the fit and healthy joined the ranks of the habitually ill airline passenger, whereas the older and feeble sat almost comatose.

Nowadays, the art of air quality and quantity manipulation is so sophisticated as to graciously allow customers enough oxygen, for a couple of hours after takeoff at most, to enable them to maneuver their cutlery, and find their mouths during supper. After they are watered and fed, they are put gently to rest by cutting down the oxygen. Roughly one hour prior to landing—one and a half if they're lucky—the re-activation process commences with a few vigorous blasts of air to enable everyone to walk, instead of crawl or be wheelchaired off board. It all makes marvelous sense, since the trip is energy efficient for all. Passengers' breathing slows down considerably when comatose, thus, air intake and carbon dioxide output is reduced. The air overflow is breathed by flight attendants, thus enhancing chances to maintain some mental coherence and physical mobility. And carriers increase their profits without being forced to hike ticket prices in the cutthroat marketplace. Yes, it's a win-win situation for everyone involved.

Circadian Rhythm Disturbance and Aircrew Duty Times

While WCB awaited my notification of readiness for their proposed treatment, the union and airline management engaged me in their customary merry-go-round farce. Brother Tobias was replaced by Harry for the April 29th, meeting; he then switched places. Dates, times, and locations were changed at random before all the players agreed to meet at NorAm's medical building at 11 A.M. on May 6th. Sister Fiona took the opportunity to courier a letter to me early that morning. It contained the news that the flight attendant union's national president deemed an extension of further legal assistance to sister Andersen's worthy cause impossible due to a shortage of funds. My request, however, had been directed to brother Kevin for consideration.

Punctuality being the courtesy of kings, only Annemarie, with two of her kids, was on time. Tobias and Fiona, the latter a mountain of flesh with multi-colored talons, showed up half an hour late and Davis, the human resource manager and the only one representing NorAm, arrived ninety minutes late. But the waiting time was a joyous one, because flight attendants taking emergency training sessions in the same building gave me cordial hugs and so energized me that I beamed like a beacon when the meeting began.

Davis, without hesitation and little apology, burped, "You know you've been restricted permanently from flying, don't you?"

"Yes. I do," I answered politely, gazing at him attentively.

"That means you'll never work as a flight attendant again. You agree?"

"No. I don't," I replied gently.

Annemarie broke the deafening silence. "Tanya has been assessed by several mental health professionals as *may* never fly again, and not that she would *never* fly again."

"Well, it's not likely she'll return to work in the foreseeable future. If she's able, she should go on rehab now," Davis said, adding, when no one uttered a word, "If she can't do that she should look at the grounded retirement pension or apply for IMMS."

"Which means?" Annemarie interjected.

"Inability to Meet Medical Standards. She can take a leave of absence without pay for twelve months and then we'll review her case."

"No, that's wrong," Tobias piped up, "It's thirty-six months," and they haggled about that for a while before deciding to check the collective agreement for accurate time limits.

"Regardless," Davis said, "we'll only cover your benefits if you prepay your group insurance and sign the IMMS form. And there's no alternate employment available. So, your best bet is grounded retirement. You'll get about $800 a month."

Silently I thought, "Their f...ing engine exploded in my face. They get $175,000. And I'm to be thrown on the garbage heap? Over my dead body." The union requested ten minutes in camera to discuss the proposal.

"I'm not signing the IMMS," I said the second that Davis had shut the door behind him. "That would be signing my death warrant because they'll fire me if I'm not flying in twelve or thirty-six months, whatever the case may be. And, tell me, why wasn't I told about the retirement pension half a year ago when my WCB pension was activated? I've just lost $5000 bucks, if I wanted to retire, haven't I? It's non-retroactive, isn't it?"

No, it was not, was the union's concerned response, and I would surely go on losing it if I did not retire.

"Doesn't really matter. I'm not accepting any of this. They want to get rid of me for $800. They offer people of my seniority $40,000 plus $800 a month in pension if they are healthy and willing to retire—so the bottom line is that I'm being punished for working on a defective aircraft. And they don't want to pay for my insurance because I'm on a $775 WCB pension? They must be joking, or belong in an asylum. This is totally unethical, and I will not accept it. The system's got to change."

I was so thoroughly annoyed that I instructed the union representatives, "Tell him we can talk again once the appeal is settled, and that they ought to be ashamed of themselves for hauling me in for such a ludicrous farce!" I said, intending not to utter another word in Davis' presence.

When he rejoined us, however, he addressed me directly. "You don't necessarily have to do flight attendant rehab—but if you choose alternate employment you'd probably have to go to Toronto or Montréal." At that precise moment Juliana, Annemarie's youngest, gurgled in his ear. Feeling ridiculed, and becoming increasingly annoyed, disinterested and tired of the shenanigans, I pointed out to Davis that none of this would have been necessary if I had been monitored between 1989 and 1990.

Sister Fiona, sensing my increasing passion for an altercation, jumped in. "We'll look at the options and let you know." Davis promised to maintain the status quo until the appeal decision was known.

"That's fine. Let's *all* wait until it's settled, then," I quipped before exiting, tired of Davis' presence and knowing from my WCB file that the airline intended to play a very active role in the appeal procedure.

"So, what do you think?" I asked Annemarie out of the union rep's earshot and after Davis's departure.

"He was playing poker!"

"Yeah, that's what I thought, too. And we called his bluff!" I replied, grinning from ear to ear.

Before she left to fetch her older children from school, she handed me a book. "Read it. The guy lived what you're living. Just in a different way," and she sped off.

Sister Fiona joined me, browsed through my file for a while, and, turning toward me with a peculiar look of unspeakable astonishment on her face, burst out with, "Your claim is justified! I'll do the best I can."

By May 13th, the lawyer McCormick had been retained for me. A week later, he initiated procedures for a WCB managerial review of my pension assessment.

Meanwhile, I read Annemarie's book *Good Bye To All That* by Robert Graves, in which the author describes his life as a young British officer in the French trenches during W.W.I. After the slaughter had ceased, he returned home, sick with PTSD—or *shell shock* as it was called then—an ailment officially unrecognized by the War Office. Without financial government support and surrounded by family and friends equally callous and ignorant, he left his wife and children after twelve years of endless struggles and started to rebuild his life on the island of Majorca as a writer. *Good-bye to All That*, his first work, had a magical "get away from it all" effect on me. I booked passage on the SS *Universe*, destined to depart on a fourteen-day round trip Alaskan cruise on July 3rd—without cancellation insurance. Determined to make the journey, I made the arrangements despite NorAm's refusal to issue me a letter of employment so that I could get an airline discount.

On June 2nd the WCB Review Board informed McCormick and me that the therapeutic treatment proposed by their psychology department would assure my capability to work as a translator. Therefore, no long-term loss of earnings would result and no grounds would exist for reviewing my disability pension award percentage.

With this news, I suffered a full-fledged stress attack. Annemarie responded to my lamentations with a firm, "You cool it. You've two lawyers working for you now. Distance yourself. Think of Alaska." So I did. Until June 10th, that is, when McCormick rang, singing how marvelous, exciting, beneficial, and enjoyable WCB's proposed therapy would be for me.

"I will not take any treatment until both psychologists have signed a statement that they'll cure me and that I'll return to flying, because otherwise, it's all speculation and mind manipulation. Cavarro has now been asked to comment whether or not treatment will produce significant improvement within twelve months. Dr. Kowal already responded by saying that the time frame is indeterminable—and she's Cavarro's superior. You think she's gonna disagree? 'Til donkeys fly. I specified my demands on March 27th, and I'm still waiting for answers from Kowal and the adjudicator," I shouted, at the boiling point.

"Forget them. They're not important," McCormick responded. "She should have kept her mouth shut anyway. Doesn't have a clue what she's talking about."

"*Not a clue what she's talking about?* Why the hell is she on the list of psychologists recommended to treat me, then?" I screamed at the top of my lungs.

"Well, I don't know. But I'm doing this to save the Board face."

"*Face?* Save *the Board's* face?" I yelled, "I'll not endanger my health any further to save the Board's face. What if I end up in a mental institution? Will that save the Board's face? Or is that's what they want? I know by now they're devious and diabolical—and it's amazing that I'm still amazed about it! And I refuse to have my head examined by another one of their hired guns. I want guarantees that I'll be cured, and not simply be exposed to someone who's merely "knowledgeable" about PTSD," I shouted full force. "For heaven's sake. Every student of psychology is knowledgeable about PTSD after the first semester. You and I are knowledgeable about PTSD..."

"No," he interrupted, "I'm not. I haven't experienced it and therefore..."

"Ain't *that* charming. And I'm living it and therefore I'm not knowledgeable either. Isn't that so?" I screamed out of control. Then I began to cry.

"Forget the letter. Forget everything I said. Just calm down, will you, please?" he pleaded.

"If you want to know what it's like to live as I have over the past four years, call my friend Annemarie. She'll give you an objective opinion. She's lived this with me," I suggested, sobbing uncontrollably.

"I'll do that. And please, try not to worry. I'll go ahead with the managerial review," he said before hanging up.

It took me a while to regain my bearings. Incessantly trying to outguess my opponents' next move and preparing for counter attacks somehow got me back on my feet. On June 21st, I met with Dr. Walton, one of the world's foremost independent aircraft accident investigators who, after reading the Safety Board report, said, "You've here everything you need to prove that the engine was damaged before start-up that day. But try to get the metallurgist report—just out of curiosity." I was so excited about his analysis, I felt like hugging him, but I dug out my wallet instead. "No, no! Put that away!" he stopped me before I could open it, adding while getting up to leave, "You can't afford my wages. If you need me in court, call!"

After flying to Annemarie's on cloud nine to share his verdict, I began to pursue the release of the metallurgy lab report, but it had been carried out by NorAm, and they refused to even consider releasing it unless they were told who requested it.

My last call in the month of June went to the wage indemnity broker to inquire how my long-term disability pension was coming along. They said they were investigating my utterly bizarre case, and with that news, I braced myself for their investigation to go on to eternity—which would only serve to increase the insurer's profit margins.

With each blow and disappointment, my enthusiasm for traveling to Alaska faded, and I soon reached the point that the thought of going anywhere made me shiver. I picked up the pieces of my broken existence, however, and a day before the journey, packed a suitcase. Annemarie insisted on picking me up the next morning, July 3rd—even though she would be coming in from a long haul the night before, and would suffer from the enormous time change and its inherent circadian rhythm upheaval.

CIRCADIAN RHYTHM INTERFERENCE

Most people in the Western World are familiar with the issue of *jet lag,* the term given to the condition of being "out of sync" with the local time after having flown through several time zones. Research has revealed that this phenomenon is caused by circadian rhythm disturbance result-ing in physiological stressors such as decreased mental alertness, inter-ruption in visceral and glandular activity, variations in pulse rate and temperature, and sleep problems.

Anecdotal reports suggest that sleep deprivation and fatigue are com-mon in aircrew of all ages, and that dangerous levels of fatigue can be produced by exposure to cockpit noise and vibration, day-to-day stress, lengthy flights, irregular work schedules, circadian disruptions, and inadequate amounts of sleep. All of these factors can compromise an aviator's performances and result in impaired vigilance, judgment, situa-tional awareness, and crew coordination.[1]

Age and personality seem to be precipitating factors to circadian rhythm disturbances and its effects. Extroverted and neurotic people are said to adapt more rapidly to time changes—regardless of age.[2] For aircrew that would mean that the introverted pilot suffers most. And, research sug-gests, if between 50–60 years of age, individuals will suffer more, averag-ing 3.5 times more sleep loss per day than younger aviators.[3]

In the early 1970s, when British Overseas Air Corporation (B.O.A.C. now British Airways) conducted a study on circadian rhythms in flight crews working global routes, the researchers concluded that circadian rhythm disruption of sleep constitutes one of the most serious problems in civil aviation. When the total duty time and duration of schedules exceeded certain limits, impairment was noticeable in pilots' heart rates, for example, which varied depending on the work load, the type of air-craft flown, and the nature of approach aides and airports. When these findings were integrated with time zone desynchronization, the re-search suggested that potentially dangerous performance impairment was directly related to circadian rhythm desynchronization.[4]

Deutsche Lufthansa conducted a sleep pattern study on aircrew operat-ing polar routes between Germany and East Asia, and observed that air-crew were generally aware of the problems associated with several long haul flights: inherent time zone transitions; attempts to get enough sleep before and after flights by extending their night sleep; and supplementing nighttime sleep with daytime napping. But, the researchers concluded, even though most aircrew succeeded with this strategy, the majority of crew members could not completely compensate during the entire trip for the sleep deficit which was primarily caused by working throughout their circadian night.[5]

When the nocturnal sleep deficit—as well as the total sleep deficit accumulated during the various types of schedules—was taken into account, it appeared evident that layover periods of several days improved the crew's sleep balances, whereas short layovers did not allow crew members to find adequate sleep on routes with several long haul flights.

Because earlier research had shown that sleep loss leads to an increase in fatigue, and probably enhances stress during subsequent flights, the researchers concluded that performance could be impaired on the return flight if adequate crew rest periods (twenty-four hours or more) were not assured. Assuming that flight safety must take in account not only average crew behavior, but also the "the weakest link in the chain" risks, such as critical individual factors, the findings of this study were assumed to have operational significance.[6]

Although the research was geared to gauge sleep patterns in flight crew, the researchers noted that, when aircrew performed short duty rosters on the polar routes—traversing many time zones very quickly—an individual's circadian system was unable to adjust to a specific local time. That, in turn, resulted in a permanently desynchronized system, and generated grave sleep disturbances throughout the trip. Resynchronization after returning to home base, however, appears to be completed within a short time. Conversely, when aircrew had longer layovers in a specific time zone, the circadian system synchronized toward the actual local time and sleep would improve. After those crew members returned home, their circadian rhythmicity exhibited a dynamic readjustment to home base time, as indicated by shifts in sleep onset and by earlier wake times.[7]

In 1989, Scandinavian Airline Systems conducted a survey involving 1240 aircrew members and their health-related problems, including circadian rhythm desynchronization. The carrier concluded that time zone changes increased the frequency of sleep problems, fatigue and irritability, and that these effects of circadian rhythm disturbances could have serious consequences for flight safety. The airline suggested that improvements in scheduling systems, such as intermittent work on both long hauls and short hauls, might lessen the effect of time zone changes and the negative effects of long haul flights.

Furthermore, they suggested that, when scheduling aircrew, it may be advisable to aim for short enough layovers to prevent acclimatization to the new time zone, but long enough rest periods to allow for adequate recuperation. The survey results also demonstrated that circadian rhythm and other health problems occurred in the context of the aircraft facilities. The context includes equipment, job demands (demands such as passenger loads for flight attendants, and takeoffs and landing for pilots), work conditions, robustness of personnel, and length of service, all of which affected both transmeridian and short haul flights crews.[8]

Research has shown that the primary cause of pilot fatigue is disrupted inadequate sleep which could result in transient insomnia: a temporary disability to obtain restful sleep. This type of insomnia, they asserted, could possibly arise from sleeping in unfamiliar environments or in places not conducive to sleep due to uncomfortable noise, light or temperature levels, or bad sleeping surfaces. To combat transient insomnia, researchers suggest aviators carry with them family pictures, their favorite pillows, or some other familiar objects on trips away from home, in order to make the new surroundings more familiar and relaxing.[9]

But what happens when those gadgets fail to produce the desired effect, and the natural compensation for sleep loss and fatigue demands an unplanned, spontaneous micro-sleep and long periods of drowsiness while controlling an aircraft—a happenstance particularly frequent in long haul night operations?[10] Knowing that state-of-the-art, long-range aircraft are operated by only two aviators, what are we to think if both pilots have the potential of simultaneously falling asleep?[11]

In the airline industry, just talking about pilots sleeping in the cockpit is taboo. It's not supposed to happen—and therefore, carriers maintain, it does not occur. Sleeping while on duty spells instant dismissal for pilots and flight attendants alike.[12] Because napping is not sanctioned by Aviation Transport regulators worldwide, Don Sprucekey, spokesperson for Transport Canada might be speaking for all regulators when declaring in October 1996:

> You know, there are a lot of people that will, you know, think they have slept because of the possibility that they've had a quick snap and their eyes have quickly shut and closed. But in fact, the rules are quite explicit that snoozing in the cockpit is not allowed under regulations.[13]

He graciously ignores the fact that the Transport Safety Board of Canada's confidential reporting program is full of reports of pilot fatigue and sleeping in the cockpit, and how in rare instances, inflight napping has been disrupted by an approaching, possibly catastrophic event, such as almost flying into a thunderstorm. Similarly Sprucekey ignores that NASA, which also runs a confidential reporting line, catalogued 60,000 reports of pilot fatigue in eight years.[14]

Analyses of confidential reports to NASA's Aviation Safety Reporting System indicate that about 21% of all reported aircraft incidents are fatigue related. Furthermore, research asserted that such incidents have a tendency to occur more frequently in the early morning hours.[15]

Are you still wondering why flight attendants pay frequent visits to the cockpit, particularly during night flights? Do you still believe it's because of the aviator's charm, beauty, wit and intellect? Wrong! It's to make sure the boys are awake and with it.

Furthermore, why do you think Air Canada's pilot, during a recent strike, demanded the airline provide relief pilots on all long haul operations? That carrier, however, would be well within Transport Canada regulations if they refused to negotiate the point. Relief pilots are only called for on flights longer than twelve hours, according to Air Canada spokesperson, John Hamilton.[16]

When airline pilots claim they're too tired to land planes safely at the end of long trans-Atlantic flights to Europe, (after nine to ten hours in the air and at about 4 A.M. home base time), when the demand for their peak performance is highest, does management attribute this fatigue to the pilot's eccentric and health-deteriorating off-duty lifestyle?

As a matter of fact, John Criten, head of the Air Transport Association of Canada representing the country's 200 airlines, seems to espouse that viewpoint, exclaiming:

> If someone goes to work and is so tired that they feel they have to go to sleep at work, one, what are you doing before you came to work that made you so tired? Two, if you are getting rest and you're still tired, perhaps you should see a doctor.[17]

That research has demonstrated that giving commercial long haul pilots a sleep opportunity during long overseas flights can improve their reaction time during critical approach and land phases, appears to be inconsequential to the industry.[18] Why? Because, even though it might save lives and avoid crashes, adding relief pilots to augment existing cockpit crew would deprive shareholders of profit.

In 1989, after reviewing a number of unspecified major transportation accidents, the US National Transportation Safety Board expressed "serious concerns about the far-reaching effects of fatigue, sleepiness, sleep disorders, and circadian factors affecting transportation safety."[19]

NASA, in a study published in 1993, also asserted that sleepiness, fatigue, and circadian rhythms can have critical effects on safety margins in aviation.[20] The agency's *Z-Team*, world leaders in the study of burned out pilots, suggested that a forty minute power nap made pilots more alert for landing. American and European civil aviation regulators weren't convinced, preferring instead to await further studies. In 1995, Transport Canada—possibly influenced by Air Canada who had submitted a policy on controlled rest for two and three pilot cockpit crews for Transport Canada's evaluation—embraced the idea of napping in the cockpit. It's expected that the airline will soon make a formal application to allow its pilots to officially sleep on duty.[21]

In 1997, researchers anticipated that many of the human errors accounting for more than half of all aviation accidents were probably the direct result of fatigue-related pilot inattentiveness and failures to respond to critical information on the flight deck.[22] It is well-documented that circadian rhythm disruption and fatigue impairs quick thinking and quick action responses—and it is these very responses which could be called upon in a split second from engine-on to engine-off. A fast response may mean the difference between life and death.

To date, British Airways appears to be the only airline to publicly acknowledge that two out of five of its pilots admit to having involuntarily fallen asleep while controlling aircraft. Since these aviators are as human as everyone else cruising the skies and piloting planes, we can safely assume that their behavior is the norm.

The question, therefore, is whether pilots fall asleep at the controls because of circadian rhythm interference (along with exposure to cockpit noise and vibrations, day-to-day stress, lengthy flights, irregular work schedules, and inadequate amounts of sleep), *or* if excessive, consecutive duty days combined with long flying hours are responsible.

FLIGHT DUTY TIME LIMITATIONS

According to the International Civil Aviation Organization (ICAO) convention in 1974, "flight time and flight duty period limitations are established for the sole purpose of reducing the probability that fatigue of flight crew members may adversely affect the safety of flight."[23]

Basically two kinds of fatigue are taken into consideration. The first is transitory fatigue, resulting from a normal period of work, and the second is cumulative fatigue, caused by a delayed or incomplete recovery from normal workloads or from recurrent abnormal and excessive work periods without opportunities for recuperation. To reduce fatigue to an acceptable amount, the degree of workload has to be limited, and rest periods sufficient to provide recovery from a preceding workload before a new duty period commences ought to be provided.

Whereas conformity exists among airlines and governments on the need to limit aircrew flight duty assignments, the interpretations of this basic need fluctuate widely from country to country.[24] Thus, France (1981) and the US (1973) consider only flight time, whereas Scandinavia (1972), Japan (1973), Switzerland (1973), Germany (1974), the United Kingdom (1975), the former Soviet Union (1977), and Australia (1978), consider either flight duty time or duty time only. However, France and the United States consider only flight time—from engine on to engine off—and other countries take either flight and duty time, or duty time alone into consideration.[25]

North America flight crews commonly work duty time periods of sixteen or seventeen hours when away from home base, and fourteen to fifteen hours when at home. This means that if a flight is delayed while the crew is already on-board, they must take the aircraft to its destination if landing time is projected within that time span. At both home and overseas ports it is common practice for both operations and pilots to tamper with these time limits if a delay threatens to enable cabin crews to walk off board because their duty hour limitation has expired. One method is to forecast a less than actual flying time; the other to imprison flight attendants aboard the aircraft by taking away the loading bridge. Both are equally effective.

In the first, a walkout by flight attendants would be called illegal and would be followed with disciplinary action. In the second, cabin crew cannot escape unless they blow an emergency chute on the aircraft, which would also result in disciplinary action. People power has yet to be discovered by cabin crew and therefore sticking together in such situations to achieve adherence to strict rules has not dawned upon us. The union is useless in all aspects of its supposed functions, because it is known to side with the airlines against flight attendants, further impeding cabin crew from presenting a unified front. Often, they are forced to prolong their duty day to as much as it pleases the carriers. If flying domestic, a sixteen-hour duty day might only mean that four hours are spent in the air and the other twelve are passed by hanging around airports in-between flights. Duty time, moreover, does not equal hours paid; only time spend on-board aircraft with engines running is remunerated. But both duty hour limitations must be considered luxurious when considering that newly proposed aircrew duty times are twenty hours on long hauls, interrupted by a three hours rest period mid-air, to be followed by a twenty-four-hour layover at destination point before doing the same trip in reverse.

Without a doubt, lengthy duty periods further enhance the acute fatigue syndrome already suffered by flight attendants because of the deplorable cabin air quality and quantity on flights of much shorter duration. However, acute and short-term fatigue occurs because of intense flying activities in relatively short periods of time. These periods usually involve multiple takeoffs and landings, and the result is concentrated workload peaks over shorter time intervals. To prevent acute aircrew fatigue, figuring duty time is a far better measure than actual flying time, since the effects contributing to aircrew fatigue are not confined to the time spent on an aircraft while it is airborne, but also produced while it is on the ground.[26]

While acute fatigue is considered transitory, fatigue deriving from the accumulation of long flights and duty times acquired over extended periods is long-term or chronic fatigue—correctly described as *burnout*. Chronic fatigue is usually caused by insufficient opportunities to recuperate from excessive and recurring workloads.[27] Various countries acknowledge the concept of accumulated fatigue and attempt to prevent it by restricting the maximum amount of flying which aircrew can accumulate per week, bi-weekly, monthly, or annually, rather than in daily limitations. They also establish long-term limits in flight hours and not in duty hours.[28] Such regulation prevents flight crew from flying 170 hours within a thirty day period, which is presently legal in the US and Canada, and is in itself an invitation for disaster.

In other nations, the extent of flight time limitations to prevent aircrew fatigue is reflected in aircrew rest requirements. Scandinavia, for example, has no long-term limits to flying time accumulation, but it does have extensive provisions for mandatory rest periods. On the other hand,

France has numerous periods of cumulative limitations, but considerably fewer comprehensive rest period requirements. The United Kingdom provides complex formulae, which vary with maximum flight duty times, between nine to fourteen hours, while some provisions within German regulations are based on findings of experimental studies on the human circadian rhythm system. The reason that duty time regulations vary from country to country is to some extent attributable to the differences in the impact of geography and the time zones, the nature of flight operations, and the political and economic character of individual nations.[29]

However, ICAO's recommendation was made in 1974, and the last country to implement some sort of duty time concept was France in 1981. In the meantime, aircrew work conditions have deteriorated, not only because of decreased crew complements for pilots and flight attendants, but also because of higher and faster flying aircraft and because of deteriorating air quality and quantity for cabin crews.

Cabin crews are scheduled according to the pilots' duty hour restrictions, but labor under far worse conditions, which can impede them in carrying out their primary responsibility—to rescue passengers in an emergency. Researchers have yet to study present day, onboard conditions and the resulting psychological and physical impact on cabin crew. Until forays are made into studying these conditions and their implications, the regulations implemented in Jurassic times should be declared obsolete.

For Canada that would have been an easy task until October 1996, because it had circumvented the brain racking activity of how to create safer skies by having no aircrew duty-time limitation regulations at all.

When the Canadian Department of Transport published the proposal establishing maximum flight times and duty times, and minimum rest periods for commercial airline flight crew members on January 4, 1986, it purportedly took into consideration such fatigue-inducing factors as these: type of air carrier operation, crew complement, frequency of take-offs and landings, arrival and departure times, routes to be operated, crew rest areas, type of aircraft, and the probability of operational delays. Nevertheless, the transport minister proposed a maximum flight limitation of 120 hours in thirty consecutive days, 300 hours in ninety consecutive days, and 1200 hours in one calendar year. He reserves the right to extend the thirty-day limitation to a whopping 150 hours—from engine on to engine off.[30] The honorable minister's proposal, which became legislation, exceeds the annual permissible flying hour total of all other ICAO nations by between 200 to 500 hours annually.[31]

"Normal" flight duty time "normally" was not to exceed fifteen hours in a consecutive twenty-four hour period. This time frame, however, could be extended if the pilot-in-command thought it safe to do so "for specific, *but unspecified*, humanitarian purposes." Minimum rest periods to allow aircrew "adequate rest prior to flight duty time," were to be established by the individual air carrier. But for major carriers, a rest period of twenty-four hours had to be provided at least once within each seven consecutive day period. The smaller ones may graciously provide a rest period of twenty-four consecutive hours thirteen times within a calendar quarter in lieu of the every seven consecutive day period.[32]

The proposed 1986 regulation was noteworthy for its inadequacies, particularly in the following areas: aircrew were allowed to fly for months on end, as long as a twenty-four-hour layover was provided every eighth day; there were no formulae to reduce the size of duty periods or to increase the duration of rest periods to compensate for the complexity of operations; and there were no provisions for specific or defined daily rest periods. In addition, with the exception of the every seven days and thirteen times within a calendar quarter twenty-four consecutive hours off, the proposed legislation did not differentiate between large airplanes, small airplanes, and rotor craft.

In other words, a provision allowing individuals to work for twelve or more consecutive days with duty times of fifteen hours or more, and without adequate rest periods in between, is barely short of insanity. It also demonstrates an outstanding ignorance of fatigue generated by disruptions in circadian rhythms, and an almost unbelievable lack of awareness of on-board work conditions for flight attendants, especially with regard to on-board air quality and quantity.

When only pilots (and as always, no flight attendants) were invited to peruse the regulation's draft, they complained that the proposed duty hours were excessive and that the "loose" wording defining "duty time and adequate crew rest" would allow carriers to take advantage of the ambiguity in its interpretation. One aviator said that, "Pilots *on call*— meaning that they are available to replace those booking off sick— do not start duty times until they start flying. If, for example, a pilot was on his own time all day, but also on call, and he was not called out until 23:00, then his duty time would start at 23:00 for possibly 15 hours even though he had been awake all day prior to takeoff."

Another one asserted that,

> At even a ten-hour duty day I will have been awake for approximately twenty-seven hours at the end of my "legal" duty day! I have actually fallen asleep during such flights, and I am sure others have as well. Our employer tells us that this is just the nature of unscheduled charter business, and there is nothing that can be done to change the situation. Personally, I believe that a duty time of fifteen hours a day is far too excessive to be safe.[33]

But pilots' work conditions are not restricted to unscheduled charter business. They are similar to those imposed on all North American aircrew.

In response to the proposal, the Canadian Aviation Safety Board (CASB), while expressing approval-in-principle for the introduction of such regulations in February 1986, nonetheless commented on the lack of provisions for preventing acute aircrew fatigue, as well as the inadequate provisions for flight crew rest. Again, this concerned only pilots. The Board's perspective was greatly influenced by the preliminary findings of a study conducted to examine the history of fatigue-related accidents in Canada from 1976 through 1984 that represented only a sample of the total accidents in which fatigue was a factor.[34]

Of the 67 accidents cited by the Board, twenty-three involving fixed wing commercial aircraft operations, altogether resulting in twenty fatalities and twenty serious injuries; only six involved inflight emergencies or flight abnormalities affecting the operation of the aircraft prior to the accidents. And in those, investigators concluded, pilot fatigue exacerbated the circumstances *after* the emergency or abnormality was detected. In a further four cases it was concluded that fatigue led to errors in judgment in fuel management, which, in turn, lead to fuel exhaustion, creating an abnormal flight situation leading to an accident. The remaining fifty-seven—or fully 85% of the reported accidents—involved aircraft for which no system deficiency which would have contributed to the accident could be detected.

The Canadian Aviation Safety Board recognized that the difficulty in evaluating the effect which fatigue may have had on an individual's performance can lead an investigator to underestimate the degree of impairment of pilots' judgmental faculties. Furthermore, information from accident reports do not illustrate the fatiguing effects of certain duty cycles, such as the number of time-zones the pilot has crossed and the amount of his on-duty hours. Many accidents or incidents, however, appear to be caused by inappropriate procedures or untimely decisions made by aviators. If the pilots do not survive, the investigators may not only be inspired, but required to speculate on whether or not the deceased's judgment had been impaired and for what reasons. In other words, accidents declared to be caused by pilot error may have occurred because the pilots were "dead on their feet."[35]

Concerns about the study's validity were raised, and a question was posed. Could the accident data supplied by pilots have been distorted in an effort to mask any errors in judgment by blaming fatigue for the errors? But the opposite was discovered on at least one occasion, when a spray pilot adamantly insisted that the error which led to his accident had not been precipitated by fatigue. How could it? After all, he had slept nine hours in the previous sixty-nine. In May 1991, the TSBC sent Transport Canada an Aviation Safety Advisory on the subject of extending maximum flight duty times, because reports indicated that there was pressure on crews in both fixed and rotary wing operations to work longer than the allowed daily limits because the "unforeseen circumstance clause," the clause that pilots were free to invoke for "specific, but unspecified, humanitarian purposes."

Transport Canada responded that, in their view, air carriers were correctly interpreting the regulation.[36] This, despite the fact that between 1985 and 1992 alone, the TSBC's "Canadian Air Safety Reporter," which aircrew can contact anonymously, received over thirty-five reports relating to acute or chronic crew fatigue. Since that time, the agency received twenty-nine additional reports, twenty of those in 1994 alone, from long haul commercial airline pilots, air ambulance aircrew, helicopter pilots, and flight attendants.[37] NASA received 60,000 calls reporting pilot fatigue cases in the six years of their anonymous hotline.[38] Astonishingly, American and Canadian aviation authorities are still disinclined to listen. As long as aircrew are standing with eyes open, then aircrew are fit to fly, seems to be the conventional wisdom of the agencies elected to oversee safety in the skies.

One factor universally ignored by North American airline corporations (as befitting any self-respecting stock-exchanged corporation), is that the human organism blatantly refuses to fall asleep while the adrenaline forcefully pounds in its vein after a completed flight performance, when it has carried itself and its owner valiantly through a twenty-hour day or longer. Even when knowing that only a ten-hour layover, engine-off to engine-on, has been generously provided for rest and recuperation before another fifteen or sixteen-hour duty day begins—on domestic runs—it is impossible to fall asleep. Of course, all forms of chemical drugs to cool down the overworked system are officially prohibited by aviation agencies and airlines alike.

Recently one major North American carrier saw fit to propose to its pilots the idea that on Pacific Coast to Hong Kong flights (a duty day of approximately 15 hours, engine-on to engine-off, with a two hour inflight break), should be followed by a thirteen-hour layover, and then return to home base after a jet stream aided duty day of around 12.25 hours. This of course, meant flight attendants would work under the same conditions. This joyful proposition apparently created such upheaval in the ranks that it replaced aircraft incident conversations in global watering holes for weeks. The protesters were adamant—seventy-two hour layovers were granted for a few months.

The joy did not last. Layover-related company expenditures of around $1.5 million per annum inspired management to introduce seventeen hour layovers. A barrage of book offs due to extreme fatigue, especially by oxygen-deprived cabin crew members, was the result. Two months later, the long layovers were reintroduced. Shareholders were heart broken.

North American airlines would be deliriously happy if they could fly flight attendants around the clock. Or, alternatively, billet them near runways at one star hotels or at airport terminals, so that they stay exposed to continual aircraft noise and can be hauled back onto a plane within minutes. Better yet, the corporation could install bunks and a shower stall in aircraft bellies. That way, the entire crew—pilots and flight attendants—would be shielded from their desire for off-duty exploration, constantly under supervision, and legally available for round the clock shifts. Burn them out and throw them away is a strategy highly conducive to the bottom line. Most likely that scheme is already on the drawing board. North American governmental aviation regulatory bodies will doubtlessly agree to it, since they are successfully lobbied by the major carriers to do their bidding.

The aircrew on-duty time proposition, put forward by Canada's Ministry of Transport, was legislated in October 1996. As early as 1929, J. Hamilton, author of "Nineteen Years in the Poisonous Trades," made this prescient observation:

> For as long as the health, safety, and contentment of the working class are left largely to the goodwill and intelligence of the employing class, there will always be dark spots and neglect and ignorance and callousness.[39]

How well Hamilton's comment applied to this new piece of legislation, demonstrating how little things have changed over time.

There is one problem, however, where aviators are concerned. The airlines' neglect, ignorance and callousness takes on different proportions because pilots are responsible for safely returning aircraft to the ground, and cabin crews are responsible for rescuing passengers in an emergency. Both might be a trifle difficult when dead on one's feet. The entire aircrew on-duty time and rest period topic is, of course, particularly relevant when studies have shown that 85% of airplane "incidents" are said to have a lapse of human performance in the causal chain.[40] Therefore, if anything unpleasant happens while you are on-board an aircraft, do not blame your crew—blame the company you chose to fly with and the North American regulative bodies who have ignored the safety of the flying public by neglecting to implement conscientious legislative regulation for aircrew duty times and rest periods.

There is hope, however. Currently, there are intense discussions between civil aviation authorities, operators and pilot associations in Europe, Japan, and the U.S. about existing legal standards of flight duty limitations. The question at the center of this debate is whether or not the regulations ought to be modified to counteract the excessive mental and psychological demands for pilots on two-crew operation aircraft. European authorities have agreed that aeromedical scientific research must be conducted before any decisions on changes can be taken.[41] Well, we know what that means—"when hell freezes over"—only then will aircrew begin to labor under humane conditions.

Twenty-five years ago, aircraft manufacturers, responding to industry demands, began designing aircraft to travel extremely long distances and to be operated by a minimum crew. Neither the manufacturers, the aviation regulative bodies, nor the carriers chose to examine or even consider what effects the automated and artificial environment would have on flight crew. Charming, is it not?

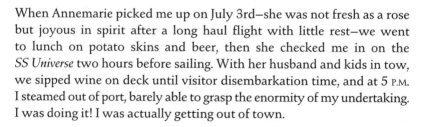

When Annemarie picked me up on July 3rd—she was not fresh as a rose but joyous in spirit after a long haul flight with little rest—we went to lunch on potato skins and beer, then she checked me in on the *SS Universe* two hours before sailing. With her husband and kids in tow, we sipped wine on deck until visitor disembarkation time, and at 5 P.M. I steamed out of port, barely able to grasp the enormity of my undertaking. I was doing it! I was actually getting out of town.

The *SS Universe* Adventure

Sailing into the first stop after a sunny 4th of July at sea we docked at Wrangell, Alaska, located in the heart of the southeast Inside Passage. It was pouring rain. Too chicken to go whitewater rafting, I looked at petroglyphs on a beach at the north end of the island before checking out the hamlet and looking for a bar, the best place to meet the locals and get a feel for the community at large.

The first one I entered smelled worse and appeared seedier than any of the third class dives I'd ever ventured into with a crowd of sailors. I backed out, thinking, "Just as well. Better get closer to the dock. Won't do to be left behind." Entering another watering hole close to the pier, my eyes fell on a pleasantly plastered fellow who looked me up and down, wondrously taking in my bright yellow oilskin coat, Nova Scotian sou'wester, and boots. "Now *there's* a virgin," he slurred.

I burst out laughing and answered, "At least to these parts," as I ordered a beer in the same breath. My intention to pick this humorous guy's brains was prematurely interrupted when his female companion, unaware that her man had just afforded me the first carefree laughter in years, hauled him out into the rain in a hurry. I found someone else to chat with while indulging in my favorite brew, and ventured back aboard minutes before the gangway was retrieved.

The following day we steamed up the Gastineau Channel and anchored opposite downtown Juneau in drizzle and 6^0C temperatures. Since a multitude of people aboard were booked on shore trips, it took me a while to get passage on one of the *Universe*'s motorized life rafts. This was the only mode of transportation to reach shore, and be tendered to the dock in the old part of town. Ashore, a bus took me and some of my shipmates close to the Mendenhall Glacier stream, where we were fitted in life vests and oilskin clothing before embarking on our journey downstream whitewater river rafting. At midway, already well-moistened, we set ashore to imbibe some local potent brew, served in preparation for the rest of the journey. Shivering and soaking wet, a kind soul at the arrival point offered me a miniature of *Wild Turkey*, and frozen to the bone, I swallowed its contents with glee. Unwilling to call it quits, I motored back aboard the *SS Universe*, changed clothing, and went ashore again.

Juneau has been spared the fire damage that many other Alaskan cities have endured, and most of the downtown buildings retain their original facades. Abundant shops and art galleries, clustered within walking distance from the dock, invited exploration. On my way back to town, I made the acquaintance of another passenger, Nancy, who asked me simply, "What're you up to?"

"Checking out town, and checking out the Red Dog Saloon," its most famous pub. And it was there that I parked myself, frozen stiff, at around 6:30 P.M., and began sipping brandy. Nancy walked in a short while later, and ordered a Chardonnay. We began to swap life stories. Nancy, a character in her own right, was a fine sport. She had been married twice—to two admirals—both of whom had found their final resting place at Arlington. We enjoyed ourselves as time flew by unnoticed.

Happily arriving at the pier in time for what we thought to be the last tender, we saw the *Universe* pull up anchor and steam out of the channel toward Skagway. While gathering our impaired thoughts, the saloon's bartender stormed down the dock bellowing, "I've already talked to them. They won't pick you up. You gotta fly to Skagway tomorrow."

"So be it," I thought.

Back to the Red Dog we went and had one for the road until the police escorted us to the station, where our identities had been verified by the ship. We were assured that it was standard procedure, and an expression of Juneau's hospitality, to have police pick up stranded cruise line travelers. They kindly found accommodation for us at the Baranof Hotel, and dropped us off there at 2:00 A.M. The receptionist had already booked our flight. It would depart at 7:00 A.M. Two hours before our departure time, I dove under a cold shower, and woke up Nancy before skipping to the coffee shop. A lone customer greeted me with a, "Which ship are you from?"

Barely able to control my laughter, I asked, "It's that obvious, is it?"

"Yep!" he replied grinning "No makeup."

Everybody in Juneau seemed to be magically interconnected. It was no surprise that the airline knew who we were and had our tickets ready when we arrived at 6:35. I didn't bother to inquire what type of aircraft I would be entrusting my life to, positive it would be a 737, since that's used worldwide for hop flights. Not even the instruction to "Come back at five to seven," aroused my suspicion. When the captain of the vessel inquired, "Got any luggage?" when we returned to the check-in desk, it dawned on me that a 737 was not in the picture.

I had bush-piloted with a friend of mine all over British Columbia, Canada, in Beavers, Cessnas, and Comanches too often not to know that this was a bush pilot's standard question for passengers. I wasn't fazed in the slightest; after all, the worst experience I had on those aircraft had been with a load of lumberjacks as they got desperately ill in heavy turbulence. Therefore, I confidently followed our skipper to the tiny Cessna parked on the dry and sunny tarmac. With not a breeze in the air, I climbed into the starboard seat behind him, which he had assigned to me, put on headsets, and with Nancy on my left, off we rolled—five people in all. Only the co-pilot's seat was vacant.

Watching the instrument panel from my vantage point, feeling the little plane bumping over the tarmac towards the beginning of the runway, I experienced an intimacy with the aircraft that is impossible to feel on larger planes. Its movements made my heart beat faster, and as we lifted off, and the ground distanced itself, my spirit soared, singing out of pure joy, "This is it! This is the only way to see Mother Earth!"

Once we crossed the coastal mountains, sun reflecting off the snow on the Mount Fairweather range and Mount Delani glittering in the distance, we could see the *SS Universe* as she made her way slowly up the dark green fjord of Taiya Inlet 5000 feet below. During the brief descent into Skagway, I focused my attention on the instrument panel and air traffic control directions for the sheer joy of it until touchdown. The flight had lasted 45 minutes. While the pilot unloaded the luggage, two of the other passengers commented, "We commute between here and Seattle, but we've never had a trip with someone who played tour guide like this guy. Most of them don't say a word. Give him a few dollars, if you can. He surely deserves it. They make lousy wages, you know."

Nancy dug out her last $10 US; I didn't have a penny on me. The pilot accepted it graciously. A little bus picked us up on the tarmac and off-loaded Nancy and me at the dock, where the *SS Universe* approached for mooring. A bit shaky after the flight, I asked Nancy, "Want to check out the Red Onion?" Naturally it was the most famous bar in town.

"No. But would you come with me to my sister's to explain things?" she replied. I did.

After that, we did not see each other again until Victoria, the last stop of the journey, because Nancy and her sister traveled on the very upper deck, while I lounged in an inside cabin at poop deck level. She found me at my favorite spot under the US flag. "I know now why I came on this trip," she said. "I was sent here as your guardian angel to get you back to flying." We hugged, and I presented her with a garnet-filled rock I had bought in Wrangell, so that she would always remember the successful accomplishment of her mission.

The Juneau adventure and the fourteen days I spent on board the *SS Universe*, performed a miracle for my self-esteem, confidence, composure, and equilibrium. Thanks to Captain Chang and his crew, thanks to my fellow passengers, but first and foremost thanks to Nancy, my cruise to breathtakingly beautiful Alaska posed the beginning of mending my broken wings. I neglected to tell my psychiatrist, my GP, and even my mother about the Juneau to Skagway flight—after all, I had not been quite sober when I took wing, and it had only been a Cessna.

Aircraft as Illness
Incubators

The jubilation over my Alaskan achievement was short-lived—a letter dated July 6th from Davis, NorAm's human resources manager, jolted me back to reality. My employment would be terminated, he threatened, if I did not qualify for the IMMS-generated leave of absence, which must be applied for by July 31st—or if the leave was granted and I had not secured alternate employment within the company at the conclusion of my leave. Fuming with indignity, I began the familiar circus of trying to get in touch with my union brothers and airline management on Monday, July 18th. "Sister Fiona never arrives before 10 A.M." I was told by a pert union staff member. At 10:30 she rang.

No, she claimed, she did not have a clue about the newest development. I gave her a synopsis and demanded that the July 31st deadline be extended. "I'll take NorAm to court if need be. They're not getting away with this," I warned.

"Hang on—I'll talk to Harry about it," she said, and minutes later she told me that the deadline extension should not present a problem. She would attempt to obtain the accident report, she said, and would set up a meeting with Harry to discuss Davis' letter. They'd keep me posted.

While in the swing of things, I got in touch with the wage indemnity brokers, who said that in order to assess my claim, my psychiatrist and my general practitioner would be asked to provide statements of my history and a current medical diagnosis. Later on that afternoon, my lawyer, McCormick, called to say that WCB insisted that I expose myself to additional psychological treatment. "It's, of course, unlawful of the Board to presume you might become better from it, however, what do you think if I forwarded documents of my choice to Dr. Kruk to get his evaluation without seeing you?" Kruk was one of the two psychologists that WCB deemed appropriate for my treatment. I consented.

My patience in trying to contact Harry ran out on the 24th when, miraculously, I reached Tobias. He said, "'I'm trying to arrange a meeting for the 26th—and don't worry about the extension. Harry's coming back from Glasgow today, and I'm going to remind him."

"My arse," I thought hanging up. After ringing Tobias again on the 25th, I discovered that he hadn't spoken with Harry. I was not to be concerned about the deadline, he said, because even though I had been predisposed to develop PTSD, the company could not terminate me.

Flying into a rage I yelled, "What are you talking about? I was not *predisposed*! I know it, and my WCB file and company file proves it!"

"Well, don't get upset now," said Tobias, retreating. "I'm off until Wednesday next week and there's plenty of time to talk things over." He disconnected. At 10:30 A.M. the following day Tobias rang, his tone changed, and he demanded to see me at the union office within the hour.

"Sorry, can't. Annemarie's at the dentist, and I'm not going without her."

"Well, I don't know when we can meet before the end of the deadline, then, 'cause I might have to fly tomorrow, you know."

"So be it," I responded, thinking, "Screw it. Its just another one of their plots to catch me alone so they can fabricate all sorts of things afterwards." Three hours later he rang again to propose a meeting on the 28th—with Harry also in attendance.

"That's fine, Tobias," I agreed, knowing Annemarie would be in town, "but I want Fiona there as well."

"Oh. I'll see what I can do. Call you later today." He didn't.

Taking the initiative of phoning him at 8:45 that evening, I learned that a meeting had now been planned for August 2nd or 3rd. "What about the deadline?" I questioned.

"Oh, don't worry about that. It'll be arranged." On August 3rd. Tobias informed me that we now would get together on August 8th. Harry and Fiona would be present, he assured me. But on the day of our meeting, only Tobias greeted Annemarie and me at the union office. The others were "busy," he said.

"Harry settled the IMMS deadline?" I inquired.

"No, I'm still working on that."

"For how many months is it, anyhow," I asked.

"Oh, I don't know. Haven't checked it out yet," he responded, candidly unashamed of his poor performance.

"Would be lovely if you did, Tobias, because I'm not signing anything until I know that. And I'm not considering retirement either, until my pension appeal has been settled, because McCormick advises against it. Why should I, anyhow? NorAm's not even paying my group insurance, and the only thing I'd get out of it would to be without a job when I'm ready to go back flying."

"But you can't!"

"Who says I can't? Don't be ridiculous," I answered. "And what's this about firing me? Davis threatens me with it three times in his letter if the IMMS isn't granted? Why threaten me, period? We only threaten when we feel threatened. And how can they? I'm sick with an injury sustained on-board aircraft? Don't they want to take any responsibility for what happened? And why doesn't the airline release the accident report? I'll tell you why!" I went on. "The engine was damaged before start-up!"

"You've proof of that?" he asked, his piggy eyes wide in astonishment.

"Of course I have," I said, and pushed the Safety Board's report over to him while relating Dr. Walton's comments.

"Mind me taking a copy?"

"I sure do mind," I quipped, snatching the file out of his porky hands before continuing my agitated spiel. "And what happened to the flight attendants we know of who had near misses, Tobias? If their experiences and mine aren't truly on-the-job accidents—I don't know what are! And I'm not taking responsibility for it. I wasn't predisposed and you know it. And I assure you, I'll be compensated for my suffering, my loss of enjoyment of life, and the loss of my career if it comes to that.

"Davis' letter just adds insult to injury!" I continued. "As far as I know right now, there's no research on PTSD in flight attendants. But, by golly, sooner or later I'll find out. And then watch out. McCormick says that NorAm is very aware of the volatility of the situation because they didn't attempt to accuse me of sloppy work performance, knowing that it wouldn't fly. Consequently, they chose another convenient avenue to get rid of me by allowing WCB to clobber me to death."

"Well, cool it now. Can't be all that bad," he said condescendingly before promising to present my concerns to NorAm—"at the earliest convenience." We parted company.

"Wonder when *that'll* be?" I said to Annemarie over lunch. "Don't you think we have here a typical example of male oppression and supremacy? They're trying to bully me onto the well-established path of female submission, aren't they? Nothing but power games and egocentrism accentuated by prolonged periods of silence to scare the prey and make her flee. 'Til donkeys fly! If they don't watch out, they've got a thing or two coming to them!"

By August 20th, brother Tobias' expertise in evasiveness merited an award of excellence. Instead of wasting more time tracking him, I hunted down Fiona and let her know the extent of my disenchantment "I want a written apology from the airline for what happened to me," I instructed her. "I also want it in writing, that they refuse to release the accident report. And I also it want in writing, that they failed to monitor me after my return to work. Furthermore, I want it in writing, that they provided inaccurate income figures to the Board—and I want it in writing that the figures which they provided are against the collective agreement. I also want a letter of employment. And," I concluded my list, "I want *you* to get this for me. Otherwise I'll sue them!"

"We better have a meeting," she responded breathlessly.

"Annemarie and I've already had one with Tobias, and it proved to be a waste—good for nothing. Haven't heard from him since, even though he promised to get answers from the company in a hurry."

"When was that?"

"August 8th. I requested your presence but was told that you were *busy*. Perhaps you want to get the minutes from him and call me back later?"

"Shall do," she said, and we disconnected. I hurried off to meet Erika at the Airport Inn.

"You won't believe this," Erika cried as she opened the door to her room, "Look what I just found in my mail folder!" She handed me a letter from NorAm's medical office dated July 28th, 1994, which stated that a passenger on her mid-May London, England flight had been ill with active infectious tuberculosis (TB). The letter kindly suggested that she be tested privately at her own expense to find out if she was infected.

"Can you believe this? Couldn't they have mailed it to me? They knew I've been on vacation from the end of June until today!" she exclaimed exasperated.

"Jessus! And if you're infected you've probably given it to Josy," (her little daughter), "And possibly a trillion others." At the time, both of us were unaware that four Vancouver flight attendants had been infected with TB that year, nor did we know that the topic of airborne diseases had been discussed on the ABC program *20/20* on May 13th, the same week that Erika had been exposed to TB. The broadcast's headline was "The Air Up There."[1]

During that televised program, a man named Bob Kahn was interviewed. He had been traveling with his wife on a MD-80, along with a passenger who was later diagnosed with infectious tuberculosis. Shortly after the flight, Mr. Kahn tested positive for the disease—his wife showed no symptoms. Mr. Kahn maintained that other passengers contracted the disease as well. San Francisco's Department of Health was reportedly investigating if Mr. Kahn and other passengers contracted TB on that flight. On another flight carrying a passenger with contagious TB, ten out of twenty-five passengers later tested positive for the disease.[2]

The fact that cabin crew is just as vulnerable to catch TB was documented by *Consumer Reports* investigators. They found that a flight attendant from an unnamed airline worked for several months with respiratory symptoms before being diagnosed with contagious tuberculosis. Epidemiologists believe she infected thirteen out of forty-three of her co-workers.[3] Their research could not determine whether or not she infected any passengers. Until August 1994, the U.S. Center for Disease Control in Atlanta had only investigated four cases in which a crew member or an airline passenger had been flying while suffering from active infectious tuberculosis.[4]

AIRCRAFT AS ILLNESS INCUBATORS

While we know that North American airlines are exceedingly fond of stating that airplane air is equal to, if not better than, air found in office buildings, it is noteworthy that some epidemiologists have documented the spread of measles and tuberculosis through buildings' ventilation ducts, and that this kind of disease transmission increases with the amount of recycled air.[5] Others, including Dr. Harriet Burge, a Harvard professor of environmental health, have maintained that no amount of ventilation will prevent TB transmission.[6]

Consumer Reports investigators also documented how airline passengers with respiratory problems can infect those sharing their air—meaning all people, in all cabins—unless enough outside air is supplied to dilute the contagious airborne particles distributed by coughs and sneezes.[7] Other researchers concluded that people traveling in First or Business class, receiving between 30 and 50 cfm of air, are less vulnerable to getting infected than those traveling in coach.[8] But, as Mr. Witkowski of the American Flight Attendant Union explained in the *20/20* interview,

> When we had planes—most planes—with 100% fresh air, the air used to come in totally...almost totally clean and then be exhausted every three minutes. Today, with the 50% fresh air and 50% recycled air, the plane isn't changed—completely changed until approximately seven minutes or even longer in some cases. So you have air that's less...has less quality to begin with. It's got more contaminants and it stays in the plane longer.

However, Michael Rioux, Vice President of Engineering and representative of the Air Transport Association, the air carriers' organization, happily announced during the broadcast,

> We certainly don't want to believe that we're trying to squeeze another nickel out of everybody's wallet just because we found out a way to make the airplane use less air, so what they've done is they've developed a system still maintaining—in fact improving—the ventilation flow to each passenger that's sitting in the airplane.[9]

He doesn't have to believe his spiel about the nickel. He knows that it's fact, not fiction. But the ABC News medical editor, Dr. Timothy Johnson rushed to Rioux's support by hurriedly pointing out that sophisticated filters installed to trap air contaminants are changed by the airlines according to manufacturers guidelines. Some critics, however, contend that these air filters are replaced far too infrequently to be effective.[10]

Most filters currently in use on board aircraft are capable of removing 90 to 95% of bacteria and viruses. And new filtration systems, apparently installed on Boeing 777 and 747-400s, claim to remove up to 99.99% of airborne contaminants of 0.5 microns and larger. But that still allows potentially harmful bacteria, and especially viruses from the cabin environment, to slip through because the most common pathogenic viruses—those responsible for colds, flu, croup, and pneumonia—are all considerably smaller than 0.5 microns. The practical difficulties and prohibitive costs of measuring viruses on-board aircraft, however, inhibit research and development in this area, although the techniques are available.[11] But, the carrier corporations may well reason, why hasten such a costly undertaking when, after all, passengers and cabin crew fly by choice, not by invitation?

Just how magnificent an aircraft is as a testing site for germ breeding and spreading (with or without ventilation and filtration), however, was illustrated when a jet with an inoperative ventilation system was grounded for more than four hours in Homer, Alaska, in the 70s with fifty-three people aboard. Within one week, 72% of passengers came down with influenza. All cases were traceable to one individual who developed flu symptoms during the delay.[12] On a U.S. military DC9 with its 100% ventilation and filtration system running in perfect working order and at full capacity, eighteen out of thirty-four Navy squadron members aboard caught the flu.[13]

Therefore, it can be deduced that over 50% of passengers on any given aircraft with any kind of ventilation and filtration system will be infected if only one person in the cabin carries an airborne disease. On a fully loaded Boeing 747-200, that means approximately 250 passengers could walk off the aircraft ill. Flight attendants are, of course, thought to be immune. The only official scientific cabin air quality study that has been conducted by the U.S. Department of Transportation was done around 1989. It has been reviewed with skepticism by many experts, who claim that such contaminants as air pollutants and germ transmission health threats were not adequately researched.[14] Therefore, the American Broadcasting Company commissioned a Harvard research team to collect air quality samples on twenty-two flights on ten different types of aircraft on every major American airline on domestic routes, and to test for eleven categories of contaminants, including carbon dioxide, noise levels, organic compounds and dust.[15]

The researchers brought a sinister picture to light. The high carbon dioxide levels they found was no surprise. Though no specific data were presented in the broadcast, the research provided a clear analysis of the cabin environment. The high levels of mites found in dust samples collected from seats and carpets indicated that they had permanently settled in. Extensive evidence of cat allergens, presumably brought on board by passengers, was also noted. Other substances irritating to sensitive travelers were found, such as aromas from perfumes, aftershaves, cooking, fuel, de-icing chemicals, cleaning fluids, pesticides, carpeting adhesives, insecticide, cleaning agents, ethanol and benzene, and upholstery finishes, all of which cannot be soaked up or eliminated by the ventilation system. Every one of those particles and odors can cause allergic reaction and asthma attacks in passengers.[16] Again, cabin crew was excluded from the research.

Dust samples collected by the team revealed relatively high levels of endotoxins, which are substances found in the cell walls of certain bacteria. The researchers purport that those may be causing the dry eye and scratchy throat symptoms suffered by passengers and cabin crew alike. But Mr. Rioux, the industry representative, protested wildly[17].

INFECTIOUS DISEASE TRANSMISSION

In 1992, Dr. Harriet Burge, Associate Professor of Environmental Health at the Harvard School of Public Health and one of the air quality researchers, said that,

> There are many episodes of infectious diseases that could, if you took the trouble, be directly traced to travel on aircraft. It is also possible that if someone on the flight has an active case of an infectious disease like influenza, then other people on-board will also have that disease by the end of the flight."[18]

Let's use the Ebola virus for an example. Ebola is an infectious virus spread by just breathing in air. An Ebola infection starts with a bad headache, then the stomach revolts, high fever sets in, the blood first clots, then loses that ability, and the body turns into an oozing, melting mass of virus within days.[19] When a recent outbreak in the Congo region caused hundreds of deaths, flights to that region were canceled to prevent spreading the disease to other parts of the World.

In 1990, when monkeys, imported from the Philippines to the Hazelton Research Primate Quarantine Unit in Reston, Virginia died of Ebola, panic silently arose because many people had been exposed to the creatures during their transport by aircraft and trucks. The virus was airborne—proven by the fact that non-infected monkeys, isolated in a different tract of the building, caught the disease as well. All 500 monkeys were killed by lethal injections and the building decontaminated with formaldehyde by the U.S. Army. No human being has set foot inside since, even though the military purports to have killed every single Ebola virus.[20]

Hantavirus is another virus transmitted directly through the air from people coming into contact with infected droppings from deer mice and rats. The virus can be contacted in our own back yards, if the urban development explosion continues displacing rats and mice from their habitual quarters. It can be brought on board aircraft with great ease.

Strains of the virus have caused outbreaks in Europe and Asia. During the Korean War, 3,000 United Nation soldiers were struck down with it.[21] It has now been reported all over the United States and Canada.

Plagues are another force to reckon with. There are two main forms of the disease: bubonic and pneumonic. Diseases of rats rather than humans, plagues are caused by bacteria—microorganisms not much larger than 1/1000 of a millimeter—transmitted from one rodent to another by fleas. If fleas from an infected rodent bite a person, swelling occurs at the bite mark, in the groin, or under the arm. These swellings, or *buboes,* give the Bubonic Plague its name. Pneumonic Plague is contacted by breathing in the bacteria when, for example, handling an infected rodent. The disease is then transmitted from person to person by air.

Fleas do not need a passport to make their way on-board aircraft. In 1995 many airlines proved divinely indifferent to the dangers of the bubonic plague by flying in and out of India as usual, even though a plague raged in parts of the subcontinent. During an epidemic, up to 90% of a population may be infected. If treatment with antibiotics is not administered within twelve to twenty-four hours, more than 50% of those with bubonic, and nearly 100% of those with pneumonic plague will die.[22]

Lassa fever, an acute and often fatal viral disease, must not be forgotten either. In the late 70s, when a passenger on an international flight was rushed into a Toronto hospital with a suspected case of highly contagious Lassa fever, health officials quarantined the hospital after about 700 people had been exposed to the disease. The case turned out to be a false alarm.[23] What happened to the aircraft, its crew and passengers has never been revealed.

Then there are also the diseases caused by the Marburg, Machupo, and Junin viruses—equally incurable and infectious as most of the others I've mentioned, and equally as eager to travel by airborne routes. Mr. Carl Johnson, a virologist, said on the CBS program *48 Hours,* "We're going to be so unprepared the day one of them [virus] lands on our shores and takes off that I cannot imagine the kind of panic it's going to produce in this society." Miss Jenkins, a medical anthropologist, says later on, "Oh, diseases move very quickly. Hop on a plane with a person—it's not hard for a disease to move. Diseases move with great ease."[24] I guess someone kicked her under the table, for she did not elaborate, nor was she invited to discuss the issue further.

"What about disinfecting aircraft?" you might well ask. Well, there is only a 1972 report from the International Sanitary Regulation (ISR) of the World Health Organization (WHO), in conjunction with the International Aviation Transportation Association (IATA), which examined new methods to accomplish that task. It appears as if, twenty-five years later, they are still examining. However, if public health officials suspect that an aircraft has transported a plague-cholera-smallpox-typhus-relapsing fever-chicken pox-gonorrhea-syphilis-tuberculosis-salmonellosis and/or strep-tococcal infectious passenger, they may request an aircraft disinfection.[25] But when that action is taken, after having run through a multitude of channels for consideration, the plane has most likely circumnavigated the globe a hundred times.

Concurring with the very limited documentation on the topic of aircraft as illness incubators, the Harvard research team believes they demonstrated beyond a shadow of a doubt that contaminants can be picked up throughout the aircraft.[26] When contaminants can be picked up, so can bacteria and microorganisms. The day the ABC *20/20* episode aired, the Air Transport Association, who a few weeks earlier had released their own study in which they noisily tooted that the cabin air was perfectly fresh and health-promoting, released a statement saying that they looked forward to reviewing the team's findings.[27] In airline industry lingo that means that they'll still be looking forward to reviewing Harvard's study when pigs fly unless they're forced into action.

Until then, one has the benevolent advice of Dr. Timothy Johnson, ABC's News Medical Editor, as a guideline. He proposed, when asked how passengers can increase their chances to deplane as disease-free as when boarding, that they should try to avoid being exposed to someone who is coughing and sneezing. It appears that the doctor has yet to travel on an aircraft that is packed solid, where seats are dished out before one is able to examine one's neighbors for any obvious or invisible health deficiencies, and where there is no possibility of escape to a more conducive location, should the person be undesirable, if only by apparent health indicators.

As a remedy for special allergies Dr. Johnson recommends you travel with appropriate medication.[28] But that, alas, might be a trifle difficult when not knowing what sort of critters, viruses and odors stream through the ventilation system or harbor in the upholstery or carpets on a particular plane or flight, since that mostly depends upon the route the aircraft has recently flown—information that, in turn, is often unknown to both passengers and flight attendants.

It is vital to pass on one piece of advice for air travelers, which escaped Dr. Johnson's attention. Take along your own blanket and pillow—even on short trips. At least you know where they've been. Blankets handed out on-board, unless wrapped in plastic and sealed, have embraced a multitude of people who have coughed, farted, jerked off, burped, sneezed, urinated and snotted into them—you do not wish to know how many times—before they end up around your body. They are cleaned only once in a blue moon. This gives bacteria and viruses more than adequate time to prosper and multiply. Your own pillow is a must for the same reasons.

But while you contemptuously wave your own blanket and pillow in front of a flight attendants' eyes when she or he is offering you one, be gracious. The attendant is only trying to make sure that you're comfortable with what has been provided. And as long as people want to travel around the world for $99, passengers will be offered dark-colored blankets and light-colored pillows that create the illusion of cleanliness and may hide a sullied past. With those bargain basement flying prices (paid by your cabin crew to begin with), you should accept both graciously and gratefully if arriving on board unprepared. Of course, it goes without saying that you must live with the potential consequences.

How does cabin crew fare in this airborne infection-loaded environment, disregarding the issuing of questionable pillows and blankets, and the subsequent collecting and folding task demanded by airline management? Well, as far as regulations for cabin crews' protection from infectious airborne diseases are concerned, the situation is similar for all other physical or psychological illnesses potentially contracted or acquired on board an aircraft. There are none. And as early as 1972, in the days when 100% fresh air circulated in passenger cabins, researchers report that airline medical officers were regularly faced with unusual illnesses in aircrew members due to the constant contact with foreign populations, as well as to the viruses and bacteria carried in foreign foods and water.[29]

Because pilots' contact with the on-board populace is practically nil, for once, flight attendants are the focus of that study. The probability of contracting an airborne disease is vividly demonstrated by the boys' reluctance to admit passengers to the flight deck. Though it was a practice once regarded as an easily-granted flight attendant request, it is now often denied because of their fear of flight deck contamination. The boys know how to protect themselves. To consider that cabin crew—most of whom regularly visit the cockpit if for nothing else but a breath of fresh air—also could be contaminated with a multitude of viruses, seems yet not to have dawned on them.

At an International Labour Organisation conference in Geneva in 1977, hosted under the auspicious title *Occupational Health And Safety In Civil Aviation*, conferees heard that

> Very little has been done in the area of flight crews occupational health and safety [whose] problems can clearly be divided into those arising in the air, where there can be no real comparison with other industries, and those arising on the ground.[30]

Those present discussed all the ailments that cabin crew suffer, and pilots, because of their oxygen-drenched and sheltered kennel, do not. In the proceedings from the conference we find this succinct observation:

> It is possible, in conventional aircraft, to fly right round the world—well within the incubation period of most infectious diseases. As a result, airport workers may be at some risk to these as visitors from infected areas [who] arrive at the airport often without showing any signs of illness. Besides the potential risk of infection involved in the transport of human beings and animals, the rodent and insect vectors of certain diseases may infest an aircraft on an international journey, and measures may have to be taken against them for the protection of the airline staff.[31]

The conference participants also determined that air transport has been responsible for outbreaks of influenza when it appears simultaneously in many parts of the world, and for influencing the mutant strains of the influenza virus which occur from time to time. They also asserted that many communicable diseases for which there are no vaccines—including Marburg and Lassa fever, which came into prominence around 1977—could be spread wonderfully well by aircraft.[32] Additionally, the researchers asserted that the carriage of animals may produce hazards such as zoonoses, which are any of the various diseases naturally transmitted to humans. Furthermore, they warned that poisonous chemicals may leak and affect crew.[33]

Despite these documented findings, the airlines still maintain, twenty years later, that there is no conclusive correlation between the cabin air which constitutes an aircraft's *natural* environment, and the health of flight attendants and passengers. U.S. Aviation authorities sing the same tune when they reassert that a link between air circulation and health is difficult to prove, because no data base can be established for passengers health before they board a plane.[34] This might be a viable argument where the public is concerned—after all, the day has yet to dawn when airline passengers will be required to present medical certificates before being granted permission to buy tickets to Disney World. Such a *modus operandi* would not be greatly conducive to corporate finances. Therefore, the only people aware of the dismal health conditions in the sky are flight attendants, who have no proof or research on which to base their assertions, and pilots who, because of the remunerative incentives they receive, are gagged.

When earning up to $247,000 as a Boeing 747 captain, it is easy to understand a pilot's complacency unless he or she is moved by exceptional ethical values. Thus, flight attendants are the ones who put their health on the line. Why, you must be asking yourself, don't they object? If they protest against the abysmal work conditions under which they labor, they will be harassed and prosecuted with such expertise—expertise aided by their own flight attendant unions—that they soon disappear between the cracks. Because the vast majority of flight attendants are unemployable in earthly pursuits, a fact which they are intuitively aware of, they would rather live to die with cancer or whatever they contract in their time in the skies, than to protest against the conditions imposed on them by carriers, pilots and their unions.

Therefore carriers such as Deutsche Airbus can get away with the eloquent statement that "Stale air, at least, has offered no cause for passenger complaint for a long time."[35] No. Of course not! Who in their sane mind would inquire about an airline's ventilation and filtration system cleaning policies before climbing aboard? Who, unless they are mentally challenged, would think that the stale air could be an indicator of what I have termed the aircraft illness incubator? Who would, without deeming oneself to be obsessively paranoid, believe that the conditions were caused by the lack of oxygen and cleanliness? The very concept is rejected by the average person—with the exception of flight attendants. They receive neither media coverage nor researchers' attention. Furthermore, as has been documented time and time again, their union officers are not interested in working on the membership's behalf.

We can be certain that the world's commercial airlines are aware of the health risks associated with cabin air quality and quantity because they conducted a symposium on aircraft air in California in the spring of 1995. Dr. C. Thibeault, Air Canada's Chief Medical Officer, delivered a symposium paper, "Cabin Air Quality: Myth vs. Reality," in which he states,

> As people became concerned about indoor air quality when energy efficient buildings came about, they also became concerned about cabin air quality with the newer generation aircraft. However, it soon became obvious, as incident reports came in, that crews and passengers were confused about the different elements of air quality. Even though there hasn't been

much research on the subject so far, the basic knowledge about pressurization, ventilation, filtration, and air conditioning have been around for a long time, but deserve to be reviewed again to set the stage for a reasonable discussion based on facts as opposed to emotions. We believe that the perceived problem related to Cabin Air Quality is multifactorial and that the review of the different factors involved will go a long way towards orienting future work and discussions.[36]

The question we must ask of Dr. Thibeault is *who* perceived the "perceived problem related to Cabin Air Quality?" *Who* should be addressed in the discussion to be based on "Facts as opposed to emotions?" On *which* facts and on *whose* emotions? There are no empirical cabin crew studies available on psychological makeup or on their perceptions of air quality-quantity. What does exist are only a handful of studies conducted on air crew's menstrual cycles, pregnancies, relative metabolic rate and heart rate variations, and work expenditure compared with the earthbound population.

If cabin crews' and passengers' problems with the air are truly a figment of their imaginations, why does Dr. Thibeault suggest, in an article jointly written with Drs. Kikuchi and Pinto-Ferreiar for the Aerospace Medical Association, that the specifications for the Very Large Airplane (VLA), presently on manufacturers' drawing boards, with a capacity of 600–1000 passengers, should provide 19 cfm airflow and 10 cfm fresh air supply per passenger? Why do they recommend levels of less than 1000 ppm carbon-dioxide, and ozone levels of less than 0.1 ppm? Why, suddenly, is a relative humidity of as close to 30% a desirable goal? Why do Dr. Thibeault and his colleagues suggest that high efficiency particulate air filters (HEPA) be installed and properly maintained on the VLA? And why do they recommend that VLAs maintain a cabin altitude as close to sea level as possible? Why suggest all these changes when, according to Thibeault, the quality and quantity of air presently found on aircraft is not harmful to passengers and cabin crew? Why indeed.[37]

Passengers have remained largely ignored by researchers except for studies describing physical ailments exacerbated by air travel. One study describes "Economy Class Syndrome," a venous problem caused by the cramped seating arrangements particularly evident in economy class.[38] Another explores contraindications for aircraft travel which include contagious or communicable disease, coronary occlusion, anemia, pneumothorax, cardiac decompensation, wired jaws or trismus, perforating eye lesions, mental disturbance and bladder or bowel incontinence because these conditions can be complicated by the reduced air pressure in passenger cabins.[39] None, however, have been conducted on passengers' psychological ailments.

So then, whose emotions are Dr. Thibeault referring to in his address to the air quality/quantity symposium? Pilots are not supposed to be emotional whatsoever, so of course, he must be referring to cabin crew. They are the only ones who do know that there's something awfully wrong with the air up there. The vast majority of passengers don't have a clue what's happening to them when they take wing. Flight attendants also have unions whose officers, mainly males who have occupied their union positions for an eternity, notoriously act as *employer* advocates rather than membership advocates.

What better way is there to attack the mainly female cabin crew's psychological integrity than by blaming their complaints about the air up there on their innate emotional fragility, as insinuated by Air Canada's Chief Medical Officer. One could not wish for a more enlightening statement to reflect the level of esteem and confidence North American airlines maintain toward their inflight service personnel. And is it not reassuring that the air quality problem *will be discussed* in the future? In air carriers' terms that means discussions could drag on for the next twenty years. Those discussions—given the length of their duration—will not prevent the long-term repercussions from oxygen starvation, intense carbon dioxide, radiation, and ozone exposure, hypoxia, and the effects of airborne microbiological diseases on flight attendants' health. No one has even begun to discuss the issues of the shorter term effects and the misery of paying passengers.

Cabin crews' book off rates should serve as an indication of how much is really amiss with the working environment and working conditions. Approximately 50% of Canadian flight attendants book off at least once a year for more than 14 days, and approximately 20% are on long-term disability. This excludes WCB claimants.[40] Compared to the lower percentages of book offs for pilots, who are considered to be highly motivated, those high percentages appear to be unjustifiable, unless we consider cabin crew as an inherently unhealthy species. But how could that be, when every single one of them passed a pre-employment examination conducted by their airline's medical officer, who certified that they were in superb physical and mental health? Doubtlessly, Canadian flight attendants' illness rates are similar to those experienced in the U.S. Comparable figures with earthly workforces are unavailable because with whom should one compare them? Coal miners? Steel workers? Office staff? British blue collar workers in the auto industry?

Flight attendants' health risks, well-known to the carriers since 1972, become an even more insidious problem when we realize that most, if not all, North American airlines closed their medical clinics to cabin crews a long time ago.[41] Why? It is so much more conducive to allow the public health care system to take care of their disease-stricken cabin personnel. Not only is it cost-efficient, it also conveniently eliminates all documentation of the causes for flight attendant illness, thus allowing North American carriers to continue to do what they have perfected to a fine art—willfully and knowingly endangering the health and well-being of cabin crews and passengers on a perpetual basis. Without this supporting documentation, the corporations have only to plead innocence or ignorance unless proven guilty of neglect. But by whom?

At the Geneva International Labour Organization Conference in 1977, the essential work of flight attendants was described:

> "they have a considerable role to play over and above the obvious one of attending to the physical needs of the passengers. They have the responsibility for maintaining the morale of passengers and keeping order in case of an emergency, operating safety equipment in the passenger cabin and controlling emergency evacuations on the ground if necessary. With the introduction of wide-bodied aircraft carrying hundreds of passengers, their safety role has become [even] more prominent."[42]

As the failure to improve their working conditions continues, flight attendants, regardless of age, seniority, color, race or religion, can only pray that their oxygen-deficient, germ-loaded, radiation, ozone, carbon monoxide and dioxide-infested working environment will not doom them an untimely, lingering, and gruesome death. On an uplifting note however, shareholders of any self-respecting stock exchanged airline corporation will see an increase in profit if they can, at the greatest speed possible, get rid of cabin attendants before they reach the top pay scale.

Remember Erika? Well, she decided to go ahead with her London flight the following day knowing that, if contagious tuberculosis had been in her system since May 13, 1994, infecting a few others in the process had not made a difference to NorAm. So why should it to her? Especially since it would cost her twenty hours flying-time pay plus tax-free expenses.

That settled, we spent a lovely evening gabbing about life in the fast lane before I returned to my home and continued to await sister Fiona's summons to a meeting.

The Road to Recovery

After the usual shuffling around of dates and times, Annemarie and I finally met with Fiona and Tobias on August 30th. Tobias revealed that Davis, upon my request, had checked my income figures used for the WCB pension and declared that perhaps they were not justified. "That's interesting, Tobias. I called payroll a few days ago, and they said that they couldn't find them. Peculiar, isn't it? And tell me. Does Davis have any decision-making power or should headquarters be involved?" I asked.

"Well, NorAm's afraid of a lawsuit and reluctant to release information— and let's not pull out the heavy guns yet. We'll plan strategy today. But now they say that you're trying to hide behind me," he answered smoothly.

"That's weird. Why should I want to hide behind you—of all people? You've only been involved the last couple of months? And why would I want to hide behind anyone, period?" I responded, astonished.

He chose not to answer, instead presenting us with twenty-four questions he intended to ask the company. The list began: "Why does NorAm have no efficient and competent *handlers* for crew members following a major incident or accident? Why is Tanya being continually treated as a pain, and being tormented to get to work or get off the blotter?"

As he read out number twenty-two, he added, "They want to fire you, you know. But I'm trying to persuade them otherwise."

"Why on Earth are you doing that? Let them fire me! Then I can sue them for unlawful dismissal," I fired back, aghast.

"You can't take NorAm to court," Fiona piped up.

"Of course, I can. Just watch me," I said, smiling at her. We went on to number twenty-three.

"Why does the company argue that flight attendants are predisposed to PTSD when they are not screening for such predisposition in their hiring process?"

"Get off it, Tobias. How can they screen for something that hasn't been researched? Besides, it would take away the possibility of declaring flight attendants insane when something happens to us. All those I know who are on long-term illness because of inflight injuries, ranging from electrical shock to turbulence, have been accused of having been mentally *and* physically predisposed and incapacitated before we joined the airline.

Of course that's a crock. It's fabricated in the hope of rattling our psyches sufficiently enough to make us doubt ourselves and go away so that NorAm won't have to pay. You get it?"

Neither he nor Fiona responded. Tobias read number 24. "Why is NorAm not aware of Post Trauma Syndrome handling, has no program in place, and has not yet learned from Tanya's accident and handling?"

"Good. When can you get the answers?" Brother Tobias promised to get them soon.

In the bothersome silence that prevailed from the beginning of September, only one sorrowful event on the 8th, jolted me into attention. On that day, the news came that a USAir Boeing 737, during its approach to Pittsburgh airport had nose-dived into a ravine for reasons unknown. After eyewitnesses' reports about limbs, suitcases, and aircraft parts hanging from trees around the accident scene, Dr. John Carr, a psychologist, was asked, "What can people do to get back into the air if they've survived an accident or if they've had to do the cleaning up after such a catastrophe?"

"It's of utmost importance that they get as much information as possible about why the accident happened. It gives them the tools necessary to evaluate the risks of flying and to decide whether or not they want to fly again," he advised. With those words, USAir's misfortune perversely turned into my blessing. I got up from my chair trembling, and fetched a drink to salute the dead and to celebrate, for I finally knew the reason for my obsession to acquire the accident report of Flight 113.

Those losing their loved ones in the USAir Boeing 737, in United Airline's 737 crash at Colorado Springs in March 1991, and in the Air Eagle accident in Indiana in October 1994, and those scraping up or trying to match torn off limbs of the deceased, had to wait until November 1996 before the news emerged: Boeing acknowledged that uncommanded rudder hardovers on Boeing 737s might have caused the accidents.

The manufacturer, however, had no intention of following the FAA's recommendations for changing the rudder design, or for recalling any of the approximately 2,700 737 aircraft in use worldwide. The 70 reports of 737 flights briefly thrown off course in a manner that suggested rudder malfunctioning, and numerous other rogue rudder incidents reported by 737 pilots in the 1970s and 80s, were by and large dismissed as a minor nuisance.[1] American Airlines, Northwest, Delta, United Air Lines and USAir, however, in late 1995 purported to have resolved the problem by having included stall training in their Boeing 757 simulator for pilots' recurrent sessions.[2] Previously, stall training had only been afforded to military pilots.

As my spirits were lifted by my increased understanding of it all, I waited patiently to hear from Tobias or Fiona, but it was Harry who phoned on the 13th, to see how I was doing, and to assure me, when I complained about Tobias' tardiness, "Don't worry! He'll call. It's a precedent-setting case, and we'll take good care of you," He then cheerfully bade me good-bye, freeing the line for Shirley to tell me that she was leaving the Workers' Assistance to join the ranks of WCB lawyers. Someone competent would take over my file, she told me.

Next, Tobias rang, grumpy and annoyed. A NorAm flight attendant who suffered from severe effects of an electrical shock sustained some years earlier on-board a DC9 had just threatened to sue the union for misrepresentation and defamation of character.

"Well, what I want from you might not please you, either," I said to him. "I want another meeting to find out what is—and is not—acceptable according to labor laws and human right provisions, if and how I'm protected by the collective agreement, and how much abuse I have to take from my employer."

"You know what," he responded. "From now on we'll get everything in writing. Perhaps we'll even hire a lawyer to deal with NorAm, and go public with your case. And if they refuse to release the accident report, we'll call for a MOT (Ministry of Transport) audit. Anyhow, as soon as Davis is back from Toronto. He's out there all week. I'll arrange a meeting and I'd like you to come along. Is that all right with you?" Obviously believing that he had lulled me into a sense of security and a softer mood, he apologized on behalf of all union officers for the inadequate handling of my "situation."

I grinned broadly, but said nothing, nor did I acknowledge his rhetoric other than to say that I looked forward to hearing from him again. He said that he would call in one week, and we parted on an amiable note.

Of course, I did not hear from him in a week, but I managed to catch him at home on the 27th, suffering from what he perceived as a horrible experience the previous day, when he had flown in from Tokyo on NorAm's inaugural Japanese flight. "There's far too little crew, and passengers are horribly impolite; they yell and scream at flight attendants. You've no idea," he whined.

"Doesn't surprise me," I chirped. "You've seen Japan Air crews get off the bus. There must be twenty in the back end alone. So what do you expect? We're only nine on the same run doing the same service! No wonder people are upset!"

"Explain that to Maryanne Wald," he replied unhappily.

"Maryanne Wald?" I asked, aghast. As usual I thought of her and visualized her as Miss Piggy because of her uncanny resemblance to the TV puppet in both features and stature.

"Yes. She designed the service," he enlightened me.

I could barely contain myself from bursting into laughter. It made such perfect sense: a long-time union hotshot and one of the laziest in-charges of all times planned NorAm's elaborate service to and from Japan.

"You must be joking! She knows only two things—how to delegate and how to create trouble for passengers and crew!" I said, knowing from personal experience and that of others about Miss Piggy's uncanny ability to instigate friction. If it wasn't so disturbing for those working with her, or passengers paying to meet her, it would be hilarious. Her personality radiated with such negative vibrations that she created tension among passengers and crew alike; within minutes of most encounters, she had everyone on edge and quickly coerced into dancing to her fiddle.

So extraordinarily gifted was she with haughtiness, arrogance, and feelings of superiority, that one passenger saw no other way to respond but to deck her. Admittedly this is a wrong move at the best of times, but on an aircraft, physical assault is particularly frowned upon, and the police always awaiting at destination point. Flight attendants on board that particular aircraft, and throughout the system, cheered the passenger as a hero, jubilant and grateful that he had dared what many had been tempted to do innumerable occasions. It was a blessing that Miss Piggy often booked off, or chose to work on special assignments on the ground, such as she had for the creation of the Japan service. The outcome of her work, however, was less of a blessing. It had turned into a service almost impossible to complete, with crew running themselves ragged, especially the experienced flight attendants. (The Japanese attendants were fresh out of training school and didn't have a clue what it was all about to begin with.) Unfortunately though, if passenger complaints sailed in, cabin crew would, of course, be blamed—and not Miss Piggy.

"Well, Tobias, while you were out and about, I spoke to Davis's gofer."

"Oh, yeah? He left a message on my voice mail," he answered, yawning deeply.

"Yes, I told him I'd be present at your meeting with Davis to get answers to the questions." That upset him so much that he yelled back that I had no say in that, or any other matters pertaining to my affairs—only union reps had the power to rule them.

"Is that so?" I responded evenly. "I am not at all pleased about that. So, what're you going to do to change that?" I asked, ready for an argument.

"Tanya, if you don't behave, Harry and I won't play with you anymore. So don't aggravate me."

"Well, that's no big loss, since I haven't received any help from you guys so far. But I do want answers to my questions," I responded matter of factly.

"I'm not paid to answer your questions," he replied, getting testy.

"Then perhaps someone should be hired by the union to get me those answers," I fired back acidly.

"Now, now," he chimed, resorting to his usual placating tone, "I'll try to arrange a meeting and call you tomorrow, OK? Gotta go to bed now. Bye," and he hung up to get his beauty rest.

Two days later he rang back. A tentative meeting for October 3rd, had been arranged.

"Can't do. Annemarie is flying".

"Then we'll postpone. I'll keep you posted," he said without hesitation. On October 6th, late at night, because he had just returned from a NorAm-sponsored three-day PTSD seminar on the East coast, he called to advise me that a tentative meeting was now scheduled for October 18th. "And take your folder along, would you? I've lost yours—think my wife threw it in the garbage."

The following day I contacted Janice, a former NorAm flight attendant who now worked as a criminal lawyer. A week later, Annemarie and

I met at her office, and she agreed to supervise the union's actions for me, viewing the task as a "labor of love." An hour later, Annemarie and I headed for the closest brasserie to celebrate.

When Tobias called on October 14th, to say that the October 18th meeting had also been canceled, and would most likely not take place until November, I almost burst out laughing, but stifling the impulse, simply said, "That's fine. Anything else?"

"Yes. Davis has a message for you. He admits you're getting a raw deal, but he asked me to tell you not to rush them if the case goes to arbitration."

Now, that indicated a whole new turn of events. But I bade him adieu without making further inquiries. That same day, NorAm's claims adjudicator asked the Board about the issues presently under adjudication, and the wage indemnity brokers demanded that I see another psychologist.

"Sorry, I won't," I said. "I've been abused enough. The case can go to court."

McCormick rang to tell me that Kruk's *in absentia* evaluation of my psyche had been favorable, and he predicted that I would receive a 100% loss of earning pension from the Board. A few days later Tobias advised me that a meeting with NorAm had now been scheduled for November 8th or 10th, adding, "They're pushing for a pension. They want your case wrapped up, you know."

"You bet they would. Call me when you got a date, place and time. Got to run now," I answered and then hung up, concealing the fact that I thoroughly disliked speaking to him. I went back to study Kruk's perception of my psyche, which had arrived in the mail that morning.

As a doctor in psychology, specializing in parent–child interactions, Dr. Kruk now provided consultations to legal counsel that included: issues of custody and access; fitness to stand trial; and the psychological status of individuals secondary to motor vehicle accidents, assaults, and industrial accidents.

Part of his practice involved the evaluation of a subject's likelihood to malinger psychological distress. Beginning his report by pointing out that PTSD had been studied extensively in combat veterans, rape victims, motor vehicle accident (MVA) victims, and victims of natural disasters, Kruk noted that systematic research concerning victims of air travel accidents did not exist. Subjects were most likely to meet PTSD criteria, however, if they had previously been victims of sexual or physical assault.

He then asserted that only random treatment outcome trials concerning combat veterans and rape victims had been published. Even though they were not particularly similar to my experience, he maintained that they could reveal something about the general PTSD treatment success rate. He then used adult female rape victim data for a comparison to my case, and concluded that, when these victims were assisted in reliving the rape scene by imaginal exposure while having them listen to their tape-recorded portrayal of the assault, it had proven to be a relatively effective treatment. Roughly two-thirds of the victims returned to normal levels of anxiety and apprehensions. But when supportive therapy was administered, such as my psychiatrist provided for me, almost none of the rape victims had recuperated.

"Hell," I thought, "For this guy it's all the same. Engine exploding outside the body—undesired penis exploding within!"

Using the relevant clinical records of my file—in chronological order from the earliest to the present—Kruk noted that ten mental health professionals had assessed and/or treated me since 1988, and that most had agreed on PTSD as a primary diagnosis. Accounts of my rigidity and other interpersonal difficulties occurred predominantly in adjudicator reports. Little evidence existed, he observed, to suggest any pre-accident difficulties relating to either a personality disturbance or pre-existing psychopathology. There had not been any mention of any significant or untoward personality features until the airline-appointed psychiatrist's report of December 1990. Kruk commented that it was unclear on which data that psychiatrist had based his diagnosis of histrionic personality. Furthermore, his assessment continued, until the Board psychologist's report of February 22nd, 1991, there had not been any mention of litigation, disability or work dissatisfaction factors underlying my psychological state. In 1989, he pointed out, I had been returned to work when, in fact, I was still PTSD symptomatic.

According to Dr. Kruk, any formal personality assessment had now been compromised by the litigious atmosphere surrounding my case and by my chronic PTSD, therefore a reliable assessment of the contribution of predisposing traits to my PTSD would be unlikely. The rather stressful relations with my ex-employer and WCB, and the litigious atmosphere surrounding my case were definitely negative prognostic signs. My limited social support did not bode well for my future, either, he wrote. My exposure to multiple mental health professionals further prevented improvement, because of my defensiveness towards them. Thus, it would be unlikely that I would benefit from further treatment.

He concluded that even though it was theoretically possible that as many as 50% of similar aviation accident PTSD patients could significantly respond to an exposure-based treatment, it was hopeless in my case, because too many negative factors were present.

Nonetheless, he stated, I had not been afforded the treatment of choice—repeated prolonged imaginal reviews of the aviation accidents combined with applied relaxation and cognitive restructuring. However, since he had not seen me personally, and probably was unaware of other important facts, his statements were based on assumptions. With that final word, the good doctor had opened a loophole for WCB, who had footed Kruk's $1,100 bill. Kowal would enthusiastically grasp the opportunity to drive a truck through it.

McCormick was delighted with Kruk's assessment, certain that the Board had to grant me a 100% pension. I spewed fire and brimstone about the rape insinuation, however, and intensified my aircrew research at the university library, which I had begun early in October.

The next focus for my research presented itself with the press announcement that an Air Canada captain had been removed from the controls of a Boeing 767, bound for Halifax, Nova Scotia, from London, England, minutes before push back for takeoff, because he was intoxicated.

Alcohol and Pilots

In the early 1960s, the Federal Aviation Agency (FAA) discovered the presence of alcohol in some aviation accident victims. Before then, little attention had been given to the role of alcohol in the "general aviation community"—which includes private and commercial air charter pilots, crop dusting pilots, and flight instructors, though excluding military and airline transport pilots.

At that time, a team of researchers began to investigate the extent of alcohol involvement in aircraft accidents and found that nation-wide, of 158 fatal incidents surveyed, 35.5% involved alcohol with blood alcohol concentration (BAC) levels of 0.015% and above. Of those, 58.8% exceeded a 0.1% BAC level.[1]

Representatives of the aviation communities, disenchanted with the implication that aircraft control and imbibing alcohol went hand and hand, protested that the researchers had surveyed only those cases which were suspected of being alcohol related. The FAA, therefore, commissioned a second study in the mid-60s in which the autopsies on pilots in an undisclosed number of fatal accidents revealed that 30% had BAC levels above 0.015%, and of those, 88% exceeded the 0.1% BAC level. An undisclosed number of apparent suicides that had been classed as accidents involving alcohol were said to have been included in the survey.[2] The overall percentage of alcohol testing among pilots killed in general aviation crashes in the 1960s and 1970s appears to have varied from 30% to 80%.[3]

The U.S. National Transportation Safety Board reported that alcoholism was the direct cause in 10.5% of all fatal general aviation accidents between 1957 and 1981.[4] In 1983, it was estimated that over 400, or 8% of the approximately 50,000 general aviation accidents occurring in the U.S. between 1965 and 1975 were alcohol related.[5] However, it has been reported by other sources, that alcohol involvement rates in fatal general aviation crashes dropped from about 40% in the early 1960's to about 10% in the late 1980s. This decrease may be artificial, because alcohol testing in post-mortem examinations first became routine in the 80s, whereas in the 60s and 70s testing was only performed on selected cases.[6]

In 1985, the U.S. Federal Aviation Administration imposed a legal requirement on all civil aviation aircrew personnel to have blood level concentration levels of less than 0.04 while on the job. This regulation is much less liberal than that of the United Kingdom's, where article 57 of the Air Navigation Order (No. 2, 1985) states that "the limit of drinking or drug taking is any extent at which the capacity to act as a crew member would be impaired." However, Britain's regulatory body presently considers that a BAC level of just 0.02 be imposed on British pilots, since there is evidence that the performance of flight crew may be impaired at even such a low level.[7]

Commercial airlines consistently argue that wind, weather, and pilot error cause plane crashes. If they were to consider that pilots' judgment might have been impaired due to one too many for the road before beginning their duties, it would not be conducive to the bottom line or to the public's perception of safety in the skies. Assisting this possible deception is the difficulty of proving an aviator's BAC levels when all that remains at an accident scene may be a fluid mass of previously solid bodies intermingled with fragments of bones, hair, and teeth.

The only time that pilot intoxication has been documented and the report published happened after China Air crashed at Tokyo's Narita Airport in the mid-90s killing all aboard. In another crash investigation, the BAC level found in the remains of a United Airline's Boeing 757 captain after his aircraft collided with a mountain near Cali, Columbia on December 20, 1995, where there were no survivors, was quickly ascribed to "natural body decomposition."[8]

To determine the extent of drug and alcohol abuse in the Canadian transportation field, the Department of Transport (DoT) in 1988 commissioned a private research organization to survey 18,000 employees whose job functions and responsibilities had a direct impact on either the health, safety, or security of the public, or on persons working in the transportation industry, and where there was a potential risk of loss of life, injury, or damage to property.[9] For the air transportation sector, those participating included: flight crews, maintenance personnel, air traffic controllers, and other navigational employees, as well as dispatchers, inspectors, private pilots, airside drivers (those driving vehicles necessary to service aircraft on the tarmac), security screeners and workers. The survey was conducted by workers self-reporting alcohol and/or drug use or abuse.

Whereas just under 5% of any group admitted to heavy substance use at work, or just before going to work, less than 1% reported that accidents had been caused due to their habits. However, 2% of air traffic controllers, and 2.9% of other air navigation personnel reported that they were less likely to drink at work but more likely to report to work with a "hangover," which, admittedly, had generated dangerous situations. Because hangovers can impair performance for up to thirty-four hours after drinking, it was anticipated that as many as thirty air traffic controllers may be directing aircraft at any given time while still to some extent under the influence.[10]

Those admitting to alcohol and drug use on the job—air traffic controllers and flight attendants leading the pack—cited pressure and stress as well as boredom, fatigue, long or odd hours, shift work, or "too long away from home" as reasons. But 50% of imbibing flight attendants and 30% of drinking private pilots also cited that easy access to alcohol or drugs at work was responsible for their habit.[11] With regard to private pilots, this stimulates our curiosity, because they themselves must acquire the goodies on earth and carry them aboard for consumption. Be that as it may, commercial airline cockpit crews are nowhere mentioned, leading to the conclusion that they are listed in the "also ran" category which reports a Virgin Mary lifestyle.[12]

For reasons unknown, the Department of Transport commissioned yet another study, in the winter of 1989/90, which involved 20,000 transport workers in the air, sea, road and rail sectors of the industry. Upon its completion, the Transportation Ministry concluded that, statistically, no crisis situation existed.[13] Because fewer than fifty of the 70,000 Canadian pilot license holders had been reported to the DoT in 1989—and none for drug abuse—and because the Canadian Owner and Pilot Association (COPA) argued that existing and educational efforts, combined with the public's watchful eyes, were sufficient to deal with the very few mixing alcohol with flying, flight attendants and passengers were encouraged to believe they are as safe when flying as they would be in a baby's cradle.[14]

Because the affinity for alcohol consumption and intoxication is a universal phenomenon, independent of social, economic, professional and cultural background, it can safely be assumed that pilots worldwide imbibe just as much as other transportation workers. In fact, perhaps they imbibe more, because their job ranks second in stress among all uniformed occupations, second only to that of police officers.[15] That pilots don't freely report their amount of liquor intake, even though 12%, purportedly, admit to using alcohol for stress relief, could be related to their perception of quantities as measured by the aviator yardstick.

For example, in a survey of 341 general aviation pilots, of whom 28% held commercial licenses, many of them looked upon beer as soda water; and all of them demonstrated a certain indifference to the affects of alcohol. Their overall opinion about how much time should elapse between drinking and flying differed dramatically from that of the FAA's regulatory aspirations. Whereas the agency requires that eight hours must pass between "bottle and throttle"[17]—twelve hours for Navy personnel—a whopping 50% of pilots thought it acceptable to fly within four hours of consuming unspecified amounts of liquor.[18]

The primary reason for pilots' indifference toward alcohol consumption in combination with assuming control of aircraft is believed to originate from either an inability to control liquor intake, or a fundamental lack of knowledge about the impact of alcohol potency levels, the amounts consumed in relation to blood alcohol concentration, and the time it takes to decrease BAC levels to the mandatory 0.04%.[19]

Depending on hours spent at the watering hole and the amounts and type of liquor consumed, four hours of abstinence before taking to the skies could prove somewhat problematic. Several studies on the effects of alcohol on pilot performance, conducted in laboratory settings, showed that BAC levels of 0.04 or below could seriously hinder performance tasks necessary for controlling aircraft.[20]

Researchers document that, whereas 10% of aviators in a flight simulator with preset errors—e.g. brakes in the off position, landing gear in the up position, fuel-select switch on the auxiliary tanks, wing flaps set at 500—missed at least one error when sober. But 68% of pilots failed to detect at least one error fourteen hours after ceasing the consumption of liquor to a 0.1% BAC level or above. A comparative study of automobile drivers revealed post-alcohol impairment fifteen hours after stopping to imbibe, to a level of 1.47 BAC.[21]

We have known for many years, that an individual's blood-alcohol concentration level and consequent intoxication cannot be directly related to the level of observable impairment. Increased tolerance to alcohol due to frequent drinking, body weight, metabolic rate, types of food in the stomach, gastric motility, potency of alcoholic beverage imbibed, time span during which the alcohol is consumed, and age of the drinker can result in individuals displaying differing performances while under the influence—even when registering the same BAC levels.[22] Older individuals, however, appear to suffer cognitive performance disruption more than younger ones when at comparable BAC levels.[23]

Even when BAC is no longer measurable in the bloodstream, the aftereffects of alcohol may contribute to aviation accidents because of *positional alcohol nystagmus* or PAN—a rapid, involuntary lateral movement of the eyeball—which is associated with an inappropriate inner ear disturbance occurring without external stimulation, and can manifest up to forty-eight hours after alcohol ingestion. PAN can be initiated by head movement alone, without the necessity of establishing a turn or some other angular acceleration, and/or be provoked by increased G-forces in response to linear acceleration, or be induced by gravitational stimuli.

Moving the head down into a dark environment looking for a switch, flying from an area of adequate visual references into blackness, or flying into a cloud bank can activate PAN. The high rate of spatial disorientation followed by accidents, which are usually attributed to pilot error, may occur as a result of PAN.[24] No data appear to be available, however, to establish if there is a relationship between BAC levels and PAN occurrence. Will three or twenty pints of Lager increase the risk potential?

It doesn't really matter, because we don't even have the foggiest idea about aircrew's drinking habits or the amounts of liquor consumed during home downtime or on layovers. We only know that imbibing is one of aircrew's favorite spare time occupations—in and out of the line of duty. Beer seems to be the preferred alcohol while in foreign ports. Not only is it perceived as being less dangerous to consume prior to flying than "hard" liquor,[25] it also nicely replenishes lost body fluid, evaporated during long flying hours in up to zero degree humidity, and it has natural sedative ingredients. Chasers are generally shunned, unless such delicacies as *Apfel Schnapps* or Newfoundland *Screech* are indigenous to the layover region.

It must be pointed out that, unlike earthlings who, according to the mental health profession, drink to hide deficiencies in social adaptation, to promote identity diffusion, and to conceal fears of intimacy, feelings of emptiness, depression, anger, or other less desirable personality traits, aircrew simply drink because it is the normal thing to do as they linger in the company of peers at ports away from home. A "steady as she goes" attitude normally prevails among aircrew, but gloriously going overboard is known to happen on occasion. Because most aircrew members experience such a slip during their career, stones are rarely—if ever—thrown during or after such an occurrence. A peaceful lot to whom aggression is alien, aircrew exchange thoughts and perspectives over barrels of beer amid fun and laughter while spending time off duty in the line of duty. It's an integral part of our way of life. The notion "who doesn't drink cannot be trusted" is wildly alive, and perpetual teetotalers are viewed as conspicuous.

It can rightfully be said that we practice our drinking habits well throughout the world. The case of two American pilots arrested in the early 1990s for imbibing heavily the night before flying a passenger jet was so extraordinary that it made headlines worldwide.[26] But that does not necessarily mean that the behavior of those two aviators was exceptional. More likely, they indulged in the wrong place, at the wrong time because the length of their layover. Layovers, which are arranged by carriers according to management's perception of what constitutes an "adequate" crew rest, do not always allow for the psychological absorption of whatever aircrew experience during the course of their work cycle. That cycle may have lasted fourteen days, interrupted only by one twenty-four hour off-duty period, with five or six takeoffs and landings daily during extremely early morning hours or late at night. Most, if not all, of their work cycle may have been in conflict with their circadian rhythms.

How often during that work cycle did they encounter "tricky" situations, and when did they encounter them, since fatigue would augment the affect on their nervous system? How many near misses did they experience during their career? Were those questions asked during their trial? Most unlikely. Therefore, those pilots can neither be classified as alcoholics nor as criminals. What they did—to overindulge and miss the cut-off time—is a common aircrew method of reducing stress after experiencing a potentially disastrous incident. This method of relaxation restores the sense of invulnerability which enables them to fly fearlessly. Instead, the airline should have been charged: for neglecting human stress tolerance levels, for failing to provide adequate recuperation periods, for the lack of mental hygiene provisions for aircrew, and for perpetually scheduling pilots and flight attendants in a manner that encourages both mental and physical burn out.

Alcohol is the most widely used and abused drug in Western Civilization.[26] It can, but does not necessarily, lead to alcoholism. The use of alcohol, the only drug officially sanctioned by the airlines, seems to enable both pilots and flight attendants to maintain their equilibrium in the face of innumerable, exceedingly stressful situations they experience and accumulate throughout their careers. And whereas earthly alcoholic employees are classically identified through their deteriorating work records, civil aviation pilots, who spend 15% or less of their lives on flight deck duty,[28] can cruise around perfecting their drinking for years before a degradation of their work performance is noticed by the employer.

The detection of heavy alcohol use by an airline medical officer was routinely synonymous with an aviator's employment termination until the U.S. Federal Air Surgeon began to issue license exemptions for alcoholism in rehabilitated pilots in the early 1970s.[29] Since then, some carriers have initiated programs to assist pilots in getting on the straight and narrow, because they discovered that attempting to remove notorious problem drinkers from the bottle—rather than

permanently removing them from the throttle—is definitely more conducive to the corporate financial picture. This makes particular sense
because, at the time the drinker is discovered, he or she most likely
hovers around middle-age, holds the rank of Captain, and at this point
the airline has invested an average of U.S. $500,000 (in 1987 dollars)
in training costs for each pilot.[30]

United Air Lines (UAL) inaugurated their assistance program in the
early 1970s. Once their medical department identifies a pilot as a problem drinker, in-patient treatment at a chemical-dependency treatment
center lasting six to eight weeks is followed by mandatory Alcoholic
Anonymous (AA) meeting attendance. After a psychiatric evaluation
insures that the aviator's boozing has not resulted in significant central
nervous tissue damage, the pilot may apply for FAA's Special Issuance
recertification On average, a pilot returns to line duty four months
after entering the treatment program. To assure sobriety thereafter,
monthly meetings are held with the flight surgeon, the flight manager,
and representatives of the pilot's union who are aviators in their
own right. AA attendance is continuous, and meetings with other
recovering alcoholic pilots are encouraged. After-care monitoring is
conducted for a minimum of two years. If a pilot suspected of continued alcoholism prefers to maintain his floating way of life, however,
he is graciously retired.[31]

NorAm has a similar program with financial provisions for those
enrolled in it for the first, fifth or tenth time. I know of several pilots who
repeated the performance on a regular basis, like clockwork, for over
fifteen years before successfully weaning off alcohol. Now they are vigorously engaged in pursuing those who, in their sublime opinion, are
hurling down the self-destructive runway of alcohol abuse.

Between 1973 and 1989, United Airlines asked 199 pilots to seek treatment for alcoholism. Of those accepting, 87% returned to flight duty
with the carrier. Their rank, age and seniority are unknown; as is the
number of pilots employed by the airline. The percentage of alcoholism among airline pilots is also unknown. A general idea can be
obtained, however, when we know that by 1985, seven hundred, or
2%, of approximately 39,000 commercial airline pilots in the U.S. had
sought FAA recertification for alcoholism. When we consider that 7 to
10% of earthbound Americans are estimated to be alcohol dependent,[33]
2% seems to indicate that airline transport pilots' boozing habits fall
far below the national norm.[34]

Air Canada (AC), another major North American carrier, implemented its employee assistance program in the 1960s. In 1983, that airline's Director of Planning and Administration, Captain P.V. Palmer, stated that an active link exists between the airline's vitality and effectiveness and workers' personal well-being and job satisfaction. He also pointed out that "One out of twelve adult men suffer from depression and stress," which could lead to difficulties at work. Acknowledging that the corporation's training costs almost $20 million annually, he argued that the carrier resents prematurely losing highly-trained, experienced, and valuable employees, particularly when considering the prohibitive cost of training pilots. Thereafter, Captain Palmer's study, focused only on cockpit crew.[35]

To entice these alcohol-endangered workers to participate in the weaning-off process, a disability income of an unnamed amount is paid to them during treatment. Upon rehabilitation, through a program structured like UAL's, the Air Canada pilot, if holding the rank of Captain, must fly as First Officer for a minimum of six months. If a relapse occurs—as happens at the rate of approximately 13% at UAL, though these figures are not disclosed by Air Canada—an opportunity might be offered to repeat the *charm farm* experience (as dry-out treatment centers are called by aircrew).[36]

Air Canada's Captain Palmer asserted that *occupational stressors*—wind and weather, the loss of separation, engine failures and/or explosions, mechanical problems, bomb and hijack threats, fatigue, and whatever else of an unexpected nature happens in the line of duty—were not *stress factors* and thus were inconsequential to a pilot's psyche. These factors were therefore unrelated to their development of alcohol abuse. Instead, he purports that, "reactions to off-the-job stresses may create a habit-forming pattern leading toward alcoholism."[37] Thus, the good man concluded, pilots' off duty hours—or 85% of their working lives—seems to be detrimental to their psychological well-being. No other airline, to my knowledge, has published surveys on the topic.

Recalling the London captain's story, and others like him caught as they attempted to control an aircraft while inebriated, I remembered that all those consistently adhering to the twelve hour, cease-drinking, bottle–to–throttle rule, had a guaranteed income if they should require treatment for alcoholism. Moreover, they had a job to return to, I had no guarantee of either, and apprehensively awaited for my future to unfold at the November 10th, 1994 meeting with management.

Aircrew Ailments

The small, bald man in full uniform entered the room. At first avoiding my gaze, he eventually introduced himself to me as the base manager, while appraising me from head to toe. He nodded to Annemarie, and shook hands with Fiona and Tobias with whom he engaged in small talk until Davis arrived. He then officially opened the November 10th meeting, and turned to address me directly, "You must immediately begin to work as a gofer in the office, four days a week from 8:30 A.M. to 4:30 P.M. On the fifth day you must job hunt within the company. If you have not found work with NorAm in six months, your employment will be terminated."

I began to tremble, laid my hand upon Annemarie's and announced, "I am leaving."

"Yes, we are," she said, getting up. "Tanya's is very upset about your proposal. Would you excuse us, please." Turning to the silent union officers, she said, "You'll meet us at the Airport Inn?" They nodded in agreement. Seconds later, we were out of there.

Two hours and forty-five minutes passed before the union officers joined us. Purportedly, they had spent the time explaining to management that firing me would result in going public with my case. The company had reacted by promising to maintain the status quo until my WCB appeal had been decided—and then they would, in their words, "give me my money due." What exactly *that* meant could not be divulged at present. No minutes had been taken. Fiona and Tobias said that they would now "think things over" and contact me once they had reached a decision about where to go from here. As we left the inn, I handed them two research studies with the advice, "Better take note of this and pass it through the system. Might be of value in the next contract negotiations!" After embracing, we went our separate ways.

One of the articles, "Fear of Flying in Civil Aviation Personnel," forms part of the discussion in Chapter Eight. The other one, entitled "Health, Sleep, and Mood Perceptions Reported by Airline Crews Flying Short and Long Hauls," was conducted by Scandinavian Airline Systems (SAS) with the goal of improving aircrew scheduling, reducing health complaints by pilots and flight attendants, and providing a basis for more effective preventive medical services for aircrew.[1]

Two hundred and ten male pilots, and 480 cabin crew members (106 men and 374 women), on short as well as long haul flights, participated in the survey. For all health problems encountered in the line of duty, with the exception of dry skin and asthma, cockpit crew reported significantly less complaints than cabin crew, and female flight attendants reported experiencing more health problems than males. More than 50% of flight attendants surveyed, however, complained about dry skin; neck, shoulder and lower back pain; fatigue; eye irritation; colds and blocked noses. Only 24% of pilots reported being afflicted with similar ailments. Higher levels of coughing were clearly noted in short haul cabin crews than in cockpit crews.[2]

Both groups complained about digestive disturbances, though their symptoms differed. Whereas pilots whined about diarrhea and the urge to urinate frequently, flight attendants suffered stomach aches, nausea, constipation, heartburn and diarrhea. The latter two symptoms were most often experienced by long haul crew.[3] In response to questions about sleep and mood problems, long haul pilots especially complained of irritability, fatigue and sleep difficulties, whereas cabin crew suffered overall fatigue.

The SAS survey noted that those flying long-distance, transmeridian routes reported more health problems than short-distance personnel, and that flight attendants suffered significantly greater health discomfort than pilots.[4] Whereas pilots can while away the hours in cockpit armchairs—affording the opportunity to take the occasional mental leave of absence to recuperate, at least on long hauls—such luxury is seldom available to flight attendants, who often move incessantly for up to sixteen hours (soon to be increased to twenty hours), often conducting heavy duty tasks. In the early 70s, the labor performed by cabin crew on a London, England to Miami run was considered to be equal to that of construction and steel workers, and somewhat less than that of farmers and coal miners.[5] Since that time, flight attendants' work loads have certainly doubled.

Though not holding my breath, I had hoped these articles would give the union officers food for thought, not to mention more ammunition to negotiate working conditions and wages according to the physical and psychological stress under which cabin crew labor. When it came to my imminent concerns, however, neither Annemarie nor I could make head or tails out of the officers' mumbo-jumbo, nor what exactly they were contemplating. Nor did we know where to look for answers. Helen, the flight attendant who had assisted me in the autumn 1992 with writing my initial letters to the union's national president, ignored my pleas for help left on her answering machine. Thus stranded, and feeling like I was sitting on needles, I contacted Tobias' home a week later. Miraculously he was there.

"We haven't decided anything yet, but Harry, Fiona, and I are going to a conference in Toronto tomorrow. Your case will be discussed. But one thing is sure. I'll definitely file a grievance. Just relax. I'll call you on the 19th," he said.

Appeased by his promises, I stood by until the 21st, when my lawyer Janice advised me to hold him to his word. This presented a task of unprecedented proportion. Leaving messages for both him and Fiona all over town turned into a perpetual game of tag. Tobias' wife, exceedingly unappreciative of my insistence about speaking with her beloved, expressed her dislike of my presence in this world in florid language before issuing one of the following excuses: he either had "just stepped out; was at the union office (where he was never to be seen all day); was at home but did not have time for me: had just left for the airport; or was at the union's airport office (where no one answered the phone)." Because he was on vacation, I knew that he was in town. Senior aircrew seldom travel privately.

The same scenario was played out with sister Fiona, who apparently spent all her waking hours in arbitration. I finally resorted to questioning another airline's union officer about how to begin a grievance procedure, and about the time limitation within which it had to be filed. But he snootily replied, "I don't know. But I think it's a month. You've gotta fill out a form and give it to Harry or Tobias."

"And where do I get that form?" I inquired.

"They've gotta mail it to you, and you return it when you've filled it out."

"And then what?" I asked, unperturbed by his abruptness.

"Well, then it'll go to the base manager "

"Thanks. And to whom have I spoken?" I wanted to know.

"Oh...can't give you my name," he answered and hung up. But if what he had said was true, I thought, time was indeed, of the essence. Ringing the union's Toronto headquarters as a last recourse, I was told that sixty days were allotted to file a grievance. My panic abated somewhat.

When I finally caught up with Tobias on November 28th, I asked, "You've discussed my case in Toronto?"

"No, no. Didn't have time!" he retorted.

"That's nice. What have you decided, then?"

"Well, there's no reason to file a grievance 'cause there's no clause under the collective agreement!" he stated.

"But it says on page 92 that NorAm commits itself to provide financial assistance to cabin personnel unfit for flight duties because of serious injuries sustained in the line of duty," I protested.

"That's not important. You didn't have an accident. Only *As* and *Bs* count. And your contract is outdated!" he fired back.

"But Tobias! Everything else goes by the old contract. Why not this? And what does *A* and *B* mean?"

"We'll discuss it another time. Gotta pick up my daughter. Call you next week."

Tobias didn't call the next week. I still sought answers to my questions. "Tell me. What constitutes *an accident*?" I asked the union's national vice president on December 6th.

"There's no definition," he responded.

"O.K. then. Please answer another question. How do you interpret page 92 in the Collective Agreement?" I demanded.

"I don't know nothing about that. But I can put you in touch with someone who does."

After three more union officers admitted their ignorance, and promised to call me back as soon as they had educated themselves, I contacted the Aviation Safety Board to be told that *Accident Configuration A* meant, in colloquial terms, one's body had been reduced to toast and/or liquefaction, whereas *B* meant survival in a broken and/or toasted body. And at the university library I found out that *serious injury*, according to the Canadian Aviation Safety Board, meant an injury sustained by a person in an aircraft accident which requires hospitalization for more than forty-eight hours commencing

> within seven days from the date the injury was sustained; results in a fracture of any bone, other than a simple fracture of the nose or any fingers or toes; involves lacerations that cause severe hemorrhage or nerve, muscle or tendon damage; involves injury to any internal organs; or involves second or third degree burns, or any burns affecting more than 5% of the body surface.[6]

Psychological Injuries are Not Mentioned.

I also learned that day that WCB is free to choose claimants' income figures–figures most beneficial to their enterprise, regardless of collective agreements. While entertaining myself with this research data, the Board, in its customary fashion, waited until December 21st to forward the managerial review decision. The disability awards manager had, in collaboration with Kowal's clinical analysis of "pertinent issues mentioned in Dr. Kruk's report," ruled that "no change in Ms. Andersen's pension was justifiable." McCormick went ballistic, and so did I.

Even though it had been agreed that Kruk's evaluation would be a binding verdict for all parties involved, Kowal argued in every imaginable way against the psychologist's perception of my psyche, and conveyed in elaborate terms that my continuing failure to become healthy was due to my lack of motivation, which had been restrained by the threat of financial losses if improvement did occur. My erroneous belief that PTSD in flight attendants was untreatable, she claimed, augmented my difficulties, especially since Kruk so clearly and adequately stated otherwise. According to Kowal, my resistance to the cognitive-behavioral therapy so highly recommended by the psychologist was the cause of my misery. The positive prognosis far outweighed the negative, she claimed, if I were to seek better counseling. If I did seek such treatment, she advised, I would be perfectly capable of performing a low-stress employment activity–such as that of a part-time Spanish translator–in the sanctuary of my home.

Stating her inability to foresee any potentially harmful effects arising from appropriate treatment, if I would willingly submit to it, the Board's director of psychology acknowledged in the same breath that the continuation of present adversarial and litigious status quo would "undoubtedly result in entrenchment of Ms. Andersen's disability and deterioration of her emotional status."

In this managerial review decision, the Board transparently colluded with management in a manner described by Thomas Szasz in his book *Law, Liberty and Psychiatry,* in which workers are oppressed by the very people entrusted to help them:

> Treating patients against their wishes, even though the treatment may be medically correct, should be considered an offense punishable by law. Let us not forget that every form of social oppression has, at some time during its history, been justified on the ground of helpfulness toward the oppressed.[7]

McCormick responded with an angry flourish, claiming that WCB had now perpetrated an expensive, harmful fraud on this worker. His outburst did not change matters—which had little effect on my psyche, because I was now completely engrossed in my research. Feeling less disturbed about the fact that flight attendants held no place in the research perceptions of commercial aviation, I instead focused on pilots. By the time Jonathan, a New York friend, called on December 27th to invite me to Las Vegas for the third week in January, I had gathered enough research data and perspectives to enthusiastically reply, "I'll be there."

Blessed with a ferocious appetite for the first time in months, I jumped off the vegetarian bandwagon to share a roasted duck with the dogs on New Year's Eve. Instead of dwelling on how the union and the airline would torment me in 1995, I contemplated the different travel methods I could use to reach Las Vegas. Yup, I could go by bus, I said to myself, but that would take light years, and would also involve traveling over the Snohomish, the only pass over the Rockies stateside to reach the Midwest. I had crossed it once during the winter in my husband's huge Peterbilt double sleeper, when mayhem struck at the top of the pass. Trucks had jackknifed, a Greyhound clung to a cliff as another one hung precariously over the opposite edge. Sneaking by unscathed, we jubilantly descended through three feet of virgin snow on the empty road, surrounded by spectacular winter wonderland.

So, buses were out. That left trains, which would mean an equally lengthy journey, because I would have to travel via Seattle and Los Angeles. That only left flying. I knew that pilots had endured similar reactions to life-threatening situations as I had, and they had overcome them. I had no intention of traveling the globe by mule cart during the remainder of my earthly existence, so I booked a Seattle–Las Vegas return flight with Mark Air—full fare, without cancellation insurance—for January 17, 1995.

On January 9th, brother Tobias begrudgingly filed the grievance, demanding that, in accordance with the collective agreement, NorAm appropriately and completely pay for the trauma I had experienced. In a letter, he informed me of his monumental effort, and he also advised me that in the future we were to communicate in writing only because of what he described as my "word twisting, unreasonable, misleading, incomprehensible, untrustworthy, deceiving and manipulative behavior." Janice said that I now had grounds to sue the union for defamation of character and misrepresentation.

On January 13, the wage indemnity brokers advised me that an assessment interview with a psychiatrist had been arranged for January 26, at 8.45 A.M.

When I telephoned their offices, inquiring who would have the honor interviewing me, no one could tell,—but they promised to look into the matter, and tell me at a later date. Could I forward Kruk's report instead of going to the interview? I asked. Yes, that would be all right, they responded.

On January 17th, my affairs in order as much as they could be. I left the house to begin my Las Vegas trip at 5:00 A.M., calm and in good spirits. I was on the bus to Seattle an hour later, thrilled to be going places. Not knowing the boarding procedures at Sea-Tac Airport, I killed an hour and a half puffing away on cigarettes outside, enjoying the sunny day before venturing to the departure lounge, where numbers were called to board the plane according to passenger check-in at the gate. The last to enter the aircraft, my plan to sit by an emergency exit at the back of the Boeing 737 vanished. I was lucky enough to get a window seat aft of the wings in the nearly full plane.

Upon push back a few minutes later, it crossed my mind to ask my aisle seat neighbor to hold my hand, but I caught myself in time. When the pilot revved up the engines, released the brakes, and began the takeoff roll I softly began to cry out of pure joy. I was doing it! I was actually going to fly on a jet plane—and I was stone cold sober to boot. Over lunch my neighbor inquired, "Why did you cry during takeoff, if I may ask?" So I told him. He understood, for he had been involved with aircraft in the military and held a private pilot's license. Time evaporated, and when I looked out, we flew by the Luxor Hotel. Seconds later, we touched down.

At the Flamingo Hilton, my home away from home for the next three days, Jonathan awaited. After I checked in, I was exceedingly thirsty. I said unhesitatingly, when he asked what I wanted to do, "Go for a beer and look around." To the Barbary Coast we went to hang out at the bar, play poker, and quench my thirst. Jonathan teetotaled. Then we did the Strip until around 10 P.M., when I called it quits. Exhilarated yet bushed, I fell into bed and slept like a log for the first time in years. Jonathan, the strong and silent type, picked me up for breakfast. Later, we took a lesson at shooting craps, which left me as clueless and disenchanted as my companion.

At the matinee at the Strand, remarkable only by the display of naked flesh and little talent, I sealed my decision to off load the man who had enticed me to fly. When he disappeared for yet another lengthy visit to the men's room, I freed him from the misery of my companionship by transferring to the Barbary Coast's bar where, aided by beer and poker, I contemplated how to occupy myself the following day.

A brochure in my hotel room advertising Grand Canyon Bus Tours solved the problem. I booked a trip. But when the driver of the minibus picked me up in the morning, we soon arrived through the airport gates, where a multitude of small aircraft were neatly lined up. I realized that wires had somehow been crossed.

"This means I've gotta fly?" I asked.

"Yeah, didn't you know? "he responded condescendingly .

"What kind of aircraft?"

"A Comanche."

"So be it," I said to no one in particular.

Weigh-in completed, I climbed into the starboard seat behind the pilot, a cheerful, tall, and competent-looking guy. We took off into a cloudless and windless sky and headed toward the Canyon, where we cruised between the high plateaus for an hour before touching down atop one to enjoy a barbecue with the natives. Upon returning to Las Vegas, I bought the photograph taken of the passengers before boarding the Comanche, checked out the Tutankhamen exhibition at the Luxor, and wandered up the Strip to alight in the Barbary Coast at around seven in the evening, exhausted, but too wound up to retire.

The place appeared deserted. Plunging onto a bar stool in front of a poker machine which had given me some joy the previous day, I apologized to my neighbor for cramping his space, and proceeded to pick his brains while playing away my quarters and drinking beer. He quickly satisfied my curiosity.

"Been here for thirty years," he drawled. "Came down from Minnesota. Been hangin' wallpaper. Never gambled in my life. Seen too many people ruined by it."

"Even people living here year round?" I inquired

"Yeah, many of my co-workers live from paycheck to paycheck. It's an addiction, you know, which..." Suddenly an earth-shattering noise erupted from my machine.

"Wow! You hit a royal flush," he exclaimed. A crowd started to gather around me.

"That's *unbelievable*. First the Grand Canyon and now this," I said in awe.

"You went into the Canyon?" the bartender asked eyes wide.

"Yeah," I responded, curious about his reaction to my statement as I scooped handfuls of coins into a bucket.

"Did you fly?"

"Yeah," I replied.

"How many went in?" he asked, meaning how many aircraft.

"Why? Three."

"And how many came out?"

"Why, three," I answered intrigued.

"You were lucky! Normally three go in and two come out."

This thought sobered me, and I packed it in a few minutes later. The excitement had drained my already depleted energy resources, and I fell into bed and slept as contentedly as a kitten.

The next morning, street-smart about Mark Air operations, and "Vegas-vibration" tired, I checked in early at the gate and was one of the first to board the plane. I chose the window seat in the second row, the first blocked off for unaccompanied minors, so that I could get off quickly in Seattle. During push back, a woman of immense proportions appeared from the washroom on crutches and squeezed herself into the center seat between me and her equally obese husband in the aisle seat. The aircraft was packed solid, and I kissed my chances of survival good-bye if the unthinkable should happen. "So be it," I thought.

When the snow on coastal mountains and dormant volcanoes sparkled in the sunset, and Seattle's lights twinkled beneath our wings, I felt ebulliently happy. "I've done it! I've really done it," my heart sang.

"The only way to pass any test is to take the test. It is inevitable," the Australian Aboriginal elder, Regal Black Swan, said.[8] I had passed the test with flying colors. I had began to mend my broken wings.

Pilot Incapacitation
and
CRM Concept

"I knew it! Time heals! It always does!" O'Doherty exclaimed, one of his rare smiles lighting his features, while he glanced at the Grand Canyon photograph, with the Comanche and me in the foreground. He asked, "Where do you want to go from here?"

"Start flying on a trial basis," I proposed. He took pen and paper and, thinking aloud, began to write.

> The above patient has exposed herself to a brief desensitization program, i.e. exposure to brief flying periods. This has given her enough confidence to ask NorAm to give her some further exposure as a passenger to brief flights over a three month period. If this is successful, a graduated return to work might be considered.

Jubilant, I mailed the note (double registered) to base manager Wackmann the same day, February 10, 1995. On February 27th, Canada Post revealed that acceptance of the letter had been refused at delivery. On the 29th, they said that a Mr. *Wakeman* at NorAm had received the letter. I told them a few days later, that no one by that name worked for the airline. Canada Post promised to take another look and, on March 9th, confirmed that Wackmann had indeed, received my psychiatrist's note on Valentine's Day. Amazing, I thought, wondering if NorAm's tentacles were so far reaching as to entice Canada Post to add stress and aggravation to my life.

Meanwhile, Tobias had sent another set of brow-beating tirades in which he informed me that NorAm viewed my neglect in applying for the IMMS as grave disobedience, and that I now was absent from my duties without reason, because I neither collected wage indemnity nor WCB's wage loss benefits. And since the company had no written proof of my continuing disability, but I currently did not meet medical standards to perform the job, my lack of status placed my employment at risk, unless I supplied the carrier with proof of my disability. If I refused to return to work immediately, NorAm would cancel my wage indemnity coverage, as they had done with all other insurance in the summer of 1994 despite my willingness to pre-pay them. Furthermore, he advised that the medical office had deemed me unable to ever return to the flight attendant position and, because I had refused to retire, my rights to ever return as cabin crew were severed. If I had any questions about my status, or my responsibilities to my employer, I was at liberty to contact sister Fiona or the union in general. I faxed the quixotic letter to my lawyer Janice.

Simultaneously, the wage indemnity brokers demanded I attend an assessment interview with a Dr. Clemens, a psychiatrist, on March 7th. They would then determine if my long-term disability claim could be accepted. But the chances for that were slim, since NorAm had cut off coverage payments. To top it off, on March 4th the union forwarded NorAm's grievance decision, dated January 30th. The company reasoned that my situation and condition did not conform to the definition in paragraph 10 of the collective agreement which, purportedly, said that, "Stress, anxiety, fear of flying and all form of mental impairment are not serious injuries. Therefore, payroll protection does not apply, and the grievance is denied."

But there was not, never has been, nor is there now, such a clause in the collective agreement. Because no covering letter from my union officers accompanied NorAm's decision, I suspected they had ignored the fact and had not filed for arbitration. My quest for answers was difficult to satisfy, because Harry and Tobias seemed to have vanished.

When Annemarie rang that afternoon, I was in a fine frame of mind because of these latest developments. My thoughts about possible courses of action were diverted when she told me that, on her outbound domestic run, the first officer on the three pilot Boeing 727 had complained about chest pains and feeling hot about twenty minutes after takeoff from Vancouver. He had moved his seat away from the instrument panel, taken a breath of oxygen from his mask and, seconds later, had lapsed into unconsciousness. The captain did a 180 and landed in Vancouver without further incident. Meanwhile, the flight attendants and a doctor had cared for the First, who had regained consciousness during the latter portion of the descent. No reason for his collapse could later be detected, despite extensive medical testing—except, that his workload over the preceding three weeks had been heavy, though within NorAm's and Transport Canada's guidelines.[1]

I had experienced a similar incident of a trifle more tricky nature in the mid-80s on a L-1011. After consuming massive quantities of First Class food throughout the flight, our captain, known more for his gluttony rather than his congeniality and *savoir faire*, passed out during approach into London, England, in the mid-morning rush hour. I happened to be in the cockpit when he crumbled and, with the help of the second officer, removed him from his seat, which the Second then dove into. I got two other crew members to assist in transporting the commander to the first class galley, where we administered oxygen, but to no avail. He remained unconscious. No medical personnel were onboard. The approach, meanwhile, had turned into a leapfrogging power on–power off affair, which had us in the back counting our blessings and preparing for all eventualities. We had no choice but to leave the captain on the galley floor for landing forty-five minutes later, since he was far too heavy to be stowed in the washroom and we did not want to drag him into the cabin and upset our passengers. The impact of the landing gear hitting the ground rather forcefully did not awaken him, and he was taken off board, still unconscious, by ambulance attendants. Needless to say, we gathered at the pub upon arrival at the hotel for a debriefing, but we never learned why this pilot had collapsed on duty. He committed suicide a few months later. Annemarie's experience and my own enticed me to research inflight pilot incapacitation, to uncover if and how aviators are trained to cope with such occurrences.

PILOT MID-AIR INCAPACITATION

One of the worst scenarios in flight, besides a fire or a crash, is sudden mid-air pilot incapacitation, which means any condition affecting an aviator's health and rendering him or her incapable of performing duties associated with flying an aircraft. This includes total incapacitation or a significant impairment of any faculty due to, for example, the onset of pain or discomfort that becomes severe enough to distract attention from normal duties. It also includes any transient impairment in the flight planning stage which could prejudice proper pre-flight planning. Degrees of incapacitation may range from minor cases of physiological or psychological upsets due to mild disease or mental stress, up to a complete collapse or some acute psychological or neurological seizure.[2]

Main causes for sudden pilot incapacitation may be epileptic seizures, physiological disorders including spatial disorientation, hypoxia, (occasionally whole crews are affected by hypoxia due to pressurization deficiency), or by carbon dioxide (CO_2) intoxication caused by inadequate packaging of dry ice containers,[3] loss of consciousness induced by acceleration of high-performance aircraft, and acute coronary insufficiency, the latter occurring more frequently at the time of takeoff or landing than during cruising. Other causes for total inflight incapacitation are cerebral hemorrhages, thrombosis, hypoglycemia, and vascular accidents related to high blood pressure.[4] Sudden incapacitation of a digestive origin appears to be primarily due to hemorrhage.[5]

Most often, however, pilots' health emergencies are related to more benign symptoms such as those associated with the flu, a toothache, a cold, a headache, fatigue, an earache, faintness, vertigo and/or disorientation, back pain, loin or kidney pain, dizziness and double vision, a nosebleed, an eye injury, chest pain, coughing and sneezing attacks, and leg or foot cramps. Gastroenteritis or digestive upsets, perhaps generated by tap water imbibed in a moment of insanity, or food consumed during a lay-over, are common, as are minor incapacitations due to ingesting drugs, alcohol and medication to alleviate some of the above symptoms. Psychological disorders of a transient nature can also cause discomforts—potentially distracting a pilot's attention while controlling an aircraft.[6]

Obviously, crew members are susceptible to degrees of incapacity any-where between those extremes; and the effects of incapacitation will depend upon the circumstances at the time of occurrence. Cases of mild incapacity are probably common but, because they do not result in inci-dents or accidents, they go unrecorded. Doubtlessly, many pilots will continue to fly even though fatigued due to sleep loss, or when worried or anxious, in order not to overburden another crew member's ability to compensate for a minor impairment.[7]

How often mid-air incapacitation occurs is suggested from a survey con-ducted by the International Federation of Air Line Pilots' Association in 1988. Aviators representing more than sixteen countries and ninety-seven airlines returned 4,345 usable questionnaires. Of the respondents, 1,251 (29%) reported experiencing at least one incapacitation incident inflight where it was necessary or desirable for another crew member to take over their duties. Of those, 52% claimed that safety had not been affected, whereas 45% acknowledged that potentially it had been.[8]

Those 45% reporting that safety had been affected by a pilot's incapaci-tation, stated that it was because other crew member(s) were placed under maximum workload as a result of taking over that pilot's duties, while 15% stated that other crew members were placed under maxi-mum work load as a result of extraordinary weather or traffic or other operational conditions. And 9% stated that the other crew members did not have the necessary training or experience to operate at an acceptable level of safety. Another 8% asserted that the placement of controls or instruments made reduced crew operation less safe. And 25% reported that a safety decrement was due to some other circumstance, such as distraction, subtle incapacitation, or reduced monitoring.[9]

Those who stated that safety had not been affected by the incapacita-tion reported that it was: because the flight was routine so far as weath-er, traffic or other operating problems were concerned (32%); because another crew member took over (25%); because the incident occurred at a time of minimum cockpit workload (16%); because the incapacitation was minor in nature (14%); or because the incapacitation was of extremely short duration (9%). In concluding, the survey revealed an increase in pilot incapacitation from 27% in 1967 to 29% in 1988.[10]

It is anticipated that of the approximately 50,000 aviation accidents which occurred in the US between 1965 and 1975, 600 were associated with psychological and/or physiological impairment or incapacitation, and seventy-seven were due to psychiatric factors.[11] The most recent surveys, conducted in the 60s and early 70s, anticipate that less than 1% of all air accidents are due to sudden incapacitation.[12]

Between the years 1961–68, reportedly there were seventeen cases of fatal pilot collapse inflight in U.S. commercial aviation in the seventeen states which reported such incidents.[13] Of those seventeen cases, five resulted in fatal accidents which were attributed to the incapacitation, and in another five the safety margin is assumed to have been critical. All seventeen collapses were the result of heart disease. The average age of the thirteen captains afflicted was forty-seven, and that of the four co-pilots was thirty-five—one being only twenty-eight. Eight of the incidents occurred in the approach and landing phase and five during taxiing after landing. Only two happened while cruising.

Air France Medical Services analyzed ten sudden pilot incapacitation cases occurring between 1968 and 1988 which were caused by cardiac arrest, epileptic attacks, duodenal hemorrhages, infection, and metabolic disorder. None resulted in an aircraft accident.[14]

IATA airlines reported forty-two cases of mid-air, non-fatal, complete pilot incapacitation for the years between 1960–66. However, these figures are considered suspect because many instances of incapacitation which do not result in an accident remain unreported.[15]

The possibility of the complete collapse of a crew member is estimated to lie somewhere in the order of one in a thousand million flights.[16] But, knowing that 85 % of aircraft incidents are said to have a lapse of human performance in the causal chain, and that there only is about a 40% chance to satisfactorily explain the cause of a crash if the cockpit crew does not survive, gives reason to wonder how many accidents are related to fatal or non-fatal pilot incapacitation.[17]

Of the latter, epilepsy is considered to be the most serious, obviously because a Grand Mal seizure creates a dangerous disruption in the flight deck. A U.S. Air Force study carried out between 1970–1980 reported four cases of generalized epilepsy out of 146 inflight incapacitations. In two of those cases investigators speculated that a fragile psychological disposition, combined with the fatigue of a long haul flight and hypoglycemia, may have encouraged onset of the seizures.[18]

Food poisoning or gastrointestinal illness are the most common causes for pilot inflight impairment. Even though the symptoms of nausea, vomiting, diarrhea, dizziness, and prostration resulting in dehydration and debilitation appear to be difficult to handle while in control of an aircraft, pilots valiantly cope with them most of the time. Severe abdominal cramping, headache, chills, fever, dizziness, and myalgia may add to the malaise. In severe cases, double vision, followed by unconsciousness, may precede death. Subtropical and tropical regions are especially high risk areas for food-borne diseases, where even brushing one's teeth with anything other than vodka can be detrimental to one's health.[19]

So what's one gonna do? Carry coolers with homemade food around the world in the line of duty? Can't. No storage space aboard. "Provide an airline catering service for crew members?" one might ask. No. Airlines would rather cut off their right arm than provide aircrew with health-sustaining nourishment. Besides, it would not be conducive to the corporate bottom line. At least we can say that the *haute cuisine* presented to aircrew and passengers while flying is so saturated with preservatives that it outlasts a refrigerator's life span.

This trend of extreme preservation derives from the fear of inflight food-borne diseases that normally originate in flight kitchens or catering sources. In February 1975, on a Japan Air Lines flight between Anchorage and Copenhagen, 196 of the Boeing 747's 344 passengers, and one of the twenty cabin crew members fell ill from dining on Alaskan cheese and ham omelets. Upon arrival at Kastrup Airport, 143 passengers and the one flight attendant were hospitalized—some for up to ten days. The cockpit crew was unafflicted because they had eaten a large meal in Anchorage before picking up the flight.[20]

British Airways reported that seventy-five crew members and more than 100 passengers were stricken with salmonella poisoning in 1984 due to the aspic glaze used on hors d'oeuvres prepared at their London Heathrow Airport flight kitchen. Crew members fell ill around the world, disrupting schedules from Washington, New York, Chicago, San Francisco, Los Angeles, Nairobi, Bahrain, United Arab Emirates, and Durban, South Africa, due to lack of replacement crew.[21] And should you entertain the thought that pilots must, by government regulation, eat meals prepared in different kitchens—think again. There is no Federal Aviation Administration regulation that governs the preparation and service of meals to commercial flight crews.[22]

In twenty international flight-related, food-born disease outbreaks, specific items and organisms implicated as sources of food poisoning included *Escherichia coli* from oysters and shellfish, *Shigella sonnei* from shrimp, *Vibrio cholerae* from hors d'oeuvres made from shrimp and from powdered dairy products, *Staphylococcus* from food containing eggs, and *Salmonella typhimurium* from egg salad and turkey. Additional illnesses may result from "individual idiosyncrasies" and "chemical" toxemias due to food containing naturally toxic substances or non-bacterial poisons which have been intentionally or accidentally introduced. Food poisoning episodes have also resulted from contaminating substances placed in foods either during preparation or during service, including cabin crew food preparation activities. Poor hygienic practices and procedures, as well as insufficient cooling were implicated in most of the contamination incidents.[23]

Nevertheless, if any minor incapacitation due to whatever reason befalls an aviator during a layover, he or she better find a remedy quickly, since repercussions could be far-reaching. A relief pilot might have to be flown in, resulting in delays which would reverberate throughout the carrier's route net, and a multitude of people would be inconvenienced. (Aircraft are scheduled to fly around the clock, because only moving planes make money.) Thus, it is better for aircrew to risk a physical collapse en route rather than to risk booking off sick abroad—regardless of one's health status. This unwritten rule sometimes reaches ludicrous, if not criminal proportions.

Recently in London, England, a Boeing 747-400 First Officer (on the two pilot controlled aircraft), suffering from severe diarrhea and vomiting after flying in from India the previous day, informed his commander the night before the homebound departure that he felt incapable of working the flight. (Over 30% of crew flying to and from that subcontinent are said to be ill on rotation.) The Captain, believing in miracles, responded that he should not jump to conclusions prematurely—after all, twelve hours remained before takeoff. While taking his pre-flight shower the following morning, the Captain slipped in the bathtub cracking two or three ribs; there was no time to check for the exact number because an aircraft awaited command. His co-pilot had not improved, but valiantly diapered himself and both controlled the 747 toward home base where they landed without incident.

Perhaps instances like the above are part of the reason why, in November 1989, the International Civil Aviation Organization recommended to its members that pilots should be trained to recognize the human factors involved in flying—in particular, fatigue. The organization asserted that potential incapacity in pilots derives from a psychological nature, in which either chronic or purely transient stressors prejudice mental functions. Stress arising from professional anxiety may be so severe as to significantly impair the capacity to operate at an acceptable level, while personal anxieties are often hidden from others. Together, and even in mild form, they may produce a reduced awareness or a reduced state of alertness, and a mental preoccupation which may result in slow reaction time and an impairment of judgment.[24]

Cockpit or Crew Resource Management (CRM)

Transport Canada (TC), in an attempt to increase the aviation community's awareness of the effects of pilot fatigue on judgment and performance, launched a national safety campaign aimed at educating pilots and airline operators by way of an Aviation Safety Management Program, Flight Safety Officer's and Pilot Decision-Making Courses, and Human Factors Seminars. These programs were attended on a voluntary basis.[25]

TC's incentive prompted some airlines in the early 90s to develop Cockpit or Crew Resource Management (CRM) courses.[26] The concept itself, however, had been recommended to the industry as early as 1973, when it was discovered that transient, subtle losses of cerebral function occurred in pilots much more often than anticipated, and were potentially much more dangerous than the feared and sudden collapse in the flight deck. Subtle incapacitation of unexplored origin could cause a crash in over 50% of cases, if occurring during a critical phase of flight. Researchers asserted, therefore, that pilots required training about aviator incapacitation just as they required training in engine fire drills, ditching, and rapid decompression.[27]

But when we consider that CRM is based on other pilots supplementing or taking over when pilot incapacitation occurs, and when we know that currently there are seldom more than two aviators in the cockpit—a do-or-die situation if one of them collapses—it is not surprising that commercial airlines embraced the CRM concept, though they only administer it on a voluntary, ad hoc basis.[28] In this way, recognition and responsibility to assess whether or not to fly when fatigued or otherwise incapacitated rests with the individual, and not with the carrier.[29]

As we have seen, pilots will not book off en route unless they're close to croaking. Their reasons are simple. If they should refuse to fly while on the road, disciplinary action or loss of employment will follow, depending on the employer's investment in that particular aviator. Neither one is an enchanting proposition, especially when pilots know that other pilots are standing by—a dime a dozen—to replace them. And should an accident occur because of pilot impairment, the airline cannot be held responsible because, ultimately, it was the aviator's decision to fly. Thus, we uncover yet another win-win situation for the industry shareholder.

The main reason for CRM training, however, is to teach pilots behavioral inter-crew dynamics and teamwork to replace the well-established custom that the captain is the all powerful and exclusive decision maker.[30] Using CRM techniques, minor omissions or misjudgments by one pilot can be readily exposed and corrected by another crew member, provided that crews are trained to cross-monitor each other's actions, and that a crew complement is based upon a fail-safe concept, whereby each member is experienced and trained to accept or question one another's actions.[31] Because cockpit crews working on today's super sophisticated aircraft are viewed as information processors, the more they are focused on controlling the aircraft, and the more they are empowered with freedom of input if encountering dire straits, the better are their chances of coping successfully with unexpected events. On the other hand, processing information is based on the model of perception, then comprehension, decision, and action. Any weakening in this model may contribute to causing an accident.[32]

Failure to fly an aircraft with focused attention can have fatal consequences. This came to light in one accident investigation, where the cockpit voice recorder readout indicated that the pilots had relaxed more than the allowable amount of their attentiveness and became involved with trivial conversation. While vigorously discussing automobile prices, the busing difficulties of the United States public schools, and whether or not the then President Nixon should resign from office, the weather deteriorated and the aircraft began to lose altitude. When the altitude warning system activated (a klaxon sounded and a light flashed), the First Officer turned off the system without a break in the chatter going on between other members of the cockpit crew. Because neither the Captain nor the First Officer brought their total level of awareness back to the task of flying the aircraft (they became attention deficit), they were inhibited from appropriately responding to the stimuli to process vital information. The situation's problems multiplied to a level that they were unable to react before the aircraft crashed.[33]

Manual aircraft control, although very demanding at times, had the advantage of keeping pilots in control of the plane. But, as more and more of that control has been relinquished to automation, pilots can become complacent. As autopilot functions become more complex, pilots become more of a controller/monitor of the autopilot functions and less of an aircraft controller.[10] Automation, therefore, forces pilots into states of inactivity and complacency for hours on end. Furthermore, the humming and subtle rhythmic beat in an airborne aircraft can transport even the most alert and well-rested person into a dreamlike trance, or even into a semi-hypnotic state, in which the immediate cockpit environment, illuminated only by dimly-lit and soothing multi-colored instruments, loses all significance. Therefore, cabin crews keep a vigilant eye on the boys, especially on long hauls, so to assure that they are with it at all times rather than snoring or in a state of suspended animation.[35] However, one soul, considering himself extremely enlightened, suggested that "FAs should stop catering coffee to pilots," in order to allow pilots to attend to the instruments.

In the past, automation has been implemented without sufficient consideration given to the human–machine interface problems inherent in the designs for automated machinery. These automation problems frequently have contributed to pilot disorientation, blunders, incidents, and accidents.[36] And those may also have been compounded by pilot sudden or subtle incapacitation.[37] Due to a general absence of data available to the public, one can only guess how often these situations occur.

———————————✈———————————

Despite augmenting my knowledge about the hidden dangers involved in flying, I was determined to return to life in the skies, since living on earth seemed revolting to me. After my Las Vegas trip, I set about with a fierce determination to accomplish my goal of returning to flying. But those in power seemed as disinterested in my achievements or my aspirations, as they remained flatly intent on my destruction. Therefore, when Annemarie and I entered psychiatrist Clemens's office on March 7th, 1995, I was more acutely on guard than I wished to be, but, regardless, I answered the now familiar questions, including: "Yes, I had joined the merchant marine at the age of seventeen, and had left my first husband to go flying because he was sterile and had refused to adopt children." When he went so far as to ask me to count and add numbers from one to ten in order to test my intellectual capabilities, I declined. Instead, I asserted that the perpetual harassment from the WCB, the union, the airline and the wage indemnity brokers had prevented the beginning of my healing process and had subsequently delayed my return to my flight attendant duties. I added that I fully intended to recommence my career in the very near future. The appointment lasted less than an hour.

Annemarie commented as we drove away, "He put two and two together."

"About what?" I asked.

"Clemens figured out that you left your first husband and went flying 'cause he didn't want to adopt children. Then you found out that you couldn't have any, either. And now you'll not allow anyone to take flying away from you, too."

"And so it is," I replied and began to cry.

April 11th, 1995, a copy of Clemens's evaluation arrived, in which he stated that I showed no psychomotor agitation or retardation, no formal thought disorder, no abnormal mental content, no psychotic thought content, and no psychotic perception. Neither did I appear to be suicidal. Easily irritated and flustered by questions, and keyed up throughout the interview, he noted, I seemed to show limited insight as to the extent of my illness, since I continued to aspire to work as a flight attendant. However, his prognosis for my recovery, in view of the chronicity of my symptoms, was bleak. The wage indemnity brokers' medical advisors accepted the report as valid, and I was allotted $206.17 in monthly long-term disability benefits retroactive to November 1993.

When NorAm had not responded to my psychiatrist's letter by April 20th, Janice, my lawyer, couriered Wackmann a copy. On April 21st, he denied ever having seen the letter, and asked whether an oversight or error on my part—such as mailing it to the wrong address—was the reason. Noting my apparent progress toward a possible recovery, he said, pleased him. However, he directed, it was imperative that I see NorAm's medical officer to obtain his advice and recommendations—which was standard procedure, because all aircrew had to obtain medical clearance from the company physician when booked off for more than fourteen days. Janice mailed Wackmann Canada Post's confirmation that he had received O'Doherty's letter on February 14th, and advised him that an appointment with the carrier's medical office had been scheduled for May 15th, 1995.

Dr. Copper, a plain general practitioner, newly hired by NorAm, greeted Janice and me with a weak, clammy handshake. After guiding us to his office, he inquired about the 1988 incident. Unwilling to repeat what for me was now becoming the ancient story, Janice interceded on my behalf. He instead asked how I pictured my comeback.

"Fly around as a passenger for about three months," I said, "then short hauls once a week to begin with, and then long hauls. And I'd like permission to sit in the flight deck for takeoff and landings as often as possible."

"Why's that?" he wanted to know.

"I believe I'll regain my sense of invulnerability faster when I see what's going on," I quipped.

"Makes sense. And then what?" he replied, burying his eyes in my face.

"Do the same schedules, but fly as additional crew member (meaning in full uniform but without responsibilities), and we'll take it from there," I offered.

"And who's going to pay for this?" he chimed.

"Why, NorAm, of course. I'll do this on a voluntary basis. I can't jeopardize my pensions and go through the hell I've lived again if it doesn't work. You do know that I'm entering uncharted territory, don't you?"

"How so?" he asked innocently.

"There's no research done on PTSD in flight attendants or pilots. So, when I volunteer as a guinea pig, I think it's fair that everything continues as is. Except that I want all my group insurance covered, and full travel benefits, and all my expenses paid while on the road. And no limits on my recovery time," I proposed. (At that time, the study "Post-traumatic Stress Disorder in Airplane Cabin Crew Attendants," surveying six North American flight attendants who survived a crash in which forty-seven passengers were killed, was unavailable to me. To my knowledge, there is still no research available on general aviation or commercial airline pilots.)[38]

"Sounds quite all right to me. But how do you know there are no studies?" he questioned. And I began to tell him.

Furiously taking notes, he interrupted me midstream, with a "Yeah, but there's research done on race-car drivers."

His ignorance rendered me speechless, but Janice interrupted. "Race-car drivers are in control of their vehicles, and therefore not comparable to flight attendants," and I picked up from there, speaking as soothingly as to a newborn.

"Dr. Copper. There's research done on PTSD in crane operators. There's research done on PTSD in rattlesnake wrestlers in the pits of Texas. There's even research done on stress in the wives of pilots. There are approximately 1243 studies done on PTSD in people of all walks of life worldwide. But there are none on flight attendants or pilots. I find that utterly peculiar."

"Well...yeah. But there's lots of talking."

"That's just not good enough, Dr. Copper. And I'm trying to change that. And I'm counting on your help. I'll of course check in with you whenever you want me to. And I've no doubt that I'll make it. Besides, I would have been back years ago had it not been for the deplorable treatment I've received from WCB and the union over the past years, and had it not been for NorAm's ignorance. But let me assure you. I'll do everything in my power to ensure that what happened to me will not happen to other flight attendants worldwide."

"Well, I'm willing to let you try. But I can't make that decision. I've gotta talk it over with Dr. Norsk."

"Dr. Norsk? He's still here? Why doesn't *he* see me, then?" I questioned.

"Well...I don't know. But he can't make a decision, either. It's gotta come from Dr. Dibalt," NorAm's chief medical officer in Toronto.

"Why not ship me out *there*, then?" I asked, annoyed.

He got up without answering, thus signaling the end of the ninety minute interview.

"Perhaps NorAm's interested in saving money by doing research to prevent a repeat of Tanya Andersen," I tried once more, "After all, last year alone, four of our engines exploded mid-air with Vancouver crew aboard. God knows how many more system-wide!"

"As I said," he protested weakly, "unfortunately I can't make the decision, and I don't know if they'll want you back."

"That's where I come in," Janice said before we walked out into the sunshine after another limp and clammy farewell handshake from the company physician.

A few days later, feeling chipper and suffering from acute cabin fever, I requested my airline travel vouchers but, after numerous phone calls and inquiries all over the system, I was referred to Davis. "You've got no travel privileges until you sign the IMMS or make up your mind what else you want to do!" he barked. It was not an auspicious sign.

At the beginning of July, 1995, Wackmann requested a meeting to exchange information and update each other, and to consider future steps that would take in my own perspectives as well as that of NorAm's. If I wanted union representation I was told, I should contact brother Tobias or Harry. Janice' presence would be unnecessary, he said. When I insisted on having legal counsel present, Wackmann canceled on the grounds that the airline needed to have legal counsel present as well. On August 18th, 1995, he proposed another meeting with all internal parties associated with my present status. My lawyer responded that Tobias' letters, and other evidence on file concerning the way the union had handled my case, sufficiently justified my refusal to attend any gathering without legal counsel. The Labor Relations Board confirmed that no law prevented me from attending meetings with my employer with my lawyer present.

Shortly thereafter, a rehabilitation consultant from the wage indemnity brokers invited herself to my house, but I courteously rejected the proposed visit. She demanded, however, that I meet with her, Wackmann, and a union officer on October 30th. My lawyer responded that my medical status with the airline required clarification and, therefore, at present, nothing was to be gained by a meeting. The wage indemnity brokers reacted by cutting off my long term disability pension on November 1, 1995, on the grounds that I refused to participate in NorAm's rehabilitation program.

My WCB appeal, which had been reactivated by the Workers' Assistance lawyer on March 30th, was also still pending. Two issues surfaced: whether part-time work as a Spanish translator was suitable and reasonably available employment for me, or whether I should be paid a loss of earnings pension. One of my Spanish professors had submitted a deposition that I was unqualified for the job, because very specialized techniques, which were not taught on the West Coast, were involved in the task. Of course, I had never been tested by anyone for my Spanish or English writing or speaking abilities. I knew that NorAm, via the Workmen's Compensation Board, would do everything in their monumental power to torpedo a loss of earning pension.

Again, I was as much in limbo as I had been on October 31st, 1990—with just one major difference.

On October 13th, 1995, I had done my own cognitive-behavioral treatment by flying to China, paying full fare. While there, I took five flights, even though I was forewarned that Chinese air traffic control cherished the practice of having passengers and crew of one flight wave to another one mid-air by minimizing the distance between aircraft. In China I cruised the Yangtze River between Wuhan and Chongking via the Three Gorges.

When I returned to Vancouver on October 27th, I felt as if I owned the world. I had regained my autonomy, and a feeling of serenity and atonement, and more awareness than I had ever wished for, filled my being. The struggle continued, but at least I had mended my broken wings. Now I would try to mend my broken spirit.

Epilogue:
Mended Wings

Single-handedly mending my broken wings did not impress NorAm. Nor did it entice them to permit my reintegration into flight attendant duties, so my struggle with the airline, the wage indemnity brokers, the WCB and my union continued inexorably. My dream of good will, compassion, understanding, tolerance, patience, good humor, and broad horizons ruling the skies and the earth as well was forever shattered. To precipitate a necessary awakening , I decided to write *Broken Wings*.

In a January 1996 submission to the Worker's Compensation Appeal Board (WCB), Copper, NorAm's medical officer, now claimed I posed a threat to passenger safety. Otherwise, he stated, I was as fit as a fiddle to engage in any occupation—away from the airport—if I were realistically motivated. My lawyer and I responded that only impaired pilots posed a threat to the flying public, not a flight attendant eager to return to in-flight service after successfully curing herself of PTSD. It was to no avail, but in my stubbornness, or blindness, I continued to battle for the livelihood I saw as my birthright.

My lawyer, reasoning that NorAm's refusal obliged them to pay me a 100% loss of earning pension for the rest of my earthly existence, filed another appeal. The Board again sided against me, basing its decision on a synopsis containing gross misrepresentations of actual facts, and solely considering perceptions of my health from two psychologists: Dr. Kruk, who never saw me, and the WCB's Department of Psychology director. Dr. Koval, who saw me once.

Once more doubting the firing power of the workers' assistance lawyer, and remembering union brother Tobias' incessant babble about my claim's precedence-setting power for the flight attendant community, I again crawled to the union begging them to retain independent legal counsel for me. The national president, expressing regret about sister Andersen's steadfast refusal to entrust her immensely capable and willing brothers Harry, Tobias, and Teddie with the defense of her worthy cause, exclaimed that lack of funds prevented such procurement.

I again retained lawyer McCormick, who valiantly began to pursue my case. In April 1998, however, only one avenue to achieve our goal of a 100% loss of earning pension remained open, namely if we submitted to a WCB Medical Review Panel. Street smart, I began to contact the five mental health physicians I was to choose from for the review panel. When the answering machine messages of the first two revealed they were replacements for Dr. Kruk, my belief in an *independent* panel blew to pieces. Both logic and intuition screamed that my chances to win under such conditions were very slim indeed. The following month, reckoning evil things were brewing, I escaped to Hawaii for rest, recuperation, and undisturbed evaluation of the situation.

On the trip, I talked about *Broken Wings* with flight attendants and passengers alike, holding everyone spellbound. The discovery that other people besides Annemarie, my peers, my literary agent, and my editor, were just as mesmerized by the book soon assisted me in my decision-making process.

Shortly after returning home, a publisher offered a contract proposal too abysmal to consider. In its own way, the proposal was a blessing, because it forced my hand. If I wanted to live peacefully with myself, if I wanted to triumph over all that had been done against me, and if I wanted to help the aircrew community, I had to publish *Broken Wings*. Failure to do so—for whatever reason—would be reneging on my life's purpose. Intuitively I knew that assistance and guidance by forces unseen would be forthcoming, as it had been throughout my life, and in particular during the past decade. Would my sense of humor, my scholastic and analytical abilities, my fighting spirit and my physical health have been preserved otherwise?

My course of action thus decided, I requested a meeting with NorAm management to negotiate an out of court settlement. Seemingly weary from my relentless pursuit of the matter, they eagerly met with Annemarie and me on July 27, 1998.

Though they refused to give me a severance package, NorAm granted me unlimited travel benefits. Furthermore, the airline's WCB claims officer guaranteed payment of a 35% permanent partial disability pension for the rest of my life. My official retirement date was readjusted to May 1, 1998.

Thus, ten years after a NorAm engine exploded five feet away from my face, I unceremoniously ceased to be a flight attendant.

Annemarie, jubilant, with tears in her eyes and beaming brighter than the morning star, exclaimed as soon as we left the conference room, "Thank heavens that's over. Now you're free to publish *Broken Wings* and perform a service to humanity!"

And how did I feel—the one who was born to fly? Well, only the approaching publication of *Broken Wings* saved me from a severe depression. Oftentimes I cried during my meditations, longing for the career, the lifestyle, I'd lost. Fellow flight attendants assurances that I would now hate the job I once loved because working conditions had deteriorated so drastically, did little to assuage the pain of my grieving process. Only understanding, compassion and love from Annemarie and my editor during many an unexpected catharsis helped me on the healing path.

Six months later, knowing that *Broken Wings* was well on its way to publication, my pain lessened and now I am grateful for my experiences, rather than resentful. Healthy in body and sound of mind, I sit in my study on this fine day, surrounded by the light of love and healing, a candle flickering in the slight breeze, contemplating my next book and my life as a writer. Trille, my little black Labrador curls sleeping at my feet, paws moving as if she were, in her dreams, playing with our steadfast companion Jessie Alabama, who this spring departed to a heavenly meadow filled with dandelions in full bloom.

Notes

Broken Wings: A Flight Attendant's Journey
by Nattanya Andersen

INTRODUCTION

1. From *The World's Strangest Mysteries* (Octopus Books: London, 1987). The author notes that, "In 1912, a liner was crossing the Atlantic with a valuable cargo—an Egyptian mummy. It was the body of a prophetess who lived during the reign of Tutankhamun's father-in-law, Amenhotep IV [who reigned from 1379–1362 B.C.]. An ornament found with the mummy bore the spell [quoted above]. The liner was the Titanic." (p. 95).

2. I have used a pseudonym for this company. "NorAm" seems appropriate to describe a North American carrier.

3. A. Dyreskov, A. Skogstad, H. Hellesoy, and L. Haugli, "Fear of Flying in Civil Aviation Personnel." In: *Aviation, Space, and Environmental Medicine*. pp. 831–838. September 1992.

CHAPTER ONE

1. I.R. Hill. "The Historical Background to Aerospace Pathology." In: *Aviation, Space, and Environmental Medicine*. January 1982.

2. American Psychiatric Association. *Diagnostic and Statistical Manual of Mental Disorder*. Fourth Edition. American Psychiatric Association. Washington, D.C., 1994. And, J.P. Kahn. *A Practical Psychiatric Guide*.
Van Nostrand Reinhold: New York, 1993.

3. J.G. Gunderson and A.N. Sabo. "The Phenomenological and Conceptual Interface Between Borderline Personality Disorder and PTSD." In: *American Journal of Psychiatry*, 150:19-27, 1993. And, F.S. Sierles, *et al*. "Post-traumatic Stress Disorder and Concurrent Psychiatric Illness: A Preliminary Report." In: *American Journal of Psychiatry*, 140:9, September 1983. And, R.J. Ross, *et al*. "Sleep Disturbance as the Hallmark of Post-traumatic Stress Disorder." In: *American Journal of Psychiatry*, 146:6, June 1989.

4. R.E. Smith. *Psychology*. West Publishing Company: Minneapolis/St. Paul, 1993.

5. M.G. Warshaw, *et al*. "Quality of Life and Dissociation in Anxiety Disorder Patients With Histories of Trauma or PTSD." In: *American Journal of Psychiatry*, 150:1512–1516, 1993.

6. R.E. Smith: *Psychology* West Publishing Company: Minneapolis/St. Paul, 1993, p. 90.

7. Simon Fraser University. Burnaby, British Columbia, Canada. 1243 Post traumatic stress disorder research studies listed in computer search in the spring of 1995.

8. R.P. Lukasik. "Post-traumatic Stress Disorder in Canadian Aircraft Accident Survivors." Ph.D. Dissertation. Walden University, 1991. Order Number DA9035038.

9. M. Marks, *et al*. "Post-traumatic Stress Disorder in Airplane Cabin Crew Attendants." In: *Aviation, Space, and Environmental Medicine*. March 1995.

10. American Psychiatric Association. *Diagnostic and Statistical Manual of Mental Disorder*. Fourth Edition. American Psychiatric Association. Washington, D.C., 1994.

CHAPTER TWO

1. Canadian Transportation Accident Investigation and Safety Board. *Aviation Occurrence Reports*, vii-viii. P.O. Box 9120, Alta Vista Terminal, Ottawa, Ontario, K1G 3T8.

2. Government of Canada. *Final Report of the Board Inquiry into Air Canada Boeing 767 604/C-GAUN Accident Gimli, Manitoba,* July 23, 1983.

3. A. Skogstad, *et al*. "Cockpit-Cabin Crew Interaction: Satisfaction With Communication and Information Exchange." In: *Aviation, Space, and Environmental Medicine*. September 1995.

4. Government of Canada. *Final Report of the Board Inquiry into Air Canada Boeing 767 604/C-GAUN Accident Gimli, Manitoba,* July 23, 1983. p. 79.

5. J.D. Bremner, *et al*. "Deficits in Short-Term Memory in Post Traumatic Stress Disorder." In: *American Journal of Psychiatry*. 150:7, July 1993.

6. L. White. *Human Debris: The Injured Worker in America*. Seaview/Putnam: New York, 1983, pp.. 59-73. See also: T. Thomason and R.P. Chaykowski, editors. *Research on Canadian Workers' Compensation*. IRC Press, Industrial Relations Center: Queens University, Kingston, Ontario. 1995.

7. L. White. *Human Debris: The Injured Worker in America*. Seaview/ Putnam: New York, 1983, pp. 59-73.

8. N. Ashford. *Crisis in the Workplace: Occupational Disease and Injury*. MIT Press: Cambridge, Massachusetts. 1976.

9. A.T. Beck, *et al.* "An Inventory for Measuring Depression." In: *Archives of General Psychiatry*, 1961. And, J.C. McKinley, and S.R. Hathaway. *Minnesota Multiphasic Personality Inventory*. University of Minnesota Press: Minneapolis. 1943.

10. R.E. Smith: *Psychology*. West Publishing Company: Minneapolis/St. Paul, 1993. p.459. And, P.D. Retzlaff, and M. Gibertini. "Objective Psychological Testing of U.S. Air Force Officers in Pilot Training." In: *Aviation, Space, and Environmental Medicine*. July 1988.

11. J.C. McKinley, and S.R. Hathaway. *Minnesota Multiphasic Personality Inventory*. University of Minnesota Press: Minneapolis. 1943.

12. L. Friedman, et al. *Psychological Assessment With The MMPI*. Lawrence Erlbaum Associates: Hillsdale, New Jersey; Hove and London, 1989. p.117.

13. M. Green, *et al.* "Risk Factors for PTSD and Other Diagnoses in a General Sample of Vietnam Veterans." In: *American Journal of Psychiatry*. June, 1990. p. 147.

14. N. Cherington, and K. Mathys. "Deaths and Injuries as a Result of Lightning Strikes to Aircraft." In: *Aviation, Space, and Environmental Medicine*. July 1995.

CHAPTER THREE

1. A.H. Brownstein, and M.L .Dembert. "Treatment of Essential Hypertension with Yoga Relaxation Therapy in a USAF Aviator: A Case Report." In: *Aviation, Space, and Environmental Medicine*. July 1989.

2. G. Bogart. "The Use of Meditation in Psychotherapy: A Review of the Literature." In: *American Journal of Psychotherapy*. July 1991.

3. *Ibid.* p. 408.

4. A.H. Brownstein, and M.L .Dembert. "Treatment of Essential Hypertension with Yoga Relaxation Therapy in a USAF Aviator: A Case Report." In: *Aviation, Space, and Environmental Medicine*. July 1989.

5. V.P. Moshansky, Commissioner. *Commission of Inquiry into the Air Ontario Crash at Dryden, Ontario. Final Report*. Ministry of Supply and Services Canada. 1992.

6. E. Pukkala *et al.* "Incidence of Cancer Among Finnish Airline Cabin Attendants, 1967–1992. Obtained from the International Civil Aviation Organization (ICAO), Montréal, Canada, in 1995. The Department of Transport, Occupational Health and Safety Branch, the Airline Division of CUPE (Canadian Union of Public Employees) and the Safety Transport Board deny having any information about this issue. The survey results, however, were broadcast on CFRB, Toronto, Canada, in 1995.

7. *Ibid.*

8. *The Vancouver Sun*, August 27, 1996. Vancouver, British Columbia, Canada.

9. J.K. Grayson ,and T.J. Lyons. "Cancer Incidence in United States Air Force Aircrew, 1975–89." In: *Aviation, Space, and Environmental Medicine*. February 1996.

10. D.A. Salisbury, *et al.* "Mortality Among British Columbia Pilots." In: *Aviation, Space, and Environmental Medicine*. April 1991.

11. *Ibid.*

12. Air Transport Medicine Committee, Aerospace Medical Association. "The Very Large Airplane: Safety, Health, and Comfort Considerations." In: *Aviation, Space, and Environmental Medicine*. October 1997.

13. *The Vancouver Sun*, August 27, 1996. Vancouver, British Columbia, Canada.

14. E. Bingham, ed. "Proceedings. Conference on Women and the Workplace." Society for Occupational and Environmental Health. Washington, D.C. June 17–19, 1996.

15. A. Ashman, and R. Telfer. "Personality Profiles of Pilots." In: *Aviation, Space, and Environmental Medicine*. October 1983.

16. J.R. Novello, and Z.I. Youseff. "Psycho-Social Studies in General Aviation: I. Personality Profile of Male Pilots." In: *Aerospace Medicine*. February 1974.

17. A. Ashman, and R. Telfer. "Personality Profiles of Pilots." In: *Aviation, Space, and Environmental Medicine*. October 1983.

18. T.J. Lyons. "Women in the Fast Jet Cockpit– Aeromedical Considerations." In: *Aviation, Space, and Environmental Medicine*, September 1992. See also: J.R. Novello, and Z.I. Youseff. "Psycho-Social Studies in General Aviation: II. Personality Profile of Female Pilots." In: *Aerospace Medicine*. June 1974.

19. R.L. Dukes, *et al.* "Stereotypes of Pilots and Apprehension about Flying with Them: A Study of Commercial Aviation Scenarios." In: *Aviation, Space, and Environmental Medicine*. August 1991.

20. S.J. Sloan, and C.L. Cooper. *Pilots Under Stress*. Routledge & Kegan Paul: London and New York, 1986.

21. R.L. Dukes, *et al.* "Stereotypes of Pilots and Apprehension about Flying with Them: A Study of Commercial Aviation Scenarios." In: *Aviation, Space, and Environmental Medicine*, August 1991.

22. *Canadian Human Rights Tribunal*, Volume 5, 1989.

23. S.J. Sloan, and C.L. Cooper. *Pilots Under Stress*. Routledge & Kegan Paul: London and New York, 1986, pp. 183.

CHAPTER FOUR

1. *Canada Labour Code:* Occupational Safety and Health. CLC: 122.1.

2. J.D. Alter, and S.R. Mohler. "Preventive Medicine Aspects and Health Promotion Programs for Flight Attendants." In: *Aviation, Space, and Environmental Medicine*. February 1980.

3. *Ibid.*

4. M. Schiavo, with S. Chartrand. *Flying Blind–Flying Safe*. Avon Books: New York. 1997.

5. A.T. Lee. "Aircrew Decision-Making Behavior in Hazardous Weather Avoidance." In: *Aviation, Space, and Environmental Medicine*. February 1991.

6. Transportation Safety Board of Canada. "Aviation Occurrence Report, Weather-Related Event; Canadian Airlines International LTD. Report Number A93F0043."

7. Transportation Safety Board of Canada. "Aviation Occurrence Report, Severe In-Flight Turbulence, Canadian Regional Airline, October 22, 1993. Report Number A93W0184."

8. BCTV Evening News. British Columbia Television. December 29, 1997.

9. *Vancouver Sun*, Sunday, April 17, 1998.

CHAPTER FIVE

1. Sloan, and C.L. Cooper. "The Sources of Stress on the Wives of Commercial Airline Pilots. In: *Aviation, Space, and Environmental Medicine*. April 1985.

2. *bid.*

3. *Ibid.*

4. *Ibid.*

5. *Ibid.*

6. Sloan, and C.L. Cooper. *Pilots Under Stress.* Routledge & Kegan Paul: London, New York. 1986. pp. 139–140.

7. Sloan, and C.L. Cooper. "The Sources of Stress on the Wives of Commercial Airline Pilots. In: *Aviation, Space, and Environmental Medicine*. April 1985.

8. *Ibid.*

9. Sloan, and C.L. Cooper. *Pilots Under Stress.* Routledge & Kegan Paul: London, New York. 1986. pp. 139–140.

10. Government of Canada. "Final Report of the Board Inquiry into Air Canada Boeing 767 604/C-GAUN Accident Gimli/Manitoba," July 23, 1983.

11. *Ibid.*

12. *Ibid.*

13. "Skeptical Canadian Airlines International Pilots Study A320." In: *Aviation & Aerospace*. August 1990.

14. *Ibid.*

15. BCTV Evening News. British Columbia Television; October 2, 1996.

16. Bergeron, and D.A. Hinton. "Aircraft Automation: The Problem of the Pilot Interface. In: *Aviation, Space, and Environmental Medicine*. February 1985.

17. "Computerized A320 Makes Canadian Debut." In: *Aviation & Aerospace*. March 1990.

CHAPTER SIX

1. J.D. Alter, and S.R. Mohler. "Preventive Medicine Aspects and Health Promotion Programs for Flight Attendants." In: *Aviation, Space, and Environmental Medicine*. February 1980.

2. J.B. Clarke. "Policy Considerations of Human Immunodeficiency Virus (HIV) Infection in U.S. Naval Aviation Personnel." In: *Aviation, Space, and Environmental Medicine*. February 1990. And, B.K. Bohnker. "Performance Impairment Prior to HIV Seropositive Diagnosis: A Preliminary Navy Population-Based Study." In: *Aviation, Space, and Environmental Medicine*. March 1992. See also: Special Committee Report by the Executive Committee of the Aerospace Medical Association. "HIV Positivity and Aviation Safety." In: *Aviation, Space, and Environmental Medicine*. May 1992. And, Mapou *et al. Measuring* Performance Decrements in Aviation Personnel Infected with the Human Immunodeficiency Virus; In: *Aviation, Space, and Environmental Medicine*. February 1993.

3. CTV News, Canadian Television Corporation. November 1995.

4. B.K. Bohnker *et al.* "In-flight Anxiety Conditions Presenting with *Break-off* Symptoms." In: *Aviation, Space, and Environmental Medicine*. April 1991.

5. *Ibid.*

6. J.E. Carr. "Behavior Therapy and the Treatment of Flight Phobia." In: *Aviation, Space, and Environmental Medicine*. September 1978.

CHAPTER SEVEN

1. H.P. Goerres. "Medical Flying Fitness–a Routine Affair–But Who Examines and Assesses Psychic Health?" In: *Aviation, Space, and Environmental Medicine*. July 1975. See also, R.E. King and C.F. Flynn. "Defining and Measuring the 'Right Stuff': Neuropsychiatrically-Enhanced Flight Screening (N-EFS)." In: *Aviation, Space, and Environmental Medicine*. October 1975.

2. A.W. Black. "Psychiatric Illness in Military Aircrew." In: *Aviation, Space, and Environmental Medicine*. July 1983.

3. K. Vaandrager. "Task of a Medical Department in Civil Aviation." In: *Aerospace Medicine*. April 1972.

4. R.E. Yanowitch, III. "Medical and Psychiatric Aspects of Accident Investigation." In: *Aviation, Space, and Environmental Medicine*. October 1975.

5. C.R. Harper. "Civil Aviation in the Coming Decade." In: *Aerospace Medicine*. January 1973. And, P.A. Santy, *et al.* "Psychiatric Diagnoses in a Group of Astronaut Applicants." In: *Aviation, Space, and Environmental Medicine*. October 1991.

6. H.P. Goerres. "Medical Flying Fitness–A Routine Affair–But Who Examines and Assesses Psychic Health." In: *Aviation, Space, and Environmental Medicine*. July 1975.

7. V.B. Maxwell, and H.C. Davies, editors. "Psychiatric Disorders as They Relate To Aviation. Introduction to the Second Scientific Session of the Association of Aviation Medical Examiners, Cambridge, England." In: *Aviation, Space, and Environmental Medicine*. July 1983. See also, S.P. Baker. "Putting 'Human Error' Into Perspective." In: *Aviation, Space, and Environmental Medicine*. June 1995. And, L R Simson, Jr. "Investigation of Fatal Aircraft Accidents: Physiological Incidents." In: *Aerospace Medicine*. September 1971.

8. R.J. Ursano, and W.G. Jackson. "The Flight Surgeon and Psychiatry: Interest and Skills." In: *Aviation, Space, and Environmental Medicine*. February 1986. And, H.P. Goerres. "Medical Flying Fitness– a Routine Affair–But Who Examines and Assesses Psychic Health." In: *Aviation, Space, and Environmental Medicine*. July 1975. And, R.J. Ursano, and D.R. Jones. "The Individual vs. The Organization's Doctor: Value Conflict in Psychiatric Aeromedical Evaluation." In: *Aviation, Space, and Environmental Medicine*. November 1981.

9. C.R. Harper. "Civil Aviation in the Coming Decade." In: *Aerospace Medicine*. January 1973.

10. V.B. Maxwell, and H.C. Davies, editors. "Psychiatric Disorders As They Relate To Aviation: Introduction to the Second Scientific Session of the Association of Aviation Medical Examiners." In: *Aviation, Space, and Environmental Medicine*. July 1983.

11. K. Vaandrager. "Task of a Medical Department in Civil Aviation." In: *Aerospace Medicine*. April 1972.

12. D.R. Jones. "Psychiatric Assessment of Female Fliers at the U.S. Air Force School of Aerospace Medicine(USAFSAM)." In: *Aviation, Space, and Environmental Medicine*, October 1983.

13. H.P. Goerres. "Medical Flying Fitness–a Routine Affair–but Who Examines and Assesses Psychic Health." In: *Aviation, Space, and Environmental Medicine*. July 1975.

14. S.P. Baker. "Putting 'Human Error' Into Perspective." In: *Aviation, Space, and Environmental Medicine*. June 1995.

15. *Ibid.* See also, F.M. Townsend, and V.A. Stembridge. "Modern Concepts in Investigation of Aircraft Fatalities." In: *Journal of Forensic Science,* 3:381–400, 1958. And, R.C. Leighton-White. "Airline Pilot Incapacitation in Flight." In: *Aerospace Medicine.* June 1972.

16. R. Smith. "Psychiatric Disorders As They Relate to Aviation." In: *Aviation, Space, and Environmental Medicine.* July 1983. And, K. Vaandrager. "Task of a Medical Department in Civil Aviation." In: *Aerospace Medicine.* April 1972.

17. G. Bennett. "Psychiatric Disorders in Civilian Pilots." In: *Aviation, Space, and Environmental Medicine.* July 1983.

18. C.L. Cooper, and S.J. Sloan. *Pilots Under Stress.* Routledge & Kegan Paul: London and New York, 1986.

19. P.J. O'Connor. "Pointers to Diagnosis of Psychiatric Illness in Aircrew." In: *Aviation, Space, and Environmental Medicine.* July 1983.

20. *Ibid.*

21. "Commercial Pilot Survey Levels III to IV Air Carrier Operations." Transportation Safety Board of Canada, 1991. And, G. Bennett. "Psychiatric Disorders in Civilian Pilots." In: *Aviation, Space, and Environmental Medicine.* July, 1983.

22. *Ibid.*

23. *Ibid.*

24. G. Bennett. "Psychiatric Disorders in Civilian Pilots." In: *Aviation, Space, and Environmental Medicine.* July, 1983.

25. A.W. Black. "Psyciatric Illness in Military Aircrew." In: *Aviation, Space, and Environmental Medicine.* July, 1983. And, G.W. McCarthy and K.D. Craig. "Flying Therapy for Flying Phobia." In: *Aviation, Space, and Environmental Medicine.* December, 1985.

26. M.A. Becker. "Mental Health Intervention in Aeromedical Evacuation." In: *Aerospace Medicine.* March 1972.

27. C.L. Cooper, and S.J. Sloan. "Coping with Pilot Stress: Resting at Home Compared with Resting Away from Home." In: *Aviation, Space, and Environmental Medicine.* December 1987.

28. *Ibid.*

29. *Ibid.*

30. *Ibid.*

CHAPTER EIGHT

1. L. Rojas. "Flying Decompensation Syndrome and Fear of Flying." In: *Aerospace Medicine.* September 1974.

2. *Ibid.*

3. B. Bohnker, *et al.* "Inflight Anxiety Conditions Presenting With 'Break-off' Symptoms." In: *Aviation, Space, and Environmental Medicine.* April 1991.

4. A. Dyregrov *et al* . "Fear of Flying in Civil Aviation Personnel." In: *Aviation, Space, and Environmental Medicine.* September 1992.

5. *Ibid.*

6. *Ibid.* And, A. Skogstad *et al.* "Cockpit–Cabin Crew Interaction: Satisfaction with Communication and Information Exchange. In: *Aviation, Space, and Environmental Medicine.* September 1995.

7. Dyregrov, *et al.* "Fear of Flying in Civil Aviation Personnel." In: *Aviation, Space, and Environmental Medicine.* September 1992.

8. O'Hare. "Pilots' Perception of Risks and Hazards in General Aviation." In: *Aviation, Space, and Environmental Medicine.* July 1990.

9. A. Dyregrov, *et al.* "Fear of Flying in Civil Aviation Personnel." In: *Aviation, Space, and Environmental Medicine.* September 1992.

10. J.C. Duffy. "Emergency Mental Health Services During and After a Major Aircraft Accident." In: *Aviation, Space, and Environmental Medicine.* August 1978.

11. D. Fischer. "Airline safety surveys remain closed to public." In: *The Vancouver Sun, (Southam News),* Wednesday, January 3, 1996, p. A1.

12. KOMO News, Whatcom County, Washington, August 27, 1995; and, BCTV News, British Columbia Television, Vancouver, Canada, November 1, 1996.

13. BCTV News, British Columbia Television, Vancouver, Canada, October 5, 1996.

14. J.C. Duffy. "Emergency Mental Health Services During And After A Major Aircraft Accident." In: *Aviation, Space, and Environmental Medicine.* August 1978.

15. *Ibid.* And, J.A. Cigrang and T.T. Yasuhara. "Critical incident Stress Intervention Following Fatal Aircraft Mishaps." In: *Aviation, Space, and Environmental Medicine.* September 1995.

16. G.A. Pane, *et al.* "The Cincinnati DC9 Experience: Lessons in Aircraft and Airport Safety." In: *Aviation, Space, and Environmental Medicine.* May 1985. And, A.K. Chaturvedi, and D. Saunders. "Aircraft Fires, Smoke Toxicity, and Survival." In: *Aviation, Space, and Environmental Medicine.* March 1996.

17. "Aviation Safety In Flight: Everyone in the Back." In: Transport *Canada Aviation.* Issue 1/ 1995.

CHAPTER NINE

1. Final Report of the Board Inquiry into Air Canada Boeing 767 604/C-GAUN Accident Gimli/Manitoba July 23, 1983. Government of Canada.

CHAPTER TEN

1. M. Nelson *et al,* "The Labor Union's Perspective on Occupational Health." In: *Environmental and Occupational Medicine.* Vol. 79. 1st edition. Little Brown: Boston. c.1983.

2. J.P. Kahn. *Mental Health In The Workplace.* Van Nostrand Reinhold: New York, 1993.

3. Labour Relation Board, British Columbia, Canada. Practice Guideline No. ADJ-3. "The Duty Of Fair Representation—What Does It Mean?" Revised edition. February 22, 1994.

4. D.K. Kentsmith. "Minimizing the Psychological Effects of a Wartime Disaster on an Individual." In: *Aviation, Space, and Environmental Medicine,* April 1980. And, E.M. Smith, *et al.* "Acute Post-disaster Psychiatric Disorders: Identification of Persons at Risk." In: *American Journal of Psychiatry,* 147:2, February 1990.

5. L. White. *Human Debris: The Injured Worker in America.* Seaview/Putnam: New York, 1983, pp. 111.

6. American Psychiatric Association. *Diagnostic and Statistical Manual III.* Washington, D.C., 1987, pp. 326–327.

7. Department of Labor. *An Interim Report to Congress on Occupational Disease*. Washington, D.C., June 1980, p.3.

8. F. Capra. *The Turning Point*. Bantam Books: Toronto, New York, London, Sydney, Auckland, 1988.

9. D. Berman. *Death on the Job; Occupational Health and Safety Struggles in the United States*. New York: Monthly Review Press, 1978.

10. M. Nelson *et al*, "The Labor Union's Perspective on Occupational Health." In: *Environmental and Occupational Medicine*. Vol. 79. 1st edition. Little Brown: Boston. c.1983.

Chapter Eleven

1. L. White. *Human Debris: The Injured Worker in America*. Seaview/Putnam: New York, 1983, p. 21.

2. *Ibid*. p.87.

3. J.P. Ellman. "A Treatment Approach for Patients in Mid-life." In: *Canadian Journal of Psychiatry*, Vol. 37, October 1992.

4. B.A. van der Kolk, and O. van der Hart. "Pierre Janet and the Breakdown of Adaptation in Psychological Trauma." In: *American Journal of Psychiatry*, 146:12, December 1989.

5. S.J. Sloan, and C.L. Cooper. *Pilots Under Stress*. Routledge & Kegan Paul: London and New York, 1986.

6. D.A. Slagle, *et al.* "Community Psychological Effects Following a Non-Fatal Aircraft Accident." In: *Aviation, Space, and Environmental Medicine*. February 1986.

7. B.A. van der Kolk, and O. van der Hart. "Pierre Janet and the Breakdown of Adaptation in Psychological Trauma." In: *American Journal of Psychiatry*, 146:12, December 1989.

8. D. Wallechinsky and I. Wallace. *The People's Almanac: On Being Sane In Insane Places*. Doubleday & Company: Garden City, New York, 1975. p.1088.

Chapter Twelve

1. D. Wallechinsky, and I. Wallace: *The People's Almanac*.
The Mock Prison, Doubleday & Company: Garden City, New York, 1975. pp. 1088–89.

Chapter Thirteen

1. B.A van der Kolk, and O. van der Hart. "Pierre Janet and the Breakdown of Adaptation in Psychological Trauma." In: *American Journal of Psychiatry*, 146:12, December 1989. And, J.P. Kahn. *Mental Health In The Workplace. A Practical Psychiatric Guide*. Van Nostrand Reinhold: New York, 1993. And, The American Psychiatric Association. *Diagnostical and Statistical Manual*. Fourth Edition. The American Psychiatric Association: Washington, D.C. 1994. And, F.S. Sierles, *et al.* "Post-traumatic Stress Disorder and Concurrent Psychiatric Illness: A Preliminary Report." In: *American Journal of Psychiatry*, 140:9, September 1983.

2. R.C. Barnett *et al*, editors. *Gender and Stress: Sex Differences in Cognitive Coping with Stress*. Free Press: New York; Collier Macmillan: London: c. 1987.

Chapter Fourteen

1. S.T. Perconte, and A.J. Goreczny. "Failure to Detect Fabricated Post-traumatic Stress Disorder With the Use of the MMPI in a Clinical Population." In: *American Journal of Psychiatry*. 147:8, August 1990.

Chapter Fifteen

1. J.R. Aitken, and J.W. Benson. "The Use of Relaxation/ Desensitization in Treating Anxiety Associated with Flying." In: *Aviation, Space, and Environmental Medicine*, March 1984.

2. J.E. Sours, *et al* "The Fear of Flying Syndrome: A Reappraisal." In: *Aerospace Medicine*, 35: 156–166, 1964.

3. M.Z. Hussain. "Desensitization and Flooding (Implosion) in Treatment of Phobias." In: *American Journal of Psychiatry*, 127:11, May 1971.

4. G.W. McCarthy, and K.D. Craig. "Flying Therapy for Flying Phobia." In: *Aviation, Space, and Environmental Medicine*, December 1985.

Chapter Sixteen

1. J. Borysenko. *Minding The Body; Minding The Mind*. Bantam Books: New York. 1993. And, R.C. Barnett, *et. al. Gender And Stress: Sex Differences in Cognitive Coping with Stress*. The Free Press: New York; Collier Macmillan: London. 19

2. *Ibid.*

3. Transportation Safety Board of Canada. "Aviation Occurrence Statistics 1992–1997." In: *Aviation Safety Reflexions*. Issue 20, Winter 1998.

4. Transportation Safety Board of Canada. "Be Careful Out There." In: *Aviation Safety Reflexions*. Issue 6, June 1994.

5. Transportation Safety Board of Canada. "Aviation Occurrence Statistics 1992–1997." In: *Aviation Safety Reflexions*. Issue 20, Winter 1998.

6. Transportation Safety Board of Canada. "Separation Losses on the Increase." In: *Aviation Safety Reflexions*. Issue 18, June 1997.

7. Transportation Safety Board of Canada. "Aviation Occurrence Statistics 1992–1997." In: *Aviation Safety Reflexions*. Issue 20, Winter 1998.

8. Transportation Safety Board of Canada. "Be Careful Out There." In: *Aviation Safety Reflexions*. Issue 6, June 1994.

9. British Columbia Television Evening News, April 3, 1998.

10. T.D. Luna. "Air Traffic Controller Shiftwork: What are the Implications for Aviation Safety? A Review." In: *Aviation, Space, and Environmental Medicine*, January 1987.

11. Activity, and Mood Analyses. In: *Aviation, Space, and Environmental Medicine*, January 1987.

12. T.D. Luna. "Air Traffic Controller Shiftwork: What are the Implications for Aviation Safety? A Review." In: *Aviation, Space, and Environmental Medicine*, January 1987.

13. Transportation Safety Board of Canada. "Be Careful Out There." In: *Aviation Safety Reflexions*. Issue 6, June 1994.

14. Transportation Safety Board of Canada. "Out of Sight, Out of Mind. In: *Aviation Safety Reflexions*. Issue 8, December 1994.

15. Transportation Safety Board of Canada. Aviation Occurrence Report A97 H 002. Risk of Collision Between Avionair Inc. Swearingen Aviation Metro II C-GBXX and Air Canada Canadair Ltd. CL-600 Regional Jet C-FSKI. Ottawa/ Macdonald/ Cartier International Airport, March 12, 1997.

16. "Pilots List 150 Worst Airports." In: *The Province*. Vancouver, British Columbia. June 8, 1998.

17. G. Johnson. "Air Traffic Control Woes."
In: *Aviation and Aerospace.* June 1990. And,
J. Gallagher. "Pay Attention." In: *Aviation and Aerospace.* February 1990.

18. Canadian Pharmaceutical Association.
Compendium of Pharmaceuticals and Specialties.
29th Edition, Ottawa, Ontario, Canada, 1994.

19. V.D. LaPierre, and A. LaBelle. "Manic-like Reaction Induced by Lorazepam Withdrawal."
In: *Canadian Journal of Psychiatry.* Vol. 32,
November 1987.

20. Canadian Pharmaceutical Association.
Compendium of Pharmaceuticals and Specialties.
29th Edition, Ottawa, Ontario, Canada, 1994.

Chapter Seventeen

1. Transportation Safety Board of Canada.
"Insight: Fresh Air." In: *Aviation Safety Reflexions.*
Issue No. 2. June 1993.

2. Airline Division of CUPE: November 14, 1994.

3. "What's Happened to Airplane Air?" In:
Consumer Reports, A publication of Consumers Union.
Yonkers, N.Y. August 1994; and the
International Herald Tribune, June 7, 1993.

4. "Smokescreen Over Cabin Air Quality."
In: *Interavia,* A Jane's Information Group Publication,
Volume 47, June 1992.

5. "What's Happened to Airplane Air?" In:
Consumer Reports, A publication of Consumers Union.
Yonkers, N.Y. August 1994.

6. American Broadcasting Company. *20/20,*
May 13, 1994; and the *New York Times,* June 6, 1993.

7. "Smokescreen Over Cabin Air Quality." In:
Interavia,
A Jane's Information Group Publication, Volume 47,
June 1992.

8. *The New York Times,* Sunday, June 6, 1993.

9. Air Canada. Chapter 66. FLTOP OPERATION
page 61: A320 Tech Bulletin Paragraph 271;
A320 Bulletin No. 271 (94-09-29);
SUBJ: A320 Air Quality.

10. *International Herald Tribune;* co-published with
The New York Times and *The Washington Post,*
June 7, 1993.

11. *The Globe and Mail,* Toronto, Canada, April 20,
1994; and the *International Herald Tribune;*
co-published with *The New York Times* and
The Washington Post, June 7, 1993.

12. *The New York Times,* Sunday June 4, 1993.

13. "Smokescreen Over Cabin Air Quality."
In: *Interavia,* A Jane's Information Group Publication,
Volume 47, June 1992; and Federal Aviation
Regulation 25.831; issued November 28/1994;
emphasis mine.

14. "What's Happened to Airplane Air?" In:
Consumer Reports, A publication of Consumers Union.
Yonkers, N.Y. August 1994.

15. J. Ernsting. "Mild Hypoxia and the Use of Oxygen
in Flight." In: *Aviation, Space, and Environmental
Medicine.* May 1984.

16. "Smokescreen Over Cabin Air Quality."
In: *Interavia,* A Jane's Information Group Publication,
Volume 47, June 1992.

17. *Ibid.*

18. *Ibid.*

19. *The Weekend Sun, Saturday Review,*
Vancouver, British Columbia, June 15, 1996.

20. *The Vancouver Sun,* Vancouver,
British Columbia, Canada, March 1, 1996.

21. *The Vancouver Sun,* Vancouver,
British Columbia, Canada, August 29, 1997.

22. *Ibid.*

23. American Broadcasting Corporation. *20/20,*
September 6, 1996.

24. *The Vancouver Sun,* Vancouver,
British Columbia, Canada, August 29, 1997.

25. *Ibid.*

26. *The Vancouver Sun,* Vancouver,
British Columbia, Canada, November 14, 1998;
and *National Post,* Toronto, Ontario, Canada,
November 3, 1998.

27. *The Vancouver Sun,* Vancouver,
British Columbia, Canada, November 14, 1998.

28. *National Post,* Toronto, Ontario, Canada,
November 3, 1998.

29. *The Vancouver Sun,* Vancouver,
British Columbia, Canada, November 14, 1998.

30. *National Post,* Toronto, Ontario, Canada,
November 3, 1998.

31. *Ibid.*

32. *National Post,* Toronto, Ontario, Canada,
November 3, 1998.

33. M. Nelson *et al.* "The Labor Union's Perspective
on Occupational Health." In: *Environmental and
Occupational Medicine* 79. 1st ed. Boston: Little Brown.
c.1983;
and the Canada Labour Code: Section 122.(1)
to 129.(2) and Canada Labour Code Part II.

34. *The New York Times,* June 6, 1993.

35. *The Vancouver Sun,* Vancouver,
British Columbia, Canada, April 7, 1995.

36. *Shared Vision,* Issue 120, Vancouver,
British Columbia, Canada. August 1998.

37. "Smokescreen Over Cabin Air Quality." In:
Interavia, A Jane's Information Group Publication,
Volume 47, June 1992.

38. Airbus/Air Canada study on onboard CO_2 levels,
1992.

39. "What's Happened to Airplane Air?"
In: *Consumer Reports,* A publication of
Consumers Union. Yonkers, N.Y. August 1994.

40. *The New York Times,* June 6, 1993.

41. "Smokescreen Over Cabin Air Quality." In:
Interavia, A Jane's Information Group Publication,
Volume 47, June 1992.

42. S. van Heusden, and L.G.J. Mans. "Alternating
Measurement of Ambient and Cabin Ozone
Concentrations in Commercial Aircraft." In: *Aviation.
Space, and Environmental Medicine,* September 1978.

43. *Ibid.*

44. *Ibid.*

45. Transportation Safety Board of Canada.
Aviation Safety Reflexions, December 1993.

46. "Smokescreen Over Cabin Air Quality." In:
Interavia, A Jane's Information Group Publication,
Volume 47, June 1992.

47. Transport Canada. Consolidated Regulation: Aviation Occupational Safety and Health, Division I: General Hazard Investigation. May 1994.

48. I. Yoneda and Y. Watanabe. "Comparison of Altitude Tolerance and Hypoxia Symptoms Between Nonsmokers and Habitual Smokers." In: *Aviation, Space, and Environmental Medicine.* September 1997.

49. Transportation Safety Board of Canada. *Aviation Safety Reflexions.* Issue 1, March 1993; and G. Johnson. "Circling the Wagons." In: *Aviation & Aerospace,* October 1990.

50. *The Globe and Mail,* Toronto, Canada, April 20, 1994.

51. W.A. Crawford and L.C. Holcomb. "Environmental Tobacco Smoke (ETS) in Airliners– A Health Hazard Evaluation." In: *Aviation, Space, and Environmental Medicine.* pp. 580–586. June 1991.

52. *The Vancouver Sun,* Vancouver, British Columbia, Canada, July 15, 1997.

53. CTV News, October 10, 1997.

54. *The New York Times,* June 6, 1993.

55. "On-Board Medical Incidents." In: *Air Canada.* FAT-13/AUG 05/93.

56. *The New York Times,* June 6, 1993.

57. *The Globe and Mail,* Toronto, Canada, April 20, 1994; and *The New York Times,* June 6, 1993.

58. *The Olympian,* Olympia, Washington, April 30, 1995.

59. *The Globe and Mail,* Toronto, Canada, February 2, 1994.

60. *The Globe and Mail,* Toronto, Canada, April 20, 1994.

61. *The Globe and Mail,* Toronto, Canada, February 2, 1994.

62. *The International Herald Tribune,* June 7, 1993.

63. L. Li *et al.* "Hygienic Investigation Of Cabin On Passenger Aircraft In China." Unpublished paper presented at an air quality/quantity symposium in California in the Spring of 1995. by researchers from the *Institute of Civil Aeromedicine.* Beijing, China.

64. C.Thibeault. "Cabin Air Quality." In: *Aviation, Space, and Environmental Medicine.* January 1997.

Chapter Eighteen

1. J.A. Caldwell. "Fatigue in the Aviation Environment: An Overview of the Causes and Effects As Well As Recommended Countermeasures." In: *Aviation, Space, and Environmental Medicine.* October 1997.

2. P.H. Gander. "Age, Circadian Rhythms, and Sleep Loss in Flight Crews." In: *Aviation, Space, and Environmental Medicine,* March 1993.

3. *Ibid.*

4. R.A. McFarland. "Influence of Changing Time Zones on Air Crews and Passengers." In: *Aerospace Medicine.* June 1974. And, F.S Preston, *et al.* "Sleep Loss in Air Cabin Crew." In: *Aerospace Medicine.* August 1973.

5. A. Samel, *et al. "Sleep* Patterns in Aircrew operating on the Polar Route Between Germany and East Asia." In: *Aviation, Space, and Environmental Medicine.* July 1991.

6. *Ibid.*

7. *Ibid.*

8. L. Haugli *et al.* "Health, Sleep, and Mood perceptions Reported by Airline Crews Flying Short and Long Hauls." In: *Aviation, Space, and Environmental Medicine.* January 1994.

9. J.A. Caldwell. "Fatigue in the Aviation Environment: An Overview of the Causes and Effects As Well As Recommended Countermeasures." In: *Aviation, Space, and Environmental Medicine.* October 1997.

10. A. Samel, *et al.* "Two-Crew Operations: Stress and Fatigue During Long Haul Night Flights." In: *Aviation, Space, and Environmental Medicine.* August 1997.

11. "Pilots Asleep at the Controls." Report on *Marketplace.* Canadian Broadcasting Corporation Television. October 29, 1996.

12. *Ibid.*

13. *Ibid.*

14. *Ibid.*

15. P.H. Gander. "Age, Circadian Rhythms, and Sleep Loss in Flight Crews." In: *Aviation, Space, and Environmental Medicine,* March 1993.

16. "Pilots Union Demands Relief Staff." Vancouver Sun. August 21, 1998. Vancouver. British Columbia, Canada.

17. *Ibid.*

18. P.H. Gander, *et al.* "Age, Circadian Rhythms, and Sleep Loss in Flight Crews." In: *Aviation, Space, and Environmental Medicine.* March 1993.

19. *Ibid.*

20. *Ibid.*

21. "Pilots Asleep at the Controls." Report on *Marketplace.* Canadian Broadcasting Corporation Television. October 29, 1996.

22. J.A. Caldwell. "Fatigue in the Aviation Environment: An Overview of the Causes and Effects As Well As Recommended Countermeasures." In: *Aviation, Space, and Environmental Medicine.* October 1997. And, S.P. Baker. "Putting *Human Error* Into Perspective." In: *Aviation, Space, and Environmental Medicine.* June 1995.

23. Convention on International Civil Aviation, Annex 6, Part I, Attachment A, International Civil Aviation Organization, 1974.

24. H.M. Wegmann *et al.* "Flight, Flight Duty, and Rest Times: A Comparison Between the Regulations of Different Countries." In: *Aviation, Space, and Environmental Medicine.* March 1983.

25. *Ibid.*

26. *Ibid.*

27. *Ibid.*

28. *Ibid.*

29. *Ibid.*

30. The Safety Programs Branch. *Staff Report On Fatigue Related Accidents and Crew Flight Time and Duty Limitations.* Canadian Aviation Safety Board. July 1986.

31. Regulations of Different Countries." In: *Aviation, Space, and Environmental Medicine.* March 1983.

32. The Safety Programs Branch. *Staff Report On Fatigue Related Accidents and Crew Flight Time and Duty Limitations.* Canadian Aviation Safety Board. July 1986.

33. Transportation Safety Board of Canada. *Commercial Pilot Survey Levels III To VI.* Air Carrier Operations. Accident Prevention Branch. 1991.

34. The Safety Programs Branch. *Staff Report On Fatigue Related Accidents and Crew Flight Time and Duty Limitations.* Canadian Aviation Safety Board. July 1986.

35. S.P. Baker. "Putting *Human Error* Into Perspective." In: *Aviation, Space, and Environmental Medicine.* June 1995.

36. Transportation Safety Board of Canada. "Insight to Advance Aviation Safety." In: *Reflexions.* Issue 9, March 1995.

37. *Ibid.*

38. "Pilots Asleep at the Controls." Report on *Marketplace.* Canadian Broadcasting Corporation Television. October 29, 1996.

39. J. Hamilton. "Nineteen Years In The Poisonous Trades." In: *Harper's Monthly Magazine.* October 1929.

40. B. Pultz. "The Human A.D.: Notification of 'Human Factors' Problems Needs to be Immediate." In: *Aviation and Aerospace.* August 1990.

41. A. Samel, *et al* "Two-Crew Operations: Stress and Fatigue During Long Haul Night Flights." In: *Aviation, Space, and Environmental Medicine.* August 1997.

Chapter Nineteen–no footnotes

Chapter Twenty

1. "The Air Up There." Report on *20/20,* American Broadcasting Company. Transcript #1419, May 13, 1994.

2. *Ibid.*

3. "What's Happened to Airplane Air?" In: *Consumer Reports,* A publication of Consumers Union. Yonkers, N.Y. August 1994.

4. *Ibid.*

5. *Ibid.*

6. "The Air Up There." Report on *20/20,* American Broadcasting Company. Transcript #1419, May 13, 1994.

7. "What's Happened to Airplane Air?" In: *Consumer Reports,* A publication of Consumers Union. Yonkers, N.Y. August 1994.

8. "Smokescreen Over Cabin Air Quality." In: *Interavia,* A Jane's Information Group Publication, Volume 47, June 1992.

9. "The Air Up There." Report on *20/20,* American Broadcasting Company. Transcript #1419, May 13, 1994.

10. *Ibid.*

11. "Smokescreen Over Cabin Air Quality." In: *Interavia,* A Jane's Information Group Publication, Volume 47, June 1992.

12. "What's Happened to Airplane Air?" In: *Consumer Reports,* A publication of Consumers Union. Yonkers, N.Y. August 1994.

13. *Ibid.*

14. "The Air Up There." Report on *20/20,* American Broadcasting Company. Transcript #1419, May 13, 1994.

15. *Ibid.*

16. *Ibid.* and "What's Happened to Airplane Air?" In: *Consumer Reports,* A publication of Consumers Union. Yonkers, N.Y. August 1994.

17. "What's Happened to Airplane Air?" In: *Consumer Reports,* A publication of Consumers Union. Yonkers, N.Y. August 1994.

18. "Smokescreen Over Cabin Air Quality." In: *Interavia,* A Jane's Information Group Publication, Volume 47, June 1992.

19. "In The Danger Zone." Report on *48 Hours,* CBS News, May 4, 1994.

20. *Ibid.*

21. *Ibid.*

22. *Strange Stories, Amazing Facts.* The Reader's Digest: Pleasantville, New York, Montréal, 1976.

23. "Killer Viruses" Report on *CBC Prime Time News,* CBC, December 14, 1994.

24. "In The Danger Zone." Report on *48 Hours,* CBS News, May 4, 1994.

25. Programme of Industrial Activities, Tripartite Technical Meeting for Civil Aviation. Occupational Health And Safety In Civil Aviation. International Labor Organisation, Geneva 1977.

26. "The Air Up There." Report on *20/20,* American Broadcasting Company. Transcript #1419, May 13, 1994; and "What's Happened to Airplane Air?" In: *Consumer Reports,* A publication of Consumers Union. Yonkers, N.Y. August 1994.

27. "What's Happened to Airplane Air?" In: *Consumer Reports,* A publication of Consumers Union. Yonkers, N.Y. August 1994; and "The Air Up There." Report on *20/20,* American Broadcasting Company. Transcript #1419, May 13, 1994.

28. "The Air Up There." Report on *20/20,* American Broadcasting Company. Transcript #1419, May 13, 1994.

29. K. Vaandrager. "Task of a Medical Department in Civil Aviation." In: *Aerospace Medicine.* April 1972.

30. Programme of Industrial Activities, Tripartite Technical Meeting for Civil Aviation. Occupational Health And Safety In Civil Aviation. International Labor Organisation, Geneva 1977.

31. *Ibid.*

32. *Ibid.*

33. *Ibid.*

34. The New York Times, N.Y., Sunday June 6, 1993.

35. "Smokescreen Over Cabin Air Quality." In: *Interavia,* A Jane's Information Group Publication, Volume 47, June 1992.

36. C. Thibeault. "Cabin Air Quality: Myth vs. Reality." Air Canada Occupational Health Services, Montréal, Québec. Canada. Issued by the Ministry of Transport, July 1995.

37. Air Transport Medicine Committee, Aerospace Medical Association. "The Very Large Airplane: Safety, Health, and Comfort Considerations." In: *Aviation, Space, and Environmental Medicine.* October 1997.

38. F. Sahiar. "Economy Class Syndrome." In: *Aviation, Space, and Environmental Medicine.* October 1994.

39. R.E. Yanowitch and J.A. Sirkis. "Air Travel and the Handicapped." In: *Aerospace Medicine.* August 1974.

40. Airline Division of CUPE, Summer, 1996.

41. K. Vaandrager. "Task of a Medical Department in Civil Aviation." In: *Aerospace Medicine*. April 1972; and J.D. Alter and S.R. Mohler. "Preventive Medicine Aspects and Health Promotion Programs for Flight Attendants." In: *Aviation, Space, and Environmental Medicine*. February 1980.

42. Programme of Industrial Activities, Tripartite Technical Meeting for Civil Aviation. Occupational Health And Safety In Civil Aviation. International Labor Organisation, Geneva 1977, p.67.

Chapter Twenty-One

1. *The Province*, November 10, 1996. Vancouver, British Columbia, Canada.

2. BCTV, British Columbia Television, Vancouver, British Columbia, Canada, December 9, 1995.

Chapter Twenty-Two

1. H.L. Gibbons. "Alcohol, Aviation, and Safety Revisited: A Historical Review and a Suggestion." In: *Aviation, Space, and Environmental Medicine*. July 1988.

2. *Ibid.*

3. Guohua Li. "Pilot-Related Factors in Aircraft Crashes: A Review of Epidemiologic Studies." In: *Aviation, Space, and Environmental Medicine*. October 1994.

4. C.F. Flynn, *et al.* "Alcoholism and Treatment in Airline Aviators: One Company's Results." In: *Aviation, Space, and Environmental Medicine*. April 1993.

5. H.R. Conwell. "Alcoholism: A Behavioural Disorder in General Aviation." In: *Aviation, Space, and Environmental Medicine*. July 1983.

6. Guohua Li. "Pilot-Related Factors in Aircraft Crashes: A Review of Epidemiologic Studies." In: *Aviation, Space, and Environmental Medicine*. October 1994.

7. R. Widders and D. Harris. "Pilots' Knowledge of the Relationship Between Alcohol Consumption and Levels of Blood Alcohol Concentration," In: *Aviation, Space, and Environmental Medicine*. June 1997.

8. Associated Press, Fort Worth, Texas. "Airline Seeks Further Alcohol Tests On Pilot In Fatal Colombian Crash." circa. January 1996.

9. A. Ditter. "Grounding High Flyers." In: *Aviation & Aerospace*, May 1990.

10. *Ibid.*

11. *Ibid.*

12. *Ibid.*

13. G. Johnson. "Baseless Drug testing." In: *Aviation & Aerospace*. July 1990.

14. *Ibid.*

15. C.F. Flynn, *et al.* "Alcoholism and Treatment in Airline Aviators: One Company's Results." In: *Aviation, Space, and Environmental Medicine*. April 1993.

16. *Ibid.*

17. H.L. Gibbons. "Alcohol, Aviation, and Safety Revisited: A Historical Review and a Suggestion." In: *Aviation, Space, and Environmental Medicine*. July 1988.

18. D.K. Damkot and G.A. Osga. "Survey of Pilots and Opinions About Drinking and Flying. In: *Aviation, Space, and Environmental Medicine*. February 1978.

19. R. Widders and D. Harris. "Pilots' Knowledge of the Relationship Between Alcohol Consumption and Levels of Blood Alcohol Concentration," In: *Aviation, Space, and Environmental Medicine*. June 1997.

20. J.L. Taylor, *et al.* "Acute and 8-Hour Effects of Alcohol (0.08 BAC) on Younger and Older Pilots' Simulator Performance." In: *Aviation, Space, and Environmental Medicine*. August 1994.

21. H.L. Gibbons. "Alcohol, Aviation, and Safety Revisited: A Historical Review and a Suggestion." In: *Aviation, Space, and Environmental Medicine*. July 1988.

22. R. Widders and D. Harris. "Pilots' Knowledge of the Relationship Between Alcohol Consumption and Levels of Blood Alcohol Concentration," In: *Aviation, Space, and Environmental Medicine*. June 1997.

23. J.L. Taylor, *et al.* "Acute and 8-Hour Effects of Alcohol (0.08 BAC) on Younger and Older Pilots' Simulator Performance." In: *Aviation, Space, and Environmental Medicine*. August 1994.

24. H.L. Gibbons. "Alcohol, Aviation, and Safety Revisited: A Historical Review and a Suggestion." In: *Aviation, Space, and Environmental Medicine*. July 1988.

25. R. Widders and D. Harris. "Pilots' Knowledge of the Relationship Between Alcohol Consumption and Levels of Blood Alcohol Concentration," In: *Aviation, Space, and Environmental Medicine*. June 1997.

26. A. Ditter. "Grounding High Flyers." In: *Aviation & Aerospace*, May 1990.

27. J.A. Pursch. "Alcohol in Aviation: A Problem of Attitudes." In: *Aviation, Space, and Environmental Medicine*. March 1974.

28. F.R. Schwartz and G.J. Kidera. "Method for Rehabilitation of the Alcohol-Addicted Pilot in a Commercial Airline." In: *Aviation, Space, and Environmental Medicine*. May 1978.

29. C.R. Harper. "Airline Pilot Alcoholism: One Airline's Experience." In: *Aviation, Space, and Environmental Medicine*. May 1978. July 1983.

30. Results." In: *Aviation, Space, and Environmental Medicine*. April 1993.

31. *Ibid.*

32. *Ibid.*

33. H.R. Conwell. "Alcoholism: A Behavioural Disorder in General Aviation." In: *Aviation, Space, and Environmental Medicine*. July 1983.

34. *Ibid.*

35. P.V. Palmer. "The Air Canada Programme for Rehabilitation of the Alcoholic Employee/Pilot." In: *Aviation, Space, and Environmental Medicine*. July 1983.

36. *Ibid.* and C.F. Flynn, *et al.* "Alcoholism and Treatment in Airline Aviators: One Company's Results." In: *Aviation, Space, and Environmental Medicine*. April 1993.

37. P.V. Palmer. "The Air Canada Programme for Rehabilitation of the Alcoholic Employee/Pilot." In: *Aviation, Space, and Environmental Medicine*. July 1983.

Chapter Twenty-Three

1. L. Haugli, *et al:* "Health, Sleep, and Mood Perceptions Reported by Airline Crews Flying Short and Long Hauls." In: *Aviation, Space, and Environmental Medicine*. January 1994.

2. *Ibid.*

3. *Ibid.*

4. *Ibid.*

5. R.M. Barnes. "Physical Energy Expenditure in Long Haul Cabin Crew." In: *Aerospace Medicine.* July 1973.

6. Aviation Occurrence Reports, vii–viii, Canadian Transportation Accident Investigation and Safety Board. P.O. Box 9120 Alta Vista Terminal, Ottawa, Ontario, K1G 3T8.

7. T.S. Szasz. Law. Liberty, and Psychiatry. Collier Books: New York. 1963.

8. M. Morgan. *Mutant Message Down Under.* Harper Collins: New York. 1994.

Chapter Twenty-Four

1. Canadian Transportation Accident Investigation and Safety Board Report. Number: 85-P54026(Incident), August 1985.

2. R.C. Leighton-White. "Airline Pilot Incapacitation in Flight." In: *Aerospace Medicine.* June 1972.

3. A. Martin-Saint-Laurent, *et al.* "Clinical Aspects of Inflight Incapacitations in Commercial Aviation." In: *Aviation, Space, and Environmental Medicine.* March 1990.

4. *Ibid.*

5. *Ibid.*

6. *Ibid.* And M. James, and R. Green. "Airline Pilot Incapacitation Survey." In: *Aviation, Space, and Environmental Medicine.* March 1988.

7. R.C. Leighton-White. "Airline Pilot Incapacitation in Flight." In: *Aerospace Medicine.* June 1972.

8. M. James, and R. Green. "Airline Pilot Incapacitation Survey." In: *Aviation, Space, and Environmental Medicine.* November 1991.

9. *Ibid.*

10. *Ibid.*

11. H.R. Conwell. "A Behavioral Disorder in General Aviation." In: *Aviation, Space, and Environmental Medicine.* July 1983.

12. P. Fromm *et al.* "Air Accidents, Pilot Experience, and Disease Related Inflight Sudden Incapacitation." In: *Aviation, Space, and Environmental Medicine.* March 1988.

13. R.C. Leighton-White. "Airline Pilot Incapacitation in Flight." In: *Aerospace Medicine.* June 1972.

14. A. Martin-Saint-Laurent, *et al.* "Clinical Aspects of Inflight Incapacitations in Commercial Aviation." In: *Aviation, Space, and Environmental Medicine.* March 1990.

15. R.C. Leighton-White. "Airline Pilot Incapacitation in Flight." In: *Aerospace Medicine.* June 1972.

16. *Ibid.*

17. B. Pultz. "The Human AD. Notification of 'Human Factors' Problems Needs to be Immediate." In: *Aviation & Aerospace.* August 1990. And L.R, Simpson. "Investigation of Fatal Aircraft Accidents: *Physiological Incidents.*" In: *Aerospace Medicine.* September 1971.

18. A. Martin-Saint-Laurent, *et al.* "Clinical Aspects of Inflight Incapacitations in Commercial Aviation." In: *Aviation, Space, and Environmental Medicine.* March 1990.

19. K.N. Beers, and S.R. Mohler. "Food Poisoning as an In-Flight Safety Hazard." In: *Aviation, Space, and Environmental Medicine.* June 1985.

20. *Ibid.*

21. *Ibid.*

22. *Ibid.*

23. *Ibid.*

24. R.C. Leighton-White. "Airline Pilot Incapacitation in Flight." In: *Aerospace Medicine.* June 1972.

25. Transportation Safety Board of Canada. "Aviation Occurrence Reports: Safety Action Taken." In: *Reflexions.* Issue 1, March 1993.

26. *Ibid.* And, Transportation Safety Board of Canada. "Don't Pile It On The Pilot." In: *Reflexions.* Issue 2, June 1993.

27. C.R. Harper. "Civil Aviation Medicine in the Coming Decade." In: *Aerospace Medicine.* January 1973.

28. Transportation Safety Board of Canada. "Judgments and Decisions." In: *Reflexions.* Issue 11, September 1995.

29. Transportation Safety Board of Canada. "Aviation Occurrence Reports: Safety Action Taken." In: *Reflexions.* Issue 1, March 1993.

30. J.J. Nance. *Final Approach.* Fawcett Crest: New York. 1990.

31. R.C. Leighton-White. "Airline Pilot Incapacitation in Flight." In: *Aerospace Medicine.* June 1972.

32. R.E. Yanowitch. "Crew Behavior in Accident Causation." In: *Aviation, Space, and Environmental Medicine.* October 1977.

33. *Ibid.*

34. H.P. Bergeron, and D.A. Hinton. "Aircraft Automation: The Problem of the Pilot Interface." In: *Aviation, Space, and Environmental Medicine.* February 1985.

35. "Asleep in the Cockpit" Aired on "Marketplace." (Canadian Television Corporation, Ltd.), October 29, 1996. (Rebroadcast July 22, 1997).

36. *Ibid.*

37. M. James, and R. Green. "Airline Pilots Incapacitation Survey." In: *Aviation, Space, and Environmental Medicine.* November 1991.

38. M. Markus, *et al.* "Post-Traumatic Stress Disorder in Airplane Cabin Crew Attendants. In: *Aviation, Space, and Environmental Medicine.* March 1995.

ORDER FORM

Share *Broken Wings: A Flight Attendant's Journey* with a friend

Please send me ____ copies of *Broken Wings: A Flight Attendant's Journey*

Broken Wings: A Flight Attendant's Journey	_____	copies x $24.95 CDN = $ _____
	_____	copies x $19.95 US = $ _____
Shipping *(Canada and Continental USA only)*		$5.00 CDN or US = $ _____
Handling	_____	copies x $1.95 CDN or US = $ _____
International Orders please add $20.00 USD		= $ _____
Subtotal		= $ _____
In Canada add 7% GST		(Subtotal x .07) = $ _____
Total enclosed		= $ _____

We ship via UPS whenever possible. Please include street address and telephone number.

Name: _____

Street: _____

City: _____ Province/State: _____

Country: _____ Postal Code/Zip: _____

Telephone: (for UPS delivery) _____

E-mail: (for conformation and receipt) _____

Please make cheque or money orders payable to: Avia Publishing Inc.
205 - 329 North Road
Coquitlam, British Columbia,
Canada, V3K 3V8

Orders may be made through our website: www.brokenwings.com
U.S. and International orders payable in U.S. funds. Prices are subject to change.